Strong Winds Are Forecast

A solo, 1850 mile journey by sea kayak, to every lifeboat station in Scotland.

To Sarah
with best wishes
Nick

Nick Ray

ISBN: 978-1-7391253-0-1

DEDICATIONS

To my darling wife Karen. Thank you for your unconditional love, your enduring patience, and your unwavering belief in me.

To Mum and Dad for your love and instilling within me a passion for wildness, adventure and eternal inquisitiveness.

To my children, Chris and Beth. You each inspire me to live my best life as your forge yours with so much potential.

To my sister Steph. You have been a constant supporter of mine and your indomitable courage inspires me.

CONTENTS

ACKNOWLEDGEMENTS

To every one of the R.N.L.I. crews and volunteers of the lifeboat stations around Scotland who generously gave their time to greet me, feed me, and make me feel warmly welcome. Thank you. Through you, I saw all the good humanity has to offer.

To Julian of Sea Kayaking Scotland. Thank you for facilitating my ownership of my beloved sea kayak, *Sahwira*, and for your supportive presence throughout my journey.

To Kokatat for your generous sponsorship of protective kayaking clothing and a buoyancy aid.

To Celtic Paddles for generously sponsoring me two sets of paddles.

To YB Tracking for the generous sponsorship of a Yellowbrick GPS tracker and your support.

To Leonie of Art and Sea for creating the wonderful graphics for my kayak.

To Gael8 for your comfortable t-shirts.

To Dave of Outside Edge, Oban, for your generous discounts and support.

To Stuart and Cathy formerly of Sea Kayak Oban, for your advice and generous support in sourcing kayaking kit.

To Charlie, for your unstinting daily support with weather forecasts, and your enthusiastic encouragement throughout.

2015
A solo, 1850 mile journey by sea kayak to every lifeboat station around Scotland.

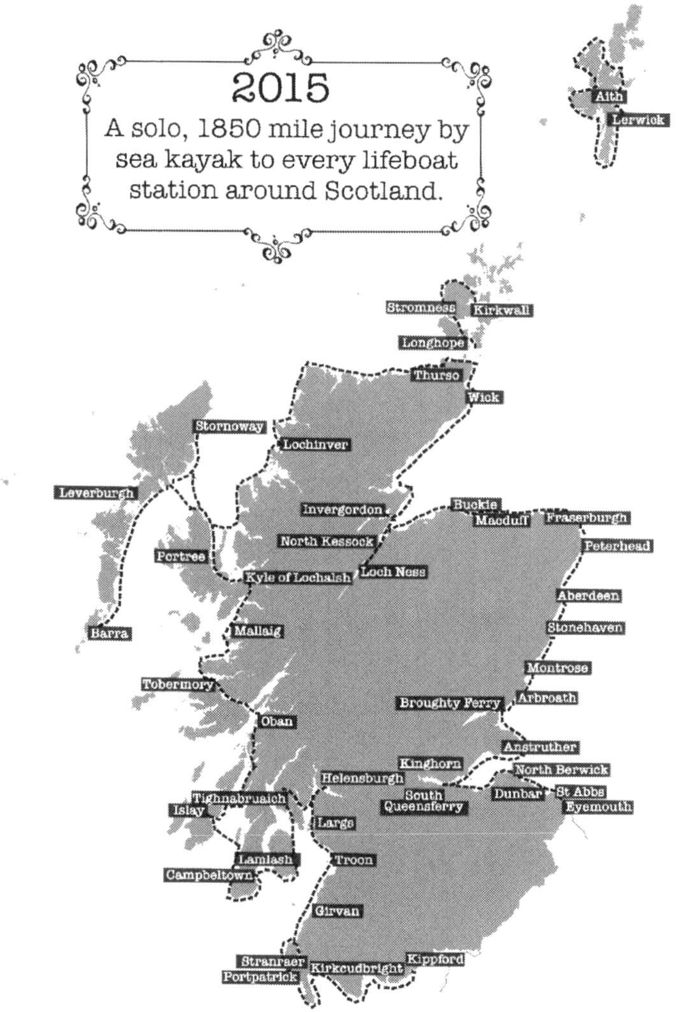

The Beginning

Chapter 1

The surrounding silence was beguiling. The new day was breaking over a wonderfully calm sea, deep orange and yellow hues infusing the inky pre-dawn sky, all perfectly mirrored across the glassy surface. Unbidden, somewhere hidden on the far shore in the gloaming, a heron squawked, its excitable screech echoing through the stillness. My reverie was disturbed. I snapped back to the reality of the moment.

How does one eat an elephant? The answer of course, is one bite at a time. Maybe not the finest riddle to begin with, so probably a more wholesome question would be how does one sea kayak two thousand and fifteen miles? The answer to this is just as simple, one day at a time. In fact, really, one paddle stroke at a time. The enormity of what lay ahead threatened to overwhelm my senses. This was the commencement of the greatest adventurous challenge in my life, to kayak to each of the then forty-seven Royal National Lifeboat Institution (R.N.L.I.) lifeboat stations dotted around the extensive coastline of mainland Scotland, and adjacent islands. By the route I'd planned, the distance was two thousand and fifteen miles.

Since conceiving the idea in the waning light of 2014, the preceding months had been a heady whirl of careful research and planning, deciding on a viable route, learning about the tidal challenges I would face, purchasing necessary equipment and clothing, seeking kit sponsors where possible, and persuading the R.N.L.I. I was competent enough to safely take the challenge on, and therefore fundraise for them without liability on their part. Not only all of this, I gave much time to the important process of examining my motivation for this massive adventure. All these factors, and more, converged into this one moment in time. It was as if all were sand in an hourglass, pouring through the narrow neck into a neat mound below. I was now the very last grain, and it was time to slip through and join the pile. The moment of embarking on my solo unsupported sea kayak voyage around Scotland had arrived.

I was on the shore of the picturesque Kippford Firth, a little-known arm of the Solway Firth, the western body of sea which separates Scotland from England. I was here because in Kippford was the first in my list of the forty-seven R.N.L.I. lifeboat stations interspersed around Scotland's rugged coastline.

This then was the beginning of my lonesome quest. I wasn't certain in this moment, but I anticipated this journey to be a genuine adventure, a personal odyssey marking my passage from my middle years to those I consider to be my later ones. The period of my life when looking back, the path is much further than the one looking ahead. Beginnings mark a moment of change. A beginning is the instant when one decides to step away from a known place, often a place of comfort and safety and embark on a new path. To *begin*, one needs to let go. To *journey*, one needs to leave home. To *adventure*, one needs to accept risk. To *live*, one needs to embrace life. None of these salient facts were lost on me that morning of my departure.

In the chilly early morning light on the pebbly shore of the River Urr Estuary, as I tentatively packed my sea kayak for the first time, I was aware of a gnawing internal tension. This was the tension between excitement at the prospect of a great adventure and the fear of the very same thing. Fear can be a debilitating emotion if I allow it to dominate my conscious awareness, and equally it can be a motivating one too. The route I'd planned, the two thousand and fifteen miles, was an eye watering distance. Until this adventure, the furthest I'd paddled on an unsupported sea kayak journey was two hundred and eighty miles, under an eighth of the distance I was now confronted with. I attempted to shift a deepening sense of gloom over the daunting mileage ahead, to the excitement and anticipation of encountering wonderful new stretches of Scottish coastline.

Such was the capricious nature of my mind, when my thinking was turned towards the possibility of enjoying new sections of Scotland's intricate coastline, I instead started to dwell on the hazards I would encounter along the way; mighty headlands with accompanying fearsome tidal races, unforgiving stretches of high cliffs with no prospect of escape, long distance open water crossings with shipping lanes to contend with, and so much more. The knotty vice-like grip of tension in my stomach was enough to cause me to stand from kneeling beside my kayak and stare out across the slowly filling waters of the Kippford Firth. Somewhere and unseen across the mud flats, the heron croaked loudly again, and I smiled. The anxiety within me diminished, and with surging excitement I looked down at my kayak and the four bulging IKEA bags full of my belongings, realising this moment was intensely real. I was embarking on a true adventure and because of this, the fears, the concerns, the anxieties, the uncertainty, and the sense of low confidence were all important aspects of the experience. Without them, I would somehow feel I was embarking upon something which was not entirely valid. I needed this tension to motivate me, to inspire me and to drive me forward.

It would be easy in a moment such as this to enquire of myself, "How did you get yourself into this?"

Indeed, how does one set about having an adventure? On this occasion, it was a simple matter of deciding to embark on a major sea kayaking journey around Scotland. Having turned fifty a couple of years earlier, I increasingly felt the urge to undertake something 'big' before age took a grip of my body. A traverse of the Scottish coastline in a sea kayak was at the top of my list. Ever since I'd read Brian Wilson's eloquently written book 'Blazing Paddles', a wonderful account of his solo sea kayak journey around Scotland in the 1980s, I wanted to emulate his achievement. It was reading his book which inspired me to take up sea kayaking in the mid-1990s and from then, search out my own journeying adventures. The first of these, in 1996, was a solo venture around the Isle of Skye, a rite of passage journey which took nineteen days to complete, ten of which were shore bound because of windy weather. That was a wonderful experience which possibly bordered on misadventure, because I knew very little about sea kayaking then, undertaking a few tricky passages with little idea of the consequences of what I was facing. This experience fired my enthusiasm for the activity to the point where I fear I may now be somewhat overzealous in proclaiming its virtues. I'd discovered a healthy pastime which enabled me to connect with the wild outdoors in a uniquely adventurous way, and which provided the wild solitude I so often desired.

Seeking adventure has been an integral part of my spirit, so much so, I rarely consider my actions to be adventurous. Making them occur is as natural a process as brewing my morning coffee. In a way, I consider it a form of artistic creativity, noticing the possibility for an escapade through pouring over Ordnance Survey maps (as I am wont to spend ages doing), or reading of somewhere new to explore. I've never been one for following guidebooks, preferring to create a route of my own from the information I glean from maps, or what I can see when out in the landscape. I have a burning desire to explore. I'm eternally curious about what might be 'out there', hidden and possibly rarely viewed by humans. I'm readily inspired by the adventures of others too. I'm not a competitive adventurer in wanting to proclaim being the first to achieve a challenge, but I do drive myself to seek adventures which have not been completed before. I think it's in my nature to be an explorer, to seek out opportunities which have not been trodden by others ahead. In truth there is little left of the physical world to explore to claim as being the first to set foot upon, and anyway, this form of colonial aspiration is not my true driving force. I think it's noticing the opportunity for an adventurous challenge and wondering firstly, has this been completed before and then, if not, is it possible? Indeed, believing anything is possible, the question really is – is it possible for *me*?

This is how I found myself standing alone on the shores of the Kippford Firth in the 5am gloaming of 1st May 2015. I wanted to see if it was possible to kayak, solo, around Scotland. With the knowledge Scotland has been traversed by kayak on innumerable occasions, the challenge ahead was purely a personal one. Was I up to the task? To add an element of uniqueness to the venture, I chose to visit each of the Scottish lifeboat stations because this would entail kayaking to some far-flung locations which are not normally included in a standard circumnavigation of Scotland. The inclusion of a visit to each of the lifeboat stations served a deeper reason too. Every adventure I embark on requires a purpose, to provide context and meaning to the undertaking. I rarely set out into the wilds with a loose expectation of simply 'seeing what might happen'. All my activities will be inspired by something or someone and there'll be questions I'll want to resolve. What is out there? What will I find at that point on the map? What will I see? Can I find historical traces of what might have existed before? Is the route I'm considering viable? Every one of the many reasons I choose, serves the purpose of legitimising any undertaking, in a way, ensuring I possess permission to indulge myself in enjoying a hearty exploit.

So it was with this journey too. I needed to bestow myself with permission to embark on an extended period away from my wife and our home, unemployed, indulgently enjoying a sea kayaking expedition in some of the finest known seas and locations in the world. Hitting on the idea of visiting all the Scottish lifeboat stations was a stroke of genius. This provided a unique expeditionary route to explore, and a viable purpose which added gravitas to the venture. The purpose of visiting the lifeboat stations was in no way intended to be exploitative to simply provide legitimacy for my undertaking. The whole idea melded several powerful motivations to afford an all-encompassing personal goal.

For much of my professional life in the outdoors, I was involved as a volunteer in various mountain rescue teams. Because of this, I've an affinity for the rescue services per se, particularly those which rely on volunteers to give their time and effort in the service of others. The R.N.L.I. is undoubtedly a national treasure and close to the hearts of millions of people in Britain and Ireland. We cannot fail to be aware of their presence when we make visits to the coast or when we undertake activities on the sea. When I worked as an instructor for Outward Bound in Aberdyfi, mid-Wales, in the mid-eighties, I was often involved in the launching of the inshore lifeboat which many of my instructional colleagues were crew members on. My affinity and connection with the R.N.L.I. was born in those far off halcyon days. My eyesight was not good enough to apply to become a member of the crew, so I had to satisfy myself with vicariously experiencing lifeboat service through the stories of my colleagues on the crew and from time to time, being involved with the launching of the lifeboat in a mad rush of excitement.

The R.N.L.I. is a charity independent of government patronage and so must raise operational funds through the generosity of the British and Irish public. It costs millions of pounds every year to provide free to all in need, the professional lifesaving service it does, which serves every corner of the British and Irish coastlines. Each lifeboat station has a dedicated voluntary fund-raising branch who work tirelessly throughout every year to raise money for the charity through ingenious means and well-tried methods. Even with their sterling work raising huge amounts of money, the charity relies on the generous good will of individuals who put themselves forward for a myriad of fund-raising events and challenges, which they undertake in return for sponsored donations from families, friends and well-wishers. We are a generous hearted nation and beloved charities such as the R.N.L.I. inspire people to extend themselves in ways they never thought possible in order to raise money. For many, these charitable undertakings are not for fame or fortune and instead fulfil our innate human capacity for compassion. In my case, I was motivated to fundraise for the R.N.L.I. because of my connection to them from my Aberdyfi days and because I understand the nature of volunteering to save the lives of those in peril.

I cannot claim my motivation was entirely altruistic though. Establishing a fund-raising purpose for my venture, provided authenticity. As a result, I was less shy when I declared my ambitious intent to my wider world and set about seeking material sponsors for the trip. It's not within my personality to ask for things if I don't think there's a valid reason for doing so. The potentially risky nature of the expedition required my overall passage plan be ratified by the R.N.L.I. before I could publicly declare my fundraising goals for them. Because the charity scrutinised my proposal, I was emboldened to publicise my intentions more widely than I would normally have done. In doing so, a deeper motivation was fulfilled, and this was the one of recognition. Fame is not the word I would use to describe this motivation. I wasn't seeking my fifteen minutes in the national limelight. However, it was self-affirming to know many people around the country were interested in my journey and were impressed by the nature of the challenge.

This self-affirmation was highlighted the night before my departure from Kippford. Members of the lifeboat crew and other volunteers met me at the local pub to celebrate my adventure ahead, and to wish me well. They bought me a fish supper and we sat around the table talking about the R.N.L.I. and what it meant to serve on the crew. This was the first of many such conversations I'd enjoy over the subsequent four months, and I relished being accepted into their closely knit group. I sensed their deep connection, and I could understand the language they were speaking, the distinctive patois rescue-service personnel use, peppered with acronyms and the habit of shortening nouns such as helicopter to 'helo'. Their pride in the D-Class lifeboat which they crewed was palpable and it was evident each of them served as volunteers for the R.N.L.I., because this strong sense of pride mattered deeply to them.

They accepted me because they were evidently as much in awe of me as I was of them. Equally, they appreciated the effort I was making for the charity they felt so passionately about. Their undisguised gratefulness was heart-warming, so I accepted their appreciation with a feeling of self-pride and the glowing knowledge I was about to do something good – and this simple fact was incredibly important. This sense of well-being emphasised the mutuality of the motivations for my venture and why it wasn't entirely altruistic. I realised there in the cosy public bar of the Anchor Hotel; this undertaking of mine was very much a shared adventure. I was going to meet and encounter many R.N.L.I. volunteers throughout my travels and through them I was going to gain invaluable support and recognition for what I was achieving.

That previous night, after making my farewells to my new friends and declining a final pint for the road, I made my way back to my lodgings, the floor of the lifeboat station crew room. As I let myself in through the side door of the station building, the pervading aroma of petrol and cleanliness assailed my senses. There was something in this smell which sparked my sense of excitement and adventure. It was reminiscent of when I assisted in the launches of the Aberdyfi lifeboat. It was a smell which evoked a sense of drama and peril, risk and attainment. The D-Class lifeboat resting on her launching trolley before me, gleamed in the stark overhead lighting and lying next to her, also gleaming and looking gracefully beautiful, was my sea kayak, '*Sahwira*'. I stood for a moment, my left hand on the starboard stern tube of the lifeboat and looked down on my kayak and the corresponding untidy pile of kit and food. For a second or two, I found it difficult to comprehend the context of what I was gazing at and then the realisation of where I was, and what I was embarking on flooded through me.

That night I slept fitfully, having taken ages to choose the place to lay out my mat and sleeping bag for fear of being in the way if there was a call-out in the night. It was as if it were a night before an important examination and I worried, true to form, I hadn't fully prepared myself. It was too late of course, and no amount of cramming would serve for what lay ahead after the next day. I needn't worry because truthfully, I had prepared for the journey, I had the information I required, and I embodied the wisdom to make sense of it all.

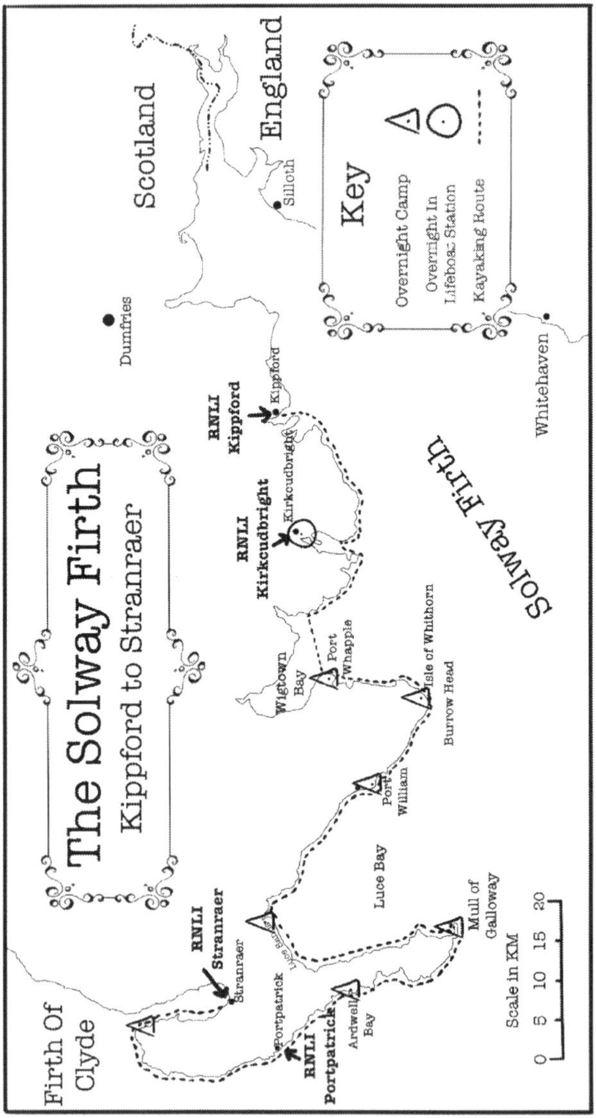
The Solway Firth
Kippford to Stranraer
Scotland
England
Key
Overnight Camp
Overnight In Lifeboat Station
Kayaking Route
Dumfries
Silloth
Whitehaven
RNLI Kippford
Kippford
RNLI Kirkcudbright
Kirkcudbright
Solway Firth
Wigtown Bay
Port Whappie
Isle of Whithorn
Burrow Head
Port William
Luce Bay
Mull of Galloway
RNLI Stranraer
Stranraer
Portpatrick
RNLI Portpatrick
Ardwell Bay
Firth Of Clyde
Scale in KM
0 5 10 15 20

The Solway Firth
Kippford to Stranraer

Chapter 2

Every kayak journey begins with a single paddle stroke. In my case, my expedition began with a hurried shove into the sea and a hasty right-hand sweep with my paddle to set me under way. There was no ceremony. A ripple of applause drifted across the water from the few bystanders who kindly gathered on the pier in Kippford to see me off and a couple of hearty shouts willing me well, echoed after me as I paddled away. There were no skirling bag pipes or the Red Arrows streaking in a multi coloured roar through the skies above. Even the gulls were notable in their absence. It was an odd experience. For such a personally significant moment, it could have been an anti-climax. Nevertheless, it was exactly the beginning I was hoping for, low key and without fuss. The sea was calm, and the day promised to be lovely throughout. It was in every way a perfect beginning to the journey I assiduously planned over the previous four months.

As I paddled away from the pier with the cheers calling out behind, I was aware of extreme discomfort in my right leg. The packing of my kayak earlier had not gone entirely to plan, and I'd resorted to placing a couple of bulky items in my cockpit with the idea (more in hope) they would nestle easily between my legs. However, in my haste to launch, I'd clambered into my cockpit without giving time to ensuring I was fully comfortable. My right foot was twisted away from the footrest where it should be securely placed, and try as I might, no amount of wiggling seemed to extricate it from the crooked position it was in. Not only was it painfully uncomfortable but I found I was now unbalanced as well. I couldn't lean my kayak too much because I feared I might capsize due to an inability to stabilise myself with my legs. The cheers from my well-wishers seemed to grow fainter as I paddled away, and I scanned my horizon ahead, seeking a likely place where I could stop and sort myself out. I didn't want to do this in full view of the folks who had come to see me off, because I didn't want them to think I was incompetent before I paddled only a few metres!

The hope I would quickly make it to a point where rearranging myself would be out of sight, were dashed when I spotted a car racing along a lane close to the shore to a viewpoint where the well-wishers and the newspaper camera man jumped out and continued to cheer me on my way. All I could do was to wave gaily and grimace a smile in response, anxiously keeping my paddle in readiness, fearful my instability would see me tip over in front of them. I was warmly grateful for their support and attention, but my right leg was losing sensation and I feared an ignominious end to my expedition, this time before it had even begun. I gave one last wave and I paddled onwards, stoically heading for the mouth of the estuary and the open seas of the Solway Firth beyond. I attempted to connect with the enormity of this moment, but any significance was dulled by my discomfort. I did wonder though if this was a portent for the journey ahead, but I didn't dwell on this too much. Instead, I paddled smoothly and easily to a small bay where I allowed myself to slowly drift to a stop and with a surge of relief, popped my spray-deck to sort out the disastrous situation within my cockpit. The pain in my leg slowly eased and I took the opportunity of calm to gaze around.

The water gently tinkled against the hull of the kayak, the sea rippled around me without a pronounced swell and the sky overhead was an eggshell blue with wisps of high cirrus indicating an impending change in the weather. The firth was lined with rolling wooded shoreline, spring green beginning to show amongst the boughs. It was all gloriously beautiful in every sense of the word. A sensation of deep peace descended, and warm satisfaction suffused every fibre of my being. I concluded everything I was experiencing in this very moment, provided the answer to what I had been pondering for so long. I realised with an onrush of explosive excitement, quite simply I was embarking on the biggest challenge I had ever undertaken and from this moment on, my life would be irrevocably altered.

It was a gorgeous day to be kayaking. Leaving the Urr Estuary and paddling into the unknown waters of the Solway Firth seemed a definitive moment. Once the village of Kippford was out of sight, I experienced for the first time the weightiness of my solitude and the enormity of what I faced. It struck me in that moment, as I forged a wake in the sea behind and the prow of my kayak sliced effortlessly through the calm waters ahead, all I needed to do was simply accept each day as a day out in my boat. I realised it would help not to think of the journey in its entirety, for to do so would make it seem impossibly huge. It was difficult to conceptualise eventually arriving in Oban, or Portree, or Castlebay, or even the far northern isles where I was particularly excited at eventually visiting. These were distant, almost mythical locations, which I would arrive at in good time. Today, the very first day of my adventure, all I had to do was reach the lifeboat station in Kirkcudbright, a mere twelve miles away.

The Solway Firth was new to me. In the years I lived in England and Wales, it was a corner of Scotland I passed in my haste to reach the Highlands without paying much attention. I'm ashamed to admit, as a sea kayaker, I purposefully overlooked this stretch of coastline in favour of the wilder Scottish west coast and the Hebridean islands. It's one of those areas which when I looked at the map, didn't hold much appeal. I held an image of a muddy grey sea inundated with exposed sand banks and mud flats. In planning for this expedition, I paid cursory attention to the technicalities of paddling here, so it was to my chagrin I found myself thoroughly tested in the first seven days when the weather and seas of the Solway taught me valuable lessons for my journey ahead.

The low-lying rocky coastline was lovely, with fringes of canary yellow gorse behind which lurked the cultivated farmland of Dumfries and Galloway. It was all very pastoral and picturesque. The coconut scent of the gorse drifted across to me on the water as I paddled along, reminding me of slathered dollops of sun cream. Much of the stretch of coastline from Kippford to Kirkcudbright is taken up by the Dundrennan military firing range. Thankfully, the day of my departure was a day when they weren't firing, otherwise I would not have been able to paddle along the coast. It would have been an embarrassing beginning to my adventure if I had attempted to sneak by, only to be hauled ashore by the range officials. All was eerily silent as I paddled underneath low cliffs adorned with military paraphernalia. I wondered what it was they fired out into the expansive waters of the

Solway Firth and what impact this had on the environment beneath the surface.

It was easy going and I realised I was covering the distance much faster than I'd expected. It's not my solo kayaking practice to pull ashore for breaks. For some reason, I'm blessed with a cast iron bladder, so the need for comfort stops is not usually a consideration. It's possible to remain in my kayak for over ten hours without discomfort, making a mad dash however, for the closest form of privacy when I land at the end of the day! I think my reluctance to land is because much of my kayaking is conducted solo. Landing ashore is when I'm most vulnerable to mishap. Consequently, I prefer not to increase the chances of this occurring. I carry snacks and a hot drink in a flask in my deck bag, so it's easy enough to sustain myself while out at sea. There are many times of course when I do choose to take a break ashore, particularly if I am keen to explore a feature I've noticed on the map. I'm not afraid of landing, even on a lee shore in a heavy swell. However, I've come to accept I'm not as agile as I once was, and the days of leaping out of my kayak as soon as my hull scrunches ashore are long gone. It means I must approach a landing with considerable caution, timing the moment of grounding my kayak when the swell is at its least potent. I suppose there's one consolation to these moments when kayaking solo, it doesn't matter if I take a tumble when I awkwardly heave myself out of my boat and end up slipping backwards into the sea in an ungainly fashion! There won't be anyone to laugh at my clumsy misfortune.

All too quickly, early in the afternoon, I found myself rounding Torr Point and the expanse of Kirkcudbright Bay opened before me. My first expeditionary day on the sea was close to ending. Like the Urr Estuary at Kippford, the waters here are shallow and at low tide there are large swathes of mud flats and sand banks. The tide had turned before my arrival and I knew I would be paddling against the flow, if I decided to make my way up through the navigable channel to the town.

This was not necessary because the lifeboat shed is situated about one mile into the bay and on its eastern shore. This is where I intended to stop for the day. It had been arranged someone from the lifeboat crew would drive out and meet me, but I did not know what time. I had a mobile phone but as with many of the remote locations along the Scottish coastline, reception was patchy. I arrived at the mouth of the bay to hear several messages ping on the phone. Listening to them I discovered they were from the lifeboat volunteer who was going to meet me, asking to call him about my intended time of arrival. Since I was only a mile away, I realised I was giving him little time to organise, and I felt a pang of guilt for not arranging this earlier. As it was, when I called him back, he was genuinely pleased to hear from me and said he would be with me as soon as he could. Being a Friday, he had to finish work first.

It was quite a moment when I eventually arrived at the Kirkcudbright lifeboat station. Set in its solitary and remote location high up on the rocky shore, it looked every inch of what one might expect of a R.N.L.I. lifeboat shed. The slipway inclined steeply to the sea from the tall and narrow grey harled building. It was easy to imagine the countless times through the ages, a lifeboat had slid down this ramp on wild and stormy nights, embarking on heroic journeys out into the Solway Firth to rescue distressed mariners. The lifeboat shed here is at least four miles from Kirkcudbright town centre, so the crew muster at their crew quarters in the town and then driven as fast as possible in the R.N.L.I. Land Rover out to the shed, the last mile or so along a rough and uneven track. It can't be a comfortable experience. The lifeboat shed is one of the oldest in Scotland and has served the community since the nineteenth century.

As I drifted to the point where the slipway dipped into the sea, I noticed within a swelling emotion of pride. This was the first lifeboat station I had paddled to and although it had not been a technically demanding day, I'd made it here in good time and without incident. This was lifeboat station number two on my list and despite knowing I had forty-five more to reach before my journey end, this was a particularly enjoyable moment. Visiting the lifeboat stations was the key purpose of the journey, so to arrive here at Kirkcudbright was in a way the moment when the purpose of my odyssey was validated. In many respects it was another moment when I acknowledged the reality of the trip. I gradually came to this realisation as each milestone was attained. Arriving at Kirkcudbright lifeboat station was an important reminder this journey was indeed real and the purpose in hand was deadly earnest.

The main door of the lifeboat station was closed, and I couldn't see anyone around to speak to. I pulled ashore, clambered out of the cockpit and dragged *Sahwira* a little further up out of the water. I was pleased with how physically fresh I felt after the twelve miles. Up by the shed was a sunny patch of closely cropped spring green grass and a picnic table positioned with an inviting view across the estuary. It was a perfect place to pitch my tent and I looked forward to my first night of camping on the trip. I phoned John, my contact for the Kirkcudbright lifeboat and he told me he would be with me in a couple of hours. It was sunny and warm, so I didn't mind in the slightest at waiting to meet him. He insisted too I bunk down in the lifeboat crew facilities in the town, from where I could explore and find a place to eat and maybe enjoy a pint. Despite wanting to camp in this glorious spot, the latter suggestion held great appeal, so I acceded to his proposal. I wandered down to my kayak and unpacked her for the first time this journey. Whoever was the person who first decided IKEA shopping bags would be suitable for carrying expeditionary kit from kayaks up to dry land, deserves a medal in my opinion. For years previously, my sea kayaking packing and unpacking process was fraught with armfuls of stuff, stumbling over slippery rocks trying not to tumble and scatter my belongings everywhere. Now all I do, is throw everything in the voluminous Nordic superstore bags and carry them with ease up the shore.

Paddling solo meant I needed to totally unpack my boat before I could carry her from where I had beached her, to where I was camping. It took a matter of minutes to empty all the compartments, strip the decks of accoutrements and unload the cockpit of the water bag and other bits and pieces. In under twenty minutes the picnic table was laden with my kit and a pan of water was on the stove, brewing for a much-desired mug of tea. I returned to *Sahwira* and hoisted her up onto my right shoulder. She's light enough to carry comfortably for quite a distance. With her balanced neatly on my shoulder I can carry her with considerable confidence over steep and slippery boulders, even up steep inclines. Carrying her the short distance over the boulders to the green sward and the picnic table proved to be no problem whatsoever.

I placed her gently on the ground next to the kit strewn table. I made lemon and ginger tea, sat down on her deck and breathed a huge sigh of satisfaction. The warmth of the sun suffused my body, and I felt a wave of serenity and pleasure wash over me. In this wonderful moment I allowed a sense of contentment envelope me. It seemed nothing was going to get in my way of achieving my goal. If every day was going to be like this one, then I was in for an extremely pleasant journey around Scotland. As I sat there lost in my thoughts, I noticed movement under the lifeboat slipway. Suddenly the graceful form of a large otter broke the surface of the muddy coloured sea. It drifted for a few seconds before sleekly diving beneath the surface, disappearing once again. I enjoyed watching it swim and feed for a while before it continued its way further along the shore and eventually out of sight. I think I might have fallen asleep because the next thing I remember was the distinctive growling of a Land Rover engine. I got to my feet to greet whoever was driving to the lifeboat shed. A dark blue Land Rover adorned with R.N.L.I. livery and a gantry with the emergency service blue lights atop, rumbled down the track through the naked early spring trees and swung into the glade where I waited.

There were two folks in the vehicle, and both seemed very pleased to see me which gladdened my heart. They clambered out and came to shake my hand, both congratulating me on successfully paddling all the way from Kippford. Then they wandered over to my pile of kit on the table and each exclaimed at the amount I was carrying.

"Does *all* of that fit in your boat?" I was asked. This question was going to be a recurring refrain throughout my trip, in just about every place where I met people.

I replied proudly, "Yes, of course. It can be a tight squeeze, but it all goes in". I went on to add, "I'm carrying a lot of food at the moment though."

"She's a beautiful canoe" said John, glancing over *Sahwira's* sleek lines with the appreciative eye of a man who has worked with boats his whole life.

I couldn't help it, and sadly I didn't alter my ways for the whole trip, but in my reply, I corrected him, "Yes, she's a beautiful kayak."

"Sorry, kayak" he corrected himself and I immediately felt awful for having been so pedantic. After all what did it matter whether she was referred to as a canoe or a kayak? Sadly though, this element of pedantry did not escape me for the next four months and each time it happened, I felt the familiar surge of guilt for embarrassing the people who had been so kind to comment about *Sahwira's* graceful shape.

I attempted to make amends, "She's an excellent expedition kayak, just right for this trip. She handles the sea well and I feel very safe when paddling her."

"Aye, that's good then" he responded with no hint of annoyance at being corrected. "What's the difference between a canoe and kayak then?"

I felt bad again. "A canoe is an open boat, like those you see in films of Canada and a kayak.... Well, a kayak is like mine here, it's closed over with a cockpit for the paddler. I wear a spray deck to keep the water out." I reached into the untidy pile on the picnic table and hefted out my sodden neoprene spray deck to show him.

"Oh aye, I see" he said.

"What does *Sahwira* mean?" asked Paula, John's companion and the local R.N.L.I. press officer.

"I'm originally from Zimbabwe" I responded, "and it means '*lifelong friend*' in Shona, the indigenous language out there."

They both looked at me with broad smiles and stated this was a wonderful name for my kayak. They didn't call her a canoe.

"You want to see the lifeboat then?" asked John.

"Yes please," I tried not to appear too eager. "She's an Atlantic-85, isn't she?" attempting to sound as knowledgeable as I could.

"Aye," was his thrifty response.

We wandered up to the shed and after unlocking the side door I was invited into the darkness inside. I was immediately assailed by the pungently sweet odour of petrol and a general background metallic smell of machinery. I was to become very familiar with these smells in my travels to all the lifeboat stations around Scotland, and every time I would feel myself stirred by excitement. It was immediately clear they were both passionately proud of their lifeboat. Indeed, I couldn't help but see her as something to be glorified, with her gleaming engines and mirror polished propellers and her clean tightly inflated orange flanks. Although obviously very much an inanimate object, she seemed to hold a spirit for life I have not seen in other craft. This was something yet again I was going to experience at just about every lifeboat station I visited, where I was shown around their lifeboat. The pride the crews effused seemed to provide a life-force for their boats, bringing them to life before my eyes. Like proud parents, John and Paula stood back while I wandered around the boat, reverently touching her every now and again, feeling the tautness of her skin, running my hand along a silky-smooth line or two, and generally admiring how neat and smart she was. Everything was spotlessly clean and well stowed. There were no extraneous items hanging around or absently tucked into corners. The lifeboat shed floor was spotless and it was clear this was just as much because of a passion for saving lives, as taking great care of the kit they have been entrusted in.

The Atlantic 85 is referred to as an inshore lifeboat. This means she is used for rescues within a 12 mile offshore limit. Her shallow draft and extremely fast manoeuvrability make her an ideal craft for the waters of the shallow Kirkcudbright seas and the rocky flanks of the Solway Firth. She carries a crew of four who sit astride saddle type seats with bracing handles to grab as the helm (the person who drives the craft) surges her with incredible skill through the rough seas towards the casualty, or as I should say in lifeboat parlance, the survivor. The boat is entirely crewed by volunteers drawn from all walks of life. These dedicated folks are willing to give up whatever they are doing at the drop of a hat, and rush to the aid of a stricken vessel in whatever weather and sea conditions they are faced with. In times gone by it will have been men from the fishing communities who would have crewed the lifeboats, but nowadays the crew were drawn from every sector of a community, many people without much boating experience. The R.N.L.I. provide extensive training at their base down at Poole in Dorset, and crew members must go through a thorough training process before they are deemed able to fully participate in a live rescue.

It transpired like Kippford; the Kirkcudbright boat had difficulty in finding young crew from the community. The local fishing fleet was heavily depleted, and many youngsters would move away once they had left school or showed little interest in the demands of being a lifeboat crewmember. An additional challenge was the 'competition' with the retained Fire Service for volunteers. In many of the rural communities of Scotland the local Fire Service teams are made up of volunteers too. These firemen and firewomen are known as retained firefighters and they receive a generous stipend for their services. The R.N.L.I. do not pay their volunteers. It's a commitment to be a lifeboat crew member with weekly training sessions, the need to be on call day and night and a dedication to performing many roles other than being on the boat during rescues. As I was to discover, those who volunteered with the R.N.L.I. performed their roles with vocational zeal.

John and Paula explained how they launched the boat down the ramp on a cable attached to the cradle. Retrieval they said could be a tricky process particularly in heavy seas. It took skill from the helm to reverse the boat back into the cradle so it could be secured and then winched back up the ramp and into the shed. I would have liked to watch the whole process of the launch and then the return. Eventually after a thorough look around, we loaded all my kit into the Land Rover and carried *Sahwira* around to the main shed door and placed her alongside the lifeboat for the night. I noticed with pride she gleamed and looked as sleekly beautiful as the lifeboat she was lying beside. It was reassuring to know she was safe and sound.

It didn't take long to reach Kirkcudbright town centre where I was given a guided tour in the Land Rover and the best pubs and eateries were pointed out. We arrived at the lifeboat crew facilities where I was invited to stay the night. It was a purpose-built building for the R.N.L.I. and consisted of a main crew room which held the computers and VHF radios for communicating with the lifeboat out at sea. I was left to my own devices after a few photos with Paula and John for their social media pages on the internet. I settled down for a long evening on my own.

Despite having ten days' worth of food, I decided to head into town for a celebratory pint and a pub meal. I felt I deserved it after completing the first full day of my journey. I discovered the town of Kirkcudbright was really very interesting and picturesque. I wandered around enjoying the sights before choosing a pub for my supper. Sadly, my choice wasn't a good one, and I sat through a mediocre burger and chips and an even more mediocre pint. I was disappointed particularly since this adventure was being conducted on limited funds, and so twelve pounds on a meal and a drink was an extravagance I couldn't waste. I determined from now on I would be far more circumspect before deciding whether to eat out or not.

Back at the base I began to settle for the night when I received a text from a good friend who I've known since my Outward Bound days in Wales. Tim lives near Carlisle and wanted to drive over to spend some of the evening with me. This was fantastic, and a couple of hours later we were sitting in a different pub enjoying a dram. Tim had met me at Ravenglass when I had unsuccessfully made the three peaks attempt in my kayak a few years earlier in 2009, and because of this, it was lovely he had joined me on my first night of this journey. After he departed, I settled down in my sleeping bag and as with the night before, sleep eluded me for a while as I mindfully played through the challenges I faced the next day. I also lay there in the dark and thought to myself this journey is going to be richly rewarding, if each day is as good as this one, my first full day of my adventure.

Chapter 3

Gathering up to date weather information was a crucial aspect of maintaining my safety throughout my journey. The simplest method was to listen to the three hourly inshore weather forecasts broadcast on VHF by the Maritime and Coastguard Agency (MCA). These broadcasts covered generalised coastal areas detailing likely weather and the sea conditions up to twelve miles offshore. It was a simple matter of switching on my VHF radio and listening to the broadcast when it was made. Over the months, listening to this broadcast became something of a ritual, and as I passed through the various Coastguard sectors around Scotland, I came to recognise the voices who recounted the weather prospects over the airwaves.

Sadly on this occasion, the previous day of warm sunshine and light winds had been an aberration. What followed for the next five days were near gales and heavy rain. The forecast when I set off from Kirkcudbright was distinctly unfavourable, but I wanted to press on. I needed to gain some momentum this early into the journey, not finding myself held up only a short distance from the start. My destination for the day was the Isle of Whithorn, with a ten-mile open water crossing of the mouth of Wigtown Bay. It wasn't an ambitious day by any means, but it would be one where serious consideration had to be accorded to route choice given the prevailing conditions.

There was a noticeable swell as I headed out towards Little Ross Island, which every now and then, was hidden behind the silently rolling waves. I felt uneasy and doubted my decision to put to sea that day. John had shown some concern when I decided to go but I had assured him the forecast winds were well within my ability to contend with and anyway, if conditions became too bad, I would make for the shore. Force six on the Beaufort Scale is probably at the top end of the wind strength I was comfortable contending with, when kayaking on my own. There are variables to this too which I would take into consideration when deciding on how to proceed. For instance, the wind direction. Would it be on my stern or my beam, or would I be paddling into the full face of it? The wind anywhere on my stern would be beneficial in terms of providing forward momentum but would mean a following sea. This isn't a major problem, but without judicious care, it might have the potential to cause me to capsize if I found myself broaching by surfing too fast down a wave. If it was head on, then it would be a slog, pure and simple. It'd be like riding a laden bicycle into a head wind, except I would also be contending with oncoming waves. The size and the nature of these waves would be determined by the fetch and whether the wind was against the tide flow or with it. The fetch is the distance of sea from the closest land from the direction the wind is blowing. The further the distance, (the fetch), the likelihood of larger waves. Wind direction and tide direction are incredibly important factors to consider when sea kayaking. If the wind is blowing in the same direction as the tidal flow, then it's likely the conditions at sea will be relatively easy. However, when the wind is blowing in the opposite direction to the tidal flow in what is known as, 'wind over tide', the sea state is likely to be rough with steep, breaking waves. If the tide is flowing strongly, then the ensuing wind over tide sea state could be nasty to kayak through, particularly when I'm on my own. These conditions are best avoided.

An additional consideration would be the wind direction in relation to the shore, particularly the shore I would be required to land on for my planned stop for the day, or out of necessity in an emergency. If the wind was blowing from seawards onto the coast, this would make for a 'lee shore'. Again, there are variables which will determine the severity of this situation. The size of the swell which would be determined by the fetch and recent weather conditions. It's worth noting the state of the sea may not always be determined by local weather conditions. When kayaking along oceanic coastlines, it might be gales hundreds of miles away which will have created the swell which crashes onto the shore I'm heading for. Understanding lee shore conditions is important when considering launching and landing, and it's the landing on a lee shore which creates the most concern. If there is a large swell and the shore is fragmented with rocks and outlying reefs, this can make a hazardous experience. A laden kayak coming into shore is vulnerable from the force of the sea and the land it is arriving on. Hefty waves can drive the boat onto the rocks and cause considerable damage, and likely be dangerous for the kayaker too. It can take considerable skill to maintain control of a laden sea kayak in lee shore conditions. A sea kayak being a long and slim boat, is directionally stable, but difficult to turn quickly, particularly when it is being driven forwards by a fearsome wave.

Sourcing the information to assist with sound decision making, is relatively easy in this age of ready access to the internet. Here, there are many weather forecasting websites which provide accurate predictions of the wind, its strength, its direction, its gusts, the precipitation, the temperature and importantly too, the forecast swell direction, size and times between the waves. A crucial source of information were the synoptic charts, the surface pressure diagrams with lines like contours we see on the television weather forecasts. These provide the context for the forecasts, and with some understanding of their meaning, it's possible to interpolate what will be occurring in the weather over the coming forty-eight hours or so. If I couldn't access the synoptic charts online, then I would listen carefully to the shipping forecast broadcast by the Marine Coastguard Agency (M.C.A.) because this would contain some detail about the pressure systems, their position and movement in relation to the British Isles. Knowing where a low-pressure system was, the value of its barometric pressure, and the direction it was moving, helped ascertain the likely weather scenario for the next day or so, particularly the wind directions and strengths. Rain and temperature variations were never a concern because adequate clothing provided protection against both.

The collating of weather information, understanding what it entails and knowing the tides, their timings and their directions, was a necessary function every evening and morning of my journey. Like many mariners with years of experience, this process was second nature and took a matter of minutes to interpret and make a rudimentary decision about whether in general, conditions were safe enough or not. Sometimes, I would pour over my map, gazing at the route ahead, attempting to anticipate the conditions I would be facing given the forecast. The variables were sometimes complex, and I would vacillate from one option to another as the permutations were explored and addressed. Even then, I often found myself standing on the shore looking out to sea towards the far horizon, agonising whether to put to sea or not.

As I paddled through the Sound between Little Ross Island and the mainland, the sea state noticeably picked up in weight and the wind was strengthening. Despite this, I set my course for the Isle of Whithorn, invisible in the gloomy weather ten miles across the mouth of Wigtown Bay. I felt uneasy but decided to press on because I had this desire not to succumb on only my second day. A mile offshore and the conditions were not easing. Reason took a hold of my drive for progress, and I slowly pulled *Sahwira* around to head along the eastern coastline into Wigtown Bay. I sighed deeply with disappointment, but I knew I had made a prudent decision. However, I really did not want to go too far into Wigtown Bay, because this would add unnecessary miles to the journey, but making a crossing of the mouth of it was out of the question in these conditions. A choice always available in situations such as this, was to pull ashore and sit the weather out.

The sea was extremely lumpy, and I felt somewhat alarmed when waves would break without warning close by. I soon acquainted myself with the frightening sound of a collapsing wave, this being a loud crack, then a slap, followed by the roaring rumble of the surf, always lasting only a few seconds. I considered making a run for Brighouse Bay which was close by, and I was tempted to turn into it and find a place to put up the tent and wait for the conditions to calm. Somehow though I couldn't bring myself to take this option and the opportunity to do so soon passed as I held my course and paddled further along the cliff lined coastline. Very soon though, I had the measure of the sea and made good progress. With the wind behind, I was being blown at a good rate of knots up into Wigtown Bay. This was unfamiliar territory. In my planning I had not examined this stretch of coastline because naively I had not considered paddling into the bay. Ahead the low-lying Islands of Fleet seemed to offer a possible haven and I paddled with renewed vigour towards them.

Despite my tenseness, I took pleasure from the rugged cliff scenery I passed, with hints of caves and interesting chasms. Normally I would have paddled close into the shore, exploring every inch, but today I wasn't going anywhere near them. The conditions were far too rough to have made any such exploration if not safe, at least pleasurable. I was cruising well but not with a relaxed paddling rhythm. It was just off high water when I reached Barlocco Isle, the first of the archipelago. I decided to cut between the isle and the main shore despite the nasty looking rough water indicating a submerged reef I would have to cross. It seemed a better option than paddling further out in the wilder seas of the bay. I was at the stage now where I was keeping an eye out for a possible campsite, because the prospect of making a crossing of the bay appeared to be diminishing. However, I was still reluctant to stop and end my day, though equally, I didn't want to head further and deeper into Wigtown Bay. Doing this would soon see me in the realm of Wigtown Sands which would undoubtedly be exposed at low water, making any kind of landing muddily difficult and unpleasant. Additionally, finding a suitable place to camp in the surrounding salt marsh at the head of the bay, would be nigh impossible.

The Islands of Fleet looked to be islands which dried out at low tide, but for the moment they were surrounded by angry choppy water. I really didn't want to stop on the eastern shore of Wigtown Bay, but looking out over to the west, the sea seemed just too rough, and I found myself tussling with the best choice to make. At the forefront of my mind was keeping myself safe and not making stupid decisions. It wasn't lost on me since I was raising money for the R.N.L.I., it would be extremely embarrassing if I ended up having to be rescued by one of their lifeboats. I was determined this would never happen. However, I've never been one to shy away from a challenge or always take the safest and easiest route. As I paddled through the rough waters of the reef and headed towards Ardwall Isle, I ran through all the options before me. I sat out of the incessant wind in the lee of the island wondering whether to land and make camp or to press on. Looking across Wigtown Bay, the far shore did not seem too far away and a quick calculation on my map showed it was just over four miles away.

I was keen to keep going and to at least reach the western shore of the bay, if not the Isle of Whithorn which had been my original plan. The sea was just as wild but the closer and longer I looked at it, the more confident I became about making the crossing in one piece. I sat in my kayak thoughtfully chewing on a snack bar and taking sips from my flask of tea. In the shelter of the island and feeling more confident by the minute, I decided the only way I would find whether I could make this crossing was to give it a go. I calculated the wind would be on my port beam (my left side) and if I needed to turn back to the shelter of the islands, I'd be able to do so without having to paddle back into the wind. I looked closely at my map and decided to cut across the bay from Murray's Isles, which would enable me to easily turn back to the shelter of the island I was behind now. Decision made, I readied myself for the crossing. It was going to be rough out there, so I made sure everything on my deck was secured or stowed away in the deck bag. Everything ready, I set off.

Emerging from behind the shelter of the islands, I was assailed by the full force of the wind and encountered the seas in their fury. What had seemed from my sheltered vantage point to be manageable conditions, turned out to be an uneven and confused sea, with a wave height of at least a couple of metres. It's easy to exaggerate the size of waves when writing about them, but sitting on the surface, any wave crest level with my head, appeared high. In this case, the heavily breaking crests of the waves were twice my head height, and when I was in the troughs, I had the feeling of being engulfed. Waves were breaking all around, and I knew it was only a matter of time before I was caught by a random breaker too. It was a type of kayaking roulette, when the further I paddled out into this crazy sea, the more I chanced the randomness of the crashing waves. As if on cue, without warning, an ominous crack by my left shoulder caught me unawares, and I had a second to brace my paddle on the rumbling white surf of the breaking wave, which pushed me sideways deeply into the trough beneath. In any other situation this occurrence would have been an exhilaration, but here a quarter of the way across Wigtown Bay on my own, it was rather alarming.

I pressed on, noticing from my GPS, despite the pounding I was receiving, I was making good progress. However, like all open water crossings, it seemed to take an age for the shore I had departed, to drop away and the shore I was heading for, to gain in size. There was what felt to be an interminable period when the perspective of both shores seemed to not alter at all. Gradually though, the western shore gained in definition, and I was able to pick out individual trees and make out discernible features on the cliffs. It was a good feeling to see the surf breaking on the shore I was heading towards, and I began to look for a suitable place to make a safe landing. Suddenly the stern of my kayak was thumped and kicked away, and I found myself going over – I was capsizing! A deep-water brace with my paddle, instinctive and at full stretch, saw me remain upright and continue my way – cursing myself for not paying attention to the heaving waves.

As I drew close to the shore, with my heart in my mouth, I could see finding a safe spot to land was going to be a challenge. The waves heaped up onto the low-lying rocks with few opportunities to land without being dashed and broken. Thankfully as if in answer to an unspoken prayer, I saw a stretch of sand surrounded by gnashing rocks. I made for this through the breaking surf, carefully matching my speed with the waves and avoiding being surfed in out of control, for this was most definitely a lee shore. *Sahwira,* laden as she was, performed perfectly, and I was able to twist myself through the gaps between the exposed rocks, hoping I was avoiding any lurking beneath the surface. Within a matter of moments, I was scrunching onto the sand and pulling my spray deck off, clambering out of my cockpit in a rather ungainly fashion, and dashing forward to grab the bow of the kayak to prevent her being dragged back out to sea in the undertow. I pulled her up over the sand and rocks until I was satisfied she was secure and unlikely to be pulled back into the breaking surf. The tide was ebbing anyway, so I didn't have to pull her up very far.

I stood for a few minutes looking back across the bay to where I'd ventured from, just over an hour previously. A surge of satisfaction swept through me, and I loudly praised myself for having made the decision to cross and doing so safely. I marvelled at my deciding to make the crossing at all! For such an important expedition as this one, I was surprised I had made the decision to venture out into the conditions as they were. I didn't think my judgement was poor and neither had I put myself at unnecessary risk, but I'd made the crossing in conditions which could have been considered marginal for a lone sea kayaker. I think because I was wearing top quality kayaking clothing, the result of generous sponsorship from Kokatat, my confidence in venturing out into rougher waters was increased. I knew I was going to stay dry, no matter what.

The tiny bay of Port Whapple I now found myself in, was fringed by woodland and it was in here, amongst the dripping trees and the sodden undergrowth, I made my first camp of the journey. Unpacking the kayak in the gathering rain I was soon under shelter and enjoying the sensuous feeling of putting on dry clothes, while a pot of water brewed on the stove for a welcome mug of tea. The moment of settling back into dry and warm shelter after a physically demanding day such as this, is one of my life pleasures. It's a reward for the expended effort, a time when I can unwind, relax and reflect on the achievements of the day. The fact this was a solitary process did not bother me, though on this occasion, I wanted to share my achievement with others. I wanted to talk with excitement about how I'd come to the decision to cross, the conditions of the crossing itself, and how I eventually made it over without major mishap (apart from the near capsize). As I reflected on my day, I realised this had been an important experience. My decision-making process and my subsequent kayaking skills had been held to account and I had come through well. I realised after today, I would face similar challenges with fortitude, and I believed I would continue to make sound decisions. I contemplated the fact I was willing to extend myself on this journey, take a risk and face challenges head on. It would've been easy to have hauled out on the far eastern shore of Wigtown Bay and waited for the conditions to ease. The fact I hadn't and subsequently now found myself safely and cosily ensconced in my tent, on my highly valued western shore of Wigtown Bay was an incredibly affirming feeling. My confidence in my ability was boosted, which was important because deep within, my self-belief in my skills was sorely tested at times.

Chapter 4

The windy conditions did not abate for another four days but despite this, I managed to make some headway each day. I paddled the eight miles from Port Whapple to the picturesque fishing village of Isle of Whithorn. Here I camped on the manicured isthmus, close to the ruins of the early medieval chapel dedicated to St Ninian. The inshore forecast each day held the same refrain – *strong winds are forecast* – and I began to despair of ever managing to find my way out of the Solway Firth.

In my extensive planning, I had intended to take only four days to reach, then round the Mull of Galloway, into the Irish Sea. I'm experienced enough to know planning a route such as this, can be a nominal paper exercise. It can take just one day of poor weather, to alter the carefully calculated plans, requiring further computation of tide times and tidal flows. Despite this depth of experience, I was beginning to doubt whether I fully comprehended the challenge I'd undertaken. If I was struggling with the conditions here at the very beginning of the journey, then how would I cope much further along, and in far more demanding coastal settings?

It didn't help to dwell on this. I accepted the best thing was to attend each moment as it occurred and not worry too much about the future. I realised if I continued to worry, I would miss out on many of the joys to be experienced ahead. It was a simple matter of living in the *'here and now'*, but it can be difficult to remember this philosophy when faced daily with strong winds and heavy seas. I found my mind continually mulling my options when I gazed at my maps, or the many moments I disconsolately stared out over a vast white crested seascape.

From the Isle of Whithorn I made it around Burrow Head, where I encountered the first big tidal race of my trip. Tide races always manage to get my heart racing and this one was no exception. Because of the windy conditions I gave up on the idea of kayaking the seventeen miles across the mouth of Luce Bay to East Tarbert on the Mull of Galloway. It was with a heavy heart I realised I was going to paddle the complete length of the extensive shoreline of Luce Bay all the way around, adding three days onto my journey.

The added difficulty to entering Luce Bay was the fact this was an active military firing range where the three services often conducted joint exercises. In my planning and preparation for the expedition I'd read many warnings about being caught out in the extensive waters of the range. As I had planned, by kayaking across the mouth of the bay I would have been outside the limits of the range and would not have needed to inform them of my presence. By keeping close to the shore of Luce Bay I managed to keep outside the limits of the range, and it was helpful there were numbered large yellow buoys which ensured I did not venture too far seawards and into the range. There was no danger of this happening because the rough offshore waters made certain I stayed close in to the shore. Despite not wanting to paddle into Luce Bay I was enjoying exploring a new stretch of the Scottish coastline. It was when I was searching for a suitable place to camp on the fourth day of my journey, I ventured too close into the shore. The wind was blowing hard, and the waves were crashing over the shallows. Believing I was just beyond the surf line, I edged my way along vainly seeking a likely looking patch of grass where I could at least put up my tent. Without warning a larger than normal wave picked me up and broke upon me, surging me sideways and out of control towards a reef of boulders. There was little I could do, apart from a desperate attempt to bring my heavy kayak to surf forwards down the wave rather than slide sideways. I didn't succeed and I realised with horror I was going to be smashed onto the rocky reef, so I prepared myself for the resulting crash.

As I feared, *Sahwira* was slammed down onto the reef with enough force for her to tremble from bow to stern. What frightened me most was the terrible sound of crunching and tearing from beneath, just behind my seat. In a matter of seconds, we were across the reef and into a deep pool of calm water beyond. With a sinking heart I turned my laden kayak towards the shore and paddled in. I was certain she had suffered catastrophic damage and she must be holed below the waterline. I had never experienced a crash such as this one in all the years I had been paddling. I clambered out and gingerly pulled her further up the shore. The wind howled around, and I knelt next to her, gently running my hand under her hull to feel for the damage I was certain would be there. To my surprise, I couldn't feel anything apart from obvious gouges in the surface gel coat. Because she was fully loaded and very heavy, I didn't want to roll her onto her side on the rocky shore, as this may have caused further damage. I decided to put to sea again and find a place to camp as soon as I could.

An hour later my tent was up next to a rancid stream reeking the foul odour of farmyard effluent. It was the only suitable place to pitch my tent and I had accepted it with alacrity because quite simply, I'd had enough of the day. When I unpacked the kayak, I was pleasantly surprised neither of the stern compartments showed any sign of leakage which meant there wasn't the likelihood of a hole in the fibreglass. Despite this reassurance, when I gently rolled *Sahwira* over, I was shocked to see she had indeed been badly injured. There was a deep and ragged sideways gash in the hull, presenting the possibility of deeper damage to the underlying layers of fibreglass. A sense of weary despair coursed through me. This was only the fourth day of my journey, and I was going to have to perform some serious repairs to my kayak. I remonstrated with myself out loud, "How could you be so fucking stupid?" My harshly delivered self-critical words served to release some of the tension locked within.

Despite the gusty conditions, there was sunny warmth left in the day and I set about cleaning *Sahwira's* wound and leaving it to dry for the rest of the afternoon. I hoped the sun was strong enough to dry the damage so I could at least affect some kind of repair. Later, as the day was ending, I filled the gash with gel coat repair paste and waited for it to dry. I sanded it down until it was difficult at first glance to determine where the repair had been made. I was pleased with myself and quietly satisfied. Rather than sink into deep despondency because of this mishap, I had resolved the problem with good results. I slept well that night despite the hundreds of sand fleas which annoyingly cavorted about the tent.

Two days later I reached East Tarbert on the Mull of Galloway. It had taken three extra days to reach this point. All the way I had contended with winds in excess of force five and sea states which made paddling uncomfortably challenging. Additionally, I had paddled across the bottom end of Luce Bay with my heart in my mouth because I had not been able to contact the military range personnel to determine whether it was safe to do so or not. What heightened my concern was the presence of a naval ship sitting in the middle of the bay, looking for all intents and purposes to be a target for some kind of exercise or about to fire its weapons itself. The various military information boards dotted around the shores of the bay had warned me in no uncertain terms how active the range was. It was a relief in more ways than one when I finally pulled ashore on the beautiful sandy beach of East Tarbert where I intended to make camp and finalise my preparations for rounding the Mull of Galloway.

Camp was made in gusty gale force winds which threatened to blow my tent over the rocks and into the sea before I could secure it. Later I wandered up the track to the lighthouse, conspicuously perched atop the Mull, overlooking the turbulent confluence of the Solway Firth and the Irish Sea. I've looked up at this iconic structure a few times when sailing past during the various Three Peaks Yacht Races I've competed in. It was an exciting moment to be visiting it from the land and the vistas it offered didn't disappoint. In the wonderfully warm glow of a late spring evening, I gazed across an alluringly calm sea to the faint smudge of the Isle of Man to the south, though try as I might, I could not distinguish any landform to the west which would have shown me Ireland.

This was the seventh day of my journey. I was still in the Solway Firth, three days after I'd planned to have moved on. Rounding the Mull of Galloway was a huge moment for two reasons. First, it was the occasion I turned the corner out of the Solway Firth and headed north, and second, it was the first of the major tidal challenges I would face on the journey.

I woke from a good night's sleep with a sense of trepidation and a strong sense of excitement too. I had not been able to listen to either the Holyhead or Belfast Coastguard weather reports on my VHF radio for a while. For some reason I couldn't pick their broadcasts up. However, the tent wasn't being buffeted by a blowing wind and when I stuck my head out from the flysheet, the day was dawning fair. I felt hopeful I was going to enjoy a settled day.

In my planning for my journey, I spent a considerable amount of time researching the tidal conditions around the Mull of Galloway. I read anecdotal tales of a mighty tide race which I needed to carefully avoid. The tides around Scotland run like rivers, except they change direction every six hours or so, and can run at different speeds during these time periods. Using predictive calculations known as tide tables, it's possible to accurately plan a kayaking route which accounts for the direction and the strengths of the tidal flows. A strong tide flowing in the direction I am travelling is helpful, conversely though, it may be impossible to paddle against the same flow.

Where tides meet headlands, are forced through narrow channels or they they flow over a shallow and uneven seabed, it's likely the speed of the water increases to such a level, it becomes almost like a rushing river with uneven rapids, swirling eddies and large breaking waves. These are known as tide races and over-falls, which are generally best avoided by solo sea kayakers. Given the right conditions, paddling through these phenomena can be exhilarating and fun. Indeed, there are some places where the tides provide play spots for kayakers to test their skills and enjoy themselves. I had no desire to linger in any of the races where I encountered them, primarily because I wouldn't have anyone to fish me out should I capsize in the turbulent waters. Capsizing in these fast moving and confused waters can be dangerous, because the ability to effectively self-rescue is reduced. Also, it's possible to be separated from my kayak, unable to regain it by swimming. The danger does not lie in being dashed on rocks but being swept out into the sea and becoming exhausted and hypothermic.

Apart from two times many years ago, when I was fooling around in my kayak, I'd never capsized on a journey or ever faced the need to self-rescue, though I admit, I've come close quite a few times. In researching the Mull of Galloway, I found myself becoming anxious at the prospect of dealing with the potentially powerful and difficult tidal conditions which sweep around the headland. I had prepared very carefully for paddling around the Mull, and I knew I needed to be at the headland, one and a half hours before the high-water time at Dover. This would ensure I would avoid the worst of the tidal flow. The tidal data for Dover is often used as a benchmark and a reference point for nautical planning around much of Britain, though it's also usual for other main ports to be referred to. Working out the tides, their times and the strength of their flow at given times, involves mathematics which has never been my strong point. I'm not a natural numbers person, so when it came to trusting my computations for tidal planning, I found myself repeatedly double checking my figures and even then, feeling unsure about getting things right. It wasn't unusual to set off not trusting myself to have made the correct calculations.

On this occasion I was as confident as I could be, and I calculated I need not set off to round the Mull until midday.

Until this time the tide was flowing from the north and would be far too strong to paddle against. This meant I had the whole morning to relax in the sunshine which felt like a rewardingly guilty pleasure. In fact, I was able to use the time to catch up on my journal and a few housekeeping chores, reorganising my packing and tidying up my deck bag. In general though it was extremely pleasurable to sit on the rocks looking out across the expanse of Luce Bay, watching the seals popping their heads through the surface of the water to squint at me with their watery inquisitive stares. As pleasant as this was, I began to get restless, and I was eager to be on my way. I revisited my scrawled computations, to see if I set off now, the tidal stream would have sufficiently weakened to sneak around the headland.

I couldn't really work this out, so I decided to go and have a look. I was confident I could eddy hop against any residual flow and this way gain an hour of paddling. I packed everything away and set off with the familiar tightness of fear and excitement pervading my senses and body. I paddled close into the rocks of the towering cliffs above. I'd heard the best way to avoid the Mull of Galloway tide race was to round the Mull so close to the cliffs, you could touch them. I was taking this advice as literally as possible. The conditions were perfect. There was a lovely warmth in the sun and there was hardly any wind at all. The sea was calm with no swell to speak of. It was an enjoyable pleasure to be able to slide my kayak along the base of the cliffs without fear of being dashed on the rocks. The cliffs were alive with Fulmars and Guillemots who squawked from their vantage points on the narrow ledges streaked with their pungent guano. There was a distinct fishy odour which pervaded these echoing surroundings.

There was no sign of any tide race, and my confidence was growing with every paddle stroke I took. At the very southern point of the Mull there was a riffle of fast-moving water with a few desultory waves which caused no concern. I allowed myself a muted whoop when I noticed the compass rose swinging gently around to point north. At long last I was rounding the Mull and finally leaving the Solway Firth. My self-congratulations were to be short lived. Keeping close into the rocks I craned my neck, gazing upwards to see if I could spot the lighthouse high above. Then ahead, I spied a tongue of water unerringly flowing towards me through a wide gap between the cliffs and a sizeable off lying rock. As I drew closer, I thought it looked tame enough to paddle hard against it, and creep into the inviting eddy a few metres above. Memories of my disaster on the Lleyn Peninsula in 2009 flooded back into my mind. Here, I'd seriously miscalculated the tides and found myself vainly fighting a six-knot tide race. I was saved from ignominy by a nearby helpful lobster fisherman who observing my futile efforts, towed me the fifty metres through the Braich y Pwll race to the haven I was desperately attempting to reach. There was no helpful fisherman close by now and I was very much on my own.

With this memory firmly in my mind, I approached the flow with some caution. I could see now, the stream was too strong to paddle against, but I thought this was only because the tide was being squeezed between the rock and the cliff. Out beyond the rock, there looked like movement in the sea but not as strong. I set about ferry gliding across the flow with my heart in my mouth, because this is an act easier said than done. In a laden kayak there's a distinct possibility of the up-stream flow piling up against the low-lying deck, flipping the kayak before I would know what's happening. I angled *Sahwira's* bow into the flow and with strong positive paddle strokes, making sure I leaned away from the main flow (presenting my kayak's hull upstream), I was across in a matter of seconds. I exhaled loudly with relief. Once across I continued my way with strong forward strokes. In the calm water *Sahwira* appeared to be effortlessly surging forward and I was sure I was through the tidal bottle neck. I looked across to the cliff and with a jolt noticed the stripe of vivid green weed on the rock face I was using as a positioning marker, was dropping ahead. I took a bearing on another marker, a similar streak of slime, and with an audible curse, I realised I was steadily losing ground. Despite deeply digging my paddles into the sea with all the power I could muster, I was being swept inexorably backwards. The tide was still in vigorous flow and yet again, I'd got it wrong – I'd been impetuous, and I was paying the price.

In desperation I angled *Sahwira* further away from the cliffs in the vain hope the further out I paddled, the weaker the stream. I found myself steadily pushed back and further out into the Irish Sea. A strong sense of fear suddenly enveloped me. I conjured an image of being swept backwards into the mighty Mull of Galloway race which I'd assiduously been avoiding. I expected any moment to find myself sucked into a maelstrom of standing waves and confused seas. Looking over my shoulder and all around, I was relieved to see no evidence to support this fear, but nevertheless I decided to turn tail and retreat to East Tarbert. The sea remained calm and once I had made the decision to retire, I started to enjoy the position I found myself in. I was a few hundred metres out from the Mull, and now had a wonderfully panoramic view of the bluff which denoted the very southwestern tip of Scotland. The beautifully appointed nineteenth century Robert Stevenson engineered lighthouse stood proud on the cliffs. I sat for a while with *Sawhira* drifting atop a weirdly swirling calm sea, taking in this splendorous scene. In the warm, bright springtime sun, I felt I could sit for ages and in fact I was tempted to do just that, while I waited for the tide to ease. Instead, I paddled to beneath the vertical cliffs again, making my way back to the haven of East Tarbert. I was trying not to berate myself too harshly for making such a rookie mistake with the tides, when suddenly I heard a voice call down from the rocks high above. I looked up to see a young man gesticulating seawards and shouting he could see a pod of Dolphins not far away. I looked as hard as I could but could not see them. He went on to tell me he was one of the R.S.P.B. wardens based at the lighthouse, and this was his job for the summer. It was strange to be shouting this conversation in this location, but it felt good to be talking to another person after four days of solitude.

Back on the beach at East Tarbert I ruefully noted my Yellowbrick GPS tracker would show the world my error of judgement, and I smiled at the thought of the jocular comments I might receive about this. I used the opportunity of my enforced free time in the warm sunshine to recharge my electrical items with my solar battery charger. I also played a game of marbles with sea smoothed pebbles around the beach. I was playing against myself, and I kept losing.

Eventually the time came (the correct time according to my original planning) to launch the kayak and try to round the Mull again. I cut across the bay to the beginning of the cliffs and edged my way around the corner. There was no movement in the sea apart from the merest of ruffles here and there, and this time I shot around the headland. I took pleasure in gliding past the stalwart bastions of this particular edge of Scotland. I was realising one of my sea kayaking ambitions and I hollered a shout of triumph when I was certain I was well around the Mull of Galloway.

I continued to make excellent progress northwards and I paddled hard and fast. I wanted to cover as much distance as I could, while the weather was fair and there was within me a drive to make up for lost time. I found it difficult to relax and to accept although I was behind the schedule I had planned, there was plenty of time to complete the journey and there was no need to push myself so hard. I didn't have a specific target for the day, but I did want to get as close to Portpatrick as possible. I considered pushing hard to make it there but dismissed this idea because it would have meant arriving late in the evening, and I wasn't sure where I would be able to camp. At this stage of the journey, I was less confident about putting my tent up in the grassy public spaces of towns – a consideration which faded as time progressed and I came to realise folks in Scotland are generally warmly welcoming of travellers and are not precious of their public spaces.

It was not long before I was crossing Port Logan Bay and rounding the headland into the stunningly picturesque Ardwell Bay. I was spoilt for choice for the perfect spot for my tent and it was an intensely pleasurable moment, pitching camp in the life sustaining warmth of the early summer evening sun. I took the opportunity to spread my belongings out in the warmth to air them. After a welcome dinner of pasta, I wandered over the low headland to look at the ruinous remains of an Iron Age broch, the first of many I would get to see on my trip. Satisfied with the successful completion of an important day, I turned in and slept soundly, without interruption.

Chapter 5

With its narrow, rocky entrance onto the Irish Sea, Portpatrick on the Galloway coast, is a picturesque, small fishing port and the home of the third lifeboat on my list. Given the wonderful reception and hospitality I had received from the previous two lifeboat stations, I was looking forward to a hot shower and the possibility of a roof over my head. It was with some excitement and anticipation I crept into the inner harbour and pulled ashore close to the lifeboat gracefully berthed on her pontoon. I had not written ahead to any of the stations or chosen to telephone them to warn them of my arrival, because it's not in my nature to bother people. I was concerned by telling the lifeboat volunteers I was on my way and giving them a potential arrival date and time, would create unnecessary worries if I were delayed for any reason. The last thing I wanted was a lifeboat tasked to search for me because I was unable to arrive on the day I said I would.

This was the first designated offshore lifeboat station of my journey. As yet I did not fully understand the differences in staffing and management between the inshore lifeboat stations and the offshore ones. In general, the offshore lifeboats operate in the seas further from the coast, often far out into British and Irish maritime waters. These offshore lifeboat stations are generally staffed full time and have at least one salaried professional and sometimes two. These being the Coxswain and the Mechanic.

The Coxswain is the senior crew member on the boat. They will have a considerable amount of experience with the lifeboat service and invariably on the boat they are leading. They are the ones who helm the boat – drive it. They are the people who make the crucial decisions out at sea during a rescue and who the crew look to for leadership. The Mechanic's role is what the title implies. The offshore lifeboats require a demanding schedule of maintenance and upkeep. They must be always service ready which requires even the smallest of defects to be immediately resolved and dealt with. Some stations are using lifeboats over fifteen years old, and this often means a constant round of servicing issues to ensure the boat is seaworthy. I didn't learn all this immediately but instead came to understand the demands of keeping a lifeboat on active duty as I travelled from station to station.

Today was the day after the General Election for the U.K. and I walked into the lifeboat station to find a television blaring out the constituency results as they came in. It was an odd experience having been away from the news and media for the last five days to return to relative civilisation. This being Scotland, all eyes were on how well the Scottish National Party were doing and as I sat there in the lifeboat crew room supping tea and munching on biscuits, I could see they were romping towards a landslide victory. Gathering from the conversations around, I sensed this wasn't a welcome development in this corner of Scotland and I kept my counsel. Politics aside, it was good to hear about the service the Portpatrick lifeboat provides and the challenges they face. Being an offshore lifeboat, their area of operation is considerably larger than the other two I had visited earlier in the week. It was interesting to learn they are one of the quieter stations on the Scottish coast which surprised me because of the busy shipping channel in the Irish Sea.

At one stage, an elderly gentleman arrived in the room who turned out to be a retired GP and a former crewman but was now a trustee of the local lifeboat committee. When he heard of my sea kayaking plans he said, "I saw some idiot a mile out in Luce Bay battling a strong offshore wind. I thought there's a shout we're going to get!"

I replied rather sheepishly, "Yes, that was me."

"Ah, good to see you got here safe and sound. I suppose you know what you're doing."

"Yup," I offered back, "the wind was blowing pretty hard as I crossed the Bay, but all the same, I was confident I'd be OK."

There then ensued a long discussion about the safety equipment I was carrying and how I would call for help if I found myself in difficulties. I'd been expecting this conversation with many of the lifeboat crews, and I was confident I had all my safety considerations covered. Not only this, but I had also presented a very clear appraisal of my risk assessments and mitigating plans with my expedition proposal scrutinised by the R.N.L.I. Headquarters in Poole. Despite this though, I couldn't help feeling I was being put on the spot and being examined in some fashion. There was an all too familiar sensation of warmth rising behind my ears, as I realised I was beginning to flush with annoyance, or possibly the embarrassment of being caught out.

In truth, the conversation wasn't a matter of convincing them I was competently safe, rather a genuine exploration of how I accounted for my wellbeing at sea, particularly since I was kayaking on my own. They were genuinely interested in what safety equipment I was carrying and my emergency procedures. In turn they described in detail the various methods at their disposal they would utilise when searching for my distress beacon or VHF call for help. It seemed the Portpatrick crew hadn't encountered many sea kayakers in the course of their work and having me drop by was an opportunity to discuss these matters.

Many people, including sea kayakers themselves, view sea kayaking as an inherently hazardous pastime and much is made of carrying essential safety equipment, undertaking training in how to use it and strongly advising against paddling solo. I hold the opinion humans inherently desire to keep themselves safe and because of this, they'll overall make sound decisions to ensure this remains the case. Unfortunately, though, even the most experienced people may one day find themselves in difficulty and require assistance. This is why we have the wide range of selfless emergency services we do in Britain.

Time and again throughout my journey, I was asked whether I was safe in what I was undertaking. I think most saw me as foolhardy and possibly madly courageous. This was often when I had to hold my irritation in check and diplomatically explain the many safety factors I'd accounted for. I often wished it were possible for folks to know without enquiring, how I never once diminished the potential for danger during my journey and I was fully prepared to meet it.

Risk and the assessment of risk is an inherent aspect of our culture here in Britain. We are encouraged to account for and mitigate even the most minor potential hazards for our own lives and the lives of others. In my view, risk is an important aspect of life. It's a life enhancer – without it, our lives would be mundane and static. Growth encompasses change and change cannot occur without accepting risk in some form or another. Every day of our lives, we move from one way of being in our world to another. Mostly these moments of change are subtle and out of our awareness – a new route to work, a new acquaintance in the office, a new recipe for dinner or a different place to buy the groceries. We make choices every day, almost every moment. There is risk involved in every choice we make – the risk things may not turn out the way we hope or expect. Of course, the great majority of these choices do not involve life or death outcomes, but risk is applied to them, nonetheless.

Because outdoor pastimes like rock climbing and kayaking are beyond the everyday experience of most people, they're perceived as being extraordinarily risky and therefore dangerous. We become inured to everyday risks in our lives such as driving a car and accept them as normal but view out of the ordinary activities with suspicion and wariness.

There were of course potentially severe hazards I faced by kayaking solo. The greatest of these was capsizing and finding myself unable to roll my kayak upright or re-enter it if I were to come out. I would be on my own without the assistance of a companion. In this situation I would be immersed in the water with the danger of fatigue and hypothermia taking hold. Another considerable danger I faced, was the threat of being run down by a large ship or other craft. Landing and launching in heavy seas were also hazards I accounted for. For all of these and more, I continuously and dynamically made assessments of the risks I faced.

The discussion petered out and I inwardly breathed a sigh of relief. I was pleased with how self-assured I had been, and assertive regarding my ability to keep myself safe. With the mugs of coffee emptied and the tin of biscuits largely depleted, I sensed it was a prudent time to move on. No offer had been made regarding me spending the night there and it was far too early in my journey to feel comfortable about asking. Anyhow, it was only midday and there was substantial northern flow remaining in the tide to help me on my way.

Before I left, the doctor took me to one side and conspiratorially offered the use of his catamaran which was berthed in Stranraer marina. This was incredibly kind of him, and I assured him I would certainly take him up on his offer if I needed to. I admitted to everyone before I left, I wasn't sure where I would be spending the night. I joked as I left, "After all, this is an adventure!" I made my way down the stairs and out into the fresh early spring air. As I paddled out of Portpatrick Harbour, I was wondering where I would be spending the night.

The tide was in my favour and along with a light south westerly wind, I effortlessly cruised up the Galloway coast. Because it was a pleasant afternoon, I considered pushing the thirty kilometres to Stranraer in the hope I could bunk down at the lifeboat station there. Having lost time in the Solway Firth, I had a strong desire to press on and cover as much distance as possible. With weather and sea conditions as benign as they were and the promise these would continue for at least another day, I was placing myself under pressure to paddle hard and fast.

The overall objective of this expedition was quite the opposite. I wanted to enjoy every moment of the Scottish coastline without scudding past and paying attention to the subtleties and beauty along the way. The idea of committing myself to improbable daily mileages did not excite me whatsoever. It had been easy to plan the journey with reasonable daily distances which would see me around my route in a minimum of two months. This of course relied on the weather being perfect every day. The reality was different and even this early into the journey, I was in the position of beginning to feel panicked about catching up and regaining momentum. I had the fullness of summer ahead of me, and yet I couldn't shake the fear I would run out of time.

I used the tide and the wind to my advantage and paddled hard for Corsewall Point, enjoying the feel of *Sahwira* knifing through the water leaving a substantial wake in her trail. I was feeling strong and a glance at my GPS showed I was averaging five miles an hour. This was wonderful. It was akin to riding the open road on a motorbike without a helmet with the wind blowing through my hair – a feeling of wild freedom.

There was a strong sense of anticipation too. This was the day I entered the Firth of Clyde, thus marking the end of the first significant leg of my journey and the beginning of the second. I had broken my journey into definable sections and so to be completing the first of these provided a feeling of achievement and a sense of progression. The Clyde was a new kayaking area for me. If I'm honest, I never really considered paddling in the Clyde because I held the view the area was industrial, lacking in wildness and the iconic beauty of the Scottish west coast. I assumed for the purposes of the journey; this was simply going to be a long leg to complete and get out of the way. However, as I rounded the top of the Rhinns of Galloway I found myself becoming excited at the prospect of entering the Firth and the new landscapes I would discover.

As if in answer to my uncertainty about the validity of the Clyde as a wild area, while I was approaching the Corsewall Point Lighthouse, I heard the giveaway slapping splash of a seal behind me. I turned to look and couldn't see anything, but my heart missed a beat when suddenly a dark shape bulleted up beside my kayak, surfaced and then dived away again. A moment of silence until I distinctly felt the stern of my kayak being knocked heavily. I twisted in my seat and saw a young seal nudging the stern-tip of my kayak. Delighted by this visit, I stopped paddling and reached for my camera, whereupon the seal splashed and disappeared. Disappointed to miss a good wildlife shot, I paddled on. Suddenly the same thing happened. I stopped paddling and again it disappeared, this time reappearing by my left paddle blade, taking a long and careful look at me with its dark, glassily languid eyes. It slipped beneath the boat and reappeared by my starboard bow. I had my camera ready and was now taking plenty of photos of this joyful encounter with this lively and friendly wild animal. I have been near to seals before, many times, but this was the closest encounter I had experienced. Resting its flippers on the front deck of the kayak it awkwardly attempted to clamber onto the boat. It almost made it before rather ungracefully sliding back into the sea. It tried once more but again to no avail. I willed it to succeed. Resting for a moment in the water, it looked back at me before suddenly effecting a boisterous splash and disappearing beneath the surface. I decided to continue my way.

What followed became a game of cat and mouse or seal and kayaker. For some apparent reason the seal began to strike the kayak by ramming into my stern with considerable force. It would then attempt to clamber onto the stern deck and a couple of times I had to quickly slap for support when its weight briefly destabilised me. The thumps into the stern hull of the kayak became increasingly severe and unsure of its ludic intentions, I began to fear being knocked over by this one seal. I paddled faster which only served to goad the seal into greater competitive action. There was no way I would be able to outpace it, but I gave it my all anyway. The seal began a new tactic too. It made lunges at my left paddle blade looking as if it wanted to take a hefty bite out of it. I was beginning to fear for the safety of my kayak and my paddles. Even though the seal looked like a juvenile I could see if it managed to take a bite it would do considerable damage with its range of teeth and powerful jaws. At one point in utter frustration, because my shouting at it to go away wasn't working, I swept my paddle in a backwards motion in a vain attempt to splash it with a sheet of cold water. As I did this, I realised the futility of my action – splashing a seal with water!

In the end, I decided to head into the shoreline skerries and paddle through the rocks. I reckoned at least this would slow the seal down and prevent it building up enough momentum to race up to the kayak and thump into it. This course of action seemed to do the trick because the seal stopped in its tracks, glared at me for a second or two, then disappeared beneath the surface. I didn't see it again. It was with considerable relief and a sense of perplexity, I kayaked past the tidily painted lighthouse at Corsewall Point. I had considered stopping here to camp but there was still plenty of time left in the day and I pressed on. Eventually I turned into Loch Ryan as rain began to descend in sweeping curtain like sheets, opening and hiding the vistas up the loch, like heavy inky grey velvet stage curtains. Realising I would arrive in Stranraer well after six in the evening, I decided to pull ashore and found a lovely campsite in the picturesque picnic spot at Lady Bay below Portencalzie. Here, I enjoyed watching the ferries departing for and returning from Ireland from the port of Cairnryan on the far side of the loch.

The following day, after a cosy night sheltered from the torrential rain, I set off on the short leg to Stranraer at the head of the loch. I arrived on the pebbly beach in front of the lifeboat station and wandered up, to discover nobody was there. I was desperate for a shower and even more desperate to get my electrical items charged up. My phone was down to the last vestiges of its battery, my GPS was about to run out of power and my camera battery was dangerously low too. Despite having a solar battery charger, I was unable to keep up with the power demands of my various gadgets. I had counted on regularly recharging these items at the various lifeboat stations I visited. The lack of a shower was a problem too, but since I was paddling alone, I could live with this. I found myself in a quandary as to what to do. The day was calm, wonderfully sunny with light winds. It was an excellent opportunity to press on and make up the time I had lost in the Solway Firth. In addition, the following day, the weather was forecast to drastically change with the arrival of further strong winds, strong enough to keep me off the water.

If I was prepared to wait for him to arrive in the late afternoon, I had the kind offer of a berth on the doctor's catamaran moored in the nearby Stranraer Marina. If I did this, I would most certainly recharge all my 'electricals' and enjoy the hot refreshing shower I craved. However, if this was what I chose to do, there'd be the distinct possibility I'd get caught in Stranraer for the next few days while the gales blew through. To aid making this decision, I wanted to have a look at the yacht, so I pulled *Sahwira* as far up as I could without ripping her hull out on the pebbly shore and set off on the long walk along the town's promenade to the marina.

The catamaran when I saw it, was huge, and would have afforded a perfect night of sheltered comfort. For a long few moments, I was sorely tempted to hang around for the doctor's arrival to accept his generous offer to stay on his boat for the night. However, my desire to press on was the greater, so I wandered back to the kayak waiting patiently on the beach. The sun was gloriously warm, and children played on the beach with shrill shrieks of joy, lending a holiday atmosphere to the day. I soon left these cries of happiness behind, as I set out across the wonderfully azure and diamond glittering bay towards the busy ferry port of Cairnryan, and my next challenge – avoiding Irish Sea ferries. This I did without difficulty, and it wasn't long before I was once again paddling along wild rocky coastline, northwards into the Firth of Clyde. I had set out from Stranraer with no eventual objective in mind, but it seemed likely I might reach the village of Ballantrae in good time, find a place to camp there and hopefully enjoy a pint in the village bar.

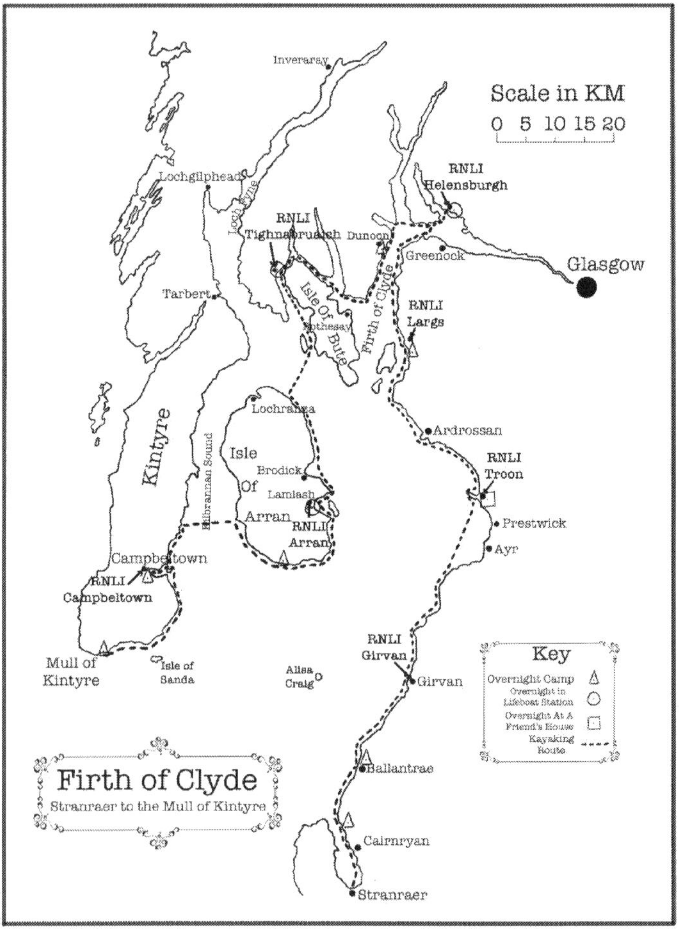
Scale in KM
0 5 10 15 20
Inveraray
Lochgilphead
Loch Fyne
RNLI
Tighnabruaich
Dunoon
RNLI
Helensburgh
Greenock
Glasgow
Tarbert
Isle Of Bute
Rothesay
Firth of Clyde
RNLI
Largs
Lochranza
Ardrossan
Kintyre
Kilbrannan Sound
Isle
Of
Arran
Brodick
Lamlash
RNLI
Arran
RNLI
Troon
Prestwick
Ayr
Campbeltown
RNLI
Campbeltown
Mull of
Kintyre
Isle of
Sanda
Ailsa
Craig
RNLI
Girvan
Girvan
Key
Overnight Camp
Overnight in Lifeboat Station
Overnight At A Friend's House
Kayaking Route
Ballantrae
Firth of Clyde
Stranraer to the Mull of Kintyre
Cairnryan
Stranraer

The Firth of Clyde
Stranraer to The Mull of Kintyre

Chapter 6

The coastline northwards from Cairnryan was steep, rocky and wild. Far different to the densely inhabited urban landscape I had somehow managed to fixate in my mind. I know in my planning I had poured over maps of this area and will have seen much of the southern Clyde coastline is sparsely habited. Despite this though, I had created for myself the idea the Clyde was synonymous with industry and high population. I was therefore enjoying this stretch of wildness and eased back on my paddling to take it in. I eyed up the attractive looking Finnarts Bay as a possible campsite, but it was both too close to the busy A77 main road and there was still plenty of time left in the warm early summer afternoon. However, a few miles on, when I arrived at the curiously named small bay of Currarie Port, I knew at first glance this was somewhere I wanted to stop. Despite this certainty, I sat in the lumpy waters just off the shore carefully considering my options. Ballantrae was only three miles further and I could make this in under an hour. If the forecast winds arrived in the night, then at least I would be safe there. As an added complication, I was running out of rations. I had resupplied (after a fashion) after visiting the small shop in Portpatrick but I didn't have enough food to last another three days and the stormy weather looked as if it might hang around for that length of time. If I became stormbound here, I would be faced with a very long walk to the closest store where I could buy food.

Yet, this spot was perfect. Truly perfect in fact. It was a totally unexpected find, with a mellow peat laden burn, languidly flowing through a series of small pools, edged with smooth boulders, out of a steeply wooded valley. The green vale with an expansive area of inviting close cropped grass, was surrounded by high and steep yellow flowered gorse covered hills. The landing on the pebbly beach was easy and I pulled *Sahwira* further up out of the reach of the rising tide. I told myself I was only going to have a look. There are at least two things in life which are impossible to do – one is to say we're only going to look at puppies, we won't get one if we don't think so. The other is to land in a beautiful location on a kayak trip and say to myself I'm only going to have a look; I'll press on if I don't like it. Before I knew it, the kayak's compartments were being unloaded and my tent was up.

Looking skywards as I often did, I could see the wispy streaks of high cirrus sweeping across the blue and far out to the western horizon, an ominous bank of cloud was beginning to build. Both these warning signs weren't enough to urge me to stay my course and press on to Ballantrae where I was assured of a haven. For the time being I was in a beautiful location, the sun was strikingly warm, and I had all my kayaking kit strewn around the tent, drying out and being refreshingly aired. Probably what was most exciting too, was the icy dip I enjoyed in a pool of fresh clear amber hued water, where I was able to wash myself and end up feeling wonderfully clean again. The beach was strewn with hundreds of pieces of smoothed driftwood which would either have made the most fantastic beach fire, or easily sold as pieces of natural art to adorn the walls and tables of wandering tourists. I did consider the fire option but decided against this, because having just enjoyed my refreshing bathe, I didn't want to go to bed with the smell of wood smoke lingering on my clothing. Instead, I set about preparing my dinner for the evening.

I've never been one to pay attention to my diet on kayaking expeditions. I'm not a gourmet who worries about menu details, so long as I'm fed and satiated. I cook with a small Trangia stove using a methylated spirit burner. It's a bomb-proof stove which is guaranteed to work come rain and wind. It may not be the most efficient and its fuel economy is questionable, but its compact reliability has won it a favoured place in my expedition kit. My cooking needs are simple. I need two small pans, one for boiling water and the other for cooking. When it comes to food, I choose easy to cook meals which require no preparation. The reason being, I need to be certain I can feed myself quickly and without fuss. This is the case when I arrive ashore wet, cold and tired and need to hastily nourish myself. Packets of microwaveable rice (no, I don't carry a microwave in my kayak) and tins of veggie chilli are a great favourite of mine as well as tinned ratatouille. Pasta and sauce are also a staple of my expedition diet.

Many tell me breakfast is an important meal and should not be avoided. I admit to being indolent when it comes to eating breakfast. It's an inconsistent process within my morning routine. Making coffee, yes. Boiling water for my vacuum flask, yes. Rustling up a bowl of porridge or muesli, no. For an inexplicable reason I chose to exclude breakfast from my important morning schedule. Neither do I stop to eat a midday lunch. I prefer to snack on the go, managing to maintain my energy levels through the day. It was rare for me to feel hungry during this trip. I think my metabolism found its rhythm and looked after me extremely well. Fluids wise, I had a five-litre water bladder attached to the back of my buoyancy aid and I filled a thermos mug with lemon and ginger tea. The latter could only be opened and drunk after I had completed ten miles of paddling. This self-imposed constraint ensured I didn't drink it too early on. I would enjoy searching the map for a likely sheltered spot at the ten-mile mark where I could stop and enjoy a twenty-minute breather.

It was rare for me to make stops ashore during a day of kayaking. My bladder and bowels seemed to be unnaturally capacious, but I think too, like my metabolism, my digestion and micturition had fallen into place with my daily routine. For the four months my bodily system worked like clockwork, only becoming a little confused when I was forced ashore for longer periods.

As a consideration, how does one go to the bathroom in the wild where there are no public conveniences to ensure the Britishly private process of voiding our bowels? As with most matters living an itinerant life in the wild, the process of urinating and defecating became a naturally regular act during my camping routine. Societally, we do not talk about our individual toiletry processes. The sea was my lavatory. The seaweed my tissue paper with a small bottle of antiseptic hand gel, my cleanser. The waves made short work of my doings and the seaweed had the excellent effect of cleansing astringency, and this too was washed away by the sea. The rocky foreshore provided many suitable toilet sites where I could rest myself comfortably and take in the spectacular scenery before me. No need for a newspaper or book. We speak of our minimum impact in wild places. This being how our presence will impact the natural settings of our overnight stops. The general rule being take nothing but photos, leave nothing but footprints, kill nothing but time. We all aspire to behave this way when we enter the natural realm. However, we are animals too and must perform what all animals must do, breathe, eat, drink, urinate, defecate, sleep and procreate. Why then I wonder, do we often view evidence of our presence in the natural realm as toxic? After all, we have the right to exist there too. Of course, it won't do to ignore the accepted conventions of not defecating near water sources or leaving your turds in places easily stumbled upon.

I find the most obnoxious remnant of human presence in a wild setting are the remains of campfires burned on grass. I'm confounded when I arrive at a beach to find two or three of these dreadful fire scars within metres of each other. Why do folks feel the need to create a fire from scratch rather than use an already 'prepared' scar? It's unthinking vandalism.

I'm certainly not against campfires. They are an important convivial element to a wild sea kayak journey. Washed up driftwood, smoothed and sculptured by the sea, makes excellent firewood. The place to enjoy a blazing campfire is down on the beach where at some stage the tide will sweep away the remains of the fire and where no damage has been done to the ground below.

That night I slept soundly, only to wake in the morning to the worrying sound of the wind fiercely tugging at the tent flysheet and the roaring of a building surf on the shingle beach. The storm had arrived. With a heavy heart I realised I was faced with a problem, and I clambered out of the tent to take a closer look. As I stood on the beach looking out over the ominous white capped seas, driving darts of rain stung my cheeks. After what seemed a considerable length of time,

I determined the rough sea appeared manageable. I decided to crack on and make my way to Ballantrae. I worked out for the three miles to the village, I would be provided with a following wind and sea and because of this welcome assistance, I counted on reaching the safety of the harbour before the worst of the weather arrived.

I was on the water by 8am and immediately experienced an alarming sense of exposure. Out there in the kayak the sea state seemed larger and more intimidating than it looked from the shore. The waves were peaking well above my head and breaking randomly around. Where they refracted off the shoreline rocks, they were noisy, wild and confused. The distance to safety was only three miles, but in this moment, it felt much further. I was aware of a nagging worry; anything could happen in that short distance. Soon after setting off along the coast towards Ballantrae, I managed to get a measure of the rumbling sea. Wave sets roared past, inviting me to catch and ride with them. There was an added challenge too, of not being pushed into the rocky coastline where rogue boulders lay in wait, out of sight in the confused sea, to nastily clip the underneath of my hull. I made steady progress and I soon got the hang of allowing the kayak to do all the work. Yet again I noticed *Sahwira's* true sea worthiness, an innate quality I was rapidly growing to appreciate. She handled the wild conditions superbly, and all she asked was to keep her heading down-wind and down-sea, with the odd paddle brace every now and again to steady ourselves. She is a Nigel Dennis, Sea Kayaking U.K. "Explorer", specifically designed for serious kayaking expeditions.

From time to time a few paddle strokes kept us moving forward, but generally I allowed the wind and the waves to determine our pleasingly steady progress. It wasn't long before Ballantrae hove into view. On peering through the driving rain at the seething shingle seafront, I found no difficulty in deciding to press on the extra mile to the shelter of the village's harbour, rather than attempt a landing on the beach.

By now the gale had increased in strength and the sea was really piling up around me. With my heart in my mouth and keeping well beyond the surf line, I crept along the shore towards a low-lying harbour wall. With a deep sigh of relief, I found myself sweeping around the harbour mole and into shelter, relishing the immediate and wonderful sense of peace after the fierce wind and raging sea. It was only a mere thirty minutes since I had departed Currarie Port. I sat for a few moments, breathing heavily before pulling ashore to make camp in a tight wee spot in the lee of the old lifeboat shed. This would be my home for the next three days.

There was a carnival atmosphere to the village's harbour front. I had arrived on the day of the first ever Ballantrae food festival. Mouth-watering aromas of sea food and other delicious dishes wafted over to me, where I sat beside my tent in a rather forlorn fashion. I was on a tight budget, which meant smelling the food was all I could afford. From time to time, visitors to the food-fayre wandered over to enquire about my purpose. They were intrigued by the R.N.L.I. bunting and the charity's flag which I draped over my tent and festooned around my camp. I had adorned my camp spot in this fashion, to both raise awareness of the nature of my expedition, and to lend an air of official importance should anyone doubt the validity of me camping there. One of these inquisitive folks was John, a resident of the village who took a great interest in my story. He sat with me and we chatted for quite a while. It transpired we shared a love for outdoor adventure, and we had a couple of mutual friends too. John was retired and a well-read local historian. He spoke passionately about Ballantrae, its past connections with the expansive waters of the Firth of Clyde and beyond, as well as its present challenges. He invited me to his home, so I could make use of his shower and for a couple of evenings we sat up late into the night, drinking distinctively smoky, peaty whisky, and animatedly discussing issues which mattered to us most. I was particularly taken by his wonderfully nostalgic accounts of creeping into the old lifeboat shed as a young boy, where he'd listen to the discussions taking place within the parliament, the manner with which the fishing community resolved their issues. John went on to describe the sometimes-fractious relationship between the tight knit community and their local laird who owned substantial swathes of the village and even the harbour. It amazed me in our modern age, some feudal rights continued to exist. In his spare time, John enjoyed creating objects of beauty from the driftwood he collected from the shoreline, and he kindly gave me a soporific tuneful flute he'd made from a lovely piece of sea tumbled wood.

An unexpected and gratifying aspect of this journey was my relationship with the social media platform of Twitter. Prior to setting off, I widely used it to advertise the adventure and my fund-raising intentions. I never imagined how popular my journey would become and I was delighted by the interest shown. I had in the region at the time of four thousand followers, most of whom of course I rarely interacted with. Yet, there were a core group of people who I regularly chatted to, and who by regularly Tweeting their encouragement, provided me with much support throughout the four months it took to paddle around Scotland. Given the ease of accessibility to the internet, even in some of the remotest locations, it was possible to lie in my tent and communicate with folks I had created an on-line friendship with all around the globe. It turned out this journey provided the opportunity to make flesh and blood connections with many Twitter friends too. As it unfolded, it wasn't uncommon at every stop I made in a harbour town or village, to meet new friends who 'followed' me on-line through this unique collaborative medium.

This was unexpected because I underestimated the power of on-line friendship. I underestimated too the interest taken in my venture. I never for one moment thought for the duration of my trip I would become a cause celebre amongst those who followed me on Twitter. Equally too, my journey garnered interest on the page I created on Facebook. To begin with, I used social media as a means of publicising my adventure and my fundraising goal for the lifeboat service. I thought it would be a simple matter of posting updates and a few photographs in the hope this would inspire folks to donate. I didn't think many people would become interested in me and in the details of my day to day kayaking expeditionary existence.

I was therefore humbled by the warm attention I received and to be honest, I was gratified too. I hadn't embarked on my adventure in a quest for fame and fortune, but the fact I was receiving plaudits from hundreds of people around the world, was an affirming experience. The awareness people were generous to give their time both on-line and to travel to meet me, emboldened me. This was an authentic validation for my venture which I truly appreciated.

A key friendship borne out of the social media 'Twitter-sphere' was the one which developed between Charles Coull and me. Charlie was a Brigadier in the British Army and also worked for the Scottish Government. He had come across my Twitter account and followed me. When I made my round Scotland plans public, he contacted me and offered to help when I reached the Ayrshire coastline. In those early stages of preparation, I wasn't certain what support I would require. When I arrived in Ballantrae and found myself shore-bound for three days, Charlie and his wife Sandra drove all the way down the coast from Troon to meet me. As I was to learn, in his inimitably generous manner, he offered to bring anything I required. As luck would have it, I was desperately short of methylated spirits for my stove and so began a lifelong friendship borne out of meths supply. When we met and walked on the hard pebbled Ballantrae beach, leaning into the driving wind, it was as if we had been friends for years. Such was the quality of our connection on Twitter, this readily translated into a genuine friendship of flesh and blood. After our meeting in Ballantrae, Charlie went on to daily text the inshore weather forecast along with an image of the atmospheric barometric chart. These were invaluable sources of weather information which assisted me many times to make important decisions about whether to paddle or not.

Likewise on another day while at Ballantrae, Anita, another on-line friend visited with her husband and brought with them a gift of whisky from Amber, a mutual Twitter on-line friend of ours who lives in Toronto. Amber, despite living in Canada became a source of genuine support. It amazed me how intuitive she became at judging the varying levels of my mood through the nature of my regular tweets.

It was clear my solitariness would not be totally devoid of warm human connections.

In the early weeks after setting off, I struggled with the notion this expedition was a worthwhile undertaking. Many times, I experienced deep pangs of guilt, berating myself for being selfish, taking time off from earning an income and being away from my wife for a long period of time. It felt incredibly indulgent I should be doing this, especially when there was little prospect of financial gain from it. I wasn't an adventure celebrity who would use this expedition to promote my lifestyle and accompanying merchandise. This was simply a personal adventure. The fulfilment of an ambition. I was scratching an itch.

I wondered if other adventurers struggled with these misgivings. How did they rationalise leaving loved ones behind for long periods of time? How did they explain their drive for adventure to their families? Did they view what they did as a selfish act, self-centred and self-indulgent? Did any of this matter to them anyway?

In these matters, I was alone. These were conundrums to ponder during my long days on the sea. The ensuing debates I held with myself swung one way and another, as I argued for and against the value of solo adventure in a person's life – in my life. There were times when I likened myself to Shackleton, Scott, Heyerdahl, and many other great adventurers who I admired and who embarked on lengthy expeditions which took them far from family and home. Of course, no sooner had I made these comparisons, I would argue in my case, my venture was no way akin to theirs for greatness or validity. For a start, there was no logical purpose to my specific undertaking except that of charitable fundraising. It wasn't as if this was an expedition to prove a geographical theory, undertake scientific enquiry, or simply be the first to kayak around Scotland. This was purely an indulgent, adult rite of passage.

And there was my answer! It was indeed a rite of passage, a life process usually reserved for the passing of youth into adulthood. For me, it was my experience of passing from adulthood into older age. The moment when I acceded the mantel of wisdom because I had lived life long enough to embody sufficient knowledge of the world, to now offer it back as insights gained through experience. The act of passing from my middle age to my older age was important because I wanted to give myself time to understand the relevance of this process.

Chapter 7

I departed Ballantrae before dawn on the fourth morning with the sun promising windless warmth as it rose from behind Bennane Head. The forecast was at last favourable, and I looked forward with hope to a long day on the sea. I set my sights on reaching Troon nearly forty miles away. On the way I would stop in Girvan to visit the lifeboat station there. It was wonderful to be on the sea again and moving onwards. The coastline bulge of Bennane Head arrived and was soon left behind, the anticipated tidal challenges there not materialising. I found my rhythm and enjoyed the fast progress I was making. There were no challenges to concern me, and I was relaxed. Out to sea the iconic volcanic plug of Ailsa Craig was a constant looming companion, watching me make my way northwards along the agriculturally rural Ayrshire coastline. I passed crowded caravan sites where static-home owners existed cheek by jowl with their neighbours, each with garden chairs out front and some with ingenious decked platforms offering unrivalled views over the Firth of Clyde.

I eventually arrived at Girvan and crept my way into the sleepy port through the impressive harbour opening, finding myself surprised by a sizeable swell which unnerved me as I made my way in. I stopped to take photos next to the Girvan Lifeboat where she was moored to a floating pontoon, before paddling further inwards and mooring alongside a greasy ladder. I climbed up this to dry land and wandered up to the lifeboat station. It was shut. I looked at my watch and realised I had arrived well before anyone would show up for work. I wasn't sure what to do. The coxswain was expecting my visit, but I had no way of contacting him and I wanted to press on for Troon. With some regret, I decided to keep going and pushed a note through the station door giving my apologies. Rather gingerly, I climbed back into *Sahwira* from the slippery, weed covered ladder, stowed the towline I used for mooring her, and headed out to sea. The island Ailsa Craig was perfectly framed by the harbour entrance, and it almost seemed it had been sitting out there patiently waiting my reappearance. A wispy puff of grey cloud hung over the pointed summit of the isle's hill giving the impression it was still a volcano.

A few miles north of Girvan I passed Turnberry Golf Club, now known as Trump Turnberry. The luxurious hotel complex appeared incongruous against the rolling Ayrshire landscape. I wondered about landing here and having a break, instead I pressed on, apologising to a small group of seals for disturbing their morning sunbathing on Brest Rocks. There were golfers and their caddies on the course, huddled together deep in conversation as I rounded Turnberry Point. I wondered if they were aware of being observed by a lone sea kayaker who was being followed by a group of bobbing selkie heads, like a pinniped Pied Piper. The seals were playing a game of follow, hide and seek with me, swimming close to the stern of my kayak only to dramatically splash underwater if I turned to look at them. As I passed the fractured ruins of ancient Turnberry Castle, I went on to wonder what the famous thirteenth century occupant would have made of the lavish golf course. I guessed Robert the Bruce, the King of Scots, might have enjoyed a round or two of golf with the rich and famous. I gently chided myself for my cynicism of great wealth.

By now the sea had calmed and I was effortlessly gliding through mirrored waters. In these wonderful conditions, every paddle stroke felt vital and powerful. My energy levels seemed boundless. I kept close to the shore, rather than choosing to cut across an expansive bay opening ahead. Ailsa Craig had dropped well behind and was out of my view, to be replaced by the looming mountains of the Isle of Arran, seemingly a lot closer than it had previously been. The coastline steepened until I was kayaking under dark wooded cliffs, atop which Culzean Castle prominently and proudly proclaimed its crenelated existence to the Firth of Clyde. Pronounced 'Cull-ayne', the castle was once a favourite holiday home to the American General Dwight D. Eisenhower and an apartment was gifted to him in recognition for his role as the Supreme Commander of the Allied Forces during the Second World War. The castle is now owned by the National Trust for Scotland. It was quite something to drift on the sea below the impressive 18thC structure.

A few miles further along the coast, just as impressive atop low rocky cliffs was Dunure Castle. Its ruinous state not diminishing the importance it must have held for the Kennedys who were the predominant owners of the estates through the ages. I stopped in the small entrance to Dunure Harbour next to the castle and easily imagined birlinns arriving there with goods and supplies for the wealthy inhabitants. I didn't linger and pressed onwards towards the low-lying Heads of Ayr, the point where I decided to set an open course for Troon eight miles distant. With powerful and long reaching strokes, I cruised through the calm sea, slicing the pliant surface like a hot knife through butter. Far to my left Arran continued to loom and barely change perspective, while between me and the island there were three anchored oil tankers. These provided a useful reference for my progress, and it was pleasing to see how quickly their red hulls and rusty white superstructures gained in definition, before I soon left them astern. It seemed surreal to look across to Arran and know in a few days I would be out there visiting the lifeboat station. To my right, a mile away along the coast were the sizeable Clyde towns of Ayr and Prestwick, though I found it difficult to differentiate them since they appeared to meld one into the other, a hazy mass of conurbation and busy-ness.

After three hours of consistent paddling, I was nearing Troon harbour. I had covered thirty-six miles since leaving Ballantrae which distance wise, was a personal best. I continued to feel strong. I picked out a figure scampering over the rocks beneath the harbour walls and realised this must be Charlie who had invited me to stay at his house for the night. I paddled in closer, and we shouted greetings to each other, with him proclaiming my speed had caught him unawares. I continued into the large harbour basin, which was eerily quiet. With the decline of the fishing fleets, so many harbours around the Scottish coast are sadly devoid of activity these days. Ahead I could see the distinctive orange of Troon Lifeboat berthed beneath an impressive gantry. As I paddled closer, I noticed the lifeboat and the quay were busy with crew and for a second, I thought in alarm they were being called out on a rescue. It was only when I saw them waving and their cheers reached me across the water, I realised they were there to greet me. I experienced a flush of embarrassed gratitude, and pride swept through me as I gulped back an irrational sob. I hadn't expected this welcome at all, so to receive it had a huge impact. I appreciated the crew were volunteers with jobs and personal lives, which they would have put on hold to give the time to be at the lifeboat station to welcome me in. This was incredibly generous.

Once I had landed and made a round of greetings with a series of firm handshakes, I was whisked up to their crew room in the adjacent station building and fed cake and tea. I seem to remember a can of cold beer being thrust into my hand too. I gazed around the room with awe. Framed photographs of yellow clad lifeboatmen through the ages adorned the walls along with certificates of merit for rescues long past, and many letters of gratitude from fortunate survivors. The hangings on the walls manifested history, camaraderie and selfless spirit. The men around me seemed larger than life too with their hearty laughter and confident chatter. Because they had gathered specially to meet me, I felt part of their crowd and my laughter joined with theirs. It was a happy time, and I basked in the self-awareness I had achieved something of worth that day.

The kayak and much of my kit was stowed in the boat house and locked away. Folks dispersed, repeating their congratulations as they climbed into their vehicles. Charlie and I followed behind and made our way to his house. Like many towns on the Clyde coastline, there was something of faded grandeur to Troon, but it seemed to be a vibrant place. It was odd to sit on a sofa and have a bed to sleep in for the night, but I certainly wasn't complaining. Despite having known each other for a short while, Charlie and I chatted like old friends. It was a convivial evening with him, his wife Sandra, their parrot and two dogs. I fell asleep quickly in a comfortable bed and slept without interruption, no wind tugging at the tent, or rain drumming a tattoo on the flysheet.

Chapter 8

An expeditionary sea kayak is a creature of great beauty and improbable capacity. There were many times during my journey when lifeboat crews would stand and with some incredulity watch me pack *Sahwira* before my departure. Invariably they would have eagerly helped carry her down to the shore, reverentially placing her on the ground. Others will have proudly carried my four IKEA bags, piled high with everything I required to comfortably sustain myself for an extended journey. There are three watertight compartments in my kayak, one in the forward section and two in the stern section. These compartments are sealed with rubber hatch covers which fit snugly and tightly on a pronounced hatch rim. Thus, properly sealed, the contents of each compartment would stay dry despite the hatch covers often being swamped by lively seas. However, in rough conditions, water will invariably work its way under the lip of a hatch cover which may not have been completely sealed. To ensure essential items such as spare clothing, sleeping bag and some foods are kept dry, they are packed inside dry bags. These are bags of various sizes, usually denoted in litres which are sealed by means of folding the opening edges together and rolling them three or four times and securing them with a plastic buckle. In a severe dunking, water will find its way into these bags, but because they're placed in a watertight compartment, it is generally assumed precious items in the bags will remain dry.

By the end of the first week of my adventure, I had my packing routine down to a fine art. Before then it took many mistakes, some rearranging and trying items out in different places in the boat. A key consideration when packing is maintaining kayak trim, so when loaded and on the water, the boat is neither bow heavy or stern heavy, nor lists to port or starboard. The accepted rule is packing heavier items close to the cockpit, so the weight is centralised. In my experience, this isn't practical because it may be necessary to place heavy items like tins of food in the narrow sections of the stern or bow because that's where they fit best. To be frank, I've never really paid much attention to the trim of my kayak. This is because she is always so heavily loaded the weight is evened out. There are rare occasions when I might deliberately make the stern heavier for a day. This when there is a strong following wind and I want the stern to be lower in the water to aid with tracking – keeping the kayak in a straight line. I have a deck bag in which I place essential safety items, snacks, and drinks. My spare paddles are secured on the stern deck of the kayak.

Packing a sea kayak requires the ability to look at an item and know where and how it'll fit in the kayak. It's a practical version of the old Gameboy game, Tetris, shifting items around so they slot together in spaces which seem improbable. In the early stages of a long journey, it's a matter of trial and error, but after years of expeditionary sea kayaking, I have established a system which works well every time. I never secure items which are difficult to fit inside a compartment to the deck of the kayak for fear of it being lost overboard. There must be a place for them and if not, then it will be discarded or something else will have to go to make room. I have a long tapered dry bag which I place my spare clothes in. This goes right up into the bow of the kayak. Tent poles and sleeping mat fit up there alongside it. My sleeping bag is compressed to the size of a medium watermelon, and this too is in a dry bag. It is placed in the forward compartment but against the bulkhead separating the cockpit. These are packed first, every time. This is because they are my essential items and I need them to remain dry at all costs. Placing them in the kayak immediately, ensures they do not lie on wet ground, in the rain or inadvertently swamped by a fast-rising tide. If there is a rising tide, I will continue to pack the forward compartment because the sea will reach this section of the boat before the others. Some food items will be packed, walking boots which I always take on a trip, my Crocs (yes, I wear them), trainers, maybe a full four litre water bag, dry bag with warm jacket and spare fleece, whisky bottle and ad hoc loose items. I will always leave space in this compartment for overflow items and a bag of rubbish because it's easier to close this hatch onto a bulging load.

The stern compartment is packed next with the tent in a dry bag, most of the food, the stove fuel, and my folding camping seat, this being slid right into the tail end of the kayak beyond the skeg box. In packing the compartments, items are placed inside in a regular sequence, and this ensures they have their place and I don't forget them. There have been times when I have been distracted when packing and the order is disturbed. It's only when I'm out on the water with no means of checking, I begin to fret about not remembering whether I packed something or not. While I'm paddling, I will run through what I recall of the morning's packing hoping to visualise the item I fear I have forgotten, being placed in the compartment, and if this does not happen, I worry about this all day long. If I stop for a break or when I arrive ashore at the end of the day, the first thing I will do is hurriedly open the compartment to see if the item is there or not. I have never left anything behind yet, but the way my memory plays tricks can cause great anxiety sometimes. I can see why mariners hold several superstitions. The breaking of my packing routine is a portent for unhappiness. I am prone to losing my reading glasses. I was absent minded with these and it's often the case I will leave them on a rock and paddle away, or more likely, place them on the stern of my kayak where they will linger like a sailor forgotten on a submerging submarine, to be eventually washed away. For this reason, I carry three spare pairs in my deck bag, in my buoyancy aid and in a small compartment I have on my foredeck.

The third compartment is behind my seat and is commonly known as the day hatch. This is my guaranteed watertight space in the kayak. This is where I pack my books, maps, passage notes, electrical items and everything else I want to ensure remains dry. My small Trangia methylated spirits stove fits in here too. This is also where emergency items are placed because it's feasible to reach into this compartment from my sitting position when I'm at sea.

Within reach in my deck bag and in pockets on my buoyancy aid are the items I want to sustain me through the day such as food and snacks, a vacuum flask with lemon and ginger tea, and boiled sweets, usually blackcurrant and liquorice. Then there are the essential emergency items which will ensure I am located and safely recovered if I had an accident. Kayaking solo along isolated coastline carries a greater element of risk, because I don't have a buddy or others to assist if trouble were to strike. Misfortune could occur in the form of a capsize and subsequent swim, an injury, or damage to the kayak. Because I was alone at sea, I needed to ensure I had the means to summon assistance as speedily as possible. My personal locator beacon (PLB) sits in my left buoyancy aid pocket. When activated, a distress signal is emitted via the global satellite network and received at a control centre in the south of Britain. They will alert the coastguard who then coordinate the search and rescue, usually with a helicopter and an R.N.L.I. lifeboat. On my right side of my buoyancy aid I have my hand-held VHF radio which I would use to transmit a 'Mayday' distress message if my life was at risk, or a 'Pan Pan' message if I was in trouble, required assistance but wasn't in imminent danger of dying. In another pocket I carry a small handheld smoke flare, and my camera. In a pocket on my back is a two-litre hydration bag with a drinking tube running over my shoulder and secured on the front. This is my drinking water for the day. I have other items too, a serrated knife for cutting lines, a signal mirror, an LED strobe light I would attach to my BA shoulder if required, and a powerful whistle. About my waist I have a fifteen-metre towline. Although I'm kayaking solo and have no need of this to tow another kayaker, this is useful if I must swim ashore ahead of my kayak and pull it in or must reverse the process when launching. This would occur if the seas were too heavy to land safely or there were only rocks to land or launch from. On the foredeck I have another line which is known as a contact tow. This is a short piece of line which is generally used to assist another kayaker in close quarters. As a solo kayaker I have used this to tether myself to my boat in extreme conditions and I've feared capsizing and becoming separated from my kayak. It's also useful as a tether when landing on a floating pontoon or alongside quays with ladders. The kayak remains tethered, floating patiently like a horse outside an American cowboy saloon.

On the stern of the kayak, I have a pair of split-paddles. These are secured under tight bungee cord and are within my reach from the cockpit should the paddles I'm using be damaged or lost. Secured on my foredeck I have an expeditionary deck bag. Attached to the left side of this is a hand operated bilge pump for clearing water from my cockpit if this became flooded. On the right side is an inflatable paddle float. This is similar in concept to a child's swimming arm band. It is placed over a paddle blade, is inflated and a buoyant outrigger is created, aiding stability if need be and when re-entering the kayak after a capsize. Atop the deck bag there is a large compass, essential for providing course direction and when holding a course. In the deck bag are my emergency flares and signal smoke, small first aid kit, emergency survival bag, handheld compass, mobile phone in a watertight bag, binoculars, sunscreen, food, snacks and hot drink. My map sits in a watertight map case, secured to my spray deck. My GPS unit is in a clear watertight bag, and this is clipped to the front of the deck bag. I use the GPS more as a daily log, providing information about my speed over the ground, average speed, and distance travelled. I used the mapping feature on the unit if I required to confirm my traditional map reading methods. I do not use hydrographic charts. For this journey I preferred to use the Nicolson's 1:250000 tourist maps of Scotland. Despite their small scale, the detail provided was more than enough to effectively navigate my way along the coast. If I required closer information, I used my GPS with 1:50 000 Ordnance Survey mapping loaded onto it.

Packing and preparing for sea was a process which took on average two hours to complete from waking to slipping free of the shore. Routine became a feature of my life during the four months. It was routine which I believe kept me safe and kept me sane. I created a pattern of existence which eased the times when they were tough and were sustainable to maintain. Without these patterns, I would have struggled to find focus when I needed to most, such as establishing camp at the end of a long day and fatigue was tugging on me to give in. My routine was such, a sequenced chain of events enabled me to swiftly set everything in order, ensuring I soon had shelter, I was changed into warm clothes, I was fed, and I had a hot drink. I find there's a dreadful temptation when the chips are down to wallow in self-pity and dither with securing a dry and warm place for the night. The wind might be driving the rain horizontally into my face, the previous miles may have been long and arduous, the approach and landing on the shore may have been hazardous and frightening, and the ground on which the tent is to stand may seem like a running quagmire. This is exactly the moment when my routine, established through easy times and tough, allows me to automatically unpack the kayak, keeping the essentials dry, set the tent and stow the kit in under fifteen minutes.

It's the same when preparing to depart when the weather is rough. Waking at four in the morning and hearing the rain drumming on the flysheet invites a strong temptation to roll over and snuggle down deeper, willing the clock to stop. My routine of twisting the valve on my sleeping mat so it deflates, thus denying any comfort, and then extricating myself from my sleeping bag and immediately compressing it and packing it away, ensures no further temptation to grab extra minutes curled up. The water goes onto the stove for coffee and while this is brewing, I dress and begin packing loose items in their respective dry bags. Each compartment of the kayak has an assigned IKEA bag, and the respective items for these are placed in them. By the time breakfast has been eaten and the pots washed, everything is packed, I'm dressed for the day, and it's time to load the kayak. My insistence on routine was such, I unpegged the tent in a certain order and tied each of the guy lines similarly. In our society we make fun of compulsive disorders, teasing people for maintaining strict routines in their lives, which on the surface appear pointless and maybe irritating. However, I understand how routine offers a sense of safety and security and it wasn't until I was well into my journey, I discovered how important this was.

From Troon I had an easy day to reach Largs. The coastline took me past Irvine, Saltcoats, Ardrossan and West Kilbride, Scottish town names I knew of but had never properly placed on a map. It was a pleasure to see them, from a sea level perspective at least. Passing Ardrossan, I stopped to chat to another Twitter friend who had cycled to the coast to meet me when I paddled past. Colin was a keen outdoors person himself, so my journey resonated with him. Again, the easiness of connecting was a natural process and we stood on the shore chatting away while *Sahwira*, like a patient child, floated in a rock pool a few metres away.

The coast from Ardrossan to Farland Head was wonderfully attractive. It was bounded with sets of skerries which provided easy haul outs for the numerous local seals. The landscape was rural, but the coastline itself held a wilder west coast feel to it, and I enjoyed a sense of steadily making my way closer to the Scottish west coast scenery I know and love so well. Portencross Castle was a pleasant surprise, well preserved and situated almost within touching distance on the rocks just above the sea. A Saltire fluttered from the ramparts far above and for a moment I wondered if I would hear a shouted roar of "Freeeeedommmm!" from within.

A couple of miles further on, the medieval quaintness of Portencross was replaced by the twentieth century industrial landscape of Hunterston B, which is one of Scotland's two remaining active nuclear power stations. I drew an audible intake of breath when I rounded the coast and saw the monstrous power station standing ahead. The day suddenly seemed to take on a dark air and I increased my pace to make it past as fast as I could. I made sure to keep well away from what appeared to be a subsurface cooling water outlet, the surface of the sea seeming as if it were boiling, with steam rising and drifting across the dark water like a scene from a horror B-movie. The long gantry pier of Fairlie hove into view and I spotted Largs not far away at the other end of Fairlie Roads, the body of water between the mainland and Little Cumbrae and Great Cumbrae islands. It was in these Roads in 1263 that King Haakon Haakonson of Norway anchored his large fleet, with the aim of bringing the Scots into submission over the disputed ownership of the Hebridean islands. The ensuing battle was more of a skirmish but has gone down in the annals of Scottish history as a great victory against the Norse, though the land ownership dispute wasn't settled until three years later.

It had begun to rain, and the wind was rising again, exactly the conditions it is said when the Viking fleet were there centuries before. My imagination was filled with images of long boats and masses of men with mighty swords and garishly painted round shields. Of course, I didn't imagine them wearing helmets with horns, because even I knew there were no 'kiss-me-quick' shops in Largs to buy them from that long ago! Joking aside, I was genuinely interested in the history of early medieval Scotland, a time when the nation was beginning to emerge as a unified country. Until this point it was a conglomerate of kingdoms where alliances were forged and broken, and feuds ran deep.

I landed ashore in front of the lifeboat station where four figures emerged from within the shed, and walked down to greet me. The Largs lifeboat is an inshore Atlantic 85 servicing the seas around the Cumbraes, out to the Isle of Bute and as far north as Cloche Point. Most of their work is dealing with leisure craft from the plush yachting marinas which abound in the area. I was invited inside for a cup of tea and given a tour of the lifeboat. It was eminently apparent they were as proud of their craft as any of the crews I had met so far. One of the crew arranged for me to camp at the Largs Marina a couple of miles southwards, back down the Fairlie Roads, so it was a hasty paddle back the way I had come for a luxurious night on a well-manicured patch of lawn, with welcome access to a hot shower and the marina bar, both of which I made good use of!

Chapter 9

Helensburgh was my goal for the next day where there was another inshore lifeboat station. I was now entering the upper reaches of the Clyde Estuary where the potential for encountering large shipping was a high possibility. I had picked up a pamphlet from the Largs Marina office with detailed passage notes for leisure craft using the upper Clyde seaways. Reading this caused some anxiety because it made things seem extremely busy up there. I decided all I needed to do was keep my wits about me. I set off in the gathering rain northwards. Largs was fast asleep when I kayaked past and I enjoyed the sensation of having the sea to myself, apart from a couple of inquisitive seals who followed me until I was well beyond the limits of the town. It was almost as if they were seeing me off the property!

I kept close into the shore because the wind was gaining in strength and blowing from the southwest. The sea was picking up too, but nothing I couldn't handle. In fact, despite the heavy rain, I was enjoying myself. The awareness this was the day I would reach the upper limit of my journey into the Clyde Estuary, filled me with a strong sense of resolve. I decided no matter what the conditions, I would make the day one to remember. The A78 ran close along the coast and for the first time this journey, I was constantly assailed by the rumble of traffic. This heavy noise quickly dropped into the background of my awareness, and I focussed on the lovely surroundings. The hills rose steeply from behind the road and there was a definite sense of wildness to the terrain. This surprised me, given the proximity to the industrial upper reaches of the estuary and the huge city of Glasgow not far away. Looking northwards it felt as if I were looking into the gaping jaws of the Highlands. The backdrop to the estuary here was magnificent; high mountains, peak after peak stretching as far as I could see. It was like a fantasy film set, where the protagonists on a courageous quest, look towards distant mountainous wild lands where they must surely travel, and high adventure awaits. Despite the traffic noise, it certainly had the feeling of a wild landscape where humans scratch a life on the littoral fringes and in the steep sided glens and are content to be surrounded by looming empty hills and mountains. To the west I could see the quintessential Isle of Bute with its manicured landscape. I was struck by how much incredible beauty there was around me.

Drawing close to Wemyss Bay, which incidentally I found myself pronouncing as Wee-muss, when it's in fact pronounced as Weems, I spotted the distinctive black and white liveried Caledonian MacBrayne ferry returning from Port Bannatyne on the Isle of Bute. It was still a mile from reaching its berth on the pier just a few hundred metres ahead of me and I found myself thinking, do I put my head down and paddle hard to cut across it, or do I ease up and wait until it's berthed? Wisely I chose the latter and turned for the small, sheltered bay by the pier. Kayaking solo is a consistent series of decisions, each one with consequences leading to the next. There isn't the opportunity to turn to a paddling colleague and ask. "D'you think we'll make it ahead of the ferry?" This is a dialogue which must occur in my own head and a decision arrived at without the validation of anyone else. This is not an onerous task and in fact adds quality to my overall experience on the sea. There is challenge in making choices where the potential outcome may be disastrous. Of course, it's wise to err on the side of caution, but sometimes, taking a risk can pay dividends. In this situation though, there was no question of attempting to outrun the ferry, especially in the difficult sea conditions as they were. Anyway, I wasn't in any hurry and it was a good opportunity to rest up out of the wild sea, take a breather and enjoy a snack.

I snuck past the berthing ferry by kayaking between the subterranean like piles of the pier and continued my way northwards, deeper into the Clyde estuary. I was enjoying myself immensely. As I passed Inverkip marina all I could see were a forest of masts hidden behind the protective and unsightly banks of its boulder strewn modern harbour. I thought suddenly of our small yacht, and a pang of homesickness caught me unawares. I had now been away from home for sixteen days and probably faced the same number again before I would see my wife when I arrived in Crinan, on the west coast. Before then I had the Isle of Arran to reach, the Mull of Kintyre to traverse and a crossing to and from the island of Islay to complete. If I allowed myself to think of what lay ahead like this, the enormity of my task appeared dauntingly insurmountable. I returned myself to contemplating what immediately lay ahead and simply reaching Helensburgh in good time.

The light house at Cloch Point hove into view, marking the moment when I would swing into the upper Clyde proper. I felt a nervous excitement at reaching this point, with the uncertainty of what I would encounter beyond. In my mind I anticipated fleets of containers ships ploughing the sea way in and out of a busy Port Glasgow. Along the shoreline leading to the lighthouse, were a cluster of what at first glance appeared to be transplanted allotment sheds. When I drew closer, I saw they were constructed not unlike

Ben Knox's romantic beach shack on the 1980s quaint Scottish film 'Local Hero', probably one of my favourite films of all time. The shacks were fashioned from pallets, driftwood and other shore scavenged treasures. A man, not unlike the character Ben of the film, sat on a rock outside one of them, warily watching as I paddled slowly past. I waved a greeting but received none in reply. I didn't mind, I suppose I admired the rebel in him, the choice he was making to live a life on the edge of society, (or this is what I assumed). The shacks didn't have the look of been hastily thrown up, because there was ingenuity and pride in their construction. A Saltire flew from a makeshift flagstaff, and another was emblazoned on one of the hut walls. It was an attractive setting, with the idea of living off grid and out of the mainstream. I didn't consider the challenges of no plumbed water or sewage disposal, neither the busy A770 right behind them. Romantic notions are excellent for discounting reality.

The upper reaches of the Clyde stretched before me when I rounded the point, the rather unkempt lighthouse welcoming me to the closing stages of the day's journey. Helensburgh was an easy eight miles away and I had plenty of time to reach there. Arriving at Gourock, I decided to make the crossing of the Clyde seaway to the Rosneath Peninsula rather than from the port of Greenock a mile further up the coast, as I had originally planned. Making sure I had my anti-collision flares close at hand, I set off into a lumpy grey sea. With the wind behind I literally surfed my way across the empty firth in a hefty following sea. Quite unusually, I was bursting for a pee, and I couldn't land fast enough amongst the rocks on the far side of the channel when I arrived, the sea piling around my waist. It was a clumsy landing, but I was close to bursting, so kayaking decorum was forgotten. Once relieved I took a moment to stand and gaze back across the Clyde to the busy seaport of Greenock and further up the narrowing estuary. It was another one of my rewarding moments of realising where I was, and how far I had come. In the planning stages for the journey, I had worried myself about crossing the Clyde at this point. Although I am an experienced kayaker, I had not paddled a great deal in waters frequented by shipping. Consequently, I had constructed ill-founded fears about what I might encounter when I arrived at this point. I was reminded of a favourite poem of mine which I often recount when talking of facing fears.

I think over again my small adventures,
My fears,
Those small ones that seemed so big,
For all the vital things
I had to get and to reach;
And yet there is only one great thing,
The only thing,
To live to see the great day that dawns
And the light that fills the world.
Anonymous (Inuit origin).

I reminded myself I had yet to cross the mouth of Gare Loch to reach Helensburgh which neighboured Faslane, the tightly guarded Royal Navy submarine base. Part of me wanted to encounter one of these underwater leviathans as they slid silently out to sea through the tight narrows of the loch. The other part was far more cautious and hoped for a quiet arrival. Setting off from my comfort break stop wasn't as easy as I hoped with a sizeable and unprotected sea crashing onto the shoreline. I'm not as agile as I once was, so my cockpit invariably filled with sea water before I managed to secure my spray deck. I carry a large sponge for these occasions and spent a few minutes, buffeted by white capped waves, mopping up the water sloshing around the bottom of my cockpit.

The intriguingly named Culwatty Bay when I rounded Rosneath Point, was cloaked in feathered black and white. A huge flock of male eider ducks, 'hoo hooing' with their distinctive soft calls were attempting to woo the attentions of their sadly drabber female companions. These ducks are a common feature during my Scottish sea kayaking trips, and their gentle communication is redolent of halcyon summer days in my kayak. I paddled clear of the bay so not to disturb them and decided to make my crossing to Helensburgh on the far shore while the way was clear. Again, I need not have been concerned about shipping traffic, I had the wind churned sea to myself.

I landed on the lifeboat station slipway where upon I was met by a Facebook friend I had not yet met in person. Susan is a keen sea kayaker and we'd made an online connection because of our shared enthusiasm for the sport. The rain was torrentially pouring stair rod fashion. Dripping wet, we found a small café where we enjoyed tea and cakes and a long chat. It was wonderful to speak with a fellow kayaker about my journey so far, sharing my experiences without any explanations. Susan was effusive in her admiration and praise which I found difficult to accept. The distance I was kayaking may have been impressive but as I attempted to say again, and again, it was merely approaching each day as a day on the water, rather than the whole.

Susan left me at the lifeboat station at 5pm when members of the crew began arriving. I received another warm R.N.L.I. reception, and we spent a convivial hour chatting in their crew room about the service they provide to their area, and some of the challenges they face. Erskine Bridge crosses the Clyde fourteen miles further up the estuary. Tragically, this high road bridge is a favoured spot for people jumping to their deaths, and many of the calls the lifeboat receive are to attend these distressing suicides. I was invited to join some of the crew for an evening of beer tasting at the annual Helensburgh Beer Festival, but I reluctantly declined both because of limited funds, and the need for a clear head the next day. I spent the night in the crew room, happy not to be in my tent while a storm raged outside. The gusty gale buffeted the walls of the station and the rain hammered against the windows like a banshee wanting to escape the deluge.

The forecast the following day was rather bleak. Strong winds from the northwest were to feature for much of the day. Heavy rain was predicted too, but this did not bother me. It was the strength and the direction of the wind which concerned me the most. I looked at my maps, working out where I would be most affected by the wind. It was forecast to be gusting above Force 5 on the Beaufort Scale. I could cope with this strength of wind, but not if I were to paddle face into it through the day. I calculated I would be sufficiently sheltered by Rosneath Peninsular as far as Loch Long. After crossing the wide mouth of this loch, I would find myself on a southerly heading which would mean the wind being on my stern. I decided to make a move and see how far I could get. It was my hope to make it all the way to Tighnabruaich on the Cowal Peninsula where there was another lifeboat station. However, given the forecast conditions, I accepted this goal was unlikely.

Two members of the crew came down to see me off, helping me down to the sodden shore with my kit, standing in the rain to observe, as I stowed it away into the kayak. Again, it felt I was being viewed as a magician who was magically making things disappear. Looking at my bulging IKEA bags; it did seem improbable *Sahwira's* slenderness would accommodate so much stuff. After firm handshakes all round, I was away, skittering across the surface of the wind flattened sea towards Rosneath Point. The rain had abated, and the cloud was climbing in wispy wreaths up the surrounding Argyll mountainsides, as if retreating from a hard-fought battle. Despite a surprisingly fierce head wind, progress was readily made along the peninsula's coastline to the beautiful community of Kilcreggan. I often play a game with myself, where I imagine buying a house in a remote and attractive location where I could happily live out the rest of my days. As I paddled along the shoreline gazing up at the substantial dwellings, set in their lush gardens with the steep hill of the peninsula behind, I could imagine myself living in one of them. The hamlet, developed as it was for wealthy Glasgow ship owners and merchants in the hey-day of the Clyde steamers, was but a stone's throw via a foot-passenger ferry from the busyness of Gourock across the Clyde. To reach the closest town of any size which was Helensburgh, would involve a seventeen-mile drive. For this reason, it was my kind of place, a challenge to reach, with a sense of remote wildness.

The neighbouring village to Kilcreggan was Cove, which I found on the other side of the aptly named headland of Barons Point. By now the conditions had considerably deteriorated. The day had become exceedingly blustery, interspersed with fierce squalls of pin-needle driving rain when the wind almost doubled in ferocity (or so it seemed). These intense windstorms gathered themselves in the high mountains which created the stunning backdrop to Loch Long, the mile and a half wide mouth of which I had to now cross. As if released from the highlands like bowling balls down a twenty-mile natural bowling alley, the squalls would shriek the length of the loch with an attendant dark cloud above them, kicking up a seething mass of rampant white horses across the surface. When these reached me, the resulting minutes of mayhem weren't at all comfortable.

I calculated the crossing would take thirty minutes which would mean encountering one or two of these squalls with no hope of shelter. I looked around and wondered if I ought to head ashore and wait for conditions to ease, and if they didn't, make camp. It was disheartening to think of ending the day so early. I looked up the loch and couldn't see any impending squalls travelling towards me. In an instant I was paddling through a cluster of expensive looking yachts, away from the shore and aiming for Blairmore Pier on the far side. There was a sizeable almost shoulder high wind driven swell, sweeping down and out of the loch. *Sahwira* was in her element and gave me no concern about her sea worthiness. She took the crackling waves on her starboard side in her stride, and I merely provided the momentum with strong and steady paddle strokes. I was just under halfway across when the first squall hit. I was aware of its impending arrival because the world around became intensely dark and cold. The wind slammed into my side, hitting the kayak and heeling her over. Instinctively I reached out leftwards, to my port side with my blade flat on the surface of the sea, supporting both myself and the kayak, hoping this was enough to prevent us being capsized. I hunched, reactively protecting my face from the icy stinging pellets of rain which were driven horizontally through the air. The sea thrashed in excitement, waves doubling in size and breaking in rushing white foam. This was far more severe than I expected and all I could do was ride the tempest out. Then, without a whimper, the squall screamed out into the open expanses of the Upper Clyde and dissipated into ephemeral rainbows which framed dark Prussian-blue curtains of rain, leaving me rather shaken in its passing. I vigorously shook my head, my hair plastered to my scalp and dug my paddles into the calming sea, aiming for the far shore. Such was the ferocity of the gust; I had been blown fifty metres off course and the pier was no longer a viable point to aim for. I endured two more squalls of equal fierceness before I made it safely to the hamlet of Strone on the far side.

My travails were not yet over. I had Holy Loch to cross where I could see the ferocious squalls working their dervish sorcery on the surface of the sea there too. Strone is a similar settlement to Kilcreggan, obviously developed as a retreat for the Glasgow wealthy. As I paddled towards Strone Point, I admired the buildings lining the shore while mentally preparing myself to face the gale blasting out of Holy Loch ahead. In line with the almost imperceptible headland, a reef of rounded pebbles stretched a hundred metres into the sea, requiring me to paddle away from the relative shelter of the shore. This resulted in being exposed to the fierce wind, and despite expecting it, I was shocked by its strength. It was as if I had slammed into an invisible wall of air, and forward movement was all but halted. My paddle was whipped out of my right hand by a strong gust which clearly informed me of the extra effort required. It was only five hundred metres from this point to an old stone pier, which I anticipated would provide desperately needed shelter. It was simply a case of ducking my head down and reaching as far forward as I could with every stroke, digging the blade into the whipped-up sea and pulling hard. One slow stroke at a time, saw me inexorably creep along the shore towards the haven of the pier. Perversely, I enjoyed the challenge, though I admit I was relieved by the complete shelter the attractive pier provided when I eventually arrived.

In the complete calm, out of the howling wind, I landed ashore and heaved myself out of the cockpit, slowly standing erect on wobbly, nerve shaken legs. I needed time to assess the situation and my options. I was under some pressure to make it as far as Dunoon on the far shore of Holy Loch to meet with a Twitter friend named Sybil and a Facebook contact named Bruce. Contacting them was difficult because of the conditions, and the fact my phone was not waterproof. This meant it was impossible to use it out at sea. Touch screen phones are an amazing development but completely useless when fingers are wet, icily cold, and like wrinkled prunes due to saltwater immersion. I could have thrown my phone far out into the raging waters of Holy Loch; such was my frustration at apps not opening and others springing open which I did not need. Eventually though, I managed to contact both, to let them know I was evaluating my options. I felt guilt at the possibility of not making it across and subsequently letting them down.

I huddled behind the pier wall, disconsolately munching a large wad of Malt Loaf, which I had foolishly stuffed into my mouth in one go. It was now a glutenous mass which I had difficulty in chewing.

"Have you come far?"

I twisted my head and looked above me, to see a middle-aged man wearing an expensive looking coat leaning over the pier wall. I smiled, tried to speak, but my glued palette prevented me forming any serviceable words.

"Gnnnf," I think I muttered, and then pointed at my mouth and emphasised my chewing action with an apologetic look.

"That's a lovely looking canoe you've got there." He carried on the conversation for the both of us.

I managed to swallow the gooey lump of sickly-sweet malt loaf and with it slowly sliding down my throat, managed to answer, "Thanks, she's a pretty new kayak, I got her only a month or so ago."

"Sorry," Said the onlooker apologetically, "kayak then." Once again, I felt bad for my pedantry.

He pressed on, "Where you off to next, it looks pretty blowy out there?"

"I'm not actually sure." I replied honestly. "That's what I need to decide in the next few minutes. I was heading for Tighnabruaich but there's no chance of that today."

"Pity." He commiserated and then seemed to lose interest when his companion joined him to look down on me on the beach. "Good luck in deciding!" he shouted, waved, and they wandered into the pub on the other side of the street.

I was tempted to follow them into the attractive looking hostelry, but my lack of funds wouldn't allow this, and anyway, I wanted to resolve my predicament. I realised it was only midday, so I had time in hand to wait and hope the conditions would begin to calm. I broke off another wad of malt loaf and wedged it into my mouth. I looked across to the opposite shore. It was less than a mile away, and yet the frenzied sea created the illusion it was twice the distance. I set about forensically studying the conditions and asked myself what was preventing me from crossing. This was a classic example of the solo kayaker's dilemma. "Do I put to sea or do I not put to sea?" In my experience, there's no formula to decision making on an expedition. Every choice must meet the demands of the situation, and these will be influenced by many factors, some known, others assumed. In this case, I started with, "What do I want?" This provided the base line from which to work. I required a focus point.

I determined I wanted to make it across to Hunters Quay on the far side of Holy Loch. Next question then, "What's preventing me?" The obvious reply being, "The strong wind and the wild sea state". This is where the variables began to occur. On first impressions, the wind is a reason I might not make it across, but was it genuinely too bad? What would be the consequences if I tried? Are they life threatening? What might occur? What are the hazards other than the wind? What is preventing *me* from giving it a try? In other words, is it fear, which is holding me back, or a lack of ability, or am I simply unwilling to give it a go?

I clambered onto the stone pier to gain a better view of the loch. I scrutinised the conditions with an enquiring eye. Yes, the wind was fierce. It was a proverbial 'hoolie' screaming down the glen from the mountains, yet it wasn't gusting as it was when I crossed Loch Long. The direction too, while on my beam if I set off, would begin to assist me before I was halfway across. I would bear away to run with the wind when I knew my angle would lead me along the shoreline past Hunters Quay. There were no true hazards I could see. Holy Loch, once an American Naval base no longer had large shipping and there was no other marine traffic in sight. There were no reefs or skerries to hinder, and the waves while white capped weren't more than a metre high. I had coped with worse already on this journey, indeed only a couple of hours earlier when I had crossed Loch Long.

I now viewed the situation differently to when I arrived half an hour before. It would be wild out there, but I would be OK. I clambered off the pier and set about launching into the maelstrom. By the time I was thirty metres offshore, I realised my choice to continue was the correct one. It looked fierce and it was indeed wild out there, but I was well within my limits of ability. I even allowed myself to gaze up the Loch into the glen and the mountains behind. It really was a stunning area!

I was arriving in the vicinity of the ferry pier at Hunters Quay when I spotted a sea kayaker a little further along the coast. I surmised this must be Bruce, my Facebook contact and a kayaker too. He looked to be in his element and thoroughly enjoying the conditions. I suddenly felt a bit of a fool for having made such a meal of the decision to cross. Nevertheless, we greeted each other with enthusiasm and surfed our way along the Dunoon seafront. It was difficult to hold a conversation in the howling wind, so as best we could we kayaked close together, to shout our questions and answers. We landed on the pebbles of the west beach and clambered ashore. An elderly couple wandered over the shingle towards us and introduced themselves as the parents of another Twitter follower who lived nearby but was working and couldn't make it himself to meet me. He had asked his parents to come down instead. I was incredibly touched by this gesture. Sybil was there too, and it was lovely to meet her for the first time. We huddled out of the wind and spent a happy hour chatting away, with me enjoying the hot soup she had kindly made.

I think much to Bruce's dismay because he was looking forward to an afternoon paddle, I decided I'd had enough of the day and wanted to stop for the night in Dunoon. I'm not certain what occurred in my thinking at that point. There was no reason to stop, the conditions were easing, and I would easily have made it another ten or twelve miles. Somehow though I had run out of steam. I pitched camp on a patch of grass next to public conveniences and had a rather desultory night, feeling soggy and dispirited. I reflected on how quickly my mood could alter, from the steely determination of the morning to the almost complete abdication in the afternoon. Even the charming company of three playful rabbits chasing each other around my tent didn't lift my spirits.

I was on my way early the following day, the weather much kinder with the promise of calming conditions. On reflection, I was pleased to have stopped in Dunoon because this afforded the opportunity to appreciate the paddle ahead. It was with a lighter heart when I rounded Toward Point and entered the romantically named Kyles of Bute. The tide was with me, and I was looking forward to this stretch of water, as did many early 20th Century Glaswegians when they headed 'doon the watter' on the Clyde steamers. The Scottish slang term *"steamin'"*, meaning to be totally inebriated, originated from these pleasure cruises. There was no chance of finding myself in that condition unless, prosaically, I could have referred to myself as being drunk on the beauty which surrounded me. I was now in the realms of Argyll's 'secret coast', a beautiful corner of Scotland which is often overlooked in favour of the iconic Highlands and Islands.

With the green pastured landscape of the Isle of Bute to my left, the steep densely forested hills of the mainland on my right, and the watery highway of the East Kyles stretching ahead, I felt I was being invited into an exclusive club. The entrance to the fjord like Loch Striven opened on my starboard beam. I crossed the Kyles channel to kayak along the Bute shoreline and was rewarded by encountering a family of three otters, an adult and two pups. They swam ahead, their sleek bodies just visible on the surface and every now and then, diving below leaving the merest rippled imprint of their presence. It's always a joy to come across otters when I'm kayaking. They're a common sight along the Scottish coastline but there's a quality to their presence in the littoral realm which ignites an unfathomable feeling within. It might be their playfulness, their intelligence, or their inquisitiveness. I consider the otter to be my totem.

The tide eased me along the shoreline, down past the short ferry crossing between Colintraive on the Argyll mainland and the Island of Bute, towards the low hummocked, rocky and intriguingly named, Burnt Islands. Arriving here awakened a flood of rewarding memories from a few years before, when I worked as an instructor on weeklong outdoor activity courses for a small cancer charity called Odyssey. We based ourselves in a large house nearby, from where we ventured into the surrounding area, guiding groups of people who were living with cancer, through various outdoor experiences, one of which was canoeing through the Burnt Islands and up into Loch Ruel. We'd stop on a small island further up the loch for bacon rolls cooked on an open fire. The week the participants spent with

Odyssey was a powerful reminder there is life to be lived, even if there is uncertainty in how much of it is left. Sadly, for some, they were not far from losing their fight with their illness and for others, they were enjoying long remission. Most of the staff delivering these courses had previously worked for Outward Bound. We were skilled in offering outdoor experiences in a manner which elicited powerful self-awareness. I remembered how privileged I felt to witness individuals' moments of sheer delight when they came to a new awareness because of achieving a challenge they believed was impossible. It was powerful and moving stuff.

I paused for a few moments amongst the small islands and allowed myself to reflect with some nostalgia on my experiences with Odyssey. Terns disturbed by my presence squawked and fluttered above, their marionette wingbeats holding them almost stationary in the sky. A couple of bright red billed oystercatchers scolded me too. My time as an outdoor personal development instructor was long past but I missed the work and the joy it gave, even if at times it was intensely demanding. Facilitating new awareness through challenging and adventurous experiences in the outdoors was a natural process for me. I think I was an effective instructor who had the ability to see opportunities for awareness, before they became apparent. There is powerful metaphoric value in outdoor activities, and Nature is a potent teacher.

From the same large house and in this same area, I once facilitated a programme for a Northern-Irish peace initiative. An eclectic group of previous paramilitary fighters, political prisoners, Ulster Constabulary, British military and people who had family members murdered, all from the troubled region, were on a long-term process of peace and reconciliation, part of which entailed the residential I was responsible for, in the wilds of the Cowal Peninsula. Mid-week we ventured out on a hike and an over-night camp. During the walk in, one of the group aggravated an historic back injury. The next day there was pressure from within the group, to shorten the day walk back to the vehicle by following an easy farm track, rather than the route I had planned, which involved traversing rugged coastal terrain. I resisted this option and insisted we continue as planned, much to the ire of the group. I saw an opportunity for individual and group learning and believed the rugged wildness would facilitate this. The man with the aggravated injury was in discomfort but not incapacitated. It did mean though, others in the group shared his load, helped him by taking his hands and everyone generally taking care of each other, by communicating what lay ahead, and offering support over steep ground. Their unhappiness at my insistence this was the route to follow was regularly expressed with undisguised anger. We eventually made it to easy ground, and I remember standing in the shade of a grove of beautifully shaped sessile oaks, listening to individuals complaining about the ordeal I had enforced upon them. I asked them to look at the people they were standing next to, and recall the others they had earlier offered help to, or when they received help from another. I then asked them, could they have conceived the quality of this support happening in their everyday lives? I invited them to consider the difficulty they had just faced and relate this to the difficulties and challenges they encountered, within their reconciliatory process. I finally asked, if they faced the reconciliatory difficulties, in the manner they had just worked together, struggling through the wild landscape, how would this be different? The silence was palpable, and then an excited chatter broke forth. This had been a powerfully valuable experience for them all and offered a breakthrough moment in their group process. It is privileged experiences such as this, with the Northern-Irish group, those with Odyssey, and my many years with Outward Bound, which continue to inspire me to seek my own self-awareness connections, through wild outdoor adventures.

With happy memories flooding my thoughts, I pulled away from the islands and headed around the childishly snigger inducing Buttock Point, into the West Kyles and the last few miles to the village of Tighnabruaich. Brightly flowered rhododendron bushes lined the shore, a reminder how humans have influenced the composite of the natural landscape. I was welcomed into Tighnabruaich by a young lad in yellow R.N.L.I. wellies. His name was Josh and he'd been placed on sea kayaker watch. The distinctive lifeboat station building was an obvious landmark in the village and when Josh showed me into their crew room, I audibly gasped at the view they had from a wonderful picture window of the whole of the West Kyles. Looking southwards I could see the length of the Bute coastline and the Isle of Arran beyond. I was left to my own devices after I accepted their kind invitation to make myself at home in the station for the night. *Sahwira was* safely tucked up alongside their Atlantic 85.

Chapter 10

My paddles creaked slightly as I pulled strongly away from the hamlet of Tighnabruaich. I had set off before eight while it seemed the village still slumbered, anxious to give myself time to reach Lamlash on the Isle of Arran, twenty-nine miles away. The conditions were calm, and the air was still, a beautiful morning to be on the water. As I neared the Isle of Bute shoreline an otter broke the surface not far off my bow, and was immediately startled by my presence and dived, not to be seen again. It always amazes how they manage to disappear without trace. *Sahwira* sliced the surface, parting the water almost gently with an ever-widening wake of delicate ripples flowing out behind. I settled into an easy rhythm and the miles dropped away. Along the Bute coastline I noticed on the map several historical features which I would have loved to explore. As always, I promised myself I would one day return to visit them. I did consider stopping on the island of Inchmarnock to have a look at a prehistoric burial cist where I had heard the remains of a woman's skeleton, known as the *Queen of the Inch* are preserved behind glass. Laziness took hold when the opportunity arose to pull ashore. I couldn't be bothered with the faff of landing, walking and launching again. I carried on my way with a guilty feeling of regret.

The crossing to the Isle of Arran was my first proper open water passage of the journey. It was only a five-mile crossing, but this was my first, greater than a few miles from one land mass to another. As usual, I had built the prospect of the crossing into a potentially fearful experience. I worried about shipping, fishing boats and unmanageable seas. As expected of course, none of these materialised and the only vessel I saw was a small lobster boat working far away, off the southern tip of Bute. The sea wallowed and rolled with the deep blueness of a fine weather day. The puffed up, crisp white clouds above, were reflected from the indigo recesses of the surrounding deep water. Ahead, the Isle of Arran looked resplendent in her mantel of spring greens and undergarments of old winter hues. She was most definitely inviting me across to join her and I paddled with confidence and a strong feeling of well-being. From time to time, I would pass a small fleet of guillemots absently floating on the surface, their heads darting left and right as I drew near, and then at the last minute they would take off with splashing wingbeats to fly low away over the sea.

In under two hours I found myself arriving in new surroundings, this being the first time I had visited Arran. Once again, I experienced a warm sense of achievement. This journey was providing many moments which validated my sense of worth and this was a good thing! I celebrated with my flask of lemon and ginger tea and an extra ration of malt loaf. I paddled as close as I dared to the Arran shoreline, enjoying matching landmarks on the map with what I was seeing. Glen Sannox was inspiring, almost causing me to stop and camp in the picturesque picnic spot by the river mouth. The mountain backdrop was jaw dropping and to view this from sea level in my kayak, added to the sense of awesomeness. In fact, I remember recounting that word in my head when I chanced upon the view, and it's one I use sparingly! I was intrigued by the playful sheep shaped bollards on the old quay at the hamlet of Corrie which I later learned from one of the Arran lifeboat crew, were placed there as recently as 1988. Eventually I arrived in Brodick Bay and after waiting for the CalMac ferry to depart,

I crossed this for the last few miles of the day and into Lamlash Bay. The sharp peak of Mullach Mor on Holy Island which guards the bay had been a welcome point of reference as I closed in to Lamlash along the coast from Brodick. By now a gusty wind had risen and my paddle to the lifeboat station slipway was an arduous effort, considering I had covered over thirty miles that day.

I clambered out of my kayak and stood stretching my aching muscles when a voice called over from the nearby pier, "You must be Nick! Welcome to Arran."

I looked up to see the beaming and healthily ruddy face of Russ Cheshire, who was a Twitter friend and runs a busy wildlife viewing and charter business using their powerful RIB. He introduced me to Elspeth his wife and we stood chatting about my day, and their life on Arran. It amazes me how strangers can meet and strike up meaningful conversations within seconds of the connection. With their RIB they also ran the passenger ferry service to and from Holy Island in the entrance to the bay. I joined them for one of these runs to collect some walkers and Russ treated me to the full power of their boat's outboards. We screamed over the waters, bouncing with satisfying thuds over the wind driven waves. After my sedate paddling pace, it was an exhilarating finish to my day. By the time we were back, the Arran lifeboat station press officer had arrived along with William the Lifeboat Operations Manager. Again, I was made to feel warmly welcome and offered the use of their crew room for the night.

The forecast was poor. I lay in my sleeping bag listening to the lilting tones of the Belfast Coastguard detail the predicted westerly winds for the next day, all over thirty knots. I checked the Windfinder app on my phone and this too told me the same story. There was a window of six hours when conditions would be OK to paddle, but after this, it was likely I would be shore bound again. I tussled with the decision. My goal from Lamlash was Campbeltown on the Kintyre Peninsula. This was a full day away and included an eight-mile crossing of Kilbrannan Sound. In the planning stages I had Kilbrannan flagged as a potential tricky piece of water because of the strong tidal stream which is purported to run through it. I didn't want to be there if the winds were blowing hard. However, I didn't want to remain stuck in Lamlash either, I wanted to press onwards. I decided to leave in the morning and make it probably as far as the western coast of Arran and wait for an opportunity to cross to Kintyre from there.

I was away at the crack of dawn, sneaking out of the lifeboat station while the rest of the small town slept. The morning was alluringly calm, and it would have been easy to forget the dire forecast. As I exited the natural harbour with Holy Island on my left, I heard the distinctive 'pfft' breathing sound of either porpoises or dolphins coming up behind. It was a delightful moment when a pod of eight porpoises cruised past, each reaching the surface for a leisurely exhalation and breath of air, their pert, triangular fins glistening in the early morning light as their backs tightly arched before disappearing below the surface again. Within an hour of departing Lamlash, the winds began to build and by the time I had reached the Sound of Pladda, I was kayaking into the teeth of a sustained force six. The sea was driven before the wind, piling up in crashing waves over jagged reefs which stretched into the Clyde like long dinosaur spines. In the confusion of breaking waves and a chaotic swell, I found it difficult to spot isolated rocks hidden just beneath the surface. I proceeded cautiously but because of the strength of the wind, I had to maintain forward momentum to prevent the kayak from losing way. I was petrified I would ram one of the hidden rocks. I could now make out the Kintyre coastline which seemed impossibly far away. I pressed onwards, experiencing a tangible sense of relief every time I made it through a reef without damage. A couple of times I was forced to head out into the deeper water to avoid a reef altogether, but this exposed me to the full force of the wind and a terrible sea.

A highlight of the morning was rounding Bennan Head where an impressive cave was set high in the cliff, beside which a stately waterfall gracefully cascaded towards the shore below. If conditions would have allowed, I might have pulled ashore to have a closer look. There was something of the movie set about the scene, and I wouldn't have been surprised to see a crowd of actors dressed in Highland Plaid, broadswords in hand, surging from the cave, and sneaking up the cliff past the waterfall. This was the only relief I enjoyed, for beyond the headland, I saw the Arran coastline stretching away with a series of fearsome reefs reaching far into the sea. They were lined up, one after the other it seemed, in a sure-fire attempt to hole my boat. There was nothing for it but to keep going and I paddled onwards. The reefs were dealt with carefully, but each time I had the feeling I was kayaking on borrowed time. I was certain any minute, I would feel the resounding and sickening crunch of the hull ramming into a semi-submerged rock. What I noticed with the rocks in these reefs were the way they must have been laid millions of years ago. They were striated perpendicularly, presenting knife blade slices of rock, which would carve into the hull of the kayak with very little effort.

Given I was not going to make it across to Kintyre, I realised the futility in pressing on in these conditions, just to gain an extra few miles. I was risking my kayak for no reason, and I decided to stop at the first opportunity. The tiny beach I landed on was bounded by a rotting mass of seaweed which was at least five metres thick from the shore. I attempted to paddle my kayak through it but to no avail. My heart sank, for I knew what was coming next. I gingerly eased out of the kayak and immediately stepped through a crusty scum of rotting weed, allowing a sickly pungent rotting egg odour to explode from the morass around me. I boaked! I took great care not to fall headlong into the stinking gunge which I slowly waded through, waist high, pulling *Sahwira* after me. My reward for this stinkingly unpleasant effort, was a sward of cropped grass and a splendid view across to the southern end of the Kintyre peninsula. I readily made camp and settled down for a long wild night in my tent.

It was a ferocious night with heavy squalls of driving rain assailing my tent so hard, at one point I dashed out and around it, to check it was securely pegged down. I need not have worried; the lightweight Wild Country *Quasar* is what we know in our outdoor parlance as 'bombproof'. My night was fitful though, with little sleep. In the morning, it was a relief when peering groggily out, I realised I wouldn't be heading off until the gale abated. I turned over and snuggled deeper into my sleeping bag for some blissful uninterrupted snoozing. One of the aspects I find most attractive about expedition kayaking, is the ease I slip into a natural rhythm of existence. Ralph Waldo Emerson succinctly describes the process. *"Adopt the pace of Nature: her secret is patience."* I create the timetable of events, but it's how I relate with Nature which sees how this timetable is fulfilled. I cast my mind back twenty days previously when I embarked on the journey and how I was driven to count the miles and push as far and as fast as I could, viewing my progress in competition with the natural forces against me. In a journey such as this, there can be no competing with Nature. To do so would have resulted in unhappiness.

The morning was fair, with light rain showers whispering through the air as the wind slowly diminished in ferocity. Rainbows would dance amongst the showers, and I enjoyed creating installation rainbow art, by moving around my camp to frame a rainbow over anything I thought would look good with one; my tent, a small cairn, and of course, beautiful *Sahwira*.

I was on my way again soon after midday and made excellent progress along the Arran coastline, through a lively deep blue sea. The reefs which had been so problematic the day before were oddly benign and allowed me passage without baring their teeth. When the moment arrived, I turned westwards and headed into Kilbrannan Sound without so much as a second thought. Apart from a couple of trawlers growling up the sound, there was nothing to alarm me, and I confidently paddled across the open waters. A steep rolling swell invited *Sahwira* to leap and dive, her prow at times burying into the sea with a resulting clapotic crescendo of water, which caught in the sunlight, immediately becoming glittering slivers of spray-painted rainbow. I stopped paddling at one stage and waited for one of the trawlers with a Belfast registration to grumble by, her crew of five lining the gunwales to gaze across at me. Our cheery waves to each other, communicated the mutually respectful bond we mariners share.

The Kintyre coast was achieved without fanfare and so marked another pivotal moment in my journey. I had crossed the Firth of Clyde. There wasn't much to 'whoop' about though, because when I turned southwards to head the final five miles to Campbeltown, I found myself in the teeth of a fiercely sustained breeze. This developed into seemingly gale force proportions, when I eventually turned into Campbeltown Loch at Macringan's Point. The surface of the sea was whipped up into a frenzy and every one of my paddle strokes was required to dig deep, and hard, to keep edging forward. To my left loomed the curiously named Island Davaar where I wondered if I might find a place to camp if this wind prevented me from progressing. It hadn't been a demanding day paddling wise, so my energy levels were high, and my reserves enabled steady headway up the loch towards the town straggled along the head of it. As was my wont, I gazed at some of the fine houses strung along the shore on the outskirts with covetous eyes. The final few hundred metres to the Severn Class lifeboat berthed alongside the Old Quay were tortuous, for the wind seemed to increase in its intensity and ferocity. It was after six o'clock in the evening and the lifeboat station was closed. I found a place to pitch my tent a mile along the shore and I wandered into the sleepy, back to the nineteen eighties, attractive town for a fish supper and a pint. I felt like celebrating!

I had chores to attend to the following day. I was severely low on fuel for my stove, and I desperately needed to stock up on food supplies. Ahead was at least a week without the likelihood of finding a shop, so I had to ensure I carried enough food for ten days. I also needed to pay a visit to the lifeboat station. Waiting for the world to come to life at nine o'clock felt odd after having lived a life governed by the tides and daylight hours. When I had purchased my supplies and fuel, I dropped by the lifeboat station to introduce myself. Both David, the coxswain, and Trevor, the mechanic, warmly greeted me and invited me into their crew room for the ubiquitous coffee and biscuits. Through mouthfuls of jammy dodgers, I recounted my experiences so far, all the while eager to get to the subject of kayaking around the Mull of Kintyre. If anyone was going to provide sound advice about this headland with a fearsome reputation, then it had to be the coxswain of the Campbeltown lifeboat. I wasn't disappointed. A serious air descended on the conversation, and we wandered over to the chart table where David described in vivid detail the tidal features, I needed to be aware of. As with much of the advice I received from lifeboat personnel and other mariners around the coastline, I had to account for it being presented from a boatman's perspective, not a kayaker's. I quickly learned too, not to become defensive when aspersions were cast as to the viability of my successful completion of a notorious stretch of sea because of the seemingly fragile nature of my vessel (and I guess, myself too).

The advice I so often sought was not an endorsement of my venture, but helpful details about any stretch of sea ahead. It was often the case I felt some trepidation when seeking advice from wizened lifeboat crew, for fear they might advise not to tackle the passage in question at all. This would then place me in a quandary because out of my respect for their wisdom, I wouldn't want to be seen to disagree. However, as a seasoned sea kayaker myself, I would understand the likelihood of my personal success over failure. This concern never materialised and every time, I received complete respect for the challenge I was undertaking. It helped too, I held my own during discussions about tidal flows and prevailing conditions as evidence I was knowledgeable and responsible for my safety.

I made my farewells and left the lifeboat station with reaffirmed knowledge the Mull of Kintyre was not a place for me in my kayak with a strong north-westerly wind. Since these were forecast for the next couple of days, I would be wise to delay my traverse of the headland until the wind direction had changed. Back at my camp, I pondered my situation and decided to press on around to the hamlet of Southend, straggled around the tip of the Kintyre Peninsula, and wait there for the opportunity to leave the Firth of Clyde behind and head northwards. I was on the water by mid-morning and enjoyed a wonderfully pleasant paddle along the buttery yellow gorse lined south Kintyre coastline. The tide swept me around into the Sound of Sanda and for the first time I saw the looming bulk of the Mull of Kintyre a few miles ahead. Despite the forecast for strong winds, the sea was surprisingly calm with none of the turbulence I had expected. The tidal flow which was sweeping me along at a pleasing six miles an hour would last another four hours, and I started to wonder if I ought to press on around the Mull while I had the opportunity in these alluringly calm conditions. I rested my paddles across my deck and perused my map. Opportunities to pull ashore and camp on the Kintyre coastline beyond the Mull headland, were limited and would undoubtedly entail a gnarly landing amongst nasty boulders. I was sure if I pushed hard, I could make it to the haven of Machrihanish before nightfall.

I vacillated. This was not what I had expected, and I had not yet prepared myself for rounding the headland. This lack of preparedness served to heighten my anxiety, yet the conditions appeared perfect for a calm sea beyond. What I couldn't be certain of, was the condition of the tide race I would encounter, out of sight a few miles further around the headland. It would be just after peak tidal flow and the race would surely be in full effect. I didn't want to combat a roaring race if it could be avoided. However, if I stopped now, I would be held here for at least another day because the forecast winds would surely arrive. While I was tussling with this choice, I swept inexorably closer to the point where the decision would be made for me, when I was committed by default to a traverse of the Mull because I had passed the last opportunity to pull ashore and camp. Indecisiveness gripped me and I once more experienced the weight of loneliness. There wasn't anyone to turn to and chat this dilemma through. I gazed around for inspiration. None was forthcoming. I was on my own and this was my decision to make.

Port na Cusaig looked in every way to be the perfect place to camp. It was also the *last* viable place to camp before I was committed to the Mull of Kintyre. It was a small white sanded beach with an attractive green sward behind. It was also hidden from any habitation and exuded a sense of peace and wildness. I sat in my kayak and gazed at it, then turned my head to look down the line of broken cliffs stretching away, the mighty Mull of Kintyre around their corner. I willed myself to make the decision. Do I stay? Or do I go? Nothing ventured, nothing gained was the axiom running through my mind and I dug my right-hand paddle blade into the water, leaned slightly in my kayak, and was under way beneath the rising cliffs, heading for the Mull. The decision, as so often happens, occurred deep within, beyond conscious awareness. It was as if my 'inner-self', fed up with cognitive procrastination, took control. Immediately, I was aware of the tide speeding me along and noticed the eddies where they formed behind boulders, as the strong current swept past them. This was a clear indication of the strength of the tide and a heavy sense of foreboding descended. The decisiveness 'my-self' had demonstrated moments earlier, quickly dissipated to be replaced with consternation. The refrain, "I'm not prepared for this right now", ran through my head and I began to paddle backwards, slowing myself down to a stop. Sweeping again with my right-hand paddle, and leaning in the same direction, I brought *Sahwira* around in an arc until I was facing the way I had come. Without delay, I paddled back to the small, secluded bay of Port na Cusaig and ran the bow of the kayak firmly up the beach, lest there be any temptation to push off out to sea again. In a matter of minutes, I was standing on the shore and any idea of pressing on around the Mull of Kintyre had finally been quashed. This isolated and tranquil beach with a lovely grassy slope and tumbling clearwater stream was my Kintyre home for the next two days. So ended my exploration of the Firth of Clyde and successful visits to eight R.N.L.I. lifeboat stations.

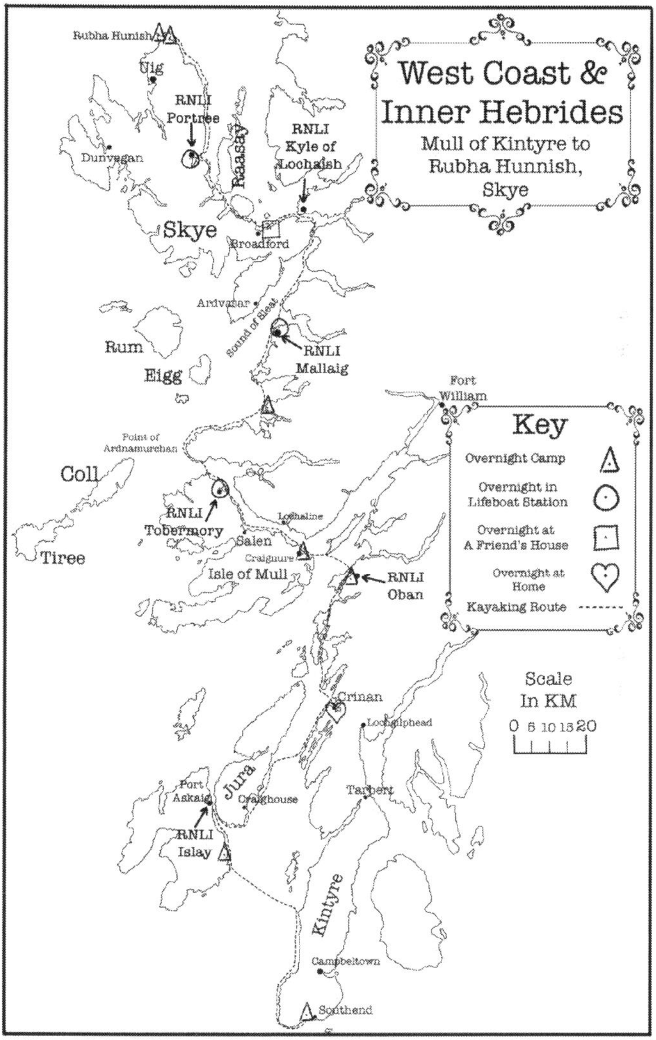
West Coast &
Inner Hebrides
Mull of Kintyre to
Rubha Hunnish,
Skye
Key
Overnight Camp
Overnight in Lifeboat Station
Overnight at A Friend's House
Overnight at Home
Kayaking Route
Scale In KM
0 5 10 15 20
Rubha Hunish
Uig
RNLI Portree
Dunvegan
Raasay
RNLI Kyle of Lochalsh
Skye
Broadford
Ardvasar
Sound of Sleat
RNLI Mallaig
Rum
Eigg
Fort William
Point of Ardnamurchan
Coll
RNLI Tobermory
Lochaline
Salen
Tiree
Craignure
Isle of Mull
RNLI Oban
Crinan
Lochgilphead
Port Askaig
Jura
Craighouse
Tarbert
RNLI Islay
Kintyre
Campbeltown
Southend

West Coast and Inner Hebrides
Mull of Kintyre to Rubha Hunish, Skye

Chapter 11

Unlike many, I am not a sea kayaker who enjoys tide races. In fact, they fill me with fear and if possible, I will steer clear of them at all costs. Because of its reputation, the Mull of Kintyre was a tidal gate I had particularly been nervous about from the early stages of planning for the expedition. So far, I had enjoyed a trouble-free circumnavigation of the Clyde but my exit from the Firth was going to be a test of my resolve and would act as a reminder of some of the sterner conditions I would face sometime further into the journey. I was pleased to have gained local information about the seas off the Mull from the Campbelltown lifeboat crew but in doing so, my fears had been exacerbated rather than allayed. I think, with mischievous glints in their eyes, they had teased about the ferocity of the tide, particularly when set against the wind. I was therefore approaching this passage with the utmost care and thorough preparation.

In preparing for my journey, I had created my own sea kayaking almanac which detailed the nautical information for my whole route around Scotland. I had a couple of pages of comprehensive data dedicated to the Mull of Kintyre, including helpful diagrams of the tidal flows at specific states of the tide cycle. To ensure I didn't find myself becoming swallowed by a raging tide race, I needed to make careful calculations using the information I had gleaned, along with the daily tide times for Dover or another constant point of reference, either Greenock or Oban. My confidence with my mathematical reasoning is low at the best of times. It was agonisingly painstaking to work through the process of arriving at a decision about what time I needed to depart my campsite, to ensure I arrived at the location of the major tide race at the safest time. This was slack water, the moment when the tide shifted from ebbing or flowing in one direction to the opposite. Generally, at slack water the tidal streams are at their weakest and any dangers they may pose will be diminished. I needed to avoid the location during the peak flow of the tide when the current would be at its strongest and the race at its most dangerous.

I worked out two possible departure times from my camp spot, the first at three a.m. and the other at three p.m. Both these times would see me arrive at the point where I was confident of safely traversing the Kintyre tide race. I had no idea of the nature of the race, how it developed and how far the disturbed water flowed. Neither did I know how close to the shore it formed. In my research I read anecdotal accounts of the race which did not fill me with anticipatory joy. Yet, I knew of many kayakers who had successfully traversed the headland, and I also knew with care, I would be fine. In a way, it was good to be on my own because I was doubly thorough with my preparations. However, in this instance I wouldn't have minded bouncing thoughts and ideas off a paddling companion.

It wasn't simply a matter of working out the tide times and flows, I had to be strategic in my decision making too. With the forecast as it was, beginning around midnight, I had a twelve-hour period of grace from the strong winds before they returned from the west, with renewed vigour for another two or three days. This was more than enough time to see me safely around the Mull and find a haven much further up the Kintyre coastline. The issue I faced concerned my passage onwards, to the island of Islay and visiting the lifeboat station there at Port Askaig. Reaching the island involved a lengthy fifteen-mile open crossing westwards from the Kintyre Peninsula. Here I would be exposed to any rough seas wrought by strong winds from the west or south-west. I was keenly aware of the slippage in my schedule and the fact I didn't want to be confined to the mainland waiting for the strong winds to blow through. If I were to make the most of these twelve hours, it would require choosing the three-a.m. departure time. The significance of this was the fact I would then be traversing the Mull and facing the tides as the sun was rising. I wasn't certain setting off on my own in the early dawn darkness to tackle one of the more notorious stretches of Scottish coastline was a wise idea. However, if I used the later afternoon time, I would possibly reach Machrihanish where I was assured of a safe camp, but I would be well short of my Islay goal. It would mean holing up there until the next available weather window. An added and important driver within my decision-making process was my desire to reach Karen and our small yacht, which was berthed at Crinan, only three paddling days away. Finding myself delayed so close to the nuptials of home would be a bitter pill to swallow. Yet, I was also aware of not allowing my marital desires to cloud my judgement. It wouldn't do to end up in a bothersome situation because I was driven to reach Karen's warm and loving companionship. Thankfully, I had a day in which to mull over my choices, because I was kept ashore by near gale force winds, though the day was filled with bright sunny weather.

Southend on the Mull of Kintyre is a collection of sprawling caravanning sites and numerous holiday homes.

The happy down beat tempo of the area belied its enormous historical significance. It was here St Columba arrived in Scotland from Ireland and the distinctive promontory of Dunaverty became one of the main strongholds of the Gaelic Kingdom of Dalriada, the precursor to the Kingdom of Alba. It was invigorating to enjoy a long walk in the bright spring sunshine, the Bluebells in the woods dancing in the strong breeze and diamonds glinting off the ruffled sea. I sought out the petrosomatoglyphs (carved human footprints on a rock) purporting to belong to St Columba marking the spot where he first preached on his arrival to the Scottish mainland. I cast a couple of coins too into the nearby wildflower adorned ancient well, whispering a wish for a fair passage around the Mull. The skull and crossbones on the medieval grave slabs in the adjacent ruined chapel served to remind me of my mortality. History oozed from the landscape while around, life was lived with holiday abandon.

Back in my secluded camp site, I enjoyed lying in the shelter of my tent soaking up the warmth of the sun. Complete and incomplete tidal machinations were strewn beside me. I was no closer to a decision about which time I would set off around the Mull. I continued to vacillate between the two choices for the rest of the day. To ease myself of troubled thinking I decided to light a small campfire on the beach and sit beside this while I enjoyed the sunset. In a matter of minutes, I had a fine collection of sea smoothed driftwood artistically piled on the sand. Moments later wisps of aromatic blue tinted smoke rose from the flickering golden flamed fire I had created. I waited for the worldly bonhomie a campfire engenders to infuse my mind, instead I experienced a painful wave of loneliness, the like I had never experienced before. My easy relationship with solitude was replaced with the ache of aloneness. I craved company, moreover, I craved the company of specific friends who I trusted and loved and who in turn intimately knew me and supported my adventurous drive and desires. I trusted their wise advice, and in their company, I have shared many exciting experiences. I craved their companionship and compassionate wisdom. The fire I had lit symbolised sharing and comradeship, and instead I was sitting beside it on my own. In an instant I had thrown the remaining pile of wood onto the flames and abruptly stood up. Looking out over the tumbled sea I suddenly came to my decision. I would set off to round the Mull at three a.m. the following morning. My desire to make headway and reconnect with Karen outweighed anything else, and I was confident I would pull this off.

Chapter 12

The strident alarm on my GPS woke me from a fitful sleep at one a.m. There was no sign of the promised dawn in the pitch blackness of my tent, but undeterred I set to, organising my kit and packing it away. I had prepared much of this the evening before, so there was no real need to hurry. I felt a developing tense excitement like the sensation I experienced before running a white-water river during my 'dinosaur days', kayaking with a reckless long neck and an equally small brain. As I sorted my meagre belongings, the knot in my stomach felt like the countless times in my youth, when I dressed and prepared myself to enter a frightening river.

I made sure I cooked myself a large bowl of porridge, mixed with muesli and honey. Quite a concoction but guaranteed to sustain me for at least the whole morning, though I had to force myself to consume it given the tension in my abdomen. Curiously, despite the dark, I was packed and ready for departure well before I had planned, which then presented the uncomfortable choice of departing before my planned time or not. Recalling my impatience on the Mull of Galloway, I opted for another pot of coffee and restraint. In fact, this eased my nerves as I sat on *Sahwira's* deck watching the lights of three ships steadily working their way up St George's Channel. Somehow seeing them out there, helped me feel less alone.

Three a.m. arrived and I launched through the small but manageable surf rolling into the bay. Just beyond the rising waves I switched off my head torch and sat for a good while, adjusting my eyesight to the dark and pondered for the umpteenth time what I was likely to encounter after I set off.

There were now the faintest of glimmers of the impending dawn, so with a couple of heavy sweep strokes and edging my laden kayak, I was on my way along the southern most Kintyre coastline, the indistinct cliffs of the Mull soon rising high above. What I noticed most was the silence. Absent were the constant calls of the seabirds, replaced with soft sleepy sighs of the waves echoing their way through the rocky, boulder strewn shoreline. I could feel the tickling pull of the tide beneath me and in the gloom, I noticed I was making good progress along the shore. Despite the danger of striking a half-submerged rock, I wanted to stick as close to the coast as possible because I feared a little further out, I would meet large standing waves and difficult water. Suddenly, not far ahead, the distinctive white splash of a breaking wave caused my stomach to spasm in a synergetic response. I strained my eyes searching for clues as to what I was approaching. I cocked my head too, attempting to catch any warning rumble of a large tide race. I could hear moving water but nothing which alarmed me and so, rather nonchalantly I paddled through the first of the tidal races of the Mull. The stern of the kayak was kicked away to the left as I passed through but nothing else to cause concern. Despite my outward calm though, every fibre of my being was tight and alert. It was almost as if I were using superhuman powers of sight and hearing to work out what was around and what lay ahead.

I began to feel a diminishing confidence and I feared capsizing in the cold early morning waters of the Irish Sea. I worked out if I did capsize, I would be swept away from the Mull of Kintyre and out into open waters. Almost as if I were caressing a reassuring amulet, I opened the left pocket of my buoyancy aid and checked to see if my PLB was there.

Before I had set off, I had also made sure that my pyrotechnic rocket and handheld flares were where I wanted them in my deck bag. I didn't want to be fumbling around for these if I was in a hurry. It was difficult to appreciate it but the tide now had me in its robust grip and I realised I was being swept along at a rapid pace. A glance at my GPS showed I was travelling at just over five miles an hour, a good speed. However, I needed to be cautious because if I didn't pay attention, at this pace I could quickly find myself in complicated circumstances. All the while around, the gloaming was lifting to be replaced with the early pink hues of a glorious dawn.

Unexpectedly, I saw the beaming light of the Mull of Kintyre lighthouse arcing out into the Irish Sea and I experienced an almost overwhelming sensation of elation. I knew once past here I would be fine, and I was relieved I had not encountered any difficulties so far. As if to counter my over confidence I saw between a large boulder and the mainland, a seething pile of white capped waves. It was clear the tide compressed by this constriction was piling up and creating a dangerously rough stretch of water to contend with. I could hear it too and the rumbling roar tightened my stomach in preparation for what I had to cope with. Looking carefully to the seaward side of the rock I couldn't make out anything which appeared to be equally as troublesome. I therefore decided to keep to the outside and edged my kayak to account for this course setting. I was shocked at how quickly the rock and the seething water were approaching and it was almost too late before I realised I was being rushed into the open jaws of a large tide race, the one I had been anticipating ever since launching an hour or so earlier. Even though it was still quite gloomy, thankfully it was light enough to make out what immediately lay ahead. In a matter of seconds, I was sucked into the race, water piling up around my kayak, waves randomly breaking around me, and unseen currents grabbing hold of my keel wishing to turn me against my will. My heart was in my mouth which was suddenly devoid of any spittle or moisture. I was paddling for my upright existence and urged myself to remain calm and not make any hasty decisions or unnecessary changes to my path. If I allowed the kayak to find her own way and moved my body to meet her random pitching and rolling and more importantly, I kept her gunwales from being loaded by an upstream current, I would be fine.

A matter of seconds after entering the race I spotted the opportunity to take a line down the edge of it, with the chance to break out of the current into the less forceful but equally unstable waters of a fierce eddy. I did not immediately rush to take this action because while I was in the main flow, as uncomfortable and frightening as this may be, I was roller-coasteering forwards, and I was able to maintain an element of control. The moment I met the line between the moving water and the upwelling and uncertain waters of the eddy, I would be at my most unstable. The eddy-edge itself was easily definable so when I crossed this, the bow of my kayak would hit the imperceptibly stationary water of the eddy and in turn slow right down, while my stern was still in the full flow of the tide race. This would result in my kayak being forcibly spun on her axis, with her upper gunwale being lowered towards the upstream flow. If I weren't prepared for this happening the gunwale would sink below the surface and the force of the water subsequently piling onto the deck of the kayak, would flip me over in a split second. I would capsize. Understanding this hydrodynamic meant I was ready with my paddles to support *Sahwira* in her turn and sudden transition from moving forward to an almost abrupt stop. In the brief seconds of this manoeuvre, I would be at my most vulnerable and I only had one chance to get it right. Paddling with others it doesn't really matter if I capsize and swim, because someone would easily rescue me and help me back into my kayak. Here on my own in the early morning gloaming, capsizing, possibly missing my roll, and the subsequent swim, would be a hazardously unpleasant experience. I was not in danger from being dashed against rocks, but in these rough and uncertain waters, a self-rescue would be a challenge, not to mention the discomfort of becoming wet and cold. Above all, it was the inconvenience of capsizing which was my concern.

I chose my moment and made my move. *Sahwira's* bow crossed the eddy line and as I knew she would, she swung hard on the edge of the water between the upwelling boils and the rumbling water train sweeping seawards. I was prepared for the almost violent lean of the kayak and my outstretched paddle, blade flat on the surface held my bodyweight, with my knees firmly in their braces under the deck, my hip flexibly meeting the movement of this manoeuvre, prevented the kayak from flipping over. In a second, I was done, and I had turned, facing the oncoming flow, sitting comfortably on the relatively calm waters of the eddy. This was not as easy as it may seem because the boils and upwelling of water from the dark depths beneath almost threatened to lift me up and force me back into the main flow. My pulse was racing but I'm sure my grin was as broad as the brim of my baseball cap.

Gingerly turning myself to face the direction I wanted to travel I paddled away from the roaring race and further out of the uncertain waters of the large eddy. Eventually I was back in a regular sea where there was no uncertainty or the need to be prepared to affect an emergency support stroke at any moment. I could relax again and knowing I had successfully navigated the main tidal race around the Mull of Kintyre, I allowed myself one of those rare moments of praising myself aloud. There was even a loud holler of success and my whoops echoed off the cliffs to my right. I don't think there was anyone to see me punch the air triumphantly. I could now really enjoy the experience of kayaking below the Mull of Kintyre cliffs. It was four thirty in the morning and I now felt safe and secure. This was an immense challenge I had taken on and had overcome. I had been cautious, but I had also been bold in deciding to paddle in the early dawn. It was a sudden realisation I had what it takes to succeed in the overall venture. Until this moment I doubted I had the ability to face this challenge – the immensity of it, the distance and the dangers.

I continued my way, hoping I would reconnect with the tidal elevator northwards. Instead, the kayak felt sluggish, and I realised with dismay when looking at the GPS, I must be in a powerful tidal back eddy. I was in fact now kayaking against the tide. I didn't want to head back out into the main race again, but this powerful current was in danger of seriously slowing me down, so I paddled closer into the shore, in the hope the stream against me would be weaker there. To compound problems, a large westerly swell made kayaking close in, a dangerous proposition. There was every chance I might be swept up in a large breaking wave onto the rocks. This was overall an inhospitable landscape for a kayaker, with very few opportunities to land safely for respite or a comfort break. In addition to the boulder lined cliffs there were many hidden skerries, which were exposed without warning by the large swell. By maintaining a high level of alertness, I worked out where these potentially destructive boomers were, by the surface patterns on the sea. Every now and then a magnificent cascade of white water would erupt either ahead, or to the side or behind me. These unpredictable boomers exploded like sea-mines, and it was my task to avoid them.

Eventually, sometime after I had left the lighthouse far behind, I felt more confident about moving further out to find the main northward flow again. I could see there was no danger of being caught in a tide race out there. Immediately on doing this, I noticed with considerable relief my speed over the ground substantially increase. I relaxed and enjoyed watching the rising sun light the sky with dawn pinks. The headlands and the subsequent rocky bays came and went. I kept my eyes out for possible landing places, looking to see if it would have been possible to make landfall and camp, if I had continued my way a couple of days ago. With this swell it was impossible to land safely, and I felt a sense of relief I hadn't pushed myself on that day. It would have been a tricky encounter, that's for sure. While passing Innean Glen where there looked to be the only possible place to land in these conditions, and even then, this would be a worrying experience, I scoured the hillside for a sight of the headstone of an unknown sailor who had been found on the shore and buried there. I couldn't see it and I certainly wasn't going to land to look more closely. Shortly later I noticed the cliff features were beginning to soften and round out. Before long I was rounding the rocky headland which guarded the southern stretch of Machrihanish Bay. I had to reawaken my alertness because of the many small reefs, seemingly intent on catching me unawares with the huge breaking swell.

By now the weather had changed, the clear skies replaced by a subdued low-lying grey cloud. The air was still and despite the rolling swell the surface of the sea was unbroken and calm. There are few things I don't enjoy when I'm sea kayaking. One of them is traversing long unbroken sandy beaches. Machrihanish promised to be one such beach and in my planning, I had assumed when I reached here, it would be a case of having to put my head down and just get past without fussing. As it transpired, I found this stretch to be a delightful experience. The swell slowly passing beneath on its way to its ignominious final rush and collapse onto the beach sands, pleasingly lifted me and lowered me down in a restful and relaxing motion. My paddling rhythm was purposeful and strong, and I was making excellent progress. The onshore transits I chose, passed by without the sense of ever lingering. I moved in as close to the shore as I dared. Landwards the sea created a rolling horizon behind which the swell became crashing surf, the only evidence of which was the occasional glimpse of spray. This was all I needed to know getting caught in these breaking waves would not be a pleasant experience at all. Towards the north end of the beach, I spotted a group of surfers sitting out at sea astride their boards just beyond the surf line. There was also one brave soul on his stand-up paddle board. As I approached, they seemed to spot the ideal wave and disappeared in a flurry of thrashing arms, catching the wave as it steeply lifted them up. The stand-up boarder waved and then manfully set off after them. The last I saw of him was his head and shoulders suddenly disappearing as if some unseen monster beneath had reached up and pulled him down. An explosion of spray behind the wave told me he had gloriously wiped out. I was determined not to follow suit, so I edged the kayak and took myself further out to sea.

The perfectly calm surface was wonderful to paddle through but with sadness, I noticed a huge amount of detritus floating in the sea. It was as if a dustbin truck had discharged its load into the ocean further up the coast and this was floating past now. I was dismayed by the amount of needless waste, drifting aimlessly, waiting for the current and the winds to guide it to destinations all along the seashore, to join the copious amounts of trash already there. Plastic, the twentieth century material humans seem incapable of existing without, made up most of the waste. Polypropylene, nylon, neoprene, and so many more materials impervious to the normal natural process of degradation, littered the waters around. The discarded items made from these materials, spend their immortal lives drifting and decaying, casting off minute particles which are inevitably ingested by the sea creatures of the oceanic ecosystem. It wasn't lost on me I was kayaking in a fibreglass kayak and many, if not all the items I was using on this trip, were made from non-biodegradable materials. One day when I no longer had a use for them, they too would require disposing of, or maybe if mindlessly forgotten on a beach, end up floating on the surface of the sea just like the rubbish I was passing now. Rather than accept culpability on the grounds I'm a consumer just as all humans are, I directed my ire at the modern-day fisherman, because much of the waste floating past was obviously cast overboard from fishing boats; a single blue glove, strands of rope, a broken plastic fish box, polypropylene netting hanging off a nearly submerged hard plastic buoy, a prawn tube and a bobbing container with probably toxic contents. I angrily wondered if fishermen didn't correlate declining fish stocks to what I self-righteously deemed their apparent poor stewardship of the sea.

Realising the harshness with which I was judging one sector of human society, I thought with sad resignation, it's not just fishermen who discount the reality of overconsumption and needless waste. We are all culpable. We ignore the association between our consumerist lifestyles and the rapid degradation of the Earth's environment. My quickness to anger and my subsequent slide into melancholy was unexpected and unwanted. Today was not the day to be absorbed by my regular bout of environmental despair and sense of hopelessness. This was a long and demanding day, and I had a long way yet to travel. I needed to focus and shake myself out of any depressive thinking. It was important to remain positive, draw on my stamina and make use of my constructive determination.

A powerful oceanic swell prevented me from taking a break on the shore. At one moment though, this decision was almost made for me when I absently dithered too close to the beach. A loud clap behind warned of a breaking wave and I looked up to see I was about to be engulfed in a collapsing wave which if it had broken over me, would have certainly imploded my spray deck and rolled me unmercifully onto the rocky shoreline. I managed with a burst of arm wrenching strength, to pull *Sahwira* up and over the lip of the crackling wave just before it folded and collapsed. As I crested the sharp peak of the wave, I was airborne for what seemed like a few weightless seconds, before the kayak thumped down into the sea behind the roller with a resounding slap. In those few seconds, I experienced fear and elation in one fluid process. The fear of being caught and wrecked by a large wave followed by the elation of gaining air and nose diving into the sea off the wave. However, despite the resulting adrenalin buzz, as I hastily paddled out beyond the break, I remonstrated with myself for my lack of concentration.

The Kintyre coastline passed by without incident after that. The sun broke through, and the day turned into a happy and warm one. Families wandered out onto the beaches and a general air of holiday and festivities, replaced the overcast gloom that had briefly attempted to take control of the day. With the remnants of the northward tide, I was making excellent progress. I judged I would make it to Glenacardoch Point, a couple of miles south of the Gigha Channel before lunchtime. I looked at the map and hoped I would find shelter around the point from the breaking surf. I needed to land ashore because by now the extra mug of coffee, drunk just before departing seven hours earlier was about to burst my bladder. I was distinctly uncomfortable.

Thankfully, my supposition there would be shelter from the swell was correct. I was able to land in a small inlet, jumping out and rushing up the shore, breathing a huge sigh at the subsequent relief. I was making excellent progress and I now had the choice of crossing to Islay, fifteen miles away or heading to the islands of Cara or Gigha slightly to the north and stopping there. I was feeling strong and there seemed no reason why I should not press on. I had already travelled over twenty miles and by any normal standards this would be a good day. However, the forecast was for strong westerlies to arrive any hour soon and I wanted to be across on Islay before these materialised. Looking south westwards,

I could see the change in the weather beginning to make an appearance, there was a bank of ominously dark cloud on the horizon. All was calm where I was now though, and the skies were clear. The decision really centred on my ability to make the crossing before the poor weather arrived. If I paddled as well as I had been during the morning, I calculated I would be across in four hours. Looking south westwards with my now practiced eye, I judge the weather front to be at least this time away. Anyhow I surmised, I would be close to the Islay shore when the worst of it kicked in and it would be easy enough to run for shelter over there, if need be.

I wandered up and down the beach a few times to get the blood flowing in my legs and chatted to a woman who was walking her dog, about the joys of living somewhere as beautiful as this location. As with the many people I met in circumstances like this, she was fascinated by the concept of my journey and full of praise for what I had achieved so far. I found myself becoming embarrassed once more by her effusions of praise, but her heartfelt wishes of luck and fortune carried weight. These meant much to me. She watched as I launched, and I turned to wave to her as I paddled away.

Islay looked a good distance away. It was impossible to pick out any definable features on the far-off low-lying hilly landscape. This was going to be my longest open water crossing to date and to be tackling it after already a full morning of paddling was a demanding expectation. As I set off across the sound in the direction of the small island of Cara, I cautioned myself not to be heroic. If I began to feel fatigued and while I still had the chance, I should camp on either Cara or Gigha and make the crossing when I could after that. In fact, I was tempted to stop on Gigha because it was an island I had wanted to visit by kayak for many years. I had last visited there in 1987 when I helped crew a yacht from Oban down to Ravenglass. Even then I had only spent a convivial evening in the pub.

I kept an eye out for shipping but apart from one small fishing boat seemingly trawling to the west of Gigha, the seas were empty. My company for the crossing consisted of the odd raft or two of guillemots and gracefully swooping herring gulls. Essentially, I was on my own and I revelled in my solitude. Suddenly a surge of pleasurable energy coursed through me. I was enjoying every minute of my day and though it was going to be a long crossing, I was relishing the challenge. I must admit I am not a fan of long open sea crossings because of the tedium I experience during them. I am a kayaker who enjoys getting close into the shore and exploring the nooks and crannies. Paddling for miles and hours through open seas does not fill me with the sea kayaking joy I seek. However, I do relish the challenge crossings pose. It is because I find them psychologically difficult, I rise to meet them with some eagerness. Today I faced this crossing with equanimity and struck a steady rhythm with my paddling, losing myself deep in my thoughts.

While there was little else to do apart from maintain a strong paddling speed and a direct heading, it was easy to switch on the autopilot and allow my mind to wander. On a day such as this, when the sun was shining, it was warm and the winds were light and the seas calm, there was great pleasure to be had in following my daydreams to see where these may lead. I do not meditate as a practice but I think when my kayaking is like this, it becomes a meditative experience. There was little to intrude on the moment and my mind was free to follow whatever path it chose. But it wasn't just about my mind and my thinking, it was also about what I was feeling in my body. I felt power surging through my muscles emanating from what seemed to be a limitless battery source. My paddling strokes were far reaching and powerful and my body felt no pain or stiffness. My back felt sturdy, and my buttocks were impervious to the discomfort of having been compressed for many hours on end. Knowing this – *feeling* this – provided even more power and a deeper sense of pleasure. Feeling healthy and robust, made me feel alive. There was far more to this realisation than the sense of wellbeing and feeling good. It was the acknowledgement I *was* indeed alive; I was breathing, I was thinking, I was feeling, and I was living the life I strived for.

There have been many times in my life when I despaired enough to consider choosing death over living. I struggled with depressive thinking daily and I have lived with clinical depression much of my adult life. I have been in hospital many times because of it, and I've required the support and care of rigorous mental health interventions. Thankfully, I had not been incapacitated by my depression for several years before this journey, though I lived with a low-grade malaise which threatened to take a grip at any time. Preventing this from happening had become a way of life. The best method I used to achieve this was to keep a check on my reality by quite literally grounding myself. This involved being aware of the earth beneath my feet, feeling the air fill my lungs, seeing the sights of the world around me and knowing because of all of these, I was OK. There were times, regularly it seemed, when my mood dipped, and my feelings of low self-worth deepened and threatened to take root. The tactics of grounding and checking out the reality did not always work in these situations. It was then I may have allowed myself to become engulfed in darkness, to feel the pain waiting for me at the bottom of a hollow emptiness. It was my experience if I allowed myself to slide all the way into a depressive episode, I would eventually make it through to the other side. Depending on the catalysts for these moments of depression, it sometimes was a frightening process. The despair I experienced was often strong enough to ignite thoughts of suicide which forever lay dormant within me. I lived with these thoughts as unwelcome companions. In the long periods of my life when I have felt strong, they have been almost banished altogether. Tenaciously though they linger, well-hidden until the moment, unbidden they make themselves known again.

I had not attempted suicide, but the desires to complete my suicide have sometimes been strong enough within me to not only cause myself concern, but concern health professionals too. Hence the admissions to inpatient psychiatric care. In the parlance of the health services, my ideations of suicide are credible. The frightening thing is, I know I don't want to die. I want to continue to live my life until its natural end. I do not want to take my own life but there is the real possibility I may choose to do so. There may be a life event, a personal occurrence which may send me into a depression so deep, I will believe there is no other solution, except to give up living. The pain, the despair, the thoughts of extreme low self-worth and more than anything, the belief I am nothing but a burden, will cause me to lose my hold on reality and I may act on the desire to end the pain I'm experiencing.

In undertaking this journey, I took myself through a thorough process of determining my state of mental health. I had to be certain I was strong enough to face the challenge and I was not setting myself up to fail, because doing so, could be just the catalyst which might send me into depths I was unable to return from. I had to be certain this trip was not a smoke screen for an ultimately darker deed. Many people asked whether I did any training before I set out on my journey. I knew they were referring to developing my physical fitness. I didn't physically train for the trip, but I wanted to tell them every day leading up to my departure, I visited my 'self' and checked in with how I was doing, ascertaining I was up to the immensity of the challenge. More to the point, was I prepared for the aftermath if I had to withdraw from the journey or it came to an early end for any reason? Was I prepared for the possibility the journey might end because I gave up through not coping? If I had one major risk assessment to make for the venture, this was it.

An important reason I was undertaking this voyage was indeed to test my resolve in the face of extreme challenge. In a way it was a pathway to vindication. If successful, I would finally realise I do hold self-worth and I am able to achieve great things. The risk of failure was huge as was the risk of a disastrous personal outcome. I was willing to accept both these risks. My confidence in this matter centred on my belief this was my time. I often referred to this journey as being a rite of passage – from my mid-age to my older-age. This was true. It was my task through this journey to discover if I was serious about living my life until its natural conclusion.

As I paddled with vigour towards the far-off island, with vitality coursing through me, I knew I was well on the way to discovering an important insight. Here, in the middle of the channel between Islay and Kintyre, I could not have felt more alive. It was a truly joyous experience. I ceased paddling and slowly drifted to a stop, simply sitting in the middle of the oceanic expanse and taking it all in. It was an incredibly powerful moment of realisation. Life is precious and must be savoured in all its shapes, forms, and complexities. Sitting there, breathing in the iodine laden air, listening to the water tinkle against the hull of the kayak, feeling the subtle movements of the sea beneath me, noticing how my body unconsciously compensated to these movements and how in tune I was to that very moment, I knew I was OK. Here I was alone, with all my darknesses and frailties, and also with all my strengths and potential to offer so much to myself and others. I realised I was not there by accident and this moment wasn't just another menial moment in my life. I had chosen to be there, and I had made it happen, totally with my own resources. I did not find myself becoming emotional and tearful as I might have done. Instead, I yelled a holler of exultation and rewarded myself in the best way I could in the moment. I issued myself an extra ration of sticky malt loaf.

A couple of miles from the Islay coast the threatening weather front finally reached me. The wind began to pick up, blowing strongly from the southwest, the sea responding by becoming unsettled and lumpy. I began to scan the shoreline for likely campsites knowing it would not be long before I would have to get myself off the water in these worsening conditions. By now of course I had been paddling for well over ten hours and I was beginning to feel fatigued. I was ready for the day to end. Ideally, I wanted to reach Proaig bothy another six miles further up the Islay coastline. This would provide me with a roof to shelter under and more importantly set me up nicely to reach Port Askaig the next day. In the worsening conditions I dug in my paddles deeper and determinedly headed onwards. Two hours later and in conditions which were now marginal, I could make out the bothy behind the shore of a wide bay enclosed by drab green hills. With renewed energy I headed straight for it. As I did so I scanned the building and its surrounds, searching for any signs of other visitors. I was hoping I would have the place to myself but there was an element of disappointment when I realised there was nobody there. I could have done with some human interaction after such a long day. Approaching the beach I'd chosen for landing; I was startled to see a fox skulking in the line of rotting seaweed fringing the high water mark. I realised with an even greater shock it was not a fox, but instead a huge otter, the size of which I'd never seen before. It was massive, looking like the kind of creature not to mess with. It remained stock still, gazing at me intently and clearly trying to work me out. I sat still in my kayak, staring back. It must have decided I was an unsavoury character because in a flash it darted across the weed and rocks and slipped into the sea without so much as a splash. In an instant it disappeared and despite continuing to sit still and scanning the surface of the sea, I never saw it again.

Feeling blessed by such a magnificent welcome I climbed out of my kayak with weakened legs and hefted her up the shore as far as I could get her. Not allowing myself to dwell on the success of my day just yet, I wandered up to the bothy to check it out and to see if it was suitable to sleep in overnight. If not, I would put the tent up instead. After I had fumbled with the rusted bolt with my cold and water wrinkled hands, the door creaked open and scraped over the flat stone threshold. Inside, the single large room was dry, clean, rustically basic and eminently suitable for a comfortable night. I heaved a sigh of relief and set about unpacking the kayak and carrying everything up to my temporary home. Finally, with *Sahwira* lying safely alongside the bothy wall I was able to undress from my kayaking attire and experience the end of day pleasure of putting on dry and warm clothes. A pot of water slowly steamed on the stove for a much-needed mug of lemon and ginger tea. Slowly a realisation and awareness of a huge sense of achievement infused me. Not only had I successfully kayaked solo around the Mull of Kintyre, but I had done this in the dawn hours. I had then gone on to paddle forty-five miles. In this moment I knew I had what it takes to undertake a sea kayaking venture of this magnitude and I was happy.

That night a storm raged around the bothy, heavy torrential rain drumming an incessant tattoo on the corrugated iron roof which the violent gale appeared intent on lifting off the eaves. It was lovely to lie warm and cosy in my sleeping bag, feeling safe and secure.

Chapter 13

The next day was a May bank holiday, and I was disappointed not to meet anyone from the Islay lifeboat crew. I had hoped I might have stopped in Port Askaig, enjoying a night of good craic in the local pub. After taking photos of their Severn class lifeboat and lingering in the hope someone might appear, I decided to press on and head back down the Sound of Islay. I had not formulated a plan for the day, so I had no notion of where I was ultimately heading for. My next determined goal was Crinan, forty miles away, where Karen was working and where we had our boat. I launched into a sweeping tide and enjoyed being whisked along at a steady nine miles an hour to the bottom end of the sound ten miles away.

I found myself seeking shelter as best I could in the lee of the shore, paddling as close to the rocky coastline of the Isle of Jura as I dared. Ahead lay a challenging crossing of the Sound of Jura back to the mainland coast, up which I could make my way northwards towards the tiny hamlet of Crinan. When the time came to make the crossing, I found myself staring across a wind churned sea, a challenging undertaking at the best of times and possibly foolish given I was paddling on my own. I hardly gave the daunting prospect ahead a second thought, as I reached forward into the sea with my paddle blades and propelled myself into the maelstrom. The wind was now on my stern which pushed me onwards, but it also kicked up a fearsome sea. Waves were breaking and collapsing around me and from time to time my deck was awash with an onrush of foam and bubbles, my kayak beneath seemingly sinking like a submerging submarine. I was paddling with the unconscious ease of someone who has perfected an acquired skill. My paddle strokes were fluid and confident and I was never in doubt about coping in the difficult conditions. Once or twice an extra fierce gust would slam into me and I felt a frisson of fear at the prospect of being knocked over, but this never happened. Two thirds of the way across, I hunkered down in the welcome lee of a couple of skerries and wolfed down a whole malt loaf. I was feeling exhilarated. Before long I was across the sound and paddling into the natural harbour of Keillmore. I'd told myself at the beginning of the day, once reaching this point I would haul ashore and make camp, leaving myself an easy paddle up the coastline to Crinan twelve miles away. In essence an easy half day of kayaking.

I sat in my kayak reluctant to leave it to search out a place to establish camp. Outside the harbour, it seemed the violence of the raging sea was attempting to break through the natural rock ramparts which guarded the lagoon. It felt the level of the sea I was sitting on was a couple of metres lower than the sea outside. I looked around, searching for a likely place to make camp. There was nowhere which jumped out as an attractive proposition. All about seemed boggy and rank. In hindsight, I think it was my state of mind at the time which caused me to see what I saw, or rather ignore what I could see. I'm sure I'd have found somewhere eminently suitable to place my tent. However, despite the raging conditions, I had a dogged determination to keep going and so again, without much of a second thought, I kayaked out into the heaving sea once more. By now I'd kayaked twenty-five miles which by my standards so far, was a decent distance to have travelled in a day, especially with the challenging conditions as they were.

Sahwira rose to meet the demands of the crashing sea without demure. I now had the full force of the wind on my port beam along with a heavily breaking swell which crashed mercilessly onto the rocky shoreline. An hour into slogging my way through the heavy conditions, I began to wonder if I'd been foolhardy to have pressed on. I told myself in recompense, the first likely place to stop and camp, I would do so. Thus assuaged, I applied myself to the task in hand with renewed vigour. Opportunities to stop came and passed by. Each time I remonstrated with myself for ignoring the succour these locations offered. The nicest of all these spots was Carsaig Bay which would not only have provided a comfortable place to spend the night, but I would be in easy walking distance of the pub in the village of Tayvallich. However, even the slightest notion of a pub meal and a welcome pint wasn't enough to draw me ashore. After Carsaig I knew, I would have one more camping opportunity and then an inhospitable shoreline all the way to Crinan. Somehow, I'd now fixated on the idea of making it home that evening. The challenge now was not my capacity for endurance, it was whether I had the daylight to make it in time. Crinan was just over five miles ahead and I'd only a couple of hours left in the day. It was going to be close.

Undeterred I pressed onwards, crossing the mouth of Carsaig Bay without so much a second glance at the inviting swathe of comfortably grassed foreshore. By now, the conditions had eased, the wind dropping in strength and the sea state, whilst not still, a far easier prospect to deal with. To keep myself from flagging because by now the distance and the effort were taking their toll, I counted off my progress in metres in my mind, playing a game where I tested whether I'd correctly judged my progress against the information on my GPS. More often than not, I was close but never spot on. It seemed an eternity but finally I rounded Ardnoe Point and paddled into Loch Crinan. I was nearly home.

It was dusk when *Sahwira's* bow scrunched onto the pebbled slipway next to the Crinan Canal. With aching stiffness, I eased myself out of the cockpit and stood rather groggily to pull the kayak out of the water. Suddenly, from nowhere, I was overcome by emotion and deep, silent sobs wracked my body. With this onrush of rawness, I realised I'd achieved something remarkable. In only two days I'd successfully rounded the fearsome Mull of Kintyre and then crossed the Sound of Jura twice, while paying a visit to Port Askaig on the western reaches of the island of Islay. The total distance was around ninety miles. If I had any questions about the validity of my venture and more importantly, whether I had the skill and courage to undertake it, these were surely now put to rest.

In a matter of minutes *Sahwira* was unpacked and gently placed high up on the shore out of reach of the highest tide. I was only metres from our berthed yacht and in the gathering dark I dumped my laden IKEA bags on the canal towpath and stepped aboard our home, calling a cheery hello as I did so.

Chapter 14

I spent three days at home with Karen, revelling in her company and enjoying the welcome rest from the daily efforts I'd been extolling. Karen was working locally, so while she was busy, I would take myself off on slow rambles through the local woods and up and down the canal tow path, always finding my way to a local café by the Crinan Canal sea locks. On the third day, while I was lingering and dragging out a pot of tea so I could use the wi-fi, a couple of weathered kayakers, still in their damp dry suits wandered in. So it was, I met Katie and Lee who were well into their kayaking circumnavigation of mainland Britain. I had been aware they were somewhere near by, having hoped to meet them when I was down at Southend on the Mull of Kintyre. We were as excited as each other for our eventual meeting and it was lovely to sit with kindred spirits to recount our relative exploits so far. As it had been for me, the unseasonable strong winds were challenging their progress and a couple of their tales of long sea crossings into the teeth of small gales, left me in awe at their guts and determination. It's an unfortunate trait of mine, but I tend to compare my achievements against those of others, and with Katie and Lee, it was easy to think of my journey so far as an inferior experience to theirs.

As it was, I'd planned to re-embark on my journey the following day, so the three of us arranged to meet on the water early in the morning and paddle together to Oban, an easy twenty-five miles away.

After my fond farewells to Karen, I caught up with the two kayakers and we made our way towards Oban. We had the notorious Dorus Mor tidal gate to navigate which we accomplished without any issues. From then it was an easy paddle up the Isle of Luing shoreline, through the Seil Sound and under the iconic gracefully arched stone 'bridge over the Atlantic'. By now the rain had settled in for the day and it was pouring down in almost tropical proportions when we paddled into Oban Bay. I had thoroughly enjoyed my time with Katie and Lee, and we warmly wished each other well for our onward journeys. As they disappeared into the rain filled gloom, I made my way to the Oban Lifeboat station where I received a warm welcome.

Shortly prior to my departure for this journey I had cause to benefit from the selfless service of the Oban lifeboat crew. We were living on our yacht at the Oban Marina on the Isle of Kerrera where we both worked. One night, in the dark early hours I was awoken by stabbing chest pains emanating from the area of my heart. Knowing a lot about first aid, from my symptoms, I diagnosed a possibly serious problem. Poor Karen, rudely woken and now beside herself with worry, phoned the coastguard who in turn called on the Oban lifeboat to attend. With professional ease and no fuss, I was eased out of our small forward cabin and taken aboard the lifeboat which rushed me across the bay to a waiting ambulance by their berth. I was then whisked up to the hospital and admitted for a few days observation. The cause of the chest pains wasn't determined because it turned out my heart was actually very healthy. About a month later, the same happened again and the whole palava with Oban lifeboat and the ambulance service was repeated. This time, after more thorough checks in hospital, it was determined I had an inflammation of the lining of my heart which painfully mimicked a heart attack. Thankfully the condition did not return, and I was pronounced fit enough to undertake my kayak journey around Scotland.

Standing in the Oban lifeboat crew room, dripping huge puddles of rainwater on the floor, I thanked them again for how professionally they'd attended my call in distress. In return, the coxswain presented me with a bottle of whisky which was clearly a special bottling with an Oban lifeboat label. I was taken aback by this gesture of kindness and again thanked them profusely for their support. The whisky lasted well into my journey and the last drops were quaffed hundreds of miles later.

It's often said Oban is the gateway to the isles, and this was certainly true for me. From here my route was now westwards, across the poetic Firth of Lorn, into the Sound of Mull and onwards to Tobermory on the Isle of Mull. Here was the fourteenth lifeboat station on my route. It took three days to reach Tobermory from Oban, one of which was shore-bound in Craignure on Mull, because of strong winds. It was a delight to eventually reach the colourful small harbour town which is a great favourite for visitors.

The afternoon I arrived the sun was shining, warmly bringing to life the vibrancy of the eye-catching sea front buildings. I was warmly welcomed into Tobermory on the sandy beach in the harbour by the indomitable Ian Stevens, the lifeboat operating manager and Popz Fairbairns, the chairman of the station. Later over tea and biscuits, Andrew McHaffie the Tobermory coxswain, showed me a film of a recent shout they attended where a disabled ship, far out in the outer Minch, was totally at the mercy of a monstrous swell. It was incredible watching the dramatic footage of the stern of the large ship being lifted clear of the heaving seas. He recounted the challenges he would have faced if it were decided the ship needed to be abandoned, and he was required to manoeuvre the lifeboat alongside to pick up survivors. Thankfully all ended well on this occasion.

I was invited to make use of their comfortable crew facilities for the night which I gratefully accepted. It's always lovely to enjoy a hot shower on a long expedition such as this. Whilst buying myself some treats from the small Co-Op supermarket in the town, I bumped into Mark Stephen, one of the presenters of the lovely to listen to, BBC Radio 'Scotland Outdoors' programme. I recognised him immediately and told him I was a huge fan of the programme, before wandering back to my kayak to munch on my family size packet of tangy-cheese puffs. A minute later, Mark appeared with his small recording device and asked if I'd be happy for an interview. I could only answer "Gnnnf?" because of a cough inducing mouthful of puffs. The interview was fun to give, and it was a lovely to hear it on the radio a few weeks later.

My sister-in-law, Aileen, lived in Tobermory and I spent the evening with her and her family and then later, for a riotous night in the Mishnish Pub with her and her teaching colleagues. I hazily remember tottering back to my lifeboat station lodgings. The next day my plans were to round the nautically famous Point of Ardnamurchan where the tides flow strongly. By this stage of my journey, I was less easily worried by the prospects of strong tides around headlands, and I fell quickly into a deep inebriated sleep.

To round Ardnamurchan Headland on a favourable tide required an early departure from Tobermory. It was difficult to leave the comfort of the lifeboat station and the guiles of the colourful island town for the open sea again. It was a moment when I found myself wondering what I was doing, as I hefted my kayak and laden bags down to the waters edge of the slipway which served the car ferry to Kilchoan on the mainland. I could easily discover an excuse to linger a day or two in the town, enjoying the friendly ambience of the lifeboat station and 'hanging out' in the popular 'Mish' as the pub was known. Strong winds were forecast to arrive in the next twenty-four hours, so there was no shame in holding on until these had blown through. Tobermory was a perfect place to be holed up. Yet, there was an unquestionable inner drive which determined I press onwards. The winds were not blowing today and there was every chance I would make good distance, so there was no question of 'skiving off'. There are times when it doesn't do to argue with a determined inner drive!

The Point of Ardnamurchan holds a daunting reputation. Sure, the uncompromising Atlantic swell sometimes finds its way through the Minch to thump with force onto the exposed headland, and yes, the tides do run strongly around the rocky bastion, sometimes creating fearsome seas. However, it is a jewel in Scotland's landscape finery with craggy cliffs backed by wild and empty country, interspersed with gleaming white sanded beaches where turquoise seas wash them clean. The peninsula is almost an island on the mainland it is so remote. I had kayaked around it once before with my good friend Phil. He and I had 'grown up' together when working for Outward Bound in Wales in the 1980's and ever since then we have shared adventures of one sort or another, including several sea kayaking trips. On this occasion in 2004 we had set off from Keppoch near Arisaig for a circumnavigation of the Isle of Rùm. We made it as far as the Isle of Eigg before turning back because of strong winds. Rather than head straight back to our start point, we decided to kayak with the wind in our favour to Fort William. The only problem was we hadn't prepared for such an option with no maps of the route and no tidal information either. Undaunted we went for it anyway and enjoyed a magnificent adventure, which include rounding Ardnamurchan in a lively and lumpy sea.

On this occasion as I drew close to the coastline of the peninsula after an uneventful crossing from the Isle of Mull, I noticed the sea state wasn't much less lively than my trip with Phil eleven years earlier. This time though, I couldn't laugh and joke with him about the enormity of the challenge. Solitude heightened my awareness. The sea was disturbed and restless, but it wasn't dangerous. I required to keep my kayaking wits about me, but this didn't mean I wasn't able to find enjoyment in the experience and I paddled close into the shoreline. The disordered swell broke onto the feet of the cliffs with irregular thumps and crashes, sending sprays of spume high above, only for it to fall as droplets of brine onto my head. With every surge towards the cliff, my kayak and I would sweep in and upwards on the wave, almost to the point of touching the rocks. The energy was exhilarating, and I felt playful. As the wave receded, there was a gut swooping sensation as *Sahwira* and I were pulled away from the cliff face, dropping into an ever-expanding trough where before there had been an upwelling of oceanic powerfulness. This was the moment I had to be most careful, for the watery chasm was about to be filled by another rushing wave, which had the potential to catch my kayak in such a manner, I would find it difficult to control. The resulting energy of the receding wave offered the momentum to sweep forwards along the rock face and with deft use of the paddle blades, I would avoid being picked up by the incoming surge and ride away into the safety of the open sea.

The sensation of dancing with the waves was pleasurable, but the greater enjoyment was gained from the intimate relationship I was developing with the sea. It was as if there were an invitation for us to be close, even though there was a feistiness to the conditions. Appreciating there was an edginess to the encounter allowed me to comprehend the sea's behaviour, understanding the patterns within this. As we encounter people, so I believe we encounter the natural world, though I think, this is something we rarely acknowledge. In human relating, it is said the outcome of our interactions is largely determined at a subconscious level, and it's when we understand this process, we may communicate far more effectively. The same is true for my life in the outdoors. I pay attention to my 'deeper level' responses to the situations I encounter, and this enables me to respond accordingly. It assists when I consider the quality of my interaction with the sea; observing the patterns of movement, feeling this movement in my body through the kayak, what the auditory signals are, and so many other experiences. Most of these observations are beyond my conscious awareness. I'm gifted with an innate ability to 'read' most conditions I encounter in a manner which enables me to respond accordingly. Today, kayaking along the mighty rock bastions of the southern Ardnamurchan coastline, I welcomed the invitation to move in close to the shoreline and dance along the rocks with a lively sea as my partner.

I had worked out the tidal flows correctly (this is always a relief), and my passage was hastened by the unseen current of water powerfully sweeping northwards out of the Sound of Mull. There was a strong level of anticipation as I traversed the cliffs, and when I rounded an outcrop to finally see the tall grey lighthouse standing aloof in the near distance, I felt a surge of happy excitement. For any mariner, rounding the Point of Ardnamurchan, so named in Gaelic as 'headland of the great seas', is a moment to be celebrated by tying a sprig of lucky white heather to the bow of the boat. It is the most westerly point of mainland Britain, proudly jutting into the Hebridean seas like a runner craning her neck forward to cross a race line first. It marked the gateway to the western reaches of my journey. The significance was important. As with the Mull of Galloway and the Mull of Kintyre earlier on, this was the closing of a chapter and the opening of another. I was eager with anticipation, boosted by enhanced confidence in my ability and an acquired comfort in the life of an itinerant expeditionary kayaker. I had no sprig of heather to affix to *Sahwira's* prow, but this did not matter. We had made it this far and in doing so, we had proved to ourselves we embodied what it takes to face the journey we were embarked on. These moments of affirmation are important in any aspect of life, even more so if they are unilaterally offered.

The lumpy chop in the sea added to the sense this moment of the journey was well earned. There was no resting on my laurels because I needed to remain alert for any tumbling waves. The sound of the surf on the rocks was a constant audible backdrop. As I rounded the point, a surprisingly large wave thumped onto the rocky ledges of the headland, powering a cascade of seething whiteness upwards, attempting to match the impressive height of the lighthouse. The perpendicular edifice in turn stood impassive, inured to the constant beating of the ocean below, disdainfully gazing down on my tiny craft bouncing and ploughing its way northwards. A small flock of busy oystercatchers were the only living witnesses to my presence. Soon the headland was easing past my peripheral vision, and then behind me. I was around!

Ahead lay the panoply of the Small Isles, the Isle of Skye and the jagged diorama of Knoydart. It was magical, as if a screen had been pulled away to expose the delights of what was yet to come. It was an uplifting moment, tantalising with the promise of easy kayaking and glorious scenery. The warm summer sunshine added to the general sense of bonhomie with the world. Sitting in a calming sea just off Sanna Point, I longingly gazed across the five short miles to the distinctive whale backed shape of the Isle of Eigg. My original plans had included a visit to the island to meet with a friend who lives there and is one of the key members of the unique island community. We had never met but Lucy and I had corresponded a fair bit, about a shared interest in Scotland's heritage. I was looking forward to both meeting her and to receiving a guided tour of the island from a community member's perspective. Eigg is an island owned by the eighty-five residents. It was one of the first community buy-outs where crofters and other residents are given first option to purchase an island or Scottish estate when it is put up for sale on the open market. They live a self-sufficient lifestyle with all their electricity requirements produced from renewable means. I was tempted to make the crossing, but the long term forecast determined caution. Gale force winds were due to arrive in the next twelve hours and I didn't want to find myself stuck on Eigg. I surmised if I kept to the mainland, I would always have the opportunity of creeping forward if possible. If I was on Eigg when the storms hit, I might find myself stuck there for several days.

Logic and heart are not the best of companions and I tussled with the choices before me. I dearly wanted to visit Lucy on her island, but instead I turned eastwards, away from Eigg, to follow the Ardnamurchan coast towards the distant wooded slopes of Moidart. I was now in kayaking waters I knew well, and I settled myself for a pleasurable day on the sea. The Ardnamurchan Peninsula is a huge swathe of Scottish wild landscape with little habitation apart from clusters of cottages overlooking a few sandy enclaves, which break the rugged rocky shore. When I think of living in a house again, it is often the dream of a simple dwelling in a location such as Inverockle, nestled into the hills at the back of a tight bay, lined with birch and alder. As I paddled past, this seemed to be as about as far as it's possible to get from the bustle of modern life on the British mainland. I drifted off into a daydream inspired by a mixture of romantic Scottish film sources; Ring of Bright Water, Local Hero, Brigadoon and dare I say it, Braveheart, where I live a heroic life of solitude and oneness with the natural world. It didn't occur to me, this is what I was actually doing.

I was almost completely lost to my isolationist reverie when I spotted three kayakers approaching from the direction of Kentra Bay. I wasn't surprised to spot them. This stretch of coastline as far as Mallaig twenty miles to the north, is a favourite destination for sea kayakers from all over Britain, because of the sheltered seas and the wonderfully wild landscapes. I looked forward to meeting them and having a chat. Sea kayaking as a recreational choice is growing in popularity but it hasn't become so popular it's commonplace to bump into other kayakers when out at sea.

There is a feeling of kinship when I come across other paddlers. I didn't want to appear too eager to greet them by paddling hard towards them, so with as much nonchalance as I could muster, I paddled just off the shoreline on an oblique heading which would see our paths cross. When I drew close enough to realise we would meet, I waved my hand in greeting, ceasing my paddling to allow *Sahwira* to slide to a stop. The three men paddled on and for a second or two, I wondered if they were going to continue without a chat. With a flourish, the paddler in a gleaming red P&H Quest kayak planted his paddle in dramatic fashion to bring himself to a stop not far off my bow. The other paddler in a white Tiderace kayak followed suit and they both demurely greeted me. The third kayaker also in a white Tiderace kayak slowed down to a stop a good few metres away.

Like dogs sniffing around each other, we opened our conversations with typical pass-timing gambits.

"Superb day for it." I said, smiling in a friendly manner.

"Yup" replied Quest kayaker, "You come far?"

"From Tobermory this morning." Was my reply, not sure whether to add I was on an extended journey. I decided not to and enquired instead, "Where you guys headed?"

"Sanna Bay, camp there, and then back to Kentra tomorrow. How about you?" Quest kayaker replied.

Before I could answer, Tiderace kayaker chipped in, "We know this area really well, this is just a bimble for us."

"Nice one." I said, unsuccessfully attempting to search for another question. This conversation wasn't exactly flowing freely.

Before I could continue Tiderace kayaker spoke again, "The forecast is looking iffy, you'd better be somewhere sheltered for tomorrow."

I bridled internally and was just about to reply when Quest kayaker picked up the theme, "It's going to be blowing over thirty knots from the west with heavy precipitation. I suggest you think about getting well into Loch Moidart, there's good camping in the lee of Shona island. Of course, you may have to ask the owner for permission first." There was no way of spotting a wry sense of irony in his eyes through his sunglasses.

In as level a tone as I could manage despite feeling irked by the assumption, I wasn't aware of the forecast, I replied, "Thanks, good suggestion and it's lovely in there, but I'll probably press on."

There was a moments silence which I hastily filled with, "Talking of pressing on…"

"Did you come around Ardnamurchan on your own?" asked the second Tiderace kayaker, who'd floated across and now joined the conversation.

"Um, yes." I looked at him warily.

"On your own?" He repeated himself and then went on, "Less than three, there should never be." He left it hanging there, the kayaking adage which implies kayaking should not be undertaken alone.

"Oh, I know what I'm doing." I said this with a smile which I hoped would convey I was confident in my ability.

"I hope you've got means for calling assistance?" Quest kayaker was obviously taking it upon himself to ensure I understood the hazards of solo kayaking. "I see you've got a radio, but P.L.B….?"

I was abrupt and cut him off, "Thanks, I'm OK. Everything's in order." I looked at the three of them, noticing for the first time how they were dressed. Each had a buoyancy aid festooned with gadgets which made them look like kayaking robo-cops. Batman's belt of gadgets had nothing on their buoyancy aids! Knives in plastic sheaths strategically placed for fast deployment, carabiners dangling from spare loops, strobe lights on each of their right shoulder straps, a VHF radio each, attached by Velcro onto the front of them. The pockets of their buoyancy aids were bulging too, no doubt full of items to be used in an emergency. Compared to them, my buoyancy aid was pitifully threadbare.

I was silent, waiting for what I knew the next question to be.

He went on, "How long you been paddling?"

"Quite a while." I replied with as little rancour as I could. I was eager to move on now.

"Well, we're all four star leaders in our club." He waited, I think for me to respond but when none was forthcoming, he continued, "We've been kayaking for over five years."

"That's great." I said and went on with faux cheerfulness, "Listen folks, been good to meet and I best be on my way. Enjoy the rest of your day and maybe see you somewhere along the coast. Cheers, all the best!" I dug my blades in and pulled away before the conversation could continue.

"Cheers."

"Bye."

I was angry and attempted to rationalise the conversation. I felt a wave of guilt at rudely and abruptly paddling away from them. The uncomfortable encounter played on my mind for the rest of the afternoon, which was a pity because my daydream of the secluded croft at Inverockle had been so much more pleasant. My sense of ire soon transmuted into bewildered sadness. I wondered why I was unable to easily connect with others in my chosen recreational activity without feeling every time I needed to qualify myself.

I can't abide the adage, "Less than three, there should never be." It limits people in such a manner they're unable to explore the possibilities of kayaking for themselves and learn the potential they hold through their own experiences. I deduced with a sigh, I'm simply a grumpy old man, the Victor Meldrew of sea kayakers!

The weather was perfect, and I began to think about where I would stop for the night. There were numerous choices, and each would offer a pleasant place to stay. I had to account for the forecast and the prevailing conditions when the weather worsened. I wasn't worried by the direction of the wind or too much by the forecast strength. However, if I were to be kept ashore for a few days, I needed a fresh water source. One option was to make my way to Glenuig where there was an inn owned and run by a sea kayaker, who also delivered sea kayak training courses and trips. I knew him vaguely but wasn't certain I could camp there without being charged for doing so and anyway, given the conversation I had just enjoyed with the two Tiderace and the Quest kayakers, I was reluctant to place myself in a location where there may be similar conversations. As much as I fancied the idea of enjoying a good pint, I chose in the end to camp beside a perfect white beach under Smirisary Hill, just north of the entrance to Loch Moidart. I knew the location well, having visited a few times when leading kayaking groups and camping there. It was a popular place for kayakers to stop, so I was prepared not to have the place to myself. When I arrived an hour or so later, it was a pleasant surprise to find I would be alone.

An hour later a group of eight sea kayakers led by a guide from a notable sea kayaking firm based near Fort William arrived on the beach. They were on a single overnight trip and they established camp on the high ground of the site. I found myself biting my tongue from suggesting they might reconsider their choice, given the forecast..I stopped myself when I remembered my conversation with the three kayakers earlier on in the day, and how I bristled at their unsolicited advice.

It was good to have people around and after they had eaten their dinner, I was invited to share the fire they had made on the beach. It was a convivial evening where the group of strangers shared stories about their lives, and I spoke a little about my journey so far. The sun set behind the Small Isles, not in a blaze of orange hues, but behind a massing bank of heavy black clouds. The smoke from their fire was already wreathed by a gathering breeze and cats' paws were spreading across the surface of the sea. The forecast gale was not far away.

I slept soundly that night, dimly aware of the storm which raged through the darkness and into the dawning gloom of the early hours. Unzipping my tent at six the next morning I was greeted with a scene not unlike a Hollywood blockbuster disaster movie. All but one of the kayaking groups' tents were destroyed, green nylon fabric spread in ripped tatters across the grass, occasionally a piece limply flapping in the strong wind and held in place by a stalwart peg. Under some of the larger sheets lay inert human forms, a macabre image of deceased soldiers covered in tarpaulins after a horrendous gun battle. Dark metallic grey clouds, seemingly emitted from the black silhouettes of the Small Isles, scudded low over a chaotic sea towards the disaster scene. In a shallow sandy gully, a waft of smoke drifted up and was whipped away by the gale. A lone figure, hunched and disconsolate, was breaking twigs of heather and feeding them into the base of a Kelly Kettle in the desperate hope that flame would catch, and water would come to the boil for a restorative hot drink.

I couldn't sit in my tent and not offer help, so I wandered across to the lonely figure who turned out to be the kayaking guide. He was in his dry suit already, quirky fleece hat of multiple colours adding a touch of brightness to a gloomy scene. His downbeat demeanour belied his good humour and when I offered him the use of my stove to boil water for his group, he declined, rather rapidly. I took the hint and not wishing to impose, retired to my tent, avoiding the temptation to keep flicking my flysheet open every few minutes to see what was happening. I didn't want to be the wild camping version of the net curtain twitcher! I made breakfast and coffee and checked the forecast on my phone. The gale seemed set and there was no chance of paddling, certainly not in the morning anyway, and probably not at all during the day. Oddly enough for such a wild and remote spot, I received an excellent signal for my phone, and I enjoyed exceptional internet connection. I wondered what Shackleton would have made of the ability to communicate in real time on an app which allowed the use of only one hundred and eighty characters with people around the world he'd never met?

I emerged from my tent when I heard voices and laughter. I assumed their spirits would be as broken as their tents but to a person, everyone in the group thought this to be one of the grandest adventures of their lives. With hilarity, they recounted how one by one during the night, the tents began to disintegrate, and how in the end there were eight bodies in one remaining tent which managed to survive until around four in the morning when that too succumbed and collapsed in a shivering heap around them. They had been strangers the day before, but it was clear this event had stripped away any pretences to create a group of unified friends. The personal development instructor within danced a wee jig! It's in these moments of adversity when the human spirit shines forth, untainted by extraneous ego. The one person not fully engaged in the conversation was the guide. He was huddled over a sputtering pressure stove frying some eggs and attempting to feed damp heather twigs into the kettle, hoping for a miracle and a full cooked breakfast for his clients. I noticed as well, his constant quick glances seawards and understood fully what he was experiencing. My heart went out to him and I thought to myself, a different time, and that might have been me.

It was certainly not my place to intervene, but I could see a problem. The conditions were dreadful, he was a single guide for eight novice kayakers, and he had a schedule to maintain where he had to return them to Fort William late in the afternoon. If he were to achieve this, he had to leave the campsite by mid-morning, maybe lunchtime at the latest. There was no hope of the wind abating by then. The route they had to travel was fully exposed to the might of the gale and the sea was a cauldron of broken waves and a running swell which mercilessly broke onto the rock-strewn shoreline. The saving grace was the fact to reach the sheltered waters and an easy run to where they were to finish, was less than a mile. However, he would be guiding them on his own, this was their first ever sea kayaking experience and a couple of them had expressed how they had been fearful during the paddle into the camp the day before. I pondered the situation. I realised I was duty bound to help him lead the group to safety. The situation was hazardous and could result in a disaster with multiple capsizes in dreadful seas and him the only person to retrieve the swimmers.

I realised my offer of assistance would be unsolicited and might result in him rejecting it out of a sense of pride. I decided if this were to happen, I would insist on my presence on the sea. Sage words of advice spoken by Roger Putnam, an inspirational manager of mine when I worked at Outward Bound Eskdale, echoed in my mind.

"Your job as an instructor is to provide peak experiences for the participants on your courses through authentic adventures, but always think as you do so, what would you say if you had to stand up in a coroner's court."

This was not my course to run or my group to manage, but by being present and having the ability to offer my assistance, I knew it was my responsibility to do so. If I didn't and a tragedy occurred, in my mind I would be culpably liable. I wandered up to the guide who was packing away his kitchen. He had performed the miracle he had been assiduously working on, producing a wonderful hot breakfast of eggs and beans for his clients. I unobtrusively offered myself as an extra pair of eyes and hands. To my relief, he accepted with alacrity.

Two hours later and we're all standing on the beach, leaning slightly into the wind which was threatening to tear paddles from unwary hands. The guide was briefing the group about what he wanted them to do. I sensed amongst them some tension, maybe excitement and a considerable amount of fear. I wasn't feeling particularly thrilled myself, but I was confident with two guides on the water, the situation was manageable.

I chose not to impinge on the guide's decisions or overall management of the group. I was happy to be directed by him and accept the role he assigned. I was the first on the sea and shocked myself at how wobbly and unstable I felt! I had been used to kayaking *Sahwira* loaded to the gunwales, with her subsequent heaviness holding her firmly in the water. Unloaded and light, she was flighty and nervous – or was that me? One by one the eight clients came out into the sea to join me. Insisting they turn the noses of their kayaks to point into the wind and hold their positions by gently paddling forward was akin to herding cats. No sooner had one person lost control of their kayak and required my assistance to move them away from the rocks, then the next followed suit.

The guide was the last onto the chaotic sea and immediately set about attempting to gather the group to make our way to the north channel entrance. No sooner had we paddled out of the lee of the bay when the full force of the wind struck us. The sea which had seemed manageable from the shore was way beyond the limit of any novice, with two metre breaking waves and a wind blowing above force five. The group were quickly scattered, and any semblance of control was given over to the elements. One of the group had caught my attention as soon as he was on the water. It was clear he was a likely candidate for a capsize. He was a tall individual who did not seem comfortable in his kayak, sitting bolt upright with no flexibility in his body whatsoever. His movements contradicted the sea. His girlfriend was twice as nervous as he appeared to be, and as soon as the call was shouted to move off, she dug her paddles in hard and made a beeline for the far shore. The problem with this was the fact she was both out of touch with the group by shooting off on her own, and she was veering away from where we were heading for. She kept yelling out, "I can't turn! I can't turn!" I had a choice, head off after her and slow her down, or stick with her partner in case he should go over.

The first capsize occurred close to the shore and the guide, in the rear of the melee was well placed to rescue the unfortunate swimmer. Seconds later, the man who I was sticking with, wobbled, wavered for a second and with graceful slow motion went over too. I was alongside him in a flash. Rescuing folks who've capsized is bread and butter for sea kayak guides and these events are usually conducted in seas which are lively and rough. He was a gallant survivor. With his hair plastered thinly on his scalp, he spluttered I leave him to swim next to his upturned kayak while I set off after his girlfriend who was vigorously paddling for the far side of the bay. It was a choice. I could only attend to one and his need was the greatest. I had to get him out of the water and into sheltered waters as soon as possible because it was likely he would capsize again if not. Deftly I emptied his kayak and helped him back in. His awkward rigidness told all I needed to know. He was petrified, and I admired him for his resoluteness. In the meantime, the guide had sorted out his capsized client and was now in hot pursuit of the demented paddler. I was able to concentrate on her boyfriend and ensure he did not capsize again. I glanced around to see what state the rest of the group were in and was relieved to see most of them had reached the entrance to the north channel and were metres away from sheltered water. I decided to attach the man to my kayak by means of a short leash and instructed him to lean onto my kayak and hold on. This way I could paddle for the both of us and there was little chance of him going over again. It wasn't easy, but we arrived at the entrance to the channel just about the same time as his girlfriend was towed in by the guide. Out of the force of the gale, the relief was instantaneous. Where moments before, there had been fear, now there was laughter and excited chatter bubbling up amongst the eight kayakers. Two had capsized but all were safe and there was no chance now anything further could happen.

I didn't linger. I could tell the guide was eager to get under way and now I had served my purpose, there was no need for my presence. The group thanked me with profusion which I found rewarding and with their good wishes for the rest of my journey calling after me, I paddled out into the maelstrom and was ashore and in my tent in under twenty minutes. It had been an eventful morning. I sat awhile mulling over the events, a mug of soup swilling in my hands, warming them up. A strong gust of wind thumped into the tent causing it to momentarily shudder. I wondered what the solution would have been if I hadn't been there to help. What would I have done? It was easy to tell myself I would have not chosen to guide the group to that location given the forecast, so I didn't. No, I wondered, what would have been the solution? In the end I decided I would have kayaked the group to the entrance to the channel and sheltered water one at a time. This way, if there was a capsize, it was a one-on-one situation and I wouldn't be worrying about others in the group on the sea at the same time. I reflected given the severity of the conditions, this is what the guide and I could have done this time around. He and I splitting the group and paddling them out four at a time. That's the luxury of hindsight and as valuable the experience for personal learning can be for the participants, it's potentially as powerful for the guide too.

The winds did not abate for another two days but the sun did make an appearance on the third day. Tucked up out of the cold blasts, I enjoyed catching up with my journal and planning the next steps of my journey. From here I would make it to Mallaig and the next lifeboat station and then I was only a day away from the Isle of Skye. No other kayakers joined me in my white beached idyll, but numerous hikers made it along the coast and a few of them sat with me and chatted about my journey and where I was heading next. It felt good to talk with them.

Chapter 15

It's always a relief to get under way again after an enforced period ashore. The wind was still gusty, and the sea was lively, but the forecast was for conditions to ease through the day, therefore I was confident to be making the decision to get going. I had a four-mile crossing of the Sound of Arisaig and then easy paddling through the popular Arisaig Skerries and onwards to Mallaig, my next port of call. The day was not going to be a demanding one and I looked forward to easing back on my paddling. I chose to arrive at an islet called Eilean á Ghaill where an Iron Age fort was marked on the map. I remembered the island from guiding trips a few years earlier and recalled noticing the fort then but because I was working, I couldn't explore it. As I drew close to the island after an uneventful crossing in rather lumpy breaking seas, I spotted a small group of red deer grazing the scant patch of grass atop the island. Their presence scuppered any chance of landing and exploring the fort, so I edged my way as close as I dared and had a good look at the substantive remains I could see from the water. What seemed to be a scree slope down one side was in fact the tumbled remains of the fort's walls. It was a fascinating spot, obviously a good defensive position but a small area for a group of people to exist on for any length of time.

Rounding the island, I suddenly encountered the five hinds I had seen, nonchalantly swimming the three hundred metre gap between the island and the mainland. They seemed to be ladies who were simply out for a morning bathe, holding their heads high out of the water and with powerful strokes with their legs, making good speed for the shore. I was entranced. I knew red deer are strong swimmers and will do so out of choice to reach good grazing, but I had never seen this happen from a close vantage point. I snapped away with my camera as they cut across my bow in the rough and tumble of the waves refracted from the rocky shoreline. I wondered how they would manage to extricate themselves from the sea because the waves weren't washing ashore in a kindly manner at all. I needn't have concerned myself because one by one, they coincided their landing with an oncoming wave and with delicate grace, each scampered up the greasy rocks to disappear into the rough land beyond my sight. I continued my way with a smile on my face, realising how fortunate I was to enjoy this encounter. It was a gift after my enforced period ashore.

The few photos I had taken, I later posted onto my Twitter feed and Facebook, not realising over the following couple of days they had gone viral, and the press were keen to publish them. It's the only time I've had a Sun newspaper's pun headline attributed to me: *"We're in at the deer-p end"*

Arriving in Mallaig felt to be a milestone and it was wonderful to be warmly welcomed by the lifeboat coxswain Michael Currie and the mechanic Tony Skea. My journey was becoming known amongst the Scottish R.N.L.I. stations and they had been anticipating my arrival, though I was gently ribbed for taking so long to make it from Tobermory only forty miles away. Mallaig is a magical harbour town. It evokes a sense of adventure because it was from here in 1996, I embarked on my solo sea kayak journey around the Isle of Skye. It is a town which is literally at the end of the railway line and from here the only passage forward is by boat. It's because of this, and the numerous choices of Hebridean destinations beyond, which make it a gateway to discovery in every sense of the word. It's not the most attractive harbour town in Scotland and its rough-edged appearance eschews a sense of the wild west, where there's a frontier between what we are used to and what may be possible.

I was invited to join the crew on their regular weekly training exercise that evening. Their boat is a Severn Class lifeboat, the largest in the R.N.L.I. fleet and is served by a complement of seven crew. It is a powerful and agile craft, with a top speed of twenty-five knots and an operational range of two hundred and fifty nautical miles with the ability to carry twenty-eight survivors. Incredibly, the Severn is self-righting too, which means if she were to be thrown over by large seas, she would return to an upright position. I attempted not to give myself away, but I was very excited at the prospect of going out to sea on this boat.

The crew gathered, and I was introduced as the crazy kayaker paddling around Scotland and I bathed in the murmurs of warm acknowledgement. Mallaig being a fishing port, many of the crew in the room were men of the sea, and so I felt a sense of validation from their assent. As I dressed myself in the heavy-duty yellow foul weather clothing, put on the iconic yellow wellies emblazoned with R.N.L.I., hefting the heavily substantial life jacket over my shoulders, then clunking its safety catch into place, awoke within a long-remembered thrill of excited anticipation. This is what I experienced when preparing to head out on a mountain rescue call out. I recalled how in these moments, all senses were alert with professional assiduousness to detail, accompanied with a frisson of fear. For the crew chatting and laughing while they enrobed around me, this was an everyday moment, but for me I was returning to what I once was, a member of a group intent on providing a valuable service which involved an element of personal risk. Of course, on this occasion I was only dressing for a training exercise, but the memories this awakened, stirred within a powerful sense of useful belonging, something I had not experienced for many long years.

Walking along the quay to the berthed lifeboat a woman's voice shouted out, "Nick!" I turned to see a person I had not met before but knew very well from our connection on Twitter. Jo was one of my key supporters for my journey and was on holiday. Meeting her in this setting seemed pertinently apposite. We managed the briefest of chats and I took the obligatory 'selfie' of us together while the lifeboat crew looked on with bemused amusement. Michael gently nudged me and teased me about my infamy and in response I inanely grinned and felt redness infuse my cheeks. Aboard the lifeboat good natured joshing was replaced by quiet determination. Each crew member knew their role and we were soon motoring out of the harbour entrance, a crowd of holiday makers eagerly watching our departure, their mobile cameras held aloft to capture the moment for mega-byte posterity.

As we left the harbour behind us, Michael atop the flying bridge opened the throttles and the boat surged forward in a roar of power which took me by complete surprise. I steadied myself and leaned into the movement, ensuring I did so without reaching to grab a rail. Around me crew went about their tasks with balanced ease, tidying lines and stowing fenders. I wanted to be everywhere at the same time to observe what was happening. The weekly training exercise is an opportunity for crew to assume duties they require practice with, helming the boat, navigation, monitoring the engines, and communication. Michael and Tony were busy imparting their knowledge and wisdom with individuals attending to their personal development. It is one of the remarkable aspects of the highly professional life saving service the R.N.L.I. provide; it is performed by volunteers drawn from all walks of life in a local community. This means for example, challenging navigational decisions are made by a coffee shop owner, or the lifeboat helmed in rough seas by the refuse lorry driver. They assume these responsibilities with equanimity, performing them to as high a standard as any professional mariner with many years' experience.

The evening was spent searching a section of the Sleat coastline on the Isle of Skye, practicing man-overboard drills, using the emergency tiller to steer the boat on a given course, and firing rocket flares. Not wishing to be an idle bystander, I involved myself as best I could, using the boat hook to retrieve the 'casualty', holding the lines for the emergency tiller and keeping an eager look out when we were manoeuvring close to the shore by the Point of Sleat. All too soon the evening of training ended, and we were roaring across the expansive Sound of Sleat back to Mallaig. I stood on the quarterdeck mesmerised by the powerful plumes of waves erupting from beneath the stern of the lifeboat. The engines roaring and thrusting us along at full speed. Around I could see the islands of Eigg, Rum, Skye and far into the mountainous depths of the Knoydart peninsula. This was a landscape which I thought I knew intimately, but until I spent an evening with the Mallaig lifeboat crew, I hadn't realised how beautifully dramatic this scene was.

The debrief of the evening's training took place back in the crew room, everyone once more garbed in their everyday clothes. Training ended, and the cold beers were passed around and conversations turned to community matters, family details, work issues and general banter. I sat silently, beer in hand and soaked the moment in. For the crew, serving on the lifeboat wasn't just about providing a life-saving service, it was about belonging.

I departed Mallaig the next day with a heavy heart. I had been warmly welcomed and included and it was tough to say goodbye. This was a reminder of my itinerant status. However, it wasn't long after leaving when kayaking past the gaping mouth of Loch Nevis, I reconnected with the excitement of exploration from a sea level perspective. I recalled nineteen years earlier I had kayaked the same route on my first day as a solo expedition kayaker. The sea then was rough, breaking and washing around my waist, the wind and tide driving me barely in control, up the Sound of Sleat. I was a naïve sea kayaking adventurer then and I wonder if this naivety has ever left me.

I paddled close into the Knoydart coastline taking pleasure from seeing the remote homesteads which dotted the littoral landscape. High mountains formed a panoramic backdrop, their craggy flanks steeply dropping to meet the sea in a tangle of boulders and bracken. Out in the Sound of Sleat, yachts of varying sizes driven by reefed crisp white sails, ploughed their way through a lively white crested sea. The sun shone on a scene which was cinematic in its grandeur. The strong southwest wind drove me forward, the tide easing my passage too. A patch of rough water as I crossed the entrance to Loch Hourn to the Sandaig Islands caught me by surprise, but this was the only tidal anomaly I faced until I reached the infamous Kyle Rhea narrows a few miles hence. I stopped briefly to stretch my legs at the picturesque bay and group of islands named Sandaig, my kayak being driven hard up the shore by the piling waves. I hadn't realised until this point how large the sea had become. Sandaig was the site of Camusfearna, the cottage where Gavin Maxwell had lived with his otters which formed the basis for his wonderful book, "Ring of Bright Water". I'm certain it was watching the 1960's film of this book as a child which implanted a latent desire to live a life of simplicity on the Scottish coastline and this is where my love for otters originates from too. Sadly, the cottage burned down but there remains a memorial to one of the otters which I found moving to see.

I was briefly tempted to make camp at Sandaig but I had an appointment for the evening and had to press on. It was imperative I made it to the Kyle Rhea narrows before the tide turned against me, otherwise I would have probably not been able to make it through. The tide here can run up to seven knots. With the wind pushing me onwards I made it with time to spare and eased my way through the narrow body of sea which separates the Isle of Skye from the mainland. In days gone by, cattle driven to and from markets were swum across the narrows which must have been an impressive sight when the tide was flowing. There is a small car ferry which connects Skye with the mainland and is the last manually operated turntable ferry in Scotland. Watching it crab across the strong flow in the narrows is an impressive display of seamanship. When immersed in stunning scenery as I had been since leaving Mallaig, it may have been easy to become a little accustomed to the beauty and wander off in a daydream. This did not occur. The lively sea, the strongly flowing tide, the presence of playful seals and the continual anticipation for what lay beyond each small promontory helped maintain a mindful presence to my surroundings.

Turning into Loch Alsh, I found myself assailed by the gusting wind. Where it had been a source of great assistance, it was now blowing into my face and made progress considerably challenging. I managed to make it across to the small town of Kyle of Lochalsh where the R.N.L.I. have a lifeboat station. This being an inshore lifeboat, there were no crew around to meet, so I took a few photos, peered in through the door windows and carried on my way. The village is the end of the Highland rail line from Inverness and once was a busy ferry port for the trip across to the Isle of Skye. Now there is the Skye Road Bridge and the ferry is no longer in existence. Sadly, the loss of the ferry took away the reason for the village's existence and it carried a downtrodden air. I was making my way towards Breakish, a hamlet close to the village of Broadford on the Isle of Skye. I had invited myself to stay with Gordon and Morag Brown who owned and ran Skyak Adventures, providing sea kayaking training and trips. Gordon is one of the preeminent sea kayak coaches in Britain with many successful books and films on the subject to his name. I had never met either of them, though Morag and I had contact through Facebook.

After a struggle against a tough headwind, I made it up the creek to the waterfrontage of their impressive home. Both Gordon and Morag came down to greet me and welcome me in. I was feeling more than a little tired having paddled just over thirty miles from Mallaig in challenging conditions. I'm not certain I got off on the right foot with Morag when she offered to take an end of my loaded kayak to carry it up to the lawn in front of their house, and I warned her; "Be careful, it's very heavy."

Her fiery response caused me to wince with shame, "It's fine, I'm quite capable of lifting a kayak, I've been doing this long enough." It was a moment of thoughtless mansplaining on my part. Thankfully though, this moment didn't impinge on what was a delightful evening spent chatting with them and their children before I skulked off to my sleeping bag and a long much needed sleep. The next day I was going to reach Portree and the lifeboat station there.

Bidding farewell to Gordon and Morag, I set off into mirror calm seas for Portree. I was once again in waters I knew well, there were no tidal or coastal challenges to test me, and I looked forward to an easy day ahead. I cruised across Broadford Bay at a steady five miles an hour, enjoying powering myself forward with every paddle stroke slicing into the calm sea. It seemed like an act of vandalism to disturb the mirrored surface and leave a wake of whirling eddies and expanding ripples behind. I imagine from the sky above, my passage through the sea would look like a swimming water beetle's imprint. Looking northwards I had a wonderful view past the small islands of Pabay, Longay and the Crowlins up the Inner Sound with the Applecross Peninsula on the right and the island of Raasay on the left. This was a landscape I knew well, and it was lovely to be gazing over it again. My route for this expedition did not take me through it and I wondered when I would be back. Keeping close to the Skye shoreline I entered Caolas Scalpay, the shallow narrows between the island of Scalpay and mainland Skye. A little further on, just through here, I came to the entrance to Loch Ainort. Suddenly, almost with reach on my right side a bulbous head surfaced, and a fishy breath of air was exhaled with an audible sigh. Seconds later another head appeared, and a similar black body eased back into the sea, barely breaking the calmness of the surface. I found myself amongst a small pod of pilot whales and deduced with sadness these must be all that remained of a larger pod, many of which had died a couple of days before, from beaching on the rocks in Staffin Bay, fifteen miles further along the Skye coastline.

There was an air of complete calm while I sat still in my kayak and the whales slowly rose and sank around me, working their way down the Scalpay narrows. I felt immense sadness for them and projected anthropocentric emotions of loss and grief into their serene presence. I wondered if they were experiencing similar emotions as a result of the distressing experience, they would have lived through only a few days earlier. The human response to the stranding was admirable but sadly nine of the whales had succumbed to the beaching and it wasn't certain why this had occurred. Many are quick to lay the blame with the military and the use of sonar. Indeed, the local seas are used for submarine exercises. Spending the briefest of time with these graceful creatures as I did, caused me to continue my way with sombre thoughts running through my mind. Even the incredible mountain grandeur which loomed high around wasn't enough to shift a sense of contemplative gloom. With fish farms in every corner of the seascape around, I felt a depressing lack of hope for humans ever choosing to collectively behave in a manner which places the needs of all living creatures on the planet on an equal footing. Looking down Caolas Scalpay, I realised I had lost sight of the whales and slowly turned *Sahwira* towards the Narrows of Raasay a short distance away. I had so many questions running through my mind.

Kayaking through these seas with the might of Skye rising on my left and the island of Raasay on my right, I couldn't help feeling a strong sense of journeying through a timeless landscape. I was alone but gazed on a landscape which would be recognisable to a Norse mariner in the ninth century, a trader in the fifteenth century or a naval captain in the nineteenth century. The imprints of humanity will alter through the centuries and leave indelible marks on the land, but the shapes of the mountains, the ruggedness of the coast and the subtleties of the indented shoreline are the one constancy which binds the generations to place and landscape. This was a moment of significance, and even though I was a wandering sea kayaker merely passing by, I felt I belonged.

Ahead stretched for as far as I could see, a long line of dark, almost black cliffs which starkly delineated Skye from the calm sea. It was a watercolour painting where subtle shades of greys and blues washed together to create a scene of imposing beauty. Suddenly, seemingly from a hole in the cliffs, emerged the distinctive orange of the Portree lifeboat. I immediately felt a surge of disappointment thinking the boat would not be on its berth for my arrival. However, it was exciting to see the lifeboat heading out for what must surely be a 'shout'. I wondered where this was happening, given the calm conditions. The boat did not appear to be in a hurry and turned to make its way down the Sound of Raasay towards me. I looked around to see if I could spot what incident it may be attending but saw nothing untoward. I was flummoxed and continued paddling slowly, not sure whether to make myself known to them or hope they would pass by without noticing me. I would then introduce myself to the crew on their return. The lifeboat cruised further down the sound and then with obvious purposefulness turned and headed directly towards me.

"Shit!" I exclaimed under my breath, and I pulled my PLB out of the left pocket of my buoyancy aid to check it hadn't accidentally been activated. This would have been impossible, but it was still a relief to see that it hadn't. What then could be the reason for them launching and so obviously making for my position? I looked around again with alarm. I was the only one on the sea and I wondered if someone on the shore had seen me out there and with well meant concern, called the coastguard who will have launched the lifeboat. I deduced this must be the only reason and so began to think of how I would respond. The lifeboat drew closer until I noticed crew lining the guard rail on the bow – and they were waving! The realisation of what was occurring caused my face to flush and tears of gratitude to swim in my eyes. I had to wipe them, so I could focus. With a wide sweep of my left paddle, I brought *Sahwira* around, so we were face on to the approaching lifeboat which burbled closer, spurts of cooling water ejected from her exhaust. I stopped paddling and my momentum carried me alongside the dark blue starboard hull of the lifeboat which now loomed over me in manner which was akin to an embrace. Yellow clad figures looked down on me, all mouthing smiled words of greeting and congratulation. At an open gate in the guardrail amidships, a figure crouched down with an arm outstretched and, in a manner, like Stanley meeting Livingstone in deepest Africa, Donnie Nicolson and I shook hands.

"Glad to meet you Nick!" Donnie firmly shook my hand.

"And you," I responded, firmly wedging my legs in my kayak to improve my stability. I didn't want to capsize in front of them all! "Thanks for coming out to meet me."

"It had to be done." Said Donnie, "I was clocking your GPS logs and knew exactly where you were. Glad we could do this!"

He went on to introduce the rest of the crew who bent down and shook my hand one after the other. In the blur of the moment, I forgot their names as soon as Donnie told me. I performed a few drawing strokes with my left paddle and drew myself away from under the lifeboat's hull. Despite the calmness of the sea, I was worried about being knocked over by the boat. We chatted for a few minutes longer before we agreed to head on into Portree.

"Race you!" I shouted rashly and pulled away from the lifeboat with as powerful paddle strokes I could muster, the type of stroke which cause me to feel the muscles in my shoulders bunch up in knots. I was soon cruising at an easy four miles an hour, *Sahwira* slicing her way forward through the calm surface of the dark sea. The cliff line to my left appeared to readily drop behind and knolls and prominent rocks ahead, rapidly came into focus until they too were but a memory. The lifeboat gurgled slowly behind, puttering along, the voices of the crew audible but indistinguishable. I couldn't see them, but I could sense their presence close on my stern which drove me on harder and faster. I was now paddling to the extent of my fitness, long reaching, powerful strokes, regular and well placed. My breathing was even and steady and I found myself pleasantly surprised with how long I was managing to keep this pace up. Pride surfaced within and I wasn't going to show any weakness.

We neared the rounded headland of Udairn, marking the southeastern entrance to Loch Portree and as the first signs of habitation on the outskirts of the town hove into view, I exhaled a moan of dismay when I saw how far I still had to paddle. Doubt assailed me when I realised there was a mile of sea to cover before I could rest. I wasn't certain I could maintain this pace for that distance. I think Donnie at the helm sensed a wavering in my progress and he deftly drew the lifeboat alongside, shouting down from the flybridge, "See you in there!" With that the gleaming orange boat pulled away and when he was sure the wash wouldn't upset me, Donnie opened the throttles, so the lifeboat reared up like a stallion in a western movie, before surging away up the Sound of Raasay to quickly diminish in size but not in presence because the roar of the twin diesels continued to echo off the dark and looming cliffs. Relieved of the pressure to paddle beyond a speed I could sustain, I eased up and focussed on reaching the Portree harbour in under thirty minutes.

There was quite a crowd in the small Portree crew room. *Sahwira* was resting on her own in the entrance way, almost relieved it seemed to have arrived. Mugs of tea were passed around and I was the centre of attention, questions being thrown about my journey so far. It was good to feel so warmly welcomed and appreciated too. It was then I realised I had met the station mechanic John Nicolson before. A memory of a wild stormy day in 1996 when I was visiting Portree during my Skye sea kayak circumnavigation. I was wandering along the harbour front when a general shout went up for lifeboat crew. The usual crew for the lifeboat were away training on their new boat, leaving a reserve boat in Portree. There was a storm raging, and the reserve boat was requested for service but there were not enough crew to take her out. As is common practice on these occasions, the coxswain can request non-R.N.L.I. crew to volunteer to assist. John collared me and asked if I was willing to volunteer, he looked me up and down, obviously realising I had some experience of the sea given my kayaking attire. To my utter shame and regret I declined, the lifeboat was simply too big and daunting for me to consider having any useful skill to offer. I recounted this memory to John, including my sense of shame, and he laughed, remembering the event clearly, even the name of the yacht they went to assist.

I was alone in the crew room, showered and refreshed. This was to be my home for the night but not after meeting Donnie in the Pier Hotel for a few beers. Every lifeboat station I was learning, had its own personality. I discovered one of the ways to ascertain the nature of the station was to look in their fridge and cupboards in their galley. The fridge contained one small bottle of milk but was full to bursting point with cans of beer, mainly the ubiquitous Tenants Lager. The cupboards were similarly packed with enough bottles of whisky and other spirits to supply a thriving bar! I smiled to myself, it was clear the Portree crew knew how to work hard and play hard too. Donnie laughed when I shared my hypothesis about lifeboat station personalities and we settled down for a long and convivial evening, propping up the hotel bar. From time to time another crew member or someone else Donnie knew, would wander over to join us and I would briefly have to give a synopsis of my venture, each time my words becoming thicker as my alcohol intake rose. Donnie clocked early in the evening I was a Talisker drinker, and this is what I found before me on the counter, drams magically refilling and just as easily slipping down. We talked about adventure. The year before he and seven others had rowed an open skiff built in the 19thC, one hundred miles from the remote St Kilda archipelago to Portree. This amazing effort raised over £40 000 for the R.N.L.I. and a young persons' charity. He and I had made contact through Twitter because of their achievement and so our connection was established.

It wasn't too late when I wandered along the pier back to the lifeboat station. Fatigue had enveloped me, and I had made my excuses and thanks. I was looking forward to tumbling into my sleeping bag even though I suspected I would wake with a throbbing whisky head in the morning. With little panache I burst into the crew room where I was to sleep, only to find myself stumbling into a 'Community First Responders' monthly meeting from the local area and a crowd of smiling faces turned towards me. I hurriedly expressed my apologies and awkwardly made for the door, but my foot caught the leg of a plastic chair and it was sent flying to clatter into a cupboard where thankfully no whisky bottles tumbled out to shatter on the floor.

"Come away in." the man in charge of the meeting invited me to sit down with them. "You must be the sea kayaker then?"

"Oh, what a good thing you're doing," said a woman, looking up at me with admiration. "What a brave thing to do, kayak around Scotland."

I gathered the chair I had kicked and slowly sat down to join them, as carefully and as deliberately as I could. I didn't want to repeat my clumsiness. Eyes looking at me twinkled with amusement.

"You'll hhhafff to hexcuse me," I said, working my mouth carefully so as not to wurr my slurds. "But I've just been to the Pier Hotel." I think that was all the information they required.

"Ah, young Donnie's been looking after you well I see." Said the man. "Tell us, how is your canoe journey going?"

I straightened my back and solemnly looked around the gathered group, (I've no idea why this was important to do) and answered, "It's going fhine thanks. No problems soh fhar. The kayak's holding up whell." Even a couple of sheets to the wind I couldn't help my kayak pedantry.

"Ah, that's good then. Kayak, yes, I see now." He smiled and turned back to their business at hand. I managed to remain alert for the remaining hour or so of their meeting and welcomed their gracious offers of slivers of cake which had been brought for the occasion. By the time the meeting was over, and I was alone, I was almost dead on my feet.

Chapter 16

The weather held for the next day, and I made good progress twenty-four miles along Skye's spectacular northern coastline as far as Kilmaluag Bay. The high cliffs were alive with birds and their constant calling echoed around me. Memories from 1996 when I had last kayaked along the stretch of coast from Portree brought a smile to my face. I recalled meeting a fisherman in his creel boat who generously spoke with me at length about the tide race around Rubha Hunish, the far tip of this stretch of coast.

For a moment when I paddled below the impressive waterfall beside the eponymous Kilt Rock, I was the subject of over a hundred cameras pointing down at me and either filming me or snapping my image. I wondered how many social media pages I ended up on and more to the point, what was the description which accompanied it. Staffin Island and Staffin Bay hold a special place in my heart. I have kayaked along the coast here a few times and camped on the green sward behind the beach. The view from my tent, overlooking the island is one of my favourites in all Scotland. I had hoped to make camp on the headland of Rubha Hunish but the tide was in full flow against me and the wind was stronger than I wished for. I knew of a place to camp in Kilmaluag and stopped there.

The following day, the wind was gusting over thirty knots, kicking up a fearsome sea. I settled down for an enforced day of rest, frustrated at being held up at a crucial moment of my journey. Ahead lay the Minch, the body of water which separates the Outer Hebrides from mainland Scotland and the Inner Hebridean islands. Undertaking a crossing of the Minch in a kayak is one of those aspirational achievements which are added to many adventurers' bucket lists. It's an enterprise akin to Scottish mountaineers traversing the challenging Black Cuillin Ridge on Skye, or the Aonach Eagach ridge above Glen Coe in winter. To have crossed the Minch solo, well that's an achievement worthy of any seasoned sea kayaker. The point I had chosen to make the crossing was only ten miles, but nonetheless it was a serious undertaking and ensuring I was prepared for it was an important business. In my tent, continually buffeted by the gusting wind, I crouched over my notes, map and tidal atlas. It was a simple business working out the tides, their times and their flows. I was confident I had all in order, but double checked with strategies for alterations and unforeseen circumstances. I was putting my paperwork away when I heard a car pull up by my tent. I sensed this was not a tourist who had found themselves at the end of the road but someone local because of the authority it seemed the car was driven into the space and brought to a halt, as if the driver knew the parking spot existed. Unable to resist the urge to see who this might be, I unzipped the tent to be met by Donnie and his family. He had seen from my tracker I was shore bound and he had driven up to see me and bring a few extra supplies! I spent a happy day back in Portree, with him, his partner and their baby daughter.

In the afternoon of the next day, I decided to press on to a small group of islands called Fladaigh Chuain, five miles into the Minch off the coast of Skye. Stopping here for a night would provide me with a perfect stepping off point to cross the Minch to the Outer Hebrides. The tides would be tricky and with the winds as strong as they were, there was a chance I might have to turn back. With some trepidation I packed my kayak, ensuring items on the deck were well secured. I anticipated the seas would be rough through the tide races. Zipping my buoyancy aid, I thought of myself as a heroic figure about to venture forth on a dangerous errand. The rock architecture along the coast out of Kilmaluag Bay was impressive to see, with arches, grottos and hints of geodesic basalt columns. I would have liked to explore further but I was focussed on making it around the corner. I knew things were going to be wild the moment I rounded Rubha Bheanachain and ran straight into a heaving race. Blue green walls of water welled up and collapsed on themselves with disturbing regularity, all the while a river like torrent ran along the rocky shore in the direction I was heading. This was far more powerful than I had anticipated, fearing one misplaced paddle stroke would see me slide sideways into the sea. It was another moment when I felt vulnerably alone. *Sahwira* took the race in her stride, riding the piling waves with panache and confidence. A minute or so later, I too began to get the measure of the seas and relaxed.

There was no let up after the promontory of Rubha na h-Aiseig as I had hoped. In fact, the sea appeared wilder and more confused as the tidal stream widened, continuing a head long rush for the point of Rubha Hunish a mile away. I could see the islands I wanted to reach but between them and me lay a sea which looked unwelcoming and dangerous. I gave up on the notion of reaching them and made every effort to escape the tide race into calmer waters closer to the shore on my left. This was easier thought of than achieved and with some alarm, I realised I was being carried on a powerful current beyond a viable landing spot and towards the headland where once more steep waves rose and collapsed on themselves. Not unlike paddling a river, I thrust the nose of the kayak into slacker water and allowed the powerful stream to push her stern around until I was facing 'upstream' and able to paddle forwards out of the current into the large eddy. Once out of the rush, calm once more descended, except my pulse rate, which took a few moments to slow to normal.

The camp spot I found on Rubha Hunish was perfect, and the warm early June sunshine made it all the finer. I pitched my tent on the feather cushioned softness of pillowed grass. I couldn't wait for the coming night when I would slide into my sleeping bag on the luxuriously soft grassy mattress. It was like making up a bed at home with freshly laundered linen, and wanting to curl up in the duvet there and then. Once all was organised and I had my customary lemon and ginger tea in my thermos mug, I wandered the eight hundred metres to the end of the headland. I was grateful for fate bringing me to this spot, for within me a joy for all I loved about sea kayaking, journeying, exploring and immersing myself in wild coastal Scotland, was emanating forth. It was almost erotic in nature, a feeling of excited tenderness issuing from deep within me. My chest was ready to burst with well-being and happiness, and my senses were enlivened, so much so, I was certain I could hear the wingbeats of the lark trilling high above. My solitude heightened my pleasure. I was alone, the only human in this expansive landscape, not an insignificant dot, but very much a part of this timeless diorama. I stepped along the very edge of the sea pinks fringed cliffs, gazing down onto the restless seas thumping onto the dark enduring rocks far below, each breaker flinging spume and crescendo skywards towards me. Gulls, fulmars, guillemots, auks and kittiwakes wheeled in the air below, above and around, their collective strident communication the signature tune to my adventure. Behind, on a low hummock of moss, a bonxie (great skua) eyed me with suspicion, willing me as a street pugilist would, to step forward so it could take to the air and teach me a lesson or two. I didn't oblige. Walking to a point where I could go no further, I lowered myself into a natural armchair of cropped grass and supped my tea.

Rubha Hunish is the north-westerly point of Skye, a low-lying promontory thrusting from the island into the Minch, a finger reaching out, pointing the way to the Outer Hebrides beyond. This was the perfect vantage point to observe my journey yet to unfold. Alluringly reclining along my horizon ten miles distant, were Na h-Eileanan Siàr, the Western Isles. Their individual shapes and distinctive form were familiar. Their names rolled off my tongue as I spoke them out loud when I counted off the islands from south to north; "Far distant Barra is hidden, maybe that's Eriskay, that's South Uist for sure, Benbecula, there's North Uist, is that Benreray? Mountainous Harris ahead, and Lewis too." It was difficult to stifle the romance these names conjured within, evoking a view of a life slower in pace and absent of avarice. Lived by a people lyrical and poetic, with hearts and spirits of tenacious warmth and a vibrant joy for life. A surge of desire to explore the islands filled me with excitement. To reach them though, I had the Minch to contend with. This was the challenge I faced and one which filled me with trepidatious awe. As an oceanic body of water, it is known as the 'Inner Seas Off the Western Coast of Scotland' and is an important passage for freighters, oil tankers and other ships. A traffic separation scheme operates in the Little Minch. North bound ships sail close to the Skye coastline and southbound traffic, close to the Outer Hebrides. This was probably my greatest concern. I feared more than anything being run down by a ship. The tides, the races, the rough seas and heavy surf landings, were worrying, but none anywhere as much as the prospect of finding myself in the powering path of an ocean-going ship. With my skill and judgement, I believed I could contend with the natural elements. However, with a ship and relying on the vagaries of there being an attentive watch-keeper aboard, was an element of risk I felt little control over. Avoidance was the best solution.

There was no evidence of shipping while I sat gazing out over the splendorous scene before me; the white capped tide race flowing west and southwards through the five-mile gap between the headland and the robust looking island group of Fladaigh Chuain, the Cleats and Lord Macdonald's Table. I gazed at them and smiled as a memory flitted into my awareness. In 2006, my adventure buddy Phil and I embarked on a hastily planned kayaking trip from Skye to the Shiant Isles, twelve miles to the north in the Minch. We were muddled in our preparations and hurried in our departure, not appreciating the strength of the tide when it began to flow against us when we were mid-Minch. Defeated by time, gathering darkness and growing fatigue, we turned and made for the island of Fladaigh Chuain, landing exhausted and thirsty. While making camp, Phil called out, "I'm making tea, d'you have the water?"

"No, I thought you had it!" was my wary reply.

Two seasoned adventurers had made the simplest of errors and embarked on a major sea kayak trip without a supply of fresh water. We had enough in our drinking bottles for a mug of tea each and that was it. There was no source of water on the island, only brackish puddles surfaced with an oily scum. Thankfully though, we had six bottles of Black Isle Brewery ale! When we made landfall the next day we ensured from then on, our waterbags were always topped to brimming and ever since then, this has been my personal practice even if am assured there is a fresh water supply at my destination.

The forecast for the following day was looking good. Light winds were expected, and the corresponding sea state would be slight. There would be little to prevent me from setting off on my crossing in the early morning. From where I was sitting, the distance was fourteen miles to the island of Scalpay where I could make out the red and white bands of the lighthouse on its shore. With Fladaigh Chuain as a stopping off point for rest, the open water crossing of the Minch would only be ten miles. I smiled to myself, that was a mere three hours of paddling. I would be across and amongst the Outer Hebrides before lunch! With that happy thought, I hefted myself to my feet and ambled back to my tent, making sure to steer clear of the pugilist bonxie still waiting for me.

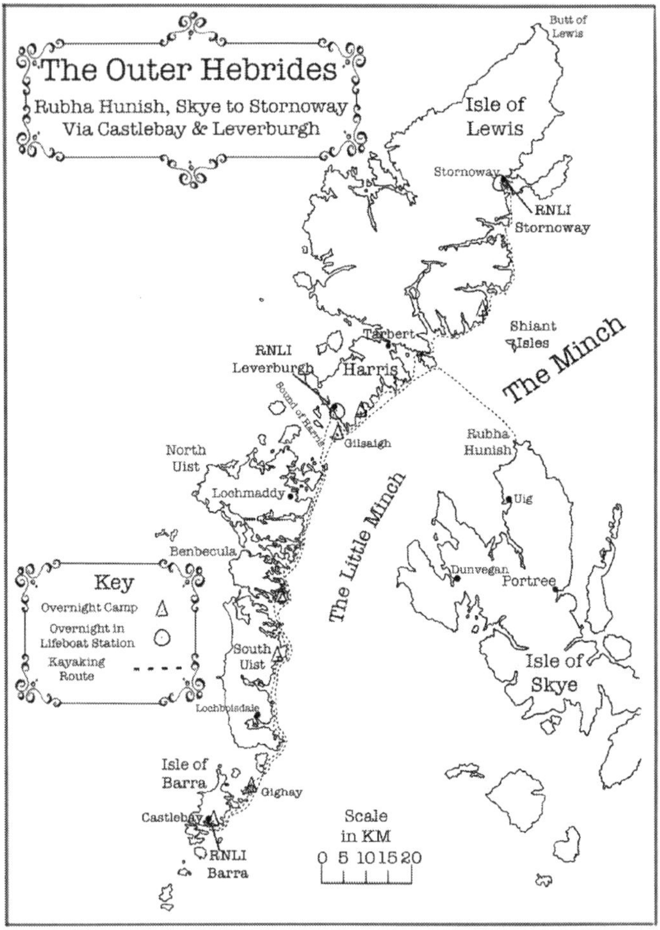
The Outer Hebrides
Rubha Hunish, Skye to Stornoway
Via Castlebay & Leverburgh
Butt of Lewis
Isle of Lewis
Stornoway
RNLI Stornoway
Tarbert
Shiant Isles
The Minch
RNLI Leverburgh
Harris
Sound of Harris
Gilsaigh
Rubha Hunish
North Uist
Lochmaddy
The Little Minch
Uig
Benbecula
Dunvegan
Portree
Key
Overnight Camp
Overnight in Lifeboat Station
Kayaking Route
South Uist
Isle of Skye
Lochboisdale
Isle of Barra
Gighay
Castlebay
RNLI Barra
Scale in KM
0 5 10 15 20

The Outer Hebrides Rubha Hunish, Skye to Stornoway, via Castlebay and Leverburgh

Chapter 17

Four o'clock and I was wide awake, and by six o'clock I was sliding my kayak into the sea, embarking on my crossing of the Minch. Two irate oystercatchers who had been constantly yelling at me while I packed, continued to shout their angry abuse until I was out of earshot. I wanted to settle my nerves because I had some tricky waters to cut through before reaching my first haven of the morning, the island of Fladaigh Chuain five miles away. I timed my departure to arrive at the Rubha Hunish headland as close to slack water as possible. Despite my meticulous mathematical machinations in the tent the night before, I was dismayed to find a pronounced flow in the sea pushing me faster than I would have liked towards the headland. Despite this momentary pulse of alarm, I allowed myself to absorb the magnificence of the scenery. The cliffs I had walked along the evening before now loomed above, the sea restless at their base but not unduly violent. The rate of flow picked up and I found myself in a roller coaster wave train, speeding towards the closing headland. I anxiously scanned the sea before me but could see no white crests and I relaxed a little. The tide was doing its work, all I had to do was ride it out.

With suddenness I broke free of the Skye shoreline. The prominent Rubha Hunish headland was behind and ahead lay five lumpy miles of sea and the beckoning islands of the Fladaigh group. This was it; a major element of my journey was about to take place and the significance of this moment wasn't lost on me. In just over four hours I would be arriving on the shores of Scalpay in the Outer Hebrides. This would be the fulfilment of a long-held dream of mine, to kayak across the Minch. I set off, determined paddle strokes establishing a worthy speed. There was no need to rush, simply cruise and enjoy the crossing. Around me little auks and guillemots bobbed on the surface of the sea, their little legs working double time to keep them moving. As usual, I found myself wishing they would be less nervous of my presence and not skitter away across the surface when I got close to them. I wanted to enjoy their company.

Looking left, southwards down the Minch, I spotted what seemed to be the top of a ship's superstructure. I wasn't certain because the large swell was doing a great job at hiding it. I stopped paddling to take a better look and sure enough, I could make out the bridge and antennae of a large ship heading towards the channel I was crossing. It was a good distance away because I couldn't see the hull. I vacillated. My instinct warned me to hold my position until the ship had passed, but my impatience encouraged me to make a dash for it. The tussle between these two clouded my ability to calculate the odds and I chose to listen to my impatience. I didn't want to hang around for the twenty minutes it would take the ship to reach me. I set off again, this time reaching forward with long and powerful strokes, *Sahwira's* prow surging through the sea like a destroyer in a North Sea WW2 convoy, plumes of sea water spraying back into my face. In a matter of minutes, I pulled up, back paddling with force to bring myself to a stop. This isn't how I wanted to make my crossing of the Minch, not through a mad dash with fear and panic tugging at my thoughts. I wanted to cross at my leisure, enjoy the experience and relish the achievement.

I could now make out most of the ship and idly back-paddled, holding my position half a mile off the Skye coastline. I felt vulnerable despite knowing I was out of the ship's route. My VHF was switched on and I had made sure the anti-collision flares were within reach in my deck bag. The light oil or chemical carrier, festooned with complicated looking pipework cruised past, almost silently ploughing a creaming furrow through the sea. I noted how it would have been difficult to have heard the ship if visibility was reduced. The speed of its arrival and its passage past me alarmed me too. From the moment I had spotted its superstructure to the point it was across my bows couldn't have been more than ten minutes. I was relieved to have made the wise decision to not outrun it and I was also pleased to experience this encounter. It was a salutary lesson and one to embody for the likely shipping encounters yet to come during the rest of my journey.

Arriving amongst the cluster of islands of the Fladaigh Chuain group was like walking into a party already in full swing and not knowing how to join in. The sky was thronging with birds of all species, wheeling, spinning, circling, diving, soaring, or joyfully flapping in a cacophony of noise where no one call could be distinguished from another. Equally on the surface of the sea, there were rafts of sea birds, shouting and yelling out to each other, swimming in random configurations which belied individual species collaboration. Hauled out on the rocks of Fladaigh Chuain, several slick coated grey seals appeared to be a disinterested audience to the avian spectacle about them. For myself, I was mesmerised. The surface of the sea, now calmed in the lee of the island, was littered with the detritus of bird life, patches of cocaine white guano were splattered about like a Pollock painting and myriad gossamer down feathers floated with the lightest of contact with the water. Amongst these were twigs and bits of reed which must have been dropped from beaks overloaded with nest building material.

I made my way along the island, overwhelmed by the fecundity of life around. I was an interloper and wanted to be out in the open Minch away from the private party I'd gate crashed. I set forth, into the Minch. The sea conditions were lumpy but not uncomfortable. The kayak rode the movement with ease and my paddling was rhythmically steady. I settled down to enjoy the three hours of paddling ahead. Gazing northwards, the Shiant Isles looked invitingly near, and I smiled at the prospect of visiting them in a couple of weeks when I made my way back to the Scottish mainland after visiting the lifeboat station in Stornoway. Until then though, there was so much more to see and enjoy! My point of reference was Eilean Glas lighthouse on the island of Scalpay, one of the earliest light houses to be built in Scotland. To the right of Scalpay gawked the dark entrance to Loch Seaforth, gaping like the mouth of a feeding basking shark. The mountainous terrain around the entrance to the loch, imbued a sense of journeying towards a mythical land. It was easy to imagine what the ancients would have made of such an experience when travelling in light skin craft across the sea towards the Hebridean islands. I'm sure what I was feeling would not have been far off the awe they might have experienced too. The Minch is a symbolic stretch of water for me. It delineates one world from another, a liminal boundary between a world of haste and consumerism and another of slowness and self-sufficiency. To reach the Western Isles one must travel by boat, ferry or by plane. There are no bridges or tunnels. Their separateness has kept alive the ancientness of Scotland, the Gaelic language and a close interrelation with the natural world, on the land and on the sea. The landscape of the Hebrides is rich with the heritage of humans who made them their home through the ages. There is a sense the Outer Hebrides have much to teach us because of this heritage, there is a wisdom to be gained regarding how we may live a harmonious life, almost at the pace Nature intended for us.

Romantic notions of ancient birlinns or prehistoric skin boats aside, I was aware I was a small kayak in a vast body of water. This realisation didn't fill me with the fear I assumed it might. Mid-point, well out of reach of any adjacent coastline, I didn't experience doubt about the wisdom of my position. I was unlikely to capsize, there was tidal movement around but none which would disarm me, and I was alone, no ships as far as my eyes could see. My oceanic solitude was liberating. I was here where no rules could contain me. Any choice I made was mine to make, the consequences mine to bear. The goals I had set for the day were fluid in nature, attainable but not essential. What mattered most was the quality of the experience. This was the reward I gained for placing myself in this place, for accepting the risks and facing the hazards. For overcoming my fears and concerns. I was beyond the reach of the limitations I normally set myself in life. Out here I was realising my potential, proving to myself once again, I am capable of so much more than I realise.

Eilean Glas lighthouse drew steadily closer. The rhythm of my paddle strokes didn't diminish and *Sahwira* ploughed a steady path through the rumpled sea. Features on the land grew in definition. I could make out trees, houses, and roads. Eventually I could hear the surf on the shore and the scolding of the oystercatchers as they chased each other over the rocks. Without fanfare, I arrived in the Outer Hebrides – I had kayaked across the Minch. I turned to look from where I had come and was shocked to notice how indistinct and far away the Skye landscape seemed. A glow of pride welled up within, this was another realisation of a long-held ambition. It's never my style to boast of my achievements but I knew I could be proud to announce I had kayaked solo across the Minch.

There was no time to bask in my self-adulatory glory, so I swung the kayak around to follow the shoreline, now on my right, southwards. The Isle of Barra was my ultimate destination, but this was at least three days paddling away. I hadn't decided on my end point for this day, concentrating only on crossing the Minch. I had the rest of the afternoon and settled conditions to see me well on my way southwards. I pulled onto the small beach beside the lighthouse to stretch my legs and to formally acknowledge my arrival in the Hebrides. The sheep on the hillside above stopped grazing long enough to give me a stare in recognition of my achievement. I raised my mug of lemon and ginger to them in return.

The route southwards was straightforward as far as the Sound of Harris sixteen miles away. There were no navigational or tidal concerns to keep me on my toes. I was feeling strong and reckoned I would make it as far as Rodel, on the northern flank of the Sound of Harris, for my stop for the night. The eastern coastline of the island of Harris is rugged with few suitable places to land a kayak and make a camp. There are no beaches to speak of and only a few inlets and tiny harbours. I would be kayaking familiar waters and I had a good idea of the likely places to stop. I decided I would choose where to camp as and when the moment arose. For the time being, I was keen to press on and reach as far as I could.

This was an unfortunate aspect of this journey, I sometimes tended to 'put my head down' and paddle hard to make up the distances. The result was missing out on the exploratory nature of the adventure and enjoying the landscape I was kayaking along. I was on a mission! After crossing the entrance to Loch Tarbert, the miles dropped away and so did the headlands; Rubha Bhocaig, Rubha Chliuthair, Meall Ruadh, Rubha Chuidhtinis, Rubha Bhalairiop and finally Rubha Reinis. Fifteen miles of paddling into a strengthening wind saw me wearily arrive at the northern edge of the Sound of Harris. I was close to my limit for the day and needed to find a place to stop. I had the ideal place in mind which required a few more miles of determination. An hour later I was pulling my kayak up a steep pebbly beach on the small island of Gilsaigh in the Sound of Harris. I knew this spot well having camped here with sea kayaking clients in my time as a guide for Clearwater Paddling based on the Isle of Barra. I had covered thirty-five miles from leaving the Isle of Skye which was just another far off landmass when I looked back across the Minch. It was a rewarding moment when I had my camp established, my food on the go, and a celebratory dram of Oban Lifeboat whisky in my cup. An arctic tern wasn't happy with my presence on the island and while I ate my supper it hovered over me with jerky wingbeats and screeched its annoyance. When I deigned to stand, it would dive with some accuracy for the crown of my head, causing me to flinch every time.

I was tired and despite the relatively early hour I decided to go to bed. While cleaning my teeth, I noticed the Leverburgh Lifeboat was out in the Sound. By its slow progress, I guessed it was out on their weekly training exercise. It was my plan to visit the station on my return leg up the Hebridean chain once I had visited the station on Barra. I rinsed my mouth wondering if the lifeboat was heading in my direction. I couldn't tell, so I climbed into my tent, zipped it up, snuggled into my sleeping bag and was out cold for the rest of the night. It wasn't until I reached Leverburgh a week later I discovered they had indeed visited and no amount of shouting and blasting the boat's horn was able to wake me from my deep sleep. I missed out on a present of cold beers!

Chapter 18

I set off early into freshening south-westerly winds. The run down to Lochmaddy beneath unremitting cliffs passed by smoothly. There was no temptation to deviate into the harbour and I pressed on, now kayaking a stretch of coastline which was unknown to me. The crags, sheer rock walls and bog laden hinterland were devoid of human life. It amazed me how I could travel for hours and not see another soul. The sea birds were my constant companions. My schedule for the day demanding a punishing pace which didn't allow time to explore the intriguing watery passageways amongst the archipelago including Grimsay, Ronay and the Flodaighs. I had often gazed at this Hebridean Venice on the map, imagining paddling in and out of the creeks and the tight channels, exploring the intricacies of the hidden islands. It was with reluctance I chose the seaward route and sadly avoided the inside passages. The wind was gaining in considerable strength causing me concern about the viability of making the thirty miles I had set myself for the day. Any thought of easing up on my paddling speed and enjoying my surroundings, gusted away with one particularly heavy blast of wind.

The Minch to my left was grey and menacing, a heavy sea was running from the south. I was pleased to have made it across to the Hebrides when I did, knowing a few days of unstable conditions lay ahead. Headlands came and went. Islands were passed, features were ticked off on the map one by one. It was with a sense of shame I kayaked past Benbecula without really noticing. By now it was raining, and I had my hood up, where all I could see through the gap under the peak was the world I existed in. Black rocked skerries became short term goals to attain, faded red lobster pot buoys were transit markers and my watch and GPS on my foredeck were constantly appraised to offer reassurance about my progress. I bent forward into the wind, reading the seas with aplomb and taking perverse pleasure from the battering I was receiving from the driving rain. The fresh water streaming from my forehead through my moustache and over my lips was a welcome change to the normal salty brine. My face was washed and refreshed.

As the afternoon drew towards early evening, I started to keep an eye out for likely camp spots but any time I spotted one, I decided to push on, trusting there would be another further ahead. I scanned my map for locations with the word *'Acarsaid'*, because this was Scots Gaelic indicating harbour or haven. It was my experience on even the wildest of coastlines, this was a reliable indication of a place to pull ashore with a kayak. Passing the entrance to Loch Sgioport, I had the wild Uisinis landscape laid out in front. Hecla loomed out of the dissipating clouds, seeming like a heather clad Everest, such was its grandeur in relation to the flat Uist and Benbecula landscape around about. Tendrils of blue grey mist were wreathed around the summit, giving an impression of mystic and awe. The rain had ceased, and I drew back the hood of my jacket, my world suddenly lightening and widening in perspective. I joined the world again from within my paddling hermitage. I knew five miles ahead, around the Uisinis headland, was a bay where there was a bothy managed by the Mountain Bothies Association. In fact, I had long wanted to stay there. Immediately ahead though, was a perfect place to camp in a tight bay with invitingly green swards of cropped turf behind.

Without a second thought, I pressed on around Rubha Heallacro and under the nineteenth century Stevenson lighthouse standing proud on the cliffs above. A sea kayak allows me to explore the rarely seen delights of the Scottish coastline. I doubt if many people have enjoyed the unique experience of wandering beneath the high cliffs of Uisinis, the birds calling to each other from their white streaked nesting ledges and the sea solemnly washing the base with a lazy swell. It was another moment of privilege, the acknowledgement I was fortunate to enjoy this opportunity. My pace had slowed, I knew I had reached the end point for my day, and it was a relief to turn into Bàgh Uisinis, Uisinis Bay. At first, I believed I had inadvertently passed through a time warp and travelled to an age far in the past when Scotland was truly wild. I was taken aback by the expansiveness and the wildness of the landscape before me. The wide boulder strewn bay was enclosed by an amphitheatre of dark heather clad mountains, wisps of light cloud drifting serenely around their upper flanks. A bealach (saddle) led intriguingly away from this human uninhabited auditorium, with a promise of something unknown beyond. The panorama was too wide to take in and I swung my head slowly, absorbing the subtle shapes of the mountains, their spurs and ridges, their gullies and re-entrants.

I fumbled with the watertight map case, reaching into it with my sodden fingers and pulling the neatly folded document out. With difficulty I unfolded it without it being blown out of my hands into the sea, and studied the terrain laid out before me. In a language I am unable to interpret and with naïve mispronunciation, I read out the names of the features arranged in their glory before me. The mountains first, south to north; Beinn na Tobha, Beinn nan

Caorach, then the Bealach Crosgard leading to the mighty Beinn Mhor, Beinn Choradail, down to Geann Usinis and then climbing high again to the high summit Hecla. As if to congratulate me on my map reading, the silhouette of a Golden Eagle swept out from behind Hecla's ridge and effortlessly cruised southwards to gain lift from the other mountains. It was a magnificent sight. The names of the natural features held a sense of antiquity. Gaelic, or even old Norse, descriptions of the landscape or attributed to a long-gone person, immortalised and as enduring as the cliffs around. This landscape empty of humans now, was once a thriving place where people lived, grew crops and tended their livestock. The wildness I was enjoying gazing over, exists because of human tragedy and the policy of clearing the land of tenant farmers in favour of wholesale sheep farming. The community managed South Uist Estate covers 93 000 acres and stalking deer (trophy hunting) in this rough land, is a major income stream.

Despite the expansiveness of the beach, finding a suitable place to land wasn't easy. Large boulders made a damage free arrival near impossible. I managed, carefully easing myself onto my lifeless legs and even then, stumbling the first few steps over slippery weed covered rocks. I had travelled thirty-three miles and I was pleased with my effort. After pulling my kayak as far over the rocks as I could so she was out of reach of the sea, I wandered along the beach in search of the bothy. This it turned out, was set on a low ridge some distance from the shore up a steep and very boggy path. It was a picturesque affair, low and snugly built from local stone. The door creaked and scraped open as bothy doors ought to do, and inside was a well-ordered single room with a wooden sleeping platform, a wood burning stove and a table area for food preparation and cooking. It was wonderfully compact and cosy, exactly where I would have loved to stay for a few nights while exploring the surrounding country. Sadly though, my heart wasn't in it. Despite eagerly anticipating this visit and the possibility of a roof over my head for the night, when the moment arrived, I longed for the familiar comfort of my tent. I think the fact I would have to lug my kit up the steep slope and through the bog influenced my change of heart. I stepped outside and closed the door, making a vow I would one day return with good friends to enjoy this incredible facility.

I made camp on a small patch of grass by a gurgling stream. The view I enjoyed while cooking my dinner was one of the finest of my journey so far. The tranquillity suffused my thoughts which were ranging as expansively as the seascape before me. I leaned back in my camp chair, absorbing all I was experiencing, the sound of the surf on the beach, the wind blowing across the heather, the busybody oystercatchers chirruping to each other, the sanderlings skittering ahead of each incoming wave, and the bubbling of my pasta dinner in the pot on the stove by my side. This was my present life, and it was intensely satisfying.

After dinner I went exploring. Marked on the map were three souterrains. A souterrain is a subterranean structure from the late Iron Age. Archaeologists suggest they were underground larders and possibly, places of refuge. They were created by digging a tunnel and maybe a chamber, then lining these with rock or wood. Some were linked to buildings and others were set in isolation in a community. They are relatively common relics in the Scottish landscape but to have the opportunity to explore one was a rare occurrence. I guessed because of the remote location of these remains, they might exist in the state they have for fifteen hundred years, and I was keen to have a good poke around. Finding them was a challenge though. The heather did all it could to grab at my legs, and with foot placements unseen, I often tumbled forwards, sideways and backwards, ending up in awkward tangled heaps. After the hours of sitting in my kayak, it was good to be striding across the open hill, stretching limbs which had remained largely inactive for the last few weeks. I had chosen to search out the souterrain marked the furthest away on the map with the idea of visiting the others on my walk back. I wasn't certain what to look for but when I chanced upon an area of ground clear of heather and bracken around which, were unnaturally placed stones and boulders, I guessed I must be in the right area. I had forgotten to bring my GPS, so I was relying on my latent map-reading skills to establish my location on the hillside.

I'm not an archaeologist by any means, but a life of living and working in the outdoors, with an active interest in our human heritage, has imbued an awareness of what is natural occurrence and what is human influence. It wasn't long before I picked out a distinctive circle of stones which I hoped would be the remains of an Iron Age roundhouse. I guessed there was a good chance the souterrain would be attached to the roundhouse, if this indeed was what I was looking at. I scanned the land around, searching for anomalies in the ground, any indication there might be an entrance to an underground passage. Then I spotted something, an odd mound running away from below the rough circle of stones. I rushed down to investigate and with an excited whoop, I spotted a void in the ground. This had to be the entrance I was hoping for because there appeared to be a lintel protecting the top of the opening. Placing my camera and binoculars on a nearby flat rock, making a metal note not to forget them, I knelt, switched on my head torch and peered inside. I gasped with excitement. There was an obvious tunnel, lined with intact rough dry- stonework. I couldn't see a collapse of any sort or an indication one was imminent, so I stuck my head into the hole and wiggled my way forwards.

The musty scent of dry earth filled my nose and with it a bile of panic rose within. I don't suffer from claustrophobia, but I do have to calm myself when squeezing into tight spaces. Accompanying the cloying fear of becoming trapped was an innate fear of snakes and scorpions. I had learned from an early age in Zimbabwe to show a healthy respect for what may lie beneath when lifting rocks or entering enclosed spaces. The fact I was in the Outer Hebrides, was not enough to dissuade my childhood autonomic response. Of course, I didn't find myself face to face with an irate cobra as I wriggled my way further in. I found it difficult to gain a sense of the souterrain, its purpose and its significance. However, touching the stonework and looking at it untouched since the day it was laid, filled me with reverential awe. These stones had been purposefully laid by people two thousand years before my arrival in the bay by kayak. They had planned this structure, discussed it and created it. They will have used it, storing grain, produce and possibly meats. It might be they hid in here too, huddled out of sight of the danger they were threatened with, whispering fearfully about what might happen. Such fantasies are difficult to maintain when my nose is filling with dirt and my eyes become itchy with dust, so I decided to retreat, reversing in a struggled wriggle, my legs flailing in the open air as they attempted to find purchase. I hadn't managed to make my way to the very end of the tunnel, but I wasn't worried about this. I had seen what I wanted and was pleased to have made the effort to explore.

I sat down by the entrance and gazed eastwards. The Minch was laid out before me, a body of water I was becoming intimately acquainted with. The southern reaches of Skye were catching the dipping sun and an orange glow was infusing the far-off hills. A huge cruise liner was entering the traffic separation zone, and this too was changing colour like a chameleon from bright white to orange-red, sparkles of light glinting from the acres of glass within its structure. The juxtaposition between the Iron Age presence around me and the twenty-first century maritime condominium couldn't have been clearer. What changes us humans have wrought on this planet of ours. Not wishing to become too philosophical and realising I was in danger of running out of daylight, I set off down the hill, making a beeline for my camp. The plan to visit the other souterrains dispensed with. It was when I was a few hundred metres from my tent I remembered my camera and my binoculars! It was dusk by the time I was settling in for the night, and this being almost midpoint of the summer, it was after eleven o'clock. I fell asleep within seconds of laying my head on my pillow of spare clothes.

I arrived on the Isle of Barra coastline after midday. From Lochboisdale southwards, I was kayaking familiar waters again and this helped the miles to slip by. I counted off well known features, islands and skerries without referring to my map. The wind was on my nose all day but never strong enough to cause discomfort. It was an unremarkable passage, a few seals along the Eriskay shoreline, no sightings of dolphins as I crossed the Sound of Barra, and sadly no mighty sea eagles when I passed the islands of Gighay and Hellisay. I never failed to see one or two in this location and their absence caused me to look at the relatively new huge fish-farm tucked close into the south shore of Hellisay with suspicion.

Rubha Bhruairnis was where I made Barra landfall and I was welcomed by two otters swimming through the wrack amongst the skerries. They were unconcerned by my presence and swam out into the open sea, across my bow to disappear behind a skerry a few metres beyond. They reminded me why I loved kayaking around the Barra coastline so much. I could clearly see Maol Dòmhnaich, the proud guardian of the entrance to Castlebay and I knew I was nearly done for the day. I was looking forward to arriving and to catching up with good friends, for it is here where I worked as a guide for Clearwater Paddling, running my first trip with them in 2009. Chris and Katie Denehy have created one of the finest sea guiding outfits in the world, offering authentic sea kayaking expeditions in some of the wildest and incredibly stunning locations around Scotland. Katie grew up on Barra and they use her family home as a hostel and run the business from a house they built on the adjacent land. In an age where there's an increasingly regimented approach to sea kayaking leadership and group management, Chris' approach to the sea kayaking journeys he offers is wonderfully refreshing. He trusts his guides to provide powerful experiences without compromising safety. As a guide, I always felt I had permission to evoke intense adventurous experiences by leading clients into coastal settings which are often considered the reserve of seasoned paddlers. It's one of the most rewarding experiences of my outdoor leadership life when leading a group beneath the mighty five hundred feet high cliffs of western Mingulay and watching and listening to their expressions of complete wonder and awe. I wasn't surprised, I was feeling the same! Allowing people to become feral while overseeing their safety, is a sure way to invite them to immerse themselves fully in the wild and natural world. When they do, magic occurs!

I was beginning to flag as I rounded the last headland leading onto the entrance of Castlebay. The wind had been on my nose most of the day and it was taking its toll on my energy reserves. Since leaving Skye, I had paddled over ninety miles in three days, a distance I was not used to covering in a relatively short space of time. Then to lift my spirits, the Barra lifeboat emerged with a roar from behind the small island of Orasaigh, crashing through the lumpy sea towards me. Portree lifeboat's gesture was being emulated and a rush of gratitude caused me to choke back unexpected sobs. This level of recognition by the volunteer crew, giving up their time during a working day to greet a sea kayaking stranger, was a powerful realisation. The crew dressed in their 'yellows' waved from their positions around the boat. I stopped paddling to allow them to draw up beside me and many words of welcome and congratulations were shouted down. The lifeboat pulled away and I watched as the crew efficiently set about deploying the 'Y-boat', an inflatable tender with an outboard engine which is used to reach survivors on the shore, or to search in waters too shallow for the Severn lifeboat. Once afloat and with two crew aboard, the engine roared into life with a puff of blue smoke, and they skimmed over the surface towards me. Greetings were once again made, and this time accompanied with firm handshakes. Their task was to photograph me kayaking in towards Castlebay with the lifeboat alongside. It turned out to be a case of them taking photos of me, taking photos of them. Castlebay is the main town on the Isle of Barra and is unique in having a restored fifteenth century castle on a sizeable rocky islet in the bay. It is a prominent feature when one enters the bay from the sea and it's difficult not to be impressed by its presence. I never fail to admire it when I arrive on the ferry or kayak around the bay. Today, with the Barra Island lifeboat escorting me in, I felt like a vaunted lord making a grand entrance to the ancient capital of the southern Hebrides.

The crew and I gathered in the small crew room of the lifeboat station, up the hill from the harbour. Beers were handed around and the formal welcomes took place. There was a relief coxswain from Aberdeen, covering for the absence of the usual Barra helm. David and I joked about the chance of us meeting each other twice, though right then in the Barra crew room, it was difficult to conceive arriving in Aberdeen a thousand miles later. John MacNeil was the mechanic and he made me feel particularly welcome. He arranged for me to enjoy a complimentary dinner up at the Craigard Hotel in Castlebay which was extremely generous. The crew dispersed, and I made camp on the lawn in front of the station. It was my intention to remain in Castlebay for a couple of days to meet with Chris, Katie and Ben, catch up on chores and kayak maintenance.

Chapter 19

It was lovely to wander into the happy chaos of Clearwater Paddling and Dunard Hostel. As usual I was afforded a warm welcome and taken in as one of their own. I was given free run of the hostel which meant hot showers, use of the laundry and Wi-Fi. Ben was guiding a trip further north and wouldn't be back for another day, so I decided to hang around until he did. As things transpired, this was a period of calm in the weather with hot June sunshine and while it was lovely to sunbathe in front of my tent, I couldn't help feeling anxious about missing excellent kayaking conditions. Castlebay as a town reminded me of my younger life in Africa. There was an element of the wild-west to the place, not in a lawless sense, but in an almost untamed way, where the norms I associate with life on the mainland are not readily applied here. There are no traffic controls on the roads and yet, in their own way, the Barra drivers manage to safely exist despite single track lanes, speedy driving, and livestock wandering free as it pleases. There is an unwritten highway code which includes driving, parking and stopping to chat to friends in the middle of the road despite the line of cars building up behind. Ben arrived back from his trip and it was great to catch up with him. He is one of the most natural guides I know with an encyclopaedic knowledge of the coastal and marine ecology, an eye like an eagle able to spot wildlife normally unseen, and excellent leadership judgement. He is also an excellent camp chef, able to create a gourmet dinner in any conditions for happy sea kayaking customers.

I would have happily hung around Castlebay for a few days longer but after two days of leisure, it was time to move on. I slipped away as I had feared, into a building westerly gale, my window of opportunity for kayaking in fine weather had disappeared.

It was tough going from the outset. I struggled from Castlebay to Rubha Bhruairnis where there were no otters to greet me this time. I doubt anyway if I would have spotted them in the heavy sea. I briefly considered stopping at this low headland because beyond, I could see things were going to be just as tough. However, the thought of not making it off the island of Barra was too much to bear, I had to keep going. It was one of those paddling days when every paddle stroke had to count. The wind was relentless, sweeping low over the sea, kicking up a steep chop which broke irregularly around. Every time the nose of the kayak dived through a wave, the resulting plume of spray would whip back and soak my face. My moustache was an ideal conduit for a constant flow of briny water into my mouth. I managed to make a further four miles to the entrance to the 'Blue Lagoon' which lies between the islands of Hellisay and Gighay when I decided enough was enough. Attempting to cross the Sound of Barra to Eriskay would be foolhardy, so I decided to pull into the lagoon and camp in a spot I knew well from my guiding days. I morosely set about unpacking the boat aware of a diesel engine annoyingly chugging from further within the channel. Given my tetchy mood at having to cut the day short, this background noise was intrusive and unwelcome. Not far away a water pump sat atop a floating pontoon, and it was this which was working away. I had no idea why it was there, but this was a recent addition to the area which until the arrival of the huge fish farm on the other side of the ridge, had been a place of serenity and wild peace. In a fit of pique, I stuffed everything back into the boat, launched and paddled back out into the maelstrom.

I had no plan. I didn't know of any possible camp spots along the western shoreline of Gighay but I trusted fate and my intuition to find one. If not, then it was going to be a wild and committing crossing of the Sound of Barra. It was near impossible to paddle close to the shore because of the seas piling onto the rocks. Oystercatchers seemed to take great delight in flitting ahead, informing me with their distinctive shrieking, I was on a hiding to nowhere. Things weren't looking great when I spotted the slightest of entrants in the shore at the back of which was a narrow pebbly landing spot. Further up on the land, I saw what seemed to be a perfect patch of sheep shorn grass. My gamble had paid off, but first I had to navigate ashore. I made it without damage to myself or the kayak and soon had a comfortable camp established with a fine view across the glorious expanse of the Sound of Barra. I was pleased with myself for finding this camp and deciding not to suffer the dreadful noise of the water pump in the Blue Lagoon. Despite only having paddled ten miles, a third of what I hoped, I felt philosophically sanguine about my situation. The forecast didn't look hopeful for the wind to ease any time soon, but I had restocked with food in Castlebay and I had plenty of water. I simply had to sit this out.

The next day. White clouds of many shapes and dimensions scudded across the sky and the sea was ruffled with frothy white caps. A tugging wind rattled the tent, but it didn't seem to be as strong as the day before. I hastily struck camp and put to sea, punching through a messy swell sweeping through the Sound of Barra from the west. The sudden appearance of a basking shark beside my kayak in the middle of the channel caused me to jump. There is something about spotting the distinctive shape of a shark's fin cruising an arm's length away, it's a primal response! The tail fin slowly and gracefully sweeping from side to side was the giveaway the fin belonged to one of the largest fish species in the ocean. Basking sharks are completely harmless to humans, their food source being plankton which they swallow and sieve through their gaping jaws as they swim through the sea. I was pleased to have seen this one and sadly, it was to be the only encounter with a basking shark I would enjoy during the whole trip.

I retraced my paddling strokes northwards, traversing the landscape I had passed only a few days earlier. As with my journey then, I paddled hard and without respite, eating the miles one by one. I had no plan for where to stop for the day, I was going to see what distance I could make. I was driven to make up for lost time, cruising past one good camp spot after another. Nearing the coastline of Benbecula towards the end of the day, I chose to take the inside passage which I had avoided on my way south.

I spotted a small islet, with an attractive looking area of grass large enough to take my tent. What drew me most to the spot were the swathes of sea pinks which covered the rocks around the shore of the island. I simply had to land there and stop for the night. It was the most perfect spot I could have chosen. Making camp was a joy, almost like a scene from an early Disney film. Calmness had descended, the air was clear, and the bird song was melodic. The pinks added colour to the end of a long day.

There is something about an island. It's a place of childhood magic and dreams of adventure. I first encountered an island in literature with the Famous Five.

Then of course it was Treasure Island and after this, Black Cat Island in Swallows and Amazons, the book which inspired me most to live adventurously. Many people have dreams of a castaway existence, a simple life unencumbered by the travails of modernity. Robinson Crusoe captured the imagination of many in the eighteenth century, and people have been captivated by a dream of a story very much like his ever since. Islands are symbolic of our desire for individuality, to step out of mainstream existence and create a life of our own. To reach an island we must cross water, this act a commitment. It's a liminal boundary. Even when canoeing on the lakes in Africa as a young boy, I would gain an incredible thrill from landing on a rocky island, pretending to be the first there, my damp footprints on the grey granite the only ones to be seen before they evaporated under the blazing African sun. Every time I land on an island in my sea kayak, I get this same thrill, holding the fantasy I'm the only one to know this place, to set foot on it. Long before I altered my view on land ownership, I dreamed of owning an island and would scour the land sales on the internet to see if any came available, even the smallest would have done.

Now though, I 'owned' an island every time I set foot on one. For the time I was there, we would share a common bond of connection. This was to be my home for the next twelve hours which was long enough to provide a sense of eternal existence. The time was my own to do what I wished. No distractions. No demands. I chose to sit silently and soak in my surroundings. I wish I could say I was totally alone but a mile away was a fish farm. I chose to ignore this. Instead, the pinks drew me back to my island, and I studied their delicateness and beauty. Along with the yellow flag iris, they are my favourite flowers, evoking a sense of freedom and summer light and warmth. The fact they are robust flowers too makes them attractive. I heard a faint plop in the water, turning my head to see concentric rings forming on the calm surface of the leaden sea. Suddenly an otter broke the surface, rising head and shoulders, looking around, and then swimming along the shore towards me. Its small head followed by its back and then sinuous tail. I always think swimming otters remind me of swimming snakes. It dived before it reached close to where I was sitting, its tail the last to disappear and a trail of tiny bubbles floating to the surface amongst concentric rings. It surfaced again, driving upwards out of the sea like a synchronised swimmer and settling down, looking around again and swimming onwards, closer still. I could hear it breathing, quick puffs and then again, with a sinuous slip o'the tail, it was gone again. A minute or two later it reappeared but this time further out in the channel and was swimming away. That was my entertainment for the evening, I lay back and gazed up at the scudding clouds. Bedtime, I thought, but I couldn't be bothered to move.

Chapter 20

I'm not sure what woke me at three o'clock in the morning, but I sat bolt upright, wide awake. There was an odd twilight gloom around, so I stumbled out of my tent to have a look. My breath was taken away! The sky on the northeastern horizon was infused with deep shades of pink, while behind me it was a deep and dark shade of blue. The sea was more than mirror calm – it was like a sheet of immovable glass which perfectly reflected the evolving tableau above. It was a mesmerising spectacle and I stood in my sleeping attire, silent and overawed. There was no movement around as if the birds too were silently observing this glorious dawn. On my own, at this early hour of the morning, it felt like a hugely significant moment. I felt I ought to offer up an incantation and wished I could remember one of my favourite inspirational Outward Bound readings.

Look to this day:
For it is life, the very life of life.
In its brief course
Lie all the verities and realities of your existence.
The bliss of growth,
The glory of action,
The splendour of achievement
Are but experiences of time.

For yesterday is but a dream
And tomorrow is only a vision;
And today well-lived, makes
Yesterday a dream of happiness
And every tomorrow a vision of hope.

Look well therefore to this day;
Such is the salutation to the dawn!
Kalidasa – Sanskrit Poet

I would offer up this reading around mid-point on a course, thinking it would resonate more powerfully as the participants gained a deeper awareness of the opportunities the outdoor activities held for them. It's a poem which holds great meaning for me too and never a dawn passes me by without thinking about it.

Inexorably the sun rose beyond the horizon but not in a blaze of glory. Despite the beauty of the pink hues the day began to darken, and a pallor descended in the form of heavy-weight grey cloud. The adage, red sky in morning, sea kayaker's warning was not without reliability it seemed. I decided to make an early start, seeing as I was up already. By six in the morning, I was away, cutting through a calm sea, but with a feeling of dread about what was to occur. The optimism of the dawn had transmogrified into a gloomy wariness. The intricate loveliness of the skerries and the islands I was paddling through, lifted my dampened spirits. These were the waterways I had missed out on when paddling southwards a few days earlier. A herd of deer stood on the boggy flank of one of the islets and watched me silently paddle by. They could have only reached their place by swimming. Maybe they too were captivated by the possibilities of island living?

I didn't expect anything remarkable from the day. I was covering ground already paddled, so it was a case of making as good progress as possible. The ominous air lifted slowly to be replaced by a clearing sky.

I saw the sleeping grey seal from a distance away. It was like a bottle floating on the water, head just above the surface, its nose pointing skywards, eyes peacefully closed. This was not an unusual sight, I had come across many snoozing seals before, catching forty winks without hauling themselves ashore. Despite their apparent deep slumbers, they were alert enough to sense my presence when I drew close and dive under the sea with alarm. I always felt dreadful at having disturbed them. This seal was a couple of metres off the cliff, where the rock dropped sheer into the sea. I stopped paddling to allow my kayak to drift silently, aiming at the gap between the seal and the shore. I avoided the seawards route because I didn't want the seal to feel trapped when it awoke, as I assumed it surely would. I didn't need to use my paddles because there was sufficient momentum in the kayak to carry me beyond the sleeping creature. I kept myself still, slightly shifting my weight so the kayak angled away preventing any chance of a collision. The seal was oblivious to my presence, and I wondered if I ought to make a small sound to let it know I was near. Curiosity got the better of me and I drifted up beside it. There was a strand of bright green seaweed draped across its prickly whiskered snout and I was tempted to reach out and carefully remove it. It was gently snoring, almost silent whispered wheezes through its tight nostrils. If I had been malicious in my intent, I could have tweaked its nose with my thumb and forefinger I was that close. I expected it to wake at any moment and was prepared for the violence of its fright and the splashing which would ensue; however I was soon past it and it continued to slumber on. I very gently placed my paddle blade into the sea and furtively pulled away. The grey seal's sleep had been uninterrupted. This was a remarkable encounter which did much to gladden my heart. It's close experiences with the natural world like this one, which offer the unremitting joy I gain from sea kayaking.

My encounter with the sleeping seal sustained me for the next few hours it took me to reach the Sound of Harris. Because I had set off so early, I would be arriving in Leverburgh much sooner than planned. It was akin to being given a surprise afternoon off work. I love kayaking in the Sound of Harris. It's the stretch of sea separating North Uist from the Isle of Harris to the north. For mariners this stretch of water has a serious reputation with unpredictable tides full of guile, sandy shallows and hundreds of treacherous skerries. The tides particularly are notorious for their fickleness and their strength. Even local boatmen and women have difficulty in understanding the flows through the sound. For a sea kayaker, the Sound is a wonderful place to explore, the non-existent draft of a kayak allowing a person to delve into hidden creeks and pristine white sanded rocky bays among the islets which abound throughout. The tides may pose a challenge, but these are easily coped with. Sadly, many of the larger islands have fish farms associated with them now, so the possibility of uninterrupted tranquillity has all but disappeared. Nevertheless, these aside, it is a stunning area. In the bright sun, the sea takes on a turquoise hue and the white sands irradiate brightness, so sharp it makes one squint. To the north, the mountains of Harris provide an authoritative backdrop and to the south, the lower and rougher lands of North Uist, are a juxtaposition to the gaily coloured Sound.

Fish farms are an emotive subject. Quite simply I dislike them. They epitomise our human avarice and the wanton colonisation of wild seascapes. They industrialise the last vestiges of precious Scottish wildness and sadly, their numbers are exponentially increasing. Up and down the west coast of Scotland and around the Inner and Outer Hebridean Islands, there isn't a picturesque bay or sound which doesn't appear to be blighted by doubled strings of floating, round fish cages with their attendant diesel chugging feed barges, which are like lopsided submarine coning towers. In some bays there may be two or three fish farms. I hate fish farms for their intrusion into nature as much as I hate quarries, road developments, green field developments or any other form development which causes the loss of wildness on the land. Not only is marine aquaculture unsightly but it creates intrusive noise and seriously pollutes the environment too. The unrestricted waste released into the sea from the farmed fish is greater than the amount of sewage produced by Scotland's population of just over five million people. Aligned with this are the effects on the declining populations of wild Salmon through infestations of sea lice and the intensive use of antibiotics and toxic pesticides, the residues of which sweep unchecked through the seas with the flowing tides.

The industry is booming with huge demand for salmon products, particularly from the Far East. The Scottish Government along with the Scottish Salmon Producers Organisation are committed to doubling farmed salmon output by the 2030s. In thinking about this, I can't imagine where the hundreds of new farms will be located. It seems there'll probably not be a single stretch of the Scottish west coast unblighted by the industry.

This is as far as my angst regarding this issue reaches. I do not involve myself in campaigning for the reduction of salmon farms or their containment. Sadly, I sigh deeply and shrug my shoulders, as I suspect many other people do. This is because I feel alone in my resistance to the industry. Scotland is a small nation which requires to develop every opportunity it can to ensure its economic viability. Marine aquaculture in Scotland produces nearly one hundred and sixty-three thousand tonnes of farmed salmon a year and is the second largest producer in the European Union. The Scottish Government has identified the Scottish food and drink industry as a vital economic area for investment and development. Allied with this are the benefits to isolated communities through employment and economic investment. Many of these west coast and island communities have struggled with population decline due to few employment opportunities and the decline of the fishing fleets. The advent of industrial scale marine aquaculture has been a boon for these villages and crofting settlements. Indeed, when I arrived at the lifeboat station in Leverburgh I made a comment to Calum MacMillan, the mechanic of the lifeboat, about my disappointment at the number of noisy fish farms through the Sound of Harris, he responded in his quiet Gaelic lilt, "If it wasn't for the fish farms, Leverburgh would be dead." Thereafter, when I passed a fish farm, instead of thinking of the workers in a denigrating fashion, I saw them as fathers, mothers, daughters and sons, eking a living in a tough economic rural environment.

Ironically, Leverburgh formerly known as Obbe, came into existence in 1920 through the patronage of Lord Leverhulme, the owner of South Harris and who developed it as a fishing port to capitalise on the herring boom of the time. The shoals of herring were overfished, and the industry crashed leaving Leverburgh to struggle into the twenty first century. Fish farming then, has been its salvation. This is a story which can be repeated up and down the Scottish west coast and I feel a sense of shame when I criticise the proliferation of the fish farming industry in these remote locations. Indeed, many of my friends in Tobermory where I live now are employed by the fish farming companies or indirectly benefit by providing services to them.

My dismay at the unexpiated growth of the fish farming industry is the loss of wild space. It's almost as if the enclosures of the eighteenth century in England are similarly occurring in the quiet lochs, bays and sounds of the Scottish west coast. Anchorages and fishing grounds which once were free for all to use have now become the preserve of multi-national conglomerates with the blessing of the Scottish Government. Creel fishermen lose access to valuable reefs and find the productivity of the fishing grounds in the vicinity of large fish farms decreases due to the pressure on the environment and pollution. Recreational mariners now find once empty sheltered anchorages clogged with fish farm pens. As a sea kayaker, I have witnessed substantial changes to the west coast landscape over the last ten years. Bays which were once a favourite of mine for their sense of solitude and wild beauty have now become hives of aquaculture industry. For example, one of my favourite locations to kayak, in the Sound of Barra by the island of Hellisay, a massive farm of over twenty cages was developed in the deep water of the channel just off the southern edge of the island. The cliff I used to enjoy silently sliding beneath in my kayak, so close I could reach out and touch the sheer wall, has now been studded with mighty bolts used to anchor the massive fish pens metres away. What was once a human empty place has now become a clamorous and odorous hive of industrial farming activity. There is no escape either, because the noise reaches far beyond the confines of the settlement.

The erosion of our wild landscapes is a perpetual issue which environmentalists have been fighting for decades. Depressingly, the march of the human colonisation of wildness seems unstoppable. This is not a local Scottish issue either, but a global one. The loss of natural peaceful serenity in a secluded Scottish bay where otters can be seen playfully hunting, eider ducks drifting in distinctive black and white flocks and terns fluttering with their jerky wing beats, due to the installation of a fish farm, may seem inconsequential in the grand scheme of global exploitation, but this added together with everything else which is happening around the world; clearing forests, damming rivers, unchecked coastal development, fracking, intensive farming practices, and more besides, it is an important contributory factor in the global decline of natural wildness.

I am careful not to refer to the seemingly empty Scottish landscapes as wilderness because this is not what they are. Through the millennia these lands and sea ways have been inhabited and utilised by humans in varying levels of intensity. In fact, if the ethnologically controversial policy of the nineteenth century clearances hadn't occurred, the landscape may look very different to how it does today. It might be that now unoccupied glens leading down to empty bays would have roads and be inhabited by clusters of dwellings or even small settlements. It's a personal view of course, but I would prefer if the wildness created by the clearances is preserved and the reestablishment of nature enhanced. This position brings me into conflict with the economic requirements of the nation and the rural communities, but I do believe there is a balance to be struck between that of Nature, which is largely negated and the development of national potential.

Halfway across the Sound, I saw the Leverburgh lifeboat leave the harbour and begin her journey out towards me. This was unexpected, and I was gratified as much as I had been with the Barra and the Portree boats. The lifeboat growled through the lumpy waters, and we met just south of the main channel through the Sound. Greetings were shouted but I couldn't get close to them because the tide was fiercely running against us. It was all I could do to maintain a steady position, so we could talk. The lifeboat crew shouted they would see me back at the station and set off. I gamely followed them into the main flow, concentrating hard on not getting caught out and flipping over. It was tough work paddling against the river-like flow, my bow creaming through the sea but little progress being made to show for it. Transits on the shore helped me gain a sense of my forward progress and metre by metre I made it up the channel and eventually into sheltered water. Pulling into the harbour and finally having my hand warmly shaken was another great feeling.

I remained in Leverburgh for three nights. The gales swept through again creating seas which were too much to possibly handle. One aspect about sea kayaking in support of the R.N.L.I. and being hosted in their stations was the need to be doubly cautious about venturing forth in marginal conditions. For this reason, I always acceded to the wisdom of the crew and accepted their continued hospitality. John, the mechanic at the station was particularly welcoming and we spent many a happy hour drinking coffee and chatting while the rain and the wind thundered against the station's windows. On the third night of my stay, I was surprised to hear knocking on the station door followed by a bedraggled figure stumbling in. He looked familiar, but I couldn't place him, even when in his broad Yorkshire accent, he asked if he could doss down for the night. It was wild outside and I couldn't turn him out, but the room wasn't mine to allow strangers to sleep in. It was then he introduced himself as Alan Hinkes and I immediately placed him! Alan is one of Britain's most accomplished mountaineers and the only one to have successfully reached the peaks of all fourteen mountains in the world over eight thousand metres. He and a friend had been out on St Kilda scouting possible rock-climbing routes. They had arrived back in Leverburgh with no place to stay. His friend had found the last free bed in the local hostel which left Alan wandering the streets. He had looked through the lifeboat station window, seen me and decided to take his chance. I didn't say no, and we ended up becoming friends. His accounts of some of his mountaineering exploits kept me entertained well into the night.

Chapter 21

My decision to press on from Leverburgh was borne out of frustration. I left after lunch on a sweeping tide and a heaving sea. My journal entry for the day reads:

"With the tide in my favour I was swept down to Renish Point but it was on the edge stuff. I was relaxed, and I think I handled the sea state well but there was no margin for error."

The moment after leaving the safety of Leverburgh harbour, I knew I was in for a rough afternoon. The wind was from the southwest which accounted for the stormy seas. I have a recollection of thinking the run down to the point was like a rollercoaster near glistening, unfriendly looking rocks. I was relieved to finally make it around the headland and into the relative shelter beyond. I didn't have the strong tide to contend with, but the seas did not relent in their ferocity. The rugged coastline which had appeared benign on my journey south now took on a more inhospitable air with few opportunities for egress if I needed them. I wasn't about to give in, but I was wary of pushing my fortune. It's in conditions like these when mistakes are easily made. Rather than cut across the bays as I had done earlier on, I hugged the shoreline, avoiding the worst of the heaving seas. This added time and distance but afforded some security. The moments I felt most vulnerable were when rounding the headlands which marked the corner of each of these small bays. Compared to some of the mighty headlands I had encountered so far on this journey, these were geographically inconsequential. However, with the seas as they were and the wind piling them onto the rocks and skerries at their bases, they were a serious undertaking. The slightest miscalculation, either finding myself too close in to cope with the weight of the waves, or too far out, fighting the steep clapotic seas, could have caused serious problems.

I chose to keep as close to the shore as I dared, anxiously alert for rogue waves which might break and sweep me wrapped up in their surf, to dash me on the waiting slick black rocks. Àird Mhànais looked tricky the moment I saw it across Loch Fleòideabhagh, it seemed to be taking the brunt of the wild seas. I kept close in, watching for the seaward waves but failed to notice a boomer ahead. A boomer is created when a submerged reef is exposed by a receding sea and almost immediately covered by the following wave, the result of which is an eruption of white surf, cascading water and a crescendo of noise. The consequences of being caught by one of these are potentially severe, possibly resulting in a damaged kayak or worse. I realised my mistake too late when suddenly the sea opened beneath me to my right, like the Biblical tale of the Red Sea opening for Moses, except I was presented with an exposed kelp strewn reef, and huge rocks covered with fibreglass tearing barnacles. As quickly as the hole beneath appeared, an ominous crack to my right and level with my ear, told me all I needed to know. I instinctively leaned rightwards, paddle blade flat, to support myself on the powerful, frothy tumult about to occur. The breaking wave lifted me, and I felt myself being thrown sideward. I clenched my buttocks for the dreadful crunch of shattered fibreglass which would surely follow. Somehow, this did not happen, and I remember the exhilaration of riding a piling wave towards the base of the cliff a few metres away. Thankfully the wave's energy was spent seconds after being expended on the hidden reef and I was able to pull hard with my paddles and make it around the headland without further mishap.

I was a little shaken by the event and determined to make camp at the next opportunity. I could not afford to damage my kayak through my inattention. I found the perfect spot beside a holiday cottage with its own bay. The only method of reaching this lonely house it seemed was by boat or on foot through the boggy rough land behind. I've since learned the house was owned by one of Her Majesty's physicians.

The following day the conditions had considerably calmed, and it was a pleasant day to spend on the water. Not by design, the day was to be an exploratory one in nature. My drive to hastily cover the miles had burned away and I had a desire to amble along and wend my way through the islets and channels which abound along this section of the coast. The violence in the sea had totally disappeared and as always it was difficult to remember how bad the conditions had been, compared to the benign ripples which lapped like a kitten on the pebbly shore of my departure. Mol Bàn was another camping spot which had won my affections and it was a wrench to paddle away. I think the nature of the isolated house on the shore, surrounded by rough land, was exactly the kind of place I could see myself living.

It was early in the morning, and I thought I had the sea to myself, when from behind a Loch Tarbert island, a creel boat cruised over and the burly fisherman in his oily yellow waterproof trousers and checked shirt, asked if I was OK. I assured him I was, and he waved and chugged away. I wondered at this occurrence. Did I look as if I was in distress in any way? I did not take umbrage at his unsolicited concern, rather I was heartened how people of the sea were willing to look out for others and I happily concluded he was both an inquisitive and caring man.

These were otter rich waters. I was lucky to spot five throughout the morning, all active and happily oblivious to my passing presence. I'd given up attempting to photograph them from my kayak because the moment I retrieved my camera from my buoyancy aid pocket, some anti-paparazzi sense within the otters alerted them and they slipped off a rock or dived beneath the surface, never to be seen again. And anyway, when I came to view the photos later, the otter would be nothing more than a tiny speck or a furry brown blur. I took great joy in seeing them. Rounding the eastern coast of Scalpay took me under the slightly arched graceful road bridge, linking the island to the Harris mainland. It is a design which wouldn't look out of place as a road crossing on the M6 motorway, but here, on the remote wild coast of Harris, it was incongruous. It saddened me to see the bridge. I could understand the need for the development of a viable transport link for the island community in an age where travel was a necessity for work and the viability of the island economy. Developments such as these were an admittance on the part of society, we were giving up on a slower way of living to embrace a modern age governed by haste and demand. The development of transport links throughout the country have been an insidious erosion of a slower pace, encouraging us to live by shaving minutes and seconds off journey times and connection speeds. It's a frailty of the human condition to expect life to be better if we seemingly make living it easier through innovation and increased communications.

I paddled onwards and away from the bridge; my pace steady. I was in new territory, and it was spectacular. Rounding Rubha Crago I was presented with the splendour of the entrance to Loch Seaforth, all the world like a scene from Norse mythology. The gap leading into the loch was surrounded by high mountains. It appeared forbiddingly dark, beyond which lay an intriguing landscape of sea loch and more mountains. I wanted to linger, to paddle across to the opening and explore but time was ebbing away, and I had to press on. Still, I slowed down and absorbed the immensity of the scene, imagining the early mariners exploring the coastline and like me, wondering what lay beyond. The coast to my north seemed equally as wild and if it wasn't for a lonely creel boat working its way from pot to pot, I would have wondered if I had time travelled into another era. Away to my right the distinctive Shiant Isles were my constant companions. I used them as a gauge for my progress. I passed lochs cutting deep into the Lewisian landscape, Hebridean fjords, incised by mighty glaciers grinding their way out of an Ice Age ice cap, the weight of which the west Scottish coastline is recovering from, still rising centimetre by centimetre every year. For twelve miles there were no signs of permanent habitation, though evidence the hillsides, glens and bays were once worked and lived in was plain to see on the map. The area was trackless and empty of humans, though our influence was never far away.

Exploring wild coastline such as this, affirmed why it is I choose to sea kayak. I was reaching into a littoral realm rarely observed by others. The local fishermen would know this coastline intimately, but everyday folks probably would not even know this existed. It is merely a line on a map, delineating the outline of the largest island in the Outer Hebridean chain. Few would even give this section of the line on the map a second thought, eyes probably glancing to place names and tourist features. Spreading an Ordnance

Survey map of the area out and reading this like a book, would offer a plethora of intriguing questions. This is what it does for me. There was almost too much to take in, my wild country senses were on overload!

Waterfalls tumbled off high cliff edges, cascading Rapunzel tresses which tinkled into the sea. Where the fresh water mixed with the salt, bubbles scootered across the sea's surface. Sometimes a stream would simply meet the sea in a run of rapids over the shoreline rocks, reminding me of garden centre water features. The life giving dark peaty fresh water rushed headlong into the sea, ending a short journey from the rough, boulder and boggy hinterland of Lewis. These moments when streams met the sea, triggered internal reflections within me. First, I'm mesmerised by the tumbling rills and falls as they cascade over the speckled gneiss or dark basalt rocks which fringe the shore. Second, as if I were an ancient being, I view these places as spiritually unique, an opportunity to encounter a liminal threshold. This, even more so where the conjoining of fresh and salt was hidden from only those humans who travelled to these places. There is magic in the unseen, and when discovered by chance, life is enriched by the specialness of it all.

I enjoyed lingering beneath the high waterfalls, especially those I could paddle under and delight in being drenched by the cold shower, drumming a hard tattoo on my kayak deck and sounding incredibly loud as the water thudded onto the hood of my kayaking jacket. This playfulness indicated the comfort I was experiencing about the journey. Sure, I was way behind in time, but I was making good progress. I was enjoying myself!

I was soon past the lighthouse atop the headland Gob Rubha Uisinish and I looked at the map for a suitable spot to close the day and camp. My eyes immediately set on what seemed to be the perfect place, the wide bay and glen of Mul Thàgaraidh. I dug my paddles more forcefully into the surface of the slight sea and set off towards my destination for the day.

The wide bay was one of large grey rounded rocks. This made landing *Sahwira* trickier than most other times, though I managed to bring her in gently with the good fortune of managing to rest her prow between two rounded rocks and allowing the surge of the following wave to slide us through the gap without so much as a scrunch, until the kayak's hull neatly rested between the rocks around. It had been a long day in the kayak, and as always when this occurred, I ungracefully clambered out of the cockpit and with wooden legs hobbled up the shore to look at my home turf for the night.

As I crested the steep beach, my breath was taken away by the beauty before me and the deep sense of peace which prevailed. It seemed I had stepped into a parallel universe where I was a lone survivor in a world empty of human life. Laid out before me was a wide, deer cropped sward of green, roughly the size of a rugby pitch. At the back of this sheep and deer fashioned lawn, stood a single cottage, sadly forlorn, seemingly clinging to its once homely usefulness with a good covering of tiles on the roof and some panes of glass still in the windows. This was one of the most perfect spots to camp I had encountered so far. It was so wonderfully tranquil, I regretfully acknowledged this was a transitory stop.

Once I had my tent up and everything stowed away, I wandered slowly up to the cottage, half expecting a figure to appear in the doorway to invite me in. I began to imagine unseen figures carefully watching me. The sense I experienced was benign without fear. I found myself walking up to the front door of the house with the greatest respect. This was once someone's home. It would be discourteous to simply walk in and poke around the empty rooms. Despite the obvious decay and the ruination of the two downstairs rooms, I shouted out, "Helloo!" Relief at the continued silence tinged with sadness too. The house was most definitely empty of human life. I stepped across a time worn flagstone and into the house, a room on either side downstairs, and from the hallway, an intriguing if somewhat spooky flight of steep wooden stairs to the first floor. The rooms were in a sadly dishevelled state, almost as if they had been vandalised, old furniture was upturned, sheets of corrugated iron were strewn about, and a layer of bird excrement covered most of the belongings in the rooms. Neither room invited me to linger, and it was difficult to imagine them once being lived in.

The stairs however were a different story. They were clean of dust and bird mess, although with a fine coating of khaki green mildew. They rose steeply into the darkness of the floor above, where I couldn't make out any discernible features. I hesitated, gamely admitting to myself I was slightly nervous of what I might encounter up there. I was aware too the stairs and the floors above were constructed of wood and I couldn't be certain of their structural integrity. My mind was playing tricks on me, inveigling me to consider the possibility of a Stephen King character lurking in the shadows. I put my foot on the first step and pressed down hard, checking the weight bearing qualities. It was sturdy enough and I slowly ascended the stairs, each footstep emitting a resounding thud. No figures loomed out of the shadows, and I was soon on the small landing between two rooms. It was the room on the left which caught my attention and caused me to gasp out loud.

Here was a low set, simple and wonky cast iron bed with a thin and obviously lumpy coir mattress. What caught my attention though, were the blankets strewn over the bed as if they had been recently slept under and cast aside by a waking occupant. On the floor at the foot of the bed, close by the door lay an old-fashioned cardboard suitcase with leather straps and rusty buckles. The suitcase was closed, though it gave the air of only recently being so, with worn leather straps dangling and untethered. The unmade bed and the suitcase were the only items in the wood slatted room. Faintly coloured strips of wallpaper hung from the sloping walls, each strip a vestige of past inhabitants' choice of decoration.

The room to the right was empty and it too, had strips of wallpaper dangling from the sloping wooden walls. I looked back into the room with the bed, and for some inexplicable reason I did not enter it. The trunk was within reach though, and I plucked up courage to lift the lid and look inside. It was empty, lined with a faded paisley pattern. I lingered a short while longer, silently taking in the tableaux, before clumping down the stairs and striding out into the welcome sunlight. There were some panes of glass in the windows and most of the tiles on the roof appeared to be in good order. It felt the house had been vacated in the last fifteen to twenty years. Who I wondered, would have lived here? There was no road access, the house was in a glen well over twelve miles from the nearest habitation. The obvious route in and out would be by boat but it would be a tough proposition launching and landing a craft off the rocky beach in foul weather.

The romanticism belied the reality. It's always easy to look upon these remote abandoned homes as the perfect hideaway and imagine living a life of wild solitude amongst the hills and glens. However, there is a reason these places become abandoned and left to crumble into ruins. Our modern age does not support a lifestyle of primitive simplicity. If any one was to choose to live here in the twenty hundreds, then they would renounce all semblance of modern connectivity or pay a heavy financial price to change this. However, there was no harm in fantasising about a life cut off from the rest of the world. In a way, this was exactly what I was achieving through undertaking this journey. For the few hours I would be camping here, this was my hideaway from the modern world I often felt I failed to connect with.

Having thoroughly explored the environs around the house, marvelling at the beauty of the setting with a burbling burn the centre piece of it all, I wandered back to my tent and prepared my dinner, treating myself to two drams instead of the one I normally rationed myself. It was all so very perfect and the contentment with my life in that moment bubbled up to burst through my chest. I woke in the middle of the night to hear the soft pinching of grass around the tent. Slowly and as silently as I dared, I peered out to be greeted with the amazing sight of a small group of red deer grazing around on the rugby pitch like lawn. "So, it's them who mow the pitch", I murmured to myself as I snuggled deep into my sleeping bag and drifted back to sleep.

From Mul Thàgaraidh, it was an undemanding nineteen miles to Stornoway. I was sad to leave this spot and even contemplated staying an extra day, but my desire to keep moving was too strong. The sea was settled, and it was an extremely pleasant day with light winds and plenty of warm sunshine. This being my final day traversing the length of the Hebridean chain, I eked the day out, sometimes ambling along, cutting through the skerry channels and enjoying the immensity of the Lewisian landscape. I was now passing the outreaches of crofting townships with their Gaelic names which invited mispronunciation. Leumrabhagh, Grabhair, Calbost, Marbhig, Cromor, and Griomsiader. There was nothing of the picturesque about these settlements. The homes were functional, usually grey harled bungalows and sometimes more traditional two up two down designs. There were no ornate gardens to speak of and no trees. It was a landscape devoid of woodland. Eponymous fish farms studded the lochs as I paddled past and despite my distaste for them, I now accepted the importance of their presence in this unemployable landscape. The communities I paddled past were indeed kept alive by the needs and requirements of these industrial fish farms.

No matter how deliberately I lingered, I soon found myself kayaking into Stornoway Harbour. Having never been here before, I was excited to arrive if a little nervous. The possibility of paddling amongst heavy shipping was not something I looked forward to and as usual I need not have worried. There was a sleepy, laid-back feel to the harbour. I drifted past the stern of the Stornoway lifeboat noticing a hefty tow rope flaked to dry over the guard rail. I surmised the crew had been out on a shout the night before.

"You must be Nick Ray!" The shout from above belonged to Murdo Campbell, the Stornoway Lifeboat coxswain. Murty as he is better known, is someone of a legend in Scottish sea kayaking circles having several 'firsts' amongst his long list of achievements. The most notable of these being the first to kayak solo the forty long miles into the North Atlantic to the isolated islands of Sula Sgeirr and North Rona, a feat which has not been replicated. I'd been looking forward to meeting him for many years. Rather than wait to unpack *Sahwira* on the pontoon, Murty insisted we carry her fully loaded up the access ramp and lift her over the rails onto the ground next to the lifeboat station. This was easier said than done because she was heavily loaded, and I was feeling fatigued after my previous days paddling. I learned he and his crew had spent the whole night rescuing a disabled fishing trawler someway north of the Isle of Lewis, and they'd towed her across to Lochinver before returning to Stornoway in the small hours. This explained the tow rope drying on the stern rail of the lifeboat. He looked none the worse for having spent the whole night at sea.

Once I'd unpacked and stowed my kayak safely alongside the building, we went up to the crew room for the ubiquitous tea and biscuits. I was invited to stay in the lifeboat station as long as I needed, a kindness I gratefully accepted. I wanted to spend a couple of days in Stornoway, taking a break to restock on supplies and plan my strategies for the remainder of my journey. I needed to decide about my return to the Scottish mainland and where I was going to make this. Murty turned out to be great company and I enjoyed sitting chatting with him whenever I could. His sea kayaking experience is extensive and I loved listening to his stories. I found his insights useful too and the advice he offered for the future legs of my voyage. I soon learned he held no preconceptions about sea kayaking expeditionary ethics, which enabled me to feel fully relaxed exploring with him the various strategies I could employ if I ran out of time, and I needed to think about curtailing my route in whatever way. It was refreshing too, to find he held the same approach to the activity as me when it came to assessing risk and paddling solo. For both of us, it was the quality of the experience, not the technicality behind it which mattered most.

Karen posted a kayaking dry suit to me because I was having a problem with the waterproof jacket I was using. In the package she had put a card which simply stated, "You're my hero." For weeks afterwards, I would repeatedly take the card out of its envelope just to read her powerfully affectionate and affirming sentiment.

When I wasn't hanging around the lifeboat station, I wandered the narrow streets of Stornoway, buying the supplies I needed and treating myself to a couple of slap-up meals. I also met with new friends who'd been following me on Twitter which was lovely. Cathy and her husband had moved to Lewis a few years earlier from the far south of England and had made a happy life for themselves on the island, both finding the relaxed and unhurried lifestyle suited them. I met with an old Outward Bound colleague which was lovely. Tim and I hadn't seen each other since the early 1990s. I was also invited into their home by complete strangers who happened to bump into me when they were returning home from attending a funeral. I just happened to be by their house, and we got chatting. I ended up staying for dinner which was a riotously funny and happy evening.

However, I couldn't remain in this Hebridean idyll forever and because it was mid-summer, I wanted to move on. I had eventually decided my route back to the mainland would be via the Shiant Isles as I had always wanted. It was exciting to think I would be camping on them the next day, 21st June and the apogee of the northern summer.

Chapter 22

Murty collected me from the lifeboat station at the early hour we had arranged, and we hurriedly loaded my kayak onto his car's roof rack and threw my kit into the boot. It was a fair distance from Stornoway to the crofting settlement of Leumrabhagh where I would set out on the nine and a half mile crossing to the Shiant Isles. I was experiencing an uneasy feeling of guilt at not paddling from Stornoway, but Murty was insistent receiving a lift to shorten the distance was well within the ethics of an expedition. I didn't need much persuading to accept his offer of a lift because it meant I would not be covering coastline I had already travelled.

We arrived at the road end by the concrete pier in the crofting hamlet. Being a Sunday, there was no sign of life, and we unloaded my kayak and kit onto the grass beside the road. Without any ceremony, Murty and I shook hands, said our farewells and he drove off. I looked out to sea and the far-off islands. They didn't appear to be too difficult to reach and the conditions were wonderfully calm. I was confident this would be a straightforward crossing. I set about packing the kayak and donning my new paddling-suit. This was the first time I had worn it, so it took some getting used to. With practiced ease, everything was stowed, and I was nearly ready for the off. All that was required were the spare paddles to be secured in their position on the rear deck. Paddles? I looked around. They were nowhere to be seen and a dreadful realisation dawned on me. I had left them at the lifeboat station!

My immediate response was one of disappointment. The conditions were perfect for the crossing and it was 21st June. I wanted to be on the islands to enjoy the long light hours of the midsummer night. The disappointment was quickly replaced with anger. I berated myself for my foolishness for not checking I had everything before leaving. I couldn't believe after all the weeks of kayaking I failed to notice I hadn't packed my paddles, fundamental items for the adventure. The anger eventually dissipated into frustration when I realised to solve my predicament, I would have to either phone Murty and ask him to collect my paddles and bring them out, or I would have to make my way back to Stornoway and retrieve them myself. I was reluctant to call Murty for two reasons. Firstly, I was embarrassed, and this was a rooky mistake to make by someone who purports to be an experienced expeditionary kayaker. Secondly, it was Sunday and he had already given his time to help me with the lift. I found myself in a quandary. I did not want to delay my crossing to the Shiants because the following day's forecast was marginal. The only way I could hope to achieve this was to phone Murty.

The desire to make the crossing outweighed my embarrassment and consideration for Murty's day of rest, so I dug my phone out of the day hatch and switched it on. No signal! I wasn't surprised but not defeated. I reckoned if I walked a couple of miles back up the road to the high point before it dropped down towards the coast, I would find a signal up there. So, still attired in my paddling-suit, I set off walking up the road. By the time I reached the point I assumed would provide a line-of-sight connection to the hoped-for certainty of a far-off phone mast, I was a sweaty mess inside my suit. I switched the phone on again and let out a cry of frustrated rage. Still no signal! For a few minutes I continued to look at the screen of the phone, willing the signal bars to begin showing. I even hoped the faint breeze would blow a signal through the ether. Magical thinking aside, I was now at a loss as to what to do. I looked around, scouting the rising ground behind the road, wondering if it was worth attempting to gain more height to find a signal. I didn't entertain this idea for long, instead deciding to head back to my kayak down by the pier and decide what to do from there. In any case, I had to accept the window for making the crossing today was closing. I could see a bank of cloud building and rolling towards me, indicating the freshening winds and heavy rain which had been forecast.

Once back at the kayak, I decided to give up retrieving my paddles that day. It was a Sunday, so there was no bus service. Equally, I didn't want to attempt to hitch hike because of the sensitivities about activity on the Sabbath. I was stuck here! Then it dawned on me. Murty would notice my YB Tracker had not shifted, and he might come back to see what was happening. He would then be able to give me a lift back to Stornoway. It occurred to me this possibility was exactly what I had been trying to avoid in the first place, that of disturbing him on the Sunday. I conceded there was little I could do about this eventuality and set about unpacking my kayak and making camp, slightly up the hill from the pier. As I did so, it began to rain.

I managed to get everything into my tent before the deluge ensued. I sat morosely in the tent deafened by the drumming of the near tropical rain on the flysheet. My spirits were dipping, and I was at a low ebb. Disappointment characterised my thinking and I realised I needed to do something to distract myself from my deepening thoughts. I was well behind with my journal, so I dug this out, and wrapped up in my sleeping bag, I was soon ensconced in writing up my memories of the preceding days. The hours slipped by and still the rain hammered down on the tent until it was late enough to consider making something to eat. It occurred it might have been divine retribution rather than foolishness on my part which had resulted in the paddles being forgotten. After all, it was the Sabbath and I had insisted on breaking it.

The next morning, Monday, I was up and away from the tent by six. I had a three mile walk to the hamlet of Glenside where I could catch the first bus to Stornoway. The rain had subsided to a steady drizzle which didn't lift my mood very much. It was the hour it took to walk to the bus top which reversed my sour mood. Fingers of wispy cloud drifted around the hillsides and through the glens like ethereal wraiths. The air was crisply clear, and the landscape was freshly laundered by the rain from the night before. It was beautiful. At the bus stop, I joined the small group of commuters waiting for their workday journey into town. Unlike commuters in the cities though, this waiting group were animatedly chatting to each other and as I arrived, greeted me with as much warmth as they did others arriving after me.

The journey into Stornoway was a convivial affair with conversations being thrown around inside the small bus from person to person. I wasn't left out either, with considerable interest being shown in what I was up to and the purpose of my kayaking expedition. However, I omitted to let on I had attempted to set off from Leumrabhagh the previous day, on Sunday. Arriving in Stornoway, I made haste to the lifeboat station only to find it locked. I was now in a hurry because I wanted to catch the next bus out of Stornoway and make my way back to my camp. Remembering the volunteer lifeboat operations manager owned a shop across the street from station, I popped across there and asked him if I could borrow a key to let myself in and collect my paddles.

It wasn't long before I was back on a bus rattling out of Stornoway along the peat fringed road southwards towards Harris. The bus dropped me off at the intersection for the road to Leumrabhagh where I would catch another bus back to Glenside. I settled down to wait. Half an hour later it dawned on me I had made another mistake. I had misread the timetable and there would not be a bus to Glenside for another couple of hours. I had no map, so I wasn't sure how far the road was to Leumrabhagh. Knowing the distance wouldn't have mattered, because I decided to set off on foot along the track anyway. I would much rather keep moving than wait at an exposed road junction with heavy traffic rumbling by. In any case, there might be the possibility of being offered a lift.

The walk was tedious and none of the drivers of the vehicles passing me seemed inclined to offer a lift. Eventually, a car did pull over and I gratefully climbed in, even though it was a short five-minute hop to the driver's home, still a long distance from where I wanted to get to. Undeterred, I pressed on. I walked past a house where a couple of sea kayaks lay on the garden lawn. A man in a checked lumberjack shirt was chopping wood in an adjoining field. By now I was feeling too tired to care much and kept walking. Minutes later I heard a car behind and then the briefest of toots from its horn. The driver pulled up beside me and asked, "Are you Nick Ray, the sea kayaker?"

I recognised the checked shirt and held one of my paddles aloft, waving it, "Yes, that's me!" My heart soared.

"Hop in" he invited. "Where are you heading for?"

"The pier Leumrabhagh" I responded, conscious of my mispronunciation of the crofting settlement's name.

"No worries" he grinned, "I saw you walk past and your paddles, so I guessed who you might be. I'm with the Stornoway kayaking club and I've been following your progress. Quite a trip you're doing."

"Thanks, it's been a good one so far – that is until I forgot my paddles at the lifeboat station." I smiled a wry, self-depreciating smile. "I'm looking forward to the Shiants though."

He laughed heartily and drove on. "It can be a dodgy crossing," he suddenly said.

"Yes, I'm pretty nervous" I agreed. I waited for a response and for the conversation to continue, but it didn't. He was pretty much silent the rest of the way to the pier and my camp spot.

After he had driven off, I felt the solitude descend on me again. The weight of coming to a decision to make the crossing now, or not, felt cumbersome. There was a strong southerly breeze and the sea seemed unsettled. I picked up my small binoculars and studied the horizon. It was lumpy out there, but I couldn't see many white horses. The tide was running southwards, and this would be in my favour. I stood a moment longer and then without any further vacillation, I set about striking camp and packing for departure. In just under an hour, I was sliding my laden kayak off the slippery pebbles next to the grey concrete pier and climbing into the cockpit. I was soon on my way, departing the Outer Hebrides and outward bound for the Shiant Isles nine miles distant.

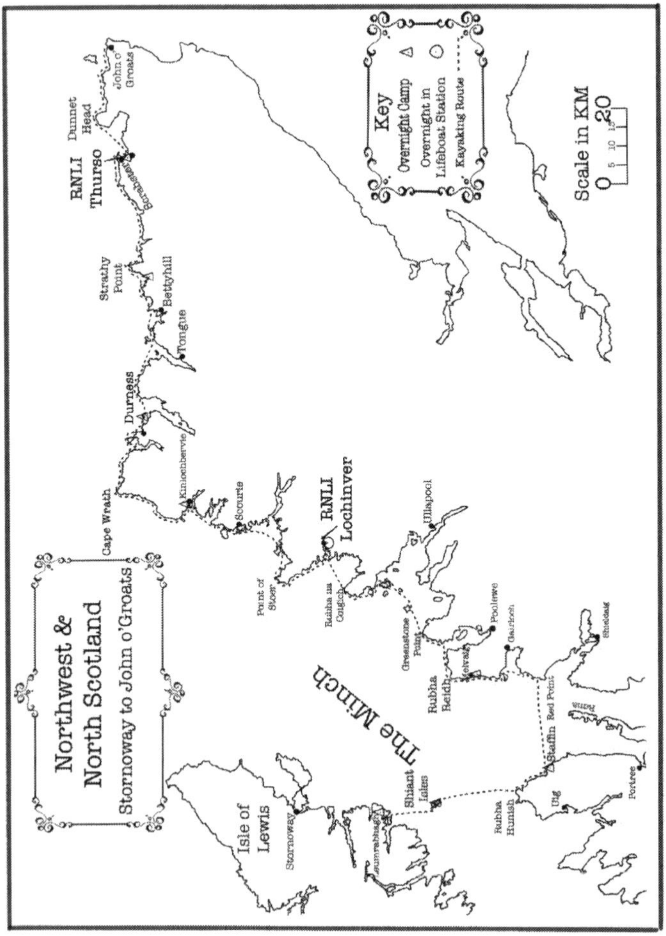
Northwest &
North Scotland
Stornoway to John o'Groats
Key
Overnight Camp
Overnight in Lifeboat Station
Kayaking Route
Scale in KM
0 5 10 15 20
The Minch
Isle of Lewis
Stornoway
Shiant Isles
Rubha Hunish
Uig
Portree
Staffin
Red Point
Rubha Reidh
Greenstone Point
Poolewe
Gairloch
Shieldaig
Ullapool
Rubha na Coigich
Point of Stoer
RNLI Lochinver
Scourie
Kinlochbervie
Cape Wrath
Durness
Tongue
Bettyhill
Strathy Point
RNLI Thurso
Dunnet Head
John o' Groats

Northwest And North Scotland Stornoway to John o' Groats

Chapter 23

Out of the shelter of Loch Sealg I encountered the lumpy conditions I had observed through my binoculars. As I suspected, the lumpiness was more akin to a sea of watery hillocks, like a drumlin strewn valley at the base of the mountains. The sea wallowed in rounded heavy lumps of water which had no rhythm to them whatsoever. If the waves were dancing, then this was Dad-dancing at its finest! Consequently, I found it challenging to paddle forwards with any consistency. *Sahwira* in response to the conditions lolloped herself, sliding into troughs in a lazy fashion, only to suddenly kick to port or starboard when a wave licked her stern or slapped her bow. In the troughs I couldn't see any land mass at all, the waves looming above at least twice my sitting height. I maintained forward momentum with irregular paddle strokes interjected with stern-rudders, sweep strokes and a good many hastily executed support strokes. Strangely, I was enjoying myself despite the incredible feeling of solitary exposure. I had come a long way since my nervous five-mile crossing to the Isle of Arran from the Cowal Peninsula many weeks previously. Fear was present though, a gnarly knot in my stomach and in my mind. The fear was in the form of large shipping which made use of the channel between the Shiant Isles and mainland Hebrides for their southward passage through the Minch. In these lumpy conditions, I knew I would be extremely difficult to spot from the bridge of any container ship or oil tanker cruising at a steady fifteen knots. It didn't help I had Murty's salutary tale of a kayaking trip he and friends were enjoying out to the Shiants when they encountered a cargo ship. They were mid-crossing and the ship bore down on them with no deviation to its course. Murty attempted to call them up on his VHF radio to no avail. In the end he realised there was no point in continuing trying and they had to paddle like buggery [sic] to get out of the path of the looming vessel. Of course, he lived to tell the tale, but it was a close-run thing. I did not want this to happen to me.

It was entirely possible it may not be a ship which might see my demise in these waters for I was now in the *Sea-stream of the Blue Men*, the realm of the mythical Blue Men of the Minch. Living in caves, deep beneath the grey seas I was now ploughing my way through, lived mermen with long grey faces wearing blue bonnets, who would prey on mariners plying the Caolas nan Eilean – the Sound of Shiant. Also known as Storm Kelpies, they could raise a stormy sea if they were enraged by a mariner's slight. It is said they might often be seen swimming closely but never within reach in a craft's wake. If this were the case, the captain of the boat would have to have their wits about them for the chief of the Blue Men would enter a sparring duel, shouting out two lines of quizzical rhyme which the skipper must emulate to complete the verse. It was an unfortunate crew if their captain failed to find the rhymes to complete the chief's stanzas because their ship would be sunk in the stormy seas the Blue Men would create. The mythology of the Blue Men is unique to this stretch of sea and the Hebrides and does not occur elsewhere around the Scottish coast. The origins of the story are unclear but there is one theory the Blue Men existed in the form of Moors or Tuaregs slaves attired in their flowing blue robes and headdresses, brought through these lands by Norse seafarers. Another historical explanation might be they were Picts crossing the Minch in kayak like craft, their heavily blue tattooed torsos visible just above the surface of the sea as they paddled. Whatever the etymology of the myth, I wasn't anxious to prove its veracity and I paddled on a steady course for the islands, which rose and fell beyond my horizon as I wallowed in the restless dark sea.

It was an enormous sense of relief to paddle into the sheltered lee of the looming flanks of Garbh Eilean, with all movement in the sea suddenly ceasing. I breathed a thankful sigh of satisfaction. I had made it across the sound without mythological mishap or being run down by modern reality. At last I was here, the islands for which I had long held a desire to reach ever since reading *Sea Room* by Adam Nicolson, the owner of these isolated Hebridean atolls. Sadly though, solitude wasn't going to be possible on this occasion, spotting a cluster of tents beside the red roofed bothy and a couple of large yachts anchored in the bay. I wasn't surprised. After all, it was mid-summer and these islands have been a draw for wild-island enthusiasts for decades. I was one of them. I set up my camp a couple of hundred metres away from the bothy and the encampment. I wasn't too perturbed by the presence of others and looked forward to possibly spending a convivial evening chatting with likeminded wilderness seekers. I wandered up to the house, which was once the shepherd's abode, to where three people were sitting on upturned fish boxes with mugs of tea in their hands. They acknowledged my arrival with suspicious hostility. I immediately sensed I wouldn't be welcome to have a look into the bothy which they had made their home. It transpired they were part of a group of environmentalists surveying the population of Black Rats, *Rattus rattus*, which were unique to the island, this being one of the very few places where they could be found in Britain. This survey was part of a project to eventually eliminate all rats on the islands because of the conflict between them and the abundant nesting sea bird populations. I wanted to chat with these young environmentalists longer, because this matter was of great interest, but I sensed I was intruding. I walked on from the bothy to explore the island on my own.

Climbing to the one hundred and fifty-metre-high summit of Eilean an Taighe, I was afforded with the most spectacular views up, down and across to both sides of the Minch. The cleansed air after the previous day's heavy rainfall, allowed me to enjoy a panoply of vistas in every direction I turned. I felt privileged to be where I was, and my heart swelled with emotion. This was a moment in my life I had long aspired to experience and everything I anticipated it would be, was fulfilled. Despite the presence of the ecologists by the bothy, I had the feeling of being truly alone. The sounds I could hear were those uttered by the hundreds of birds hurtling around the skies above and the whispering murmur of the surf on the rocks at the base of the vertiginous cliffs far below. So often in moments of solitude in wild locations such as this, I experience a primal awakening within and because it emerges from the depths of my core, it's a process which is difficult to describe. It's as if all my debilitating inhibitions have been locked away, and my true spirit has been set free. My heart soared and joined the sea birds above, screaming through the air as loudly and as joyfully as they were. I was liberated of internal angst and depressive pain. My eyes saw nothing but beauty and the possibilities this held. Moments like this are bodily absorbed and seared into my memory banks. In this way, when I feel the need to reconnect with wildness, I transport myself through vibrant recollections to places and times spent in them, such as this.

I sat atop the island for a couple of hours, gazing in every direction open to me. I watched a large red bulk carrier, one of the ships I had so feared when I was making my crossing earlier, make its way down through the Sound of Shiant to eventually disappear over the horizon of the southern Minch. I gazed mainland-wards, wondering about what lay ahead and the journey I had yet to complete. My mind was filled with the anticipation for new experiences and further exciting encounters. The opportunities before me seemed endless and ripe for the picking.

I descended to my camp, weaving and ducking as I rounded the northern flank of the hill to avoid a belligerent bonxie which took exception to my presence on its patch. The skua repeatedly flew at my head with alarming precision, seemingly threatening to scalp me with its fearsome beak whenever I attempted to hold my nerve and stand erect rather than ducking in pitiful fear. Every time I tried this, I couldn't help flinching at the last moment, feeling the rush of air caused by its low pass, ruffle my unkempt hair. A couple of times I turned to face the bonxie square on, eye to eye, almost as if we were gunslingers in a gold-rush town street, about to slug it out. The bonxie won every one of these encounters with me ducking down, each time instinctively flinging my arms up, to ward off the thumping blow which I feared would surely happen.

That night I slept the soundest sleep I had enjoyed for many weeks, lulled by the surf on the rocks and the continuous avian chattering from the cliffs around.

It was a sadness to depart the island idyll of the Shiants. I didn't think I had given them my attention and deep down, I felt I had cheated myself. I continued to feel an annoyance at my enforced night on Lewis because of the blunder with my paddles. This mistake denied me the two nights I wished for on the islands. This was a harsh reminder of the transiency I bore as an expeditionary kayaker. I would never develop a meaningful attachment to a place because of my nomadic existence. I wanted to stay on the islands, even for one day more, to briefly allow some deeper connection to occur. Sadly, I rigidly kept to my waning timeline and set off early in the morning.

I had not made up my mind whether to paddle across the Minch to the mainland from the islands, or to make my way down the seaway with the assistance of the tide to Skye. The sea was unsteady with a deep rolling swell. The day was hazy, and it was difficult to usefully ascertain features on the distant coastline. My confidence too was rattled from the lively seas the day before. I craved an easy day on the sea. It was no surprise then, I quickly decided to use the tide and the running swell and head for Skye. The choice made, my inner tension eased, the day became suddenly brighter. I enjoyed the company of fleets of puffins swimming comically away as I kayaked by, their legs beneath them, obviously working hard to push them through the languid sea. The guillemots were less jumpy and far more impassive as my kayak glided past them.

My destination after the Shiants was the once busy fishing port of Lochinver where there was a lifeboat station with an all-weather lifeboat. It took me four days to reach the quaint town nestling on the coast on the edge of the wild lands of Assynt with its easily recognisable mountains, including the iconic Suilven which gave the appearance of looming right over the town as I approached from the sea. I had paddled via Skye, across to the mainland north of the Isle of Rona, then northwards along the coast, stopping for a night to meet my Outward Bound friends, Chris and Fran at their Melvaig croft, before wending my way through the lovely Summer Isles and onward to Lochinver. The welcome I received from the lifeboat station team was customarily warm and generous. I was given space in their crew room for the night, and it was lovely to make use of their hot shower. I used the opportunity too to get some shopping done for vitally needed supplies, knowing full well I had a long stretch ahead where I'd have to be self-sustaining for several days.

From Lochinver I was heading for the small fishing village of Kinlochbervie high on the northwest coast of Scotland. This would be my last port of call before tackling the mighty Cape Wrath, the northwest corner of mainland Britain. Before reaching this destination though, I had the challenge of rounding the Point of Stoer to contend with. This headland jutting out into the northern Minch waters had a fearsome tidal reputation and I found myself becoming anxious about meeting it. I gleaned all I could about the seas I could expect from members of the lifeboat crew and rather unusually, I was careful to delay my departure from Lochinver to ensure I arrived at the headland when the tidal flow was its weakest. I need not have worried myself. The paddle around the bastion like headland with its distinctive lighthouse atop was a delightful experience in the bright summer sunshine. The top of the cliffs by the lighthouse are a favourite spot for keen whale watchers to gaze out into the Minch, and I was aware of countless pairs of binoculars following me as I wended my way through the almost silent skerries, a few hundred feet below. After leaving Lochinver I made it as far as the delightful hamlet of Scourie where once again I was shore-bound for a day by strong winds. From here it was an easy if gustily windy paddle to Kinlochbervie where I found shelter amongst the once thriving sheds which served the long-gone fishing fleets.

I waited in Kinlochbervie yet another day for the weather conditions to settle, before I embarked on the one challenge I had long been aspiring for, rounding Cape Wrath.

Chapter 24

The alarm I had set on my phone went off surprisingly loudly at three in the morning, trilling me to wakefulness with its bee-boppy melody. I didn't linger in the luxurious warmth of my sleeping bag and immediately set about preparing myself for the day ahead. As the water came to the boil for my first coffee of the day, I was aware of a knot of anxiety deep in my stomach. There was a palpable sense of excitement too. Rounding Cape Wrath had been high on my kayaking bucket list for many years, and it felt anomalous my opportunity to realise this had finally arrived. The feeling I was experiencing was not unlike waking on a childhood Christmas morning, when the preceding weeks and days of interminable anticipation had created a heightened level of eagerness, eventually to climax in a gift wrap tearing frenzy.

By five, before the sun had risen, I was silently slipping out of Kinlochbervie harbour through a glassily calm sea. The dipping blades of my paddles created the only sound and even this seemed muted, almost as if I were a fugitive intent on escaping the slumbering village undetected. An otter unexpectedly appeared from the depths a few metres away on my starboard bow, surfacing like a cork with a large brown crab in its jaws. I ceased paddling, allowing my kayak to drift silently by while I watched the sleek creature swim for the nearby rocky shore to devour its crustaceous breakfast. Realising the otter was quite unconcerned by my presence I continued paddling and set my course westwards out of the confines of Loch Inchard for the open sea. Cape Wrath was fifteen wild miles and four hours away.

As I was steadily leaving Kinlochbervie astern, the sun slowly lifted itself over the wild north-west Sutherland landscape to create one of those glorious sunrises which take my breath away. What with seeing the otter a few minutes earlier and now the incredible sunrise, I felt the portents for the day to be inspirationally powerful. It seemed a worthy reward for having decided to wait so long ashore for the arrival of stable conditions.

I had made an early start to the day to utilise the favourable northward flowing tide which would sweep me up to Cape Wrath. The forecast was settled, and I didn't anticipate any surprises to concern me through the day. It felt good to relax and set a steady paddling rhythm. I kept a wary distance from the coastline because there was a residual swell which heaved itself onto the rocks in crashing booms and eruptions of spray. It was one of those days at sea, when all factors converged in unison to produce sea kayaking perfection.

As I predicted, the tide picked me up as the tiny rocky island of Am Balg hove into sight. Soon after this I spotted the distinctive sea stack of Am Buachaille, *'the shepherd'*, standing proudly erect from the surrounding cliffs. Despite the early hour, the sun was climbing high into a cloudless sky and there lingered over the surface of the wallowing sea, a salt laden haze, kicked up by the surf crashing into the far-off expanse of Sandwood Bay. The atmosphere was ethereal, adding an element of mystery to the day. Indeed, the finger like sea stack appeared to ominously point in a Tolkienesque fashion, northwards to the far-off Cape Wrath headland. I was now in the firm and helpful grip of the tidal travellator, so I eased back on my paddling and enjoyed floating past the sea stack, which like the Old Man of Stoer, was a rock climber's dream. It was first climbed by the indomitable

Tom Patey in the late '60s. I snapped away with my camera, hoping to catch the perfect image.

Despite my earlier eagerness to reach the iconic headland of Cape Wrath, there was rising within me a sense of melancholy. These were my last few hours of exploring the west coast of Scotland and soon I would be turning east, marking a definitive point in my journey. It dawned on me a significant moment in my life was only a few miles away. With growing awareness, I realised I was about to complete one of Britain's great sea kayaking challenges, that of traversing the length of the west coast of Scotland. For a few brief moments, I did not want to leave the west coast seas and landscape. It's familiar territory and reaching Cape Wrath marked a liminal moment in my odyssey. From this point on I would be exploring seas previously unseen by me and ones which I held in awe. This was the infamous 'Roof of Britain' and I was fearful of what lay ahead.

I decided I didn't want to drag things out, so I picked up my pace and set myself to the task of reaching the Cape as soon as I could. I was now determined to make good time. I chose to keep well out of Sandwood Bay to avoid being sucked in by the heavy surf which I could hear thumping onto the golden sands of the extensive beach, one of the popular vistas of wild Scotland which can only be reached on foot or by kayak. Beyond the one-and-a-half-mile long strand stretched the rugged and shelter-less cliffs leading to Cape Wrath. If I looked carefully, I could just make out the pimple like speck of the lighthouse atop the far headland. Seeing this made me gulp with nervousness because it reinforced the enormity of my day and the fearsome reputation and the remoteness of the headland I had yet to round.

What normally would have taken a couple of hours only took one. With the tide and an unbroken paddling rhythm, I proceeded towards Cape Wrath at a steady six miles an hour. It felt effortless and I enjoyed the sensation of easily cruising past the rugged cliff landscape. By now the headland of the Cape was clearly defined. The lighthouse sat aloft, its perpendicular presence marking the very northwest point of human habitation on the British mainland. The name Cape Wrath is derived from the Old Norse word of *hvarf*, meaning 'turning point', the moment the ancient Norse seafarers turned their craft either eastwards for their home in Scandinavia or south-westwards for the plunder rich lands of west-Scotland and even Ireland. I was hardly a Viking in a mighty longboat, but in my own way, I was nearing my own significant turning point.

Suddenly, there appeared rushing through the sea towards me, a rounded projectile, a torpedo in fact! The water around its distinctive rounded nose was piled up as it sped towards me. I almost yelled out in shock and back paddled frantically, heaving my kayak sideward to the left in a mighty attempt to avoid being hit. The torpedo was only a matter of metres away when suddenly it dived under the surface. My panic rose again as I searched for it with wide alarmed eyes. Then it appeared, grey-green and threatening. We bore down on each other but thankfully now not on course for an explosive collision. Then as suddenly as my fear had been sparked, so was a rush of embarrassed relief. The torpedo was nothing more than a lobster pot buoy which was at the limit of its tether to the accompanying pot deep below the sea and which because of this, was being tugged frantically on its rope by the driving tide, creating the effect of a surging projectile. If it wasn't because the seas around Cape Wrath are an active military live-firing range, I would not have thought this, but for a few frightening seconds, I believed I'd heard the wrong firing dates from Charlie, and I had inadvertently paddled into a military exercise.

I soon found myself arriving at Cape Wrath. My embarrassment forgotten; I was assailed by a flood of emotion. I stopped paddling, resting my paddles on my spray deck. I sat stock still and allowed *Sahwira* to drift slowly past the high cliffs of the outlying Stac an Dùnain. It seemed to me, even the forceful tide eased its speed in reverential acknowledgement. My many long-held fears about this moment failed to materialise. There was no fearsome tide race, and neither were huge breakers crashing onto the base of the cliffs, creating a chaotic sea which would have made paddling hazardous. Instead, it was a moment of incredible serenity. It was as if I had been presented with a gift and this was a pure moment in my life to enjoy.

I gazed around. I was at the far north-western point of mainland Britain. Seawards lay thousands of miles of open North Atlantic Ocean. I felt myself at the edge of the world. Looming above me were the mighty cliffs of the Cape. I had to arch my neck to gaze up and when I did, the sense of awe was increased. Sea birds of all species studded the sky, wheeling, diving, mewing, screeching and calling. The cacophony was incredible. Razorbills floated nearby, impassively gazing at me, almost as if they were assessing my wonderment. The lighthouse which had been a distinctive point of human reference, was now out of sight. Without its visual company, my sense of solitude increased. There were no signs of human presence. In that very moment, I was the only person in existence on the sea at Cape Wrath. The enormity of this realisation flooded my already heavily stimulated senses. It felt my outdoor career, all my sea kayaking experience, indeed my life in general, had guided me to this very moment. I sat motionless, a human speck in a small sea kayak, amidst the magnificence of geography, geology, oceanography and cacophonic nature that is Cape Wrath. I could have felt insignificant, but I didn't. In fact, the opposite. I felt hugely significant. This was *my* place in the world, a completely wild, untamed landscape which had required my determination, spirit and effort to attain. This wasn't an 'Instagram' selfie moment, proclaiming my adventurous prowess. It was a moment of intimacy with the world I lived in, and more significantly, a moment of intimacy with myself.

A sea kayaking guidebook wrote of rounding cape Wrath in a sea kayak; *"Cape Wrath is as 'out there' as it gets on mainland Britain and with a lively ocean under you and soaring impregnable cliffs above you, it will feel like it! This is not a section of coastline to get caught out on. There are few landing spots, these often with the potential for big surf and challenging walk-outs. The headland of Cape Wrath is fully exposed to the Atlantic and rarely will there be a day without much swell, so whatever direction it comes from it will have an effect on how this trip goes. Ideal conditions are required, light winds and minimal swell."*

I had this description running through my mind when I had approached the headland, but now I was here, it seemed benign and almost kindly. It wasn't lost on me when I was at Lochinver Lifeboat Station a week or so earlier, I had listened to the tale, recounted in a typically understated manner by Stuart Gudgeon one of the crew during the shout, of the incredible rescue of the fish carrying ship *Norholm* conducted under these very cliffs on the 7th of

December 2014. In dreadful conditions, with seas of ten metre waves and gale force winds, the Lochinver Lifeboat, helmed by the Coxswain David MacAskill, took the beleaguered ship under tow and drew her away from certain destruction and possible loss of life on the seething rocks. This act of valour and an incredible display of seamanship by helm and crew over the twelve hours, where the tow parted twice, and the lifeboat manoeuvred in towering seas, earned David the rarely bestowed R.N.L.I. Bronze Medal and the six other members of crew, R.N.L.I. Letters of Thanks.

I'm not the only mariner to look upon the Cape with reverential awe. My friend Charlie, in his early years in the military and when he was a junior officer in the Navy, requested to be on watch on the bridge of HMS Invincible as she steamed out of the Pentland Firth, around Cape Wrath and into the expanse of the Atlantic. He described this as a deeply spiritual moment in his life when he alone was responsible for the ship as she rounded this iconic geographical point. Brian Wilson eloquently described his experience of rounding the Cape in his kayak in the '80s, *"It had for me the quality of a vision, a glimpse into the future of my journey. I felt beauty, privilege, and all the conquering awe of the first primitive seafarers who, also in manpowered boats, challenged these grim northern seas, and must have been rewarded with a view little different to this."*

Sadly, it was time to move on and I shook myself out of my reverie. I looked down at my compass and saw I was now on a south-east heading. I had turned the corner! Ahead, right under the mighty cliffs of the headland were a couple of inviting sea arches. The closest one to the base of the cliff was like a gateway, a portal to another world. It felt symbolic this was there, as if by passing through it, I was committing myself to the middle of my long journey. I paddled towards the great arch, and despite the calm conditions, I moved forwards tentatively, keeping a wary watch for rogue waves which might thrust me onto the rocks at the base of the mighty cliff. Instead though, the sea simply breathed calmly, lifting me and dropping me gently with every Atlantic exhalation as the swell arrived at this north-west bastion. The closer I got to the cliffs, the louder the cacophony of sea bird cries became, until it was almost unbearable. The pungent fishy odour of their guano was equally potent, but neither the intense noise or rancid smell could overpower this incredible experience.

Still using my paddles sparingly, as if attempting to eke out every glorious minute of my presence in this wondrous cathedral of nature's grandeur, I slowly entered the great arch and crept my way through. Cormorants dropped off greasy ledges under the roof of the arch, splashing into the feather littered sea, and then with frenzied wingbeats half-flew and half-swam away. I felt guilty at having disturbed them. I paddled forward unhurriedly, not wanting this moment to end. I wanted to linger and soak in the incredible atmosphere, one which I had experienced only once before when guiding sea kayaking clients around the west coast of the island of Mingulay at the southern tip of the Outer Hebrides. Here too the cliffs were immense with a sense of being at the edge of the known world. This time though, unlike then, I was alone. Solitude heightened my senses, so every fibre of my being was exquisitely stimulated.

Then I was through. Cape Wrath was no longer ahead, it was now astern. To view it I had to twist my body or turn my kayak. The cliff scenery ahead was no less grand but somehow, suddenly, the exposure and awesomeness had diminished. This was again like a memory from a childhood post-gift sharing and post-dinner Christmas Day. My excitement no longer existed, but instead there remained the hushed pleasure of perusing my gifts, satisfied by good food. This is almost exactly what I was feeling as I strengthened my paddling strokes and made away from the headland and set my course now along the North Coast of Scotland. I was satiated.

Chapter 25

I thoroughly enjoyed the north coast of Scotland and as so often during my voyage, I regretted not giving it the time I would have liked. My ultimate destination for this leg was Thurso, more specifically Scrabster, fifty-six miles from Cape Wrath. It took me three days to traverse this section of wild coastline with its incredible beaches, cave studded cliffs, numerous natural arches, many offshore islands, powerful tidal streams and always the unbelievable vibrancy of sea bird life. While I enjoyed experiencing the north coast, this may have been the few days during my adventure I felt my solitude slip into loneliness. Despite the wondrous sights I witnessed, or maybe because of them, I would've loved to have shared the company of a close friend. The night I camped high on the cliff, my tent pitched amongst a glorious profusion of purple orchids, overlooking the golden emptiness of Armadale Bay, I encountered a void within my experience, almost as if I was looking over the beauty before me with dispassionate, hollow eyes. This was the night before I would reach Thurso and the lifeboat station there. It was now well into early July, and I'd been paddling on my own for nine weeks. The kayaking through the north coast seas wasn't particularly demanding. The winds were kind in their moderation and apart from one impressive and frightening thunderstorm, I'd enjoyed settled weather. All that was required to reach this point, was getting the tidal flows correct and keeping a wary eye when rounding the three main headlands of the stretch. I was looking forward to reaching another lifeboat station and enjoying the company of others.

Next day I couldn't help but think of Old Holborn tobacco and rolling cigarettes. I could picture the packaging, even though I'm not a smoker. This was because the final headland of my day was Holborn Head, guarding the western entrance to Thurso Bay. Having felt like I had survived the reef breaks of Brims Ness earlier in the day, I enjoyed the three miles of lumpy but unbroken sea under the mighty cliffs of Ness of Litter and Spear Head. I was even enticed into a huge cave, entering with my customary caution to find myself in a wonderfully atmospheric cavern. It was so deep, as I ventured further in, I had to rely on my sense of hearing to guide me rather than my sight. Gurgles and splashes helped reference my position in relation to the cave walls. I had an impression of the thousands of tonnes of rock above and how I was venturing underground in my kayak.

I reached Holborn Head where a large sea stack known as Clett stood off from the cliffs, creating a long passageway through which I could paddle, cutting a couple hundred metres off the day's journey. As I entered the geo I suddenly felt destabilised. I experienced the distinct sensation of paddling downhill. In fact, I responded to this uneasiness by paddling backwards to prevent myself from rushing down the watery slope. It was an odd experience indeed. The cause of this mind blowing natural optical illusion, was due to the strata on the cliffs flanking the geo. The lines in the rock sloped upwards from sea level giving the impression they were parallel, and it was the sea's surface which was dropping away from me. Arriving at the other end of the geo, which felt like the bottom of it, I looked back and experienced the strange optical illusion again, this time it felt as if I were looking up a steep ramp of water. I shook my head in amazement and continued my way.

Exiting the geo, I paddled slap bang into a feisty tide race. It caught me completely by surprise and to add to my confusion, I couldn't work out what direction the sea was flowing. I was completely thrown! It was a nasty piece of water, a sea state which appeared intent on tipping me over. I rarely anthropomorphise nature, but in this instance, I wondered what I had done to incur this level of malevolence. The waves weren't big, but they were sharp and forceful. Their chaotic irregularity created uncertainty in my mind and my confidence in my paddling ability took a sudden dive. I found myself breathing in hurried gasps and whispering to myself over and again, "Come on Nick, keep it together. You can do this!"

I felt like I was a novice kayaker again, my paddles flailing in desperate support strokes as I steadfastly kept a semblance of forward momentum. It transpired the flow was pushing me into the bay, but I couldn't work out why there should be a tide race in this location. There was little wind to speak of, so it wasn't wind over tide. This turmoil was extremely unsettling, and I was perplexed. It was with huge relief when I eventually found my way to Scrabster Harbour without capsizing. It was a testing finish to a long stretch of eight days kayaking from Lochinver. I was looking forward to arriving at the Thurso lifeboat station, having someone to chat to, and more than anything, a long hot shower.

I paused at the entrance to the Scrabster harbour, wondering whether I could find a place to land my kayak and unload. The Thurso lifeboat was in plain sight, and I could see the station building on the quay behind her. I was reluctant to enter the harbour because I was intimidated by the seemingly enormous ships berthed around the harbour walls. It didn't seem to be a busy harbour, but I didn't want to enter unbidden, especially in my tiny kayak compared to the hefty looking offshore support vessels looming over the quays. Neither did I want to cause any embarrassment to the lifeboat station personnel if I entered and ended up being remonstrated by the harbour authorities. I paddled along the harbour mole to the beach a few hundred metres away and enjoyed the relief of climbing out of my kayak onto dry land.

I was feeling uneasy. Landing on the beach meant I was a fair distance from the lifeboat station. I glanced around noting the beach was busy with families enjoying the summer sunshine. A young lad detached himself from a family group digging holes in the sand and wandered over.

"Where you from?" he enquired, his smile ragged with tooth fairy missing teeth.

I struggled to recall the name of the place I had paddled from that morning, so responded, waving vaguely west, "Along the coast, close to Bettyhill."

He didn't respond and instead turned tail and gambolled back to his family, waving his garishly purple plastic spade above his head. I suddenly felt alone and wanted to follow him, to introduce myself to his family, to tell them of the day I had enjoyed, the incredible scenery I had experienced, and the fear I had encountered when I entered Thurso Bay. I didn't of course and instead lowered myself onto the deck of the kayak, opened my thermos mug and swigged the last of my lemon and ginger tea. I felt weary and longed for sustained human company.

Hefting myself to my feet, I dragged my kayak further up the beach ensuring it was out of reach of the tide and set off in search of the lifeboat station. Scrabster Harbour was an industrial contrast to the landscape I had been living in for the last week. A pervasive smell of diesel and fish dominated my senses as I wound my way through the sheds and warehouses, the detritus of modern fishing methods strewn about. There was an element of the exotic. After living alone, immersed in some of the wildest landscapes Britain has to offer, this seemed incredibly civilised and exciting. I found myself looking forward to spending a couple of days here, exploring the town of Thurso and relaxing in the lifeboat station. I eventually arrived at the door of the lifeboat station and let myself in. No lights were on but because the door was unlocked, I assumed someone had to be inside. The usual lifeboat station aroma of adventure invited me further in and I made my way up a flight of stairs to an open office door. I knocked politely and let myself in.

Sitting at a desk surrounded with the accoutrements which make up a lifeboat station office; framed photos of lifeboat crew from years gone by, R.N.L.I. coffee mugs, files, folders and paperwork, was a large man who exuded a knowing maritime wisdom. Was it a lingering unease from earlier? I wasn't certain, but immediately I felt a tension descend around the two of us.

I shrugged this unease off and stepped forward, offering my hand, "Hi, I'm Nick. Nick Ray, the sea kayaker who's kayaking around Scotland to all the lifeboat stations."

There was silence and my hand remained proffered in mid-air. I baulked. This was very odd, and I was uncertain. As usual in situations like this I gabble, and this is what happened now, "I've come from Armadale Bay today. It was a good paddle, easy enough. Strathy Point wasn't hard, and I got through Brimms Ness OK too. It was just coming into Thurso Bay here I found a tide race."

I stopped, hoping I had opened a communication channel.

"I'm the Lifeboat Coxswain", his reply was terse but not unfriendly. "Where are you off to next?"

"I'm heading north to Orkney and the Shetland Isles" I responded, hoping this was the beginning of a conversation where I could seek his advice about the Pentland Firth, and he would willingly impart useful wisdom which would help.

"This must be for you then" the Coxswain said, reaching to a shelf above the desk and handing me a bulky padded envelope. "I see I'm your post office now."

I took the package from him, thanking him profusely. It contained a new sea kayaking jacket which Julian my kayak sponsor had sent to replace the Kokatat jacket which had malfunctioned. My excitement at receiving this was tempered by a growing discomfort within due to the awkwardness of this encounter. I was thrown. Up until this moment I had enjoyed a convivial welcome from every lifeboat station, where there were personnel to greet me. I had assumed the same would be true here at Thurso.

"Um, is it possible for me to stay here?" I was immediately annoyed at myself for the tentative manner I asked this question.

His response was immediate. "No, this isn't a bunkhouse. Do you see any bunks here?" He waved his hand in the direction of the open door and the passage beyond.

I think I blanched at what felt to be his hostility, but I gamely pressed on, making some form of conversation. After ten minutes of awkward questions from me and thrifty answers from him, I graciously thanked him and made my farewell. He turned back to his desk as I left his office and closed the door quietly behind. I wandered out of the

R.N.L.I. building reeling from a sense of shock. I felt embarrassed and stupid for having asked if I could stay. This had been the first time I had done so because the offer of a place to lay my sleeping bag and the instruction to make myself at home, had always been forthcoming until now. I was in a quandary. My confusion muffled my ability to decide, and I wasn't certain what to do. I walked hastily back to my kayak on the beach and once more sat down on the deck, my head in my hands.

A wave of despondency enveloped me, and tears of unhappiness welled up in my eyes. I suddenly felt incredibly alone. This was a quality of loneliness I had not encountered on this journey so far and I was overwhelmed by the sadness of it. I was struck by how *really* alone I was and in fact, how isolated I had been all along through the journey. It was as if all the hours, days and weeks of solitude; assessing risks, making decisions, coping with logistics, cooking, camp setting, kayaking, and encountering myriad experiences, suddenly piled on top of me in a jumble of moroseness. I had been carrying all of this on my own without the ability to share any of it with another person. Sure, I had met plenty of people along the way so far, but never able to 'unload' or review the processes I had been going through. Right then, sitting on the deck of my kayak on Thurso Bay beach, all I wanted was companionship. Then, for the first time, I considered giving in and ending my journey right there.

Thus, began a spiral of depressive thinking which inhibited any rational response to the situation. I looked out to sea with suddenly weary eyes, berating myself for believing I had it within me to undertake a venture of this magnitude. All I believed now, was the fact I was a failure, this because of my terse engagement with the Thurso

Coxswain. I had no evidence to support this premise but as so often with my depressive thinking, there was no need for evidence. If I felt it, then that was all the truth I required. My mind raced ahead, casting doubt after doubt in its wake. What's the point of continuing if this will happen again? How could you ever assume you would be welcomed with open arms by the lifeboat crews? Is this what people think anyway, you're on an ego trip? Who are you doing this for, yourself or the R.N.L.I.?

Adding weight to my self-pity was a gnawing fear of what lay ahead. The notorious Pentland Firth with its fearsome tides had been one of those navigational challenges which had weighed heavily on me ever since I had conceived the adventure. The twelve knot tidal streams with accompanying overfalls and races were not for the faint-hearted sea kayaker, let alone any mariner. I had hoped I could have gained insights and advice about how best to proceed from someone on the lifeboat crew but instead the coxswain's words rang in my ears when I recalled his response when I had timorously asked him for this advice.

"You've no right to be going through there on your own in a canoe." I remembered him glowering at me as he said this and I was too shocked to respond with my usual pedantry.

Around, on the beach were the cheerful shouts of children playing with their families. It all seemed incongruous as I struggled with the notion of what I should do next. My knee jerk desire to give up was receding, to be replaced with a dogged determination to continue. Slowly and surely a sense of equilibrium was attained, and I realised I had to decide on what my course of action would be. I dug out my map and studied it closely, seeking inspiration from this. The facts were, I needed to resupply with food. I needed too, to recharge all my electricals. I wanted to do a laundry because my clothing was in dire need of this. Finally, I desperately wanted a shower.

I considered my options. There was enough time in the day to press on another five miles, certainly the mile or so to the shoreline below Thurso town. If I could, I would camp there and use this as a base to shop and find a friendly café where I could recharge my electrical items. The worry with this choice was the uncertainty of a suitable place to camp. I could press on a further three miles eastwards to Murkle Bay, where there was the certainty of a camping spot but a long trudge into and out of Thurso. Finally, I could find a spot close to where I was now.

One thing the Coxswain had said after he had declined my request to stay at the lifeboat station was, if I approached the Harbour Master, he would give me a key to a shower which was for the use of mariners off the ships visiting the harbour. This solved my problem about showering. This fact alone swung the decision and I heaved myself to my feet and with renewed determination, set about unpacking my kayak. The young lad who had spoken to me earlier once more ran over, but this time he simply stood and watched as I emptied each compartment and filled the IKEA bags. I didn't chat to him either, though I did look up to him from time to time and smiled. He shyly smiled back.

I spent an hour searching around the harbour fringes for a suitable place to put my tent. I was looking for somewhere out of the way, unobtrusive and with enough grass and earth to pitch the tent and peg it out. This looked as if it were going to be an impossibility because the land was covered in concrete and tarmac. In the end, I went back to where I had left my kayak and my kit, beside the Thurso sailing Club building and at the top of their slipway. Here there was the tiniest sliver of grass which would just about fit my tent. Making sure there were no broken bottles or anything else which might pierce my groundsheet (and clearing the dog shit), I had my tent up in a matter of minutes. I had created home again and it felt good. I was aware the position of my tent was by the path people used to reach the beach. I realised there would not be much privacy while I was here. Truthfully too, I was a little nervous about camping in such a public place because of security. I wouldn't be able to guarantee the safety of my kit when I walked into town. As things turned out, I need not have worried because people couldn't have been kinder. If I were sitting outside my tent, strangers would stop and chat with me, the R.N.L.I. flag draped on my tent often inviting conversation. One woman brought me a cake she had baked because she thought I needed fattening up. While I was there, I took the opportunity to have a haircut and a beard trim. It was the first time I had ever had a beard trim in my life, and for many weeks afterwards I was pleased with my new hipster style.

Forever more, I'll think of my experience in Thurso as the point where my spirits were at their lowest ebb. There wasn't to be a repeat for the rest of the journey. I was saddened by my lack of connection with the Thurso Lifeboat Coxswain, and I regret not revisiting the station to attempt to straighten things out while I had the opportunity. What I gained from this experience was an awareness of my resilience in the face of difficult challenge. I reflected on my ability to not allow adversity to overwhelm me, even though at the time this is what it felt was happening. A desperate situation like this was bound to have occurred during the four months, and I'm pleased it did so only once. I recognise I'm good at facing down the physical adventures, but the interpersonal ones are my greatest challenge.

Chapter 26

I departed Thurso beach on the third morning, heading off while the town still slumbered. A heavy fog engulfed the bay and I paddled on a compass bearing to Clardon Head, from where I could cross Dunnet Bay and set myself up for a traverse of Dunnet Head. Despite knowing I'd deliberately set a course well clear of the sea lane in to Scrabster Harbour, I kept my ears open for the car ferry from Stromness on Orkney, which I knew would be arriving about that time. This was the first real sea fog I'd encountered on my journey, and it was an eery experience totally trusting my deck compass. I was glad of my GPS mapping which reassured my sceptical mind. I hoped the fog would lift by the time I rounded Dunnet Head because this notable landmark was the northernmost point of mainland Britain. It would be nice to gaze up at the cliffs. As it was, my passage around this stretch of coastline was shrouded from sight, almost as if I were paddling in secret. The fog did little to mute the cries of the sea birds though, I just couldn't see them. Suddenly there was an incredible squawking of fear and anger above, immediately followed by a large shadow hurtling downwards through the fog towards me. A huge bundle of brown and crisp white feathers splashed with force into the sea, whereupon it split into two, when a bullying bonxie and an irate gannet separated themselves from each other's clutches. The bonxie glowered at me for a second before spreading its powerful wings and flying off into the fog. The gannet meanwhile ruffled its feathers, preened itself and then gave a look which said, "Ha, that'll teach her to mess with me!" It drifted off on the surface of the sea into the fog and I was on my own again.

I paddled out of the mist into the secluded Brough Cove where I'd arranged to meet Joanne Kaar, an artist who I'd been in close contact with on Twitter. It was still early in the morning and when I arrived, I saw two kayakers packing their sleek sea kayaks on the beach. They turned out to be Ken Nicol and his friend Shona. When I'd stayed with them on Skye earlier in my journey, Gordon and Morag Brown encouraged me to contact Ken as a highly experienced kayaker who'd provide excellent advice about the tricky Pentland Firth seas. I'd got in touch with him during my stop at Thurso, but I didn't expect him to give up a workday to paddle with me and guide me through the passage ahead. I was immensely relieved and grateful to meet him!

Joanne was there too with family and friends. She'd made a pile of incredibly tasty bacon butties which were still warm when I unwrapped them and wolfed them down. The hot strong coffee she'd brought also went down a treat. There followed an enjoyably convivial hour sitting in the weak sunshine and dissipating fog, next to the restored and substantially constructed bothy, which had originally been built for the Dunnet Head lighthouse. This was now an asset for the local community.

Sadly, the time came to leave and say goodbye to Joanne and her family, but it was exciting to be paddling away with Ken and Shona, off into the sea which I'd so long been fearing. It was wonderful too, to have their company on the water. Ken knows the Pentland Firth very well as a kayaker, so it was easy to abdicate any form of decision making and hand over the route choices for the day to him. I simply delighted in paddling with new friends, chatting about my trip so far, and listening to their stories of their lives in the far north. The fog drifted in and out for the rest of the day, sometimes breaking enough to offer tantalising glimpses of the coastline ahead. In these brief moments of clarity, I managed to get a sense of the power of the tide as it swept us along the shoreline. We pulled out of the sea at the top of 'The Merry Men of Mey' to have lunch and allow this notorious stretch of rocky tidal races to ease, as the strength of the tide died away. Despite the fog, I was able to make out a couple of the rapids which looked exciting. I was glad not to be navigating them on my own.

I never stop to eat lunch ashore when I'm kayaking solo, so it was an enjoyably novel experience to relax, comfortably sprawled amongst the boulders of the beach, chatting with my two new friends. Just over an hour later when we returned to the sea, there were only the merest of riffles to denote the Merry Men and we enjoyed an uneventful passage down to Gills Bay. Here Shona had left her car as part of the shuttle arrangement she and Ken had organised, so they could paddle with me.

I ended up thoroughly enjoying the day as a highlight of my expedition. When it came to saying goodbye at John o' Groats after we'd each devoured a huge ice cream, I felt bereft of their company.

There had never really been any doubt over the previous few days I wouldn't paddle the short but highly intense six or so miles across the Pentland Firth to the Orkney Islands. While at Thurso I'd had a long telephone conversation with Julian, my kayak sponsor, who'd become my defacto expedition advisor about the ethics of taking the passenger ferry across the Firth instead of paddling. He listened with great sympathy as I described the conflict I was experiencing, attempting to come to a decision about this. I really wanted to kayak across to Orkney, to continue and fulfil my journey by kayak. Although I was fearful of the encounter, I was keen to take on the challenge of kayaking through some of the most tidally fierce waters of Scotland. However, time was against me and I was a long way behind the schedule I wanted to be on. To cross the firth safely on my own, I required near perfect weather and sea conditions. Neither of these were in alignment and were forecast not to be for a good few days into the future. If I was set on making the crossing, I'd have a long wait in John o' Groats. The alternative was to load my boat, kit and myself on the foot passenger ferry which plied the crossing between John o' Groats and Burwick on the Orkney island of South Ronaldsay. This would see me safely across and in a better position to press onwards into the Orkney archipelago even if the weather wasn't great.

It was a huge disappointment to be considering using the ferry and not kayaking across. I felt I was letting myself down by considering this option and I was worried the many sponsors and supporters of my expedition, would be disappointed too. What others thought of my venture and what I imagined they considered were the ethics in undertaking it, deeply mattered. This often added weight to the many decisions I'd made until now. Julian gently and deftly managed to alter this perception I held, bringing me around to the realisation the adventure was mine alone, to make of it whatever I wanted it to be. This included facing the realities of time and weather which I'd always known would be challenges out of my control. With his guidance I was able to accept the inevitable and find peace with the fact I would most likely use the passenger ferry to cross the Pentland Firth.

However, even up until the last moment, I held onto the hope I could make the crossing by kayak. Indeed, when kayaking towards John o' Groats with Ken and Shona, the sea conditions were ideal for a crossing to the abandoned Island of Stroma just off the Caithness coastline. They would have left me on this island to hop across the firth the next day. However, when the moment came to make the crossing, we couldn't even see the island, so thick was the fog, and the plan was abandoned. Thus, this being the last nail in the coffin, I acceded to a crossing to Orkney on the ferry.

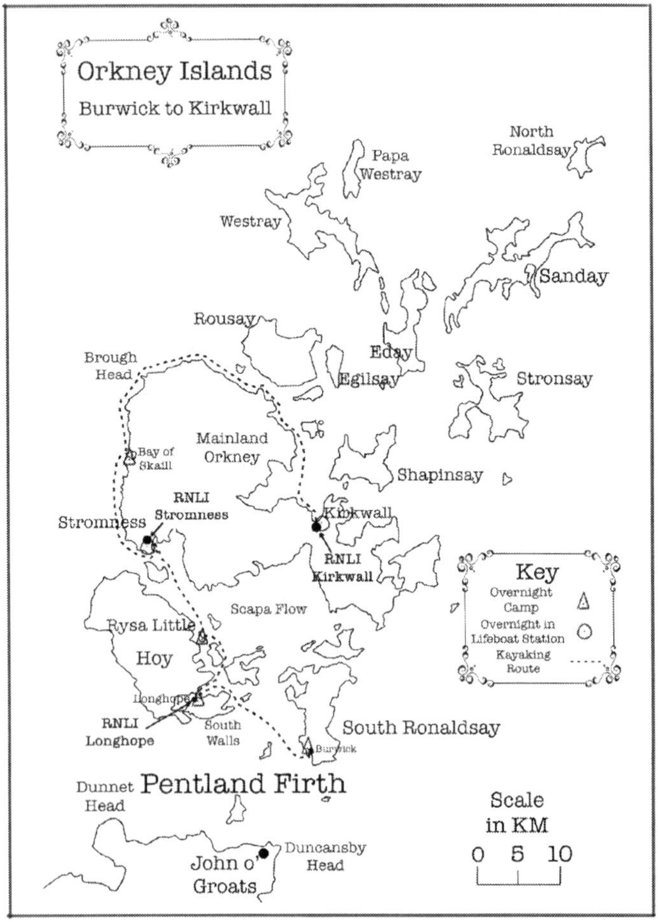
Orkney Islands
Burwick to Kirkwall
North Ronaldsay
Papa Westray
Westray
Sanday
Rousay
Eday
Brough Head
Egilsay
Stronsay
Mainland Orkney
Bay of Skaill
Shapinsay
RNLI Stromness
Kirkwall
Stromness
RNLI Kirkwall
Key
Overnight Camp
Overnight in Lifeboat Station
Kayaking Route
Scapa Flow
Rysa Little
Hoy
Longhope
RNLI Longhope
South Walls
South Ronaldsay
Burwick
Dunnet Head
Pentland Firth
Scale in KM
0 5 10
John o' Groats
Duncansby Head

Orkney Islands
Burwick to Kirkwall

Chapter 27

I was kindly gifted a complimentary passage across to South Ronaldsay where within reach of the ferry waiting room, I made camp. I couldn't make onward progress from here for the next four days because of sustained near gale force winds. For the first time on the journey, I began to experience 'tent fever', the irritation of living only in a small, enclosed space without room to wander around, sit comfortably, use a table or other modern conveniences. I found myself making use of the rather soulless environs of the ferry waiting room, as a place to sit and hang out. A positive outcome of this however, was meeting many interesting people over the four days. Two of them Lisa and Alastair have since become good friends. They were touring the islands in their beloved campervan. They kindly fed me lunch, poured me a dram of extremely fine Campbeltown malt whisky, and gifted me a tasty family size pack of potato crisps, a couple of apples and a bottle of Orkney beer. We met again when I arrived on the Island of Hoy, and years later they would visit me on another sea kayaking journey I was undertaking. One night I held a Twitter Celidh. Using You Tube films a large group of my Twitter friends and I shared our favourite traditional music tracks with each other, discovering tunes which were new and rediscovering old favourites. Despite this draining my phone battery, it was a welcome break in the tedium of my enforced South Ronaldsay existence.

Finally, on the fifth day, just as my patience was close to completely evaporating, the wind and sea state eased. I was able to leave South Ronaldsay for Longhope on the Island of Hoy only ten miles away. Gone were the fearsome wind over tide seas which I'd morosely observed from my lonely campsite vantage point. I enjoyed a fast paddle that morning over to Longhope, the strong tides sweeping me in the direction I was travelling. I arrived in the hamlet on the day of their annual regatta, where traditional sailing yawls were being raced against each other. When I landed I noticed bunting dancing breezily, with a banner proclaiming 'Welcome to Longhope'. After my travails in reaching this point, I secretly took this as a welcome for me. Indeed, I had been eagerly expected and the welcome I received at the lifeboat station, which was a buzz of happy activity, was genuinely warm and generous.

I woke with a thick head early the next morning and recalled with a groan the large number of beers bought for me at the regatta party, all of which I had willingly consumed. It had been a wonderful night and just what I wanted after my enforced four days ashore on South Ronaldsay. I had spent the evening chatting and laughing with many of the lifeboat crew about their lives on Hoy and sharing snippets about my adventures so far too. It was heart-warming the amount of interest my journey seemed to generate. Yet again, I gained an insight to the passion people hold for the R.N.L.I. and as such, are grateful for any venture which supports the charity. I guessed given the tragic history of the lifeboat here, this was not unexpected. Because of my early start the next day, I had skulked away from the party, making my way down the hill to my tent in a rather wobbly fashion.

I was up and ready by eight to meet Kevin, the lifeboat coxswain, who had generously offered to take me to the graveyard to visit the memorial to the lost lifeboat crew. In a fragile state, I rustled up a quick breakfast and hurriedly gulped down a scalding and restorative mug of coffee. Kevin arrived right on time wearing a pair of sunglasses and a wry smile. I was relieved I wasn't the only one suffering from too many Orkney Brewery Ales. We grinned to each other, agreeing it had been a good night. On the way to the cemetery, we chatted amiably about my trip and the lifeboat stations I had visited so far. I was keen to hear his account, but I couldn't bring myself to ask him about the Longhope disaster. Because of his personal connection to the story, I was sensitive about appearing too eager to hear him recount it.

I opened the gate to the cemetery, its lever latch clunking heavily as I did so. I was struck immediately, first by the serenity, and then the view. Headstones of various sizes and hues stood in perpendicular tiers facing out over the sea. The dead had a wonderful view over Kirk Hope and out to Cantick Sound. Kevin was silent as I read the information board close to the gate which detailed the Longhope Lifeboat disaster. I knew the outline of the story already but to read it again here, in the graveyard where the perished crew were buried, had quite an impact.

In the evening of 17th March 1969, the Longhope Lifeboat "*T.G.B.*" was launched with eight crew aboard into a dreadful storm with waves recorded that night of twenty metres. The lifeboat was tasked to head towards the seas off South Ronaldsay, in response to a cargo ship in distress. The Liberian registered *"S.S. Irene"* with seventeen crew had lost power and was adrift in the fearsome Pentland Firth. It is not known what occurred, but the last sighting of the lifeboat was by the lighthouse keepers on the Pentland Skerries at 9.30pm. A radio message was received in Wick from the lifeboat about the same time, after which there was silence. To begin with, hope lay with the possibility that their radio had failed but as the hours passed, despair set in. The lifeboat was never heard from again.

Early in the afternoon the next day during an extensive search, in what must have been a dreadful moment for the crew of the Thurso Lifeboat, they came across the upturned hull of the Longhope craft close to South Ronaldsay. There was clearly no hope of any survivors and the upturned Longhope lifeboat was towed to Scrabster by the Thurso Lifeboat. I could only imagine what would be going through the minds of the crew as they undertook this sombre passage. Seven bodies of the Longhope crew were later discovered in the wrecked boat but sadly the assistant mechanic, Jim Swanson, wasn't among them and he was never found. The tiny community of Brimms in Longhope consisted of thirty people. Such was the impact of this tragedy, ten children lost their fathers and seven women were widowed, two losing both a husband and a son. I have personally encountered the devastation to a small community when one of their own is lost at sea, so to lose a quarter of the population in one tragedy, didn't bear thinking about.

Thankfully there was no loss of life from the ship in distress. The *S.S. Irene* drifted ashore and was grounded at Grimness on South Ronaldsay where the Coastguard rescued the seventeen crew with rocket lines from the shore.

I followed Kevin between the tiers of headstones down to the impressive Longhope Lifeboat memorial, standing proud in the centre of the graveyard. The six-foot statue of a lifeboat man clothed in the protective garb of the day, along with a bulky lifejacket emblazoned with R.N.L.I. stood atop a neatly constructed stone plinth. He was gazing seawards, in the direction of the Pentland Firth where the tragedy occurred. His head was held high and he was stepping forward with his left foot, his arms calmly resting by his side, as if walking with composure to take his place on the waiting lifeboat. The statue eschewed quiet determination. Below his feet written onto a large bronze plaque was a brief description of the disaster and the names of the deceased, Coxswain, Daniel Kirkpatrick. Second Coxswain, James Johnston. Bowman, Daniel R. Kirkpatrick. Motor Mechanic, Robert R. Johnston. Assistant Mechanic, James Swanson. Life-Boatman, Robert Johnston. Life-Boatman, John T. Kirkpatrick. Life-Boatman, Eric S. McFadyen. Below this plaque was another inscription, this time with the words from the Christian Bible, *"Greater love hath no man than this, that he lay down his life for his fellow men."*

These words, so simply stated, struck deep into my core. I was once heavily involved in life saving as a Mountain Rescuer, serving as a volunteer and team leader on three teams in Britain and Africa. Over the years of my involvement, I undertook many rescues in varied conditions and levels of severity. Along with team colleagues after one arduous winter, nighttime incident, I was awarded the Royal Humane Society Bronze Medal for saving a man's life. Every time a summons went out for us to muster for a 'call-out', it never crossed my mind one day I may not return from a rescue. It may have been the immortality of youth which meant I discounted this possibility, but I trusted I would always make it home. This was until one time in Zimbabwe in 1997. The local Chimanimani Mountain Rescue team were tasked to search for a German hiker who had gone missing overnight deep in the Haroni River gorge, which flanks the chain of mountains forming the border between Zimbabwe and Mozambique. His girlfriend had waited through the night in their tent for his safe return and because he failed to appear, the following morning she walked out of the forest to seek help.

Five of us from the rescue team made our way through dense forest to the last known location of the missing man and set about searching the vicinity for him. The couple's tent was pitched on a slender ridge flanked on one side by a narrow and deep chasm. A fast-flowing stream flowed into this, disappearing over the lip of what seemed to be a substantial fall into mysteriously dark depths below. It was clear something was dreadfully amiss, and we needed to be hasty in our efforts to locate him. We set up an abseil and two of us went down the rope into the chasm. We found Ulf's body at the bottom of a picturesque waterfall, floating in a shallow pool, the water from the fall pattering onto his lifeless corpse. The rescue now became a retrieval.

Because of the location of the incident and the enormous task presented in retrieving his body, a Zimbabwean Airforce helicopter was dispatched with several army commandos to assist in the operation. A Huey helicopter, a veteran of the Vietnam War, noisily arrived above the ridge, whereupon the soldiers and additional members of the rescue team abseiled out to the ground below. It then flew off to wait out our retrieval of the body from the chasm. Ulf was extricated using an improvised pulley system on a stretcher which had been flown in. While a colleague Pete and I were packing the rescue gear away, the soldiers carried Ulf's body wrapped in an orange survival bag to a landing zone which had been hacked out of the forest further down the ridge, in fact where it was at its most narrow and sloping steeply downwards. The helicopter was radioed to fly in and collect us.

Pete and I arrived at the landing zone just as the drab green helicopter descended on its final approach. With horror we saw the body, a pile of equipment and the team were waiting on the uphill side of the landing zone, thus presenting us all to extreme danger because the rotor blades would be close to the ground on the up-hill side. Pete and I attempted to dissuade the soldiers from going ahead with the pickup, urging them to call the pilot and ask him to abort the landing and fly around while we rearranged everything on the down-hill side of the landing zone. This was to no avail and the helicopter clattered in, its reverberating rotors sending up clouds of dust and scattering small stones like bullets. Seeing the pile of kit was in danger of being similarly scattered, I threw myself over it, shouting out my fear someone was going to be hit by the blades, the tips of which were less than a metre from my head.

Most of the rescue party picked up the stretcher and ducking down, sprinted for the open door of the helicopter, Ulf's orange clad arm pointing skywards in rigour from the stretcher. I remember watching the shirt of one of the rescuers being plucked up by the rotor blades. I was terrified and, in that instant, accepted there was every chance I may not make it alive from this. I was lying over the pile of rucksacks and ropes, desperately working out how to ensure I could board the helicopter without being hit by the blades. It was a miracle the stretcher party had made it to the aircraft's door without incident!

One of the rescuers, a soldier named Paradzai, detached himself from the party as the stretcher was being loaded into the cabin, and crouched back towards the pile of kit. He reached out for a rucksack which I passed to him, our eyes locking for a millisecond, and he turned back to return to the open door. There was a resounding metallic 'ting'! Paradzai was whipped off his feet and flung several metres to end up lying out of sight behind a rock. Not able to observe where he was, I looked back to the helicopter to see everyone aboard wide eyed and open mouthed, staring at what must have been his body behind the boulder.

Pete and I leapt to our feet, whereupon I could now see Paradzai's legs, one of them twitching violently like an out-of-control marionette. At our insistent waving and yelling, the helicopter eventually lifted off and flew away, enabling us to rush over to him. He was in a pitiful condition, his helmet smashed open and a gaping wound to his skull with dreadful consequences to his brain. Blood and matter were spread on the ground about. There was no medical assistance we could offer and even though he was incoherently moaning, he was clearly deeply unconscious. Minutes later he began to decorticate, and I feared his death was close. I knelt next to him and spoke gently, hoping he might hear my voice. I wished him peace and told him to go well. "Peace my friend" I said repeatedly. Paradzai died minutes before the helicopter returned to collect us about half an hour later.

To say I recalled the details of my dreadful story while standing before the Longhope memorial would be untrue. However, I did imagine with considerable feeling the fear and the acceptance of death which members of the doomed lifeboat crew might have experienced the moment the catastrophe befell them, the split seconds when the monstrous seas overwhelmed their craft and the capsize occurred. These were eight every-day men who were placing themselves in a position of considerable danger with the sole purpose of going to the aid of others in distress, willingly performing a task for which they had courageously volunteered without thought of recompense.

Even though they were strangers, I connected with each of their names on the plaque, because I understood the motivation which impelled them to heed the call for help and head out into that fearsome storm that night of March, even though they must have known the danger this entailed. I was certain their motivation was not for fame or glory. I was certain too, it was a motivation which runs far deeper and because of this, can be difficult to quantify. There are sometimes insufficient words to describe the compassion people hold for strangers, which compels them to risk everything of themselves, to at least have a chance at saving a another's life. Maybe it can be best explained like this and here I paraphrase from Kurt Hahn, the founder of the Outward Bound movement; *"The experience of helping a fellow human in danger, or even of training in a realistic manner to be ready to give this help, tends to change the balance of power in a person's inner life with the result that compassion can become a primary motive."*

The memorial at Longhope was not the only tribute I encountered during my journey. There have been similar disasters with considerable loss of life to Scottish lifeboat crews; Fraserburgh, Arbroath, Stonehaven and Broughty Ferry. Yet, it was the story of the Longhope tragedy, which piqued my attention when I was planning my journey. Reaching here and paying my respects was in a way a personal acknowledgement to myself, I connected deeply with the selflessness of the R.N.L.I. crews everywhere. I shared with them the potential for loss and the acceptance of death.

In the modern age, tragedies such as the Longhope disaster are unlikely to occur again. Lifeboat design has advanced, as has the personal protective equipment crew wear out at sea, and the methods of communication including the use of GPS. The understanding of personal safety and assessing risk has altered too. However, notwithstanding this, it is not possible for lives to be saved at sea without lifeboat crew placing themselves in harms way. They must still embark on hazardous passages in conditions which are difficult to comprehend if never experienced before. Individuals must move about a heaving deck of a lifeboat to work with lines or receive survivors. The smaller inshore lifeboats must be navigated through seas sometimes immeasurably larger than the craft itself, searching for a casualty. Every time a crew member responds to their pager going off, and they don their foul weather clothing and head out to sea, they do so without considering what this means for them. Their mind is on the task at hand and the compassionate rescue of another in distress.

I stood silently next to Kevin, his surname Kirkpatrick, and read through again the names of the deceased on the plaque. His surname was repeated three times amongst those who had made the ultimate sacrifice, one of them his father. I had no words. He sighed deeply and made to move away. I nodded and simply said, "Thank you."

We walked quietly and slowly back up the slope to the cemetery entrance through the tiers of headstones, each with a grandstand view across the fields to the open seas. I thought to myself, when life comes to an end, this was a fine place to be laid to rest.

Chapter 28

Later that day, I paddled away from Longhope heading for Stromness across Scapa Flow, the next lifeboat station on my journey. On the way I spent the night on the small island of Rysa Little.

Nestled in a hollow within the surrounding low hills, Stromness was a town I had wanted to visit for a long time. It was a name which conjured an air of mystery. I knew very little about it and yet was attracted to its ubiquitous name. I imagined hundreds of years of Norse influence shaping its cultural development. I paddled slowly into the harbour attuning myself to new surroundings. I could see the Stromness Lifeboat ahead, berthed against a harbour wall. I was in no hurry and enjoyed a leisurely entrance to what appeared to be a quaint town. The drab grey houses were built gable end on to the harbour with what seemed to be narrow lanes separating them. I looked forward to exploring.

After taking photos of the lifeboat as I drifted past, I searched for a place to land but could only see a flight of stone steps leading steeply up to the quayside. These would have to do, so I drew alongside them, popped my spraydeck and gingerly extricated myself from the cockpit of my kayak, awkwardly stepping my right foot onto a slimy and weedy step. It would just be my luck if I slipped and ended up floundering in the harbour water while *Sahwira* embarrassed by my antics drifted off. I began to faff, and the kayak wobbled ominously, threatening to tip me in. As I was grunting to myself a voice from above cheerfully shouted down, "You must be the sea kayaker! Hi, I'm John, the mechanic at the station."

I looked up and shouted a greeting in return. John's warm welcome bolstered my resolve, and I was soon on dry land, *Sahwira* now tethered with my tow-line to the railing and drifting lightly, almost in relief to be rid of her embarrassingly clumsy companion. John and I shook hands warmly and he invited me over to the station for tea and biscuits. The R.N.L.I. station in Stromness is a quaint stone-built building in the middle of what appears to be a plaza, quite unlike the functional purpose-built buildings I was used to visiting. John pointed out he had a separate workshop and office on the other side of the harbour. As I had become accustomed to doing, I wandered around the lifeboat crew room gazing at photos of past crews, faces staring at me with levelheadedness. I would like to have met these people and not for the first time, I found myself experiencing a level of envy at those who did know them and had shared intimately heroic moments together.

After tea, I was invited to stay the night in the crew room, and I set about unloading the kayak from the foot of the greasy steps. This wasn't an easy task because I was fearful of dropping belongings into the sea. Thankfully, this didn't occur, and I managed to manhandle *Sahwira* up onto the quay and placed her gently off the road under a sign which stated, "No Parking". I hoped I wouldn't receive a penalty ticket for leaving a kayak on double yellow lines. With my bulging IKEA bags piled in a corner in the crew room, I began to unpeel the layers of kayaking clothing when John walked in.

"What a stink!" he exclaimed and walked around the room throwing open the windows. I was suddenly aware I did indeed carry with me the odour of an unwashed traveller and scurried for the shower room and a long hot scrub.

John didn't hold my pungency against me because a little while later he appeared in the crew room and presented a couple of bottles of Orkney Brewery 'Scapa' and gave me money to buy myself a smoked haddock patty from the local chippy. I was under strict instructions to try the patty because this was a local delicacy and not to be missed. Yet again the kindness of strangers was nearly overwhelming. I followed his instructions to the letter. Through mouthfuls of delicious smoked fish, I agreed this was indeed a delicacy to be enjoyed. I wandered aimlessly around the narrow closes, enjoying the sensation of being somewhere exotic. With this came a sense of disbelief I was there. Not for the first or the last time during my journey, I experienced the odd sensation of disembodiment, almost as if I were observing myself wandering the Stromness streets from afar. I couldn't believe I had made it this far. I was awash with memories of so many incredible experiences, at times I felt at a bursting point.

John Rae, almost my namesake, is a famous son of Stromness. I stood before his statue with some reverential awe. I knew of his history and was pleased to find myself connecting with him here. In the years of colonial exploration of the Canadian wilderness, Stromness was an important port for the Hudson Bay Company which had offices here and resupplied their ships in the port. John became well acquainted with the wild northern lands of Canada and intimately connected to the ways of the Inuit peoples. From them he learned to travel and survive in the icy landscapes, and he became the foremost arctic explorer of his time. He was called upon to assist in the search for Sir John Franklin, who, along with one hundred and thirty-four men and two ships, had gone missing during an expedition to discover the 'north-west passage', a navigable route through the arctic from the Atlantic to the Pacific. During two expeditions to find the missing explorers, Rae discovered the Northwest Passage. He later encountered Inuit hunters who had come across the remains of Franklin's party but never visited the location himself. However, because of the personal items which the hunters had collected, he ascertained this was indeed Franklin's group. Dreadfully, the Inuit had described to him how they had seen pots with human remains in them, indicating the wretched survivors had resorted to cannibalism.

In reporting this dreadful news, he incurred the disdainful wrath of Victorian Britain, especially that of Lady Jane Franklin, Sir John's widow along with an ardent supporter of hers, in the form of Charles Dickens. Despite his achievements on behalf of the nation, John Rae's reputation was never restored and he died at the age of 79, largely forgotten except by the people of Stromness. The story of his struggle with the establishment of the time deeply touched me. In reading about him, I couldn't help being inspired by his tenacity and his willingness to seek opportunities for new awareness, despite the social difficulties he faced. It was clear it wasn't fame or glory which drove him, but a deep love for wildness, a respect for the peoples of the land and a desire to explore and discover.

It was while in Stromness, I was again faced with a critical decision about my onward route. My original plans entailed paddling northwards from the town, through the Orkney Islands to North Ronaldsay, from where I would make the crossing to Fair Isle and then onwards to Shetland. I wondered what John Rae would have advised, as I tussled with the choices before me. There were several factors to consider which complicated the process of deciding. Time was not on my side. I could ill afford lengthy delays waiting for benign weather to undertake the committing crossing to Fair Isle. However, if I could make it as far as Fair Isle, I could travel on the ship which links the island with Shetland if kayaking progress onwards from there was impossible. It was not possible to kayak to Kirkwall, the next Orkney town with an R.N.L.I. lifeboat and then on to North Ronaldsay because this would involve adding on a substantial distance to the route. I had to decide in Stromness where I was heading for next. If I decided on pressing for Kirkwall, I would be giving up on kayaking to Shetland and take the ferry there instead. Despite having used the ferry across the Pentland Firth to reach the Orkney Isles, I held onto the hope I could complete the rest of my journey under paddle power alone. Once again, I found myself struggling with the ethics of my adventure.

Taking the ferry to Shetland would cut out a substantial chunk of the route, certainly diminishing the eventual mileage tally. While this wasn't a primary objective, it had been an aspiration to paddle a distance greater than two thousand miles. It would be a disappointment not to achieve this. I wanted to make the crossing between Orkney and Shetland by kayak and to visit Fair Isle too. I was not claiming any sea kayaking firsts, so these were personal ambitions. The ethics of my adventure were mine to debate, but I did feel a level of responsibility to the many people who were actively interested in my journey and supported me with their enthusiasm for the adventure. I was not beholden to anyone but myself, but there was an underlying discomfort at the prospect of turning away from the challenge to kayak to Shetland. Was it shame? I couldn't be certain.

In the end, I fudged my decision. Knowing I had a day still to decide because it would take me this to reach the point on mainland Orkney where the crux occurred. The problem with this though, was the likelihood this decision would then be made without the assistance of the internet and up to date weather forecasting. Nevertheless, I waived the importance of deciding and erred on the side of procrastination.

The morning of my departure from Stromness, I was packing *Sahwira* before a small crowd of onlookers who were intrigued by what I was doing. One of the crowd was an elderly fisherman who hailed from Fair Isle. He got wind of the route I was planning and came forward to speak with me with some urgency. He implored me to give up on the notion of kayaking to the island from North Ronaldsay. He warned me of the dangerous seas and the fearsome tide races around the island. He told me he was certain if I attempted to kayak there, I would not survive. He was earnest in his vociferousness, and I found myself on the defensive. This was the first time during my journey when I felt I had to qualify my experience and knowledge. I remained as calm as I could, countering his assertions I would find myself in grave trouble. In the end, I allowed him to seem as if he had compelled me to change my mind and I lied to him, I wouldn't make the crossing. I didn't like doing this.

I was slightly unsettled by the time I was ready to depart and after saying my farewell to John, I slipped the kayak into the harbour and climbed in. As I paddled out through the moored craft within the inner harbour, I had playing in my head the gorgeous tune written by Maxwell Davies,

"Farewell to Stromness". I would like to have had a recording of the tune playing as I paddled out of Hamnavoe and headed for Hoy Sound. It would have calmed my shaken nerves.

Looking seawards, down Hoy Sound, I was shocked by the ferocity of the breaking waves still a few miles distant. I knew with a worried heart if I could see these white horses so clearly now, the waves were likely to be substantial out there. Nevertheless, I pressed on, not wanting to eat humble pie and return to Stromness. I was confident I would cope with whatever I faced. It was a rough ride out of Hoy Sound and my nerves were jangled by the time I met the open sea. I had chosen to keep close to the shore to avoid being caught by the tide race further out in the sound. The problem with this was finding my way through sets of skerries onto which a hefty swell was forcefully breaking. Just as I was punching through one set of foaming waves, I spotted a bright yellow tennis ball bobbing on the surface as if quite unconcerned by the mayhem it was surrounded by. Immediately I altered my course to intercept the ball and managed to collect it with my first reach. I deposited it in my deck bag feeling pleased with myself at finding a trophy. This would make a lovely gift for Ziggy, an incongruous moment to think of my dog far away at home.

I paddled on and out into the roughest conditions I had encountered during my journey so far. The westerly winds over the last few days had developed a huge swell which was now beating itself against the western cliffs of mainland Orkney. This created a nastily confused clapotis ridden sea, bouncing off the walls of the cliffs stretching as far as my eye could see. I considered turning back for Stromness but the tide flowing out of the Sound of Hoy was now too strong and with the wind against the tide, the conditions were building against me. I had no option but to press on. The next haven was ten miles away. Until then, I had to keep my wits and make progress as best I could.

There was no rhythm to the sea. It was an anarchic melee of peaking waves, well over twice my sitting height, which crested without warning, with equally deep troughs where it seemed daylight struggled to reach. The accompanying noise was equally dramatic and added a suitable accompaniment to the struggle I faced. The roar was constant, every now and again punctuated by a resounding boom, when a mighty Atlantic breaker found its mark under an overhang or entering a cave. A thick haze of brine encrusted air, lingered around the base of the cliffs causing their features to become indistinct. Pinpointing my location on the map was difficult and I had to rely solely on my GPS to navigate. Everything on my deck was securely tethered and I had my deck bag tightly zipped up. It seemed I was paddling at the limit of my comfort zone and there was a real prospect of capsizing. I understood for the first time how a sea could be described as tempestuous.

Despite the conditions, I made steady progress. I paddled doggedly, the muscles throughout my body tense and responsive. It was as if my mind and body created the perfect crew. My mind focussed on what my eyes could see, working out the route to follow, how far to stay offshore, remaining alert for larger than normal waves. It played no part in conducting the body's responses to the demands of paddling through the chaotic movement of the sea. My movements were fluidly autonomous of conscious thought. I was acutely aware of my solitude in this enormous sea. I accepted the consequences a capsize would have, and while I was certain I would not die, I was fearful of losing my kayak, my equipment and my dignity. My certainty about my survival in the event of capsizing, was supported by the various means I had with which to summon rescue assistance, and the knowledge the Stromness Lifeboat was only an hour away. Despite this reassurance, I did not want to end up in the sea. The conditions were so rough, I doubted my ability to perform a self-rescue if I were unable to roll my kayak upright.

Equipped as I was for any eventuality, emboldened me to take on challenges such as the one I was encountering off the Orkney cliffs. Throughout my career in the outdoor development training industry, I facilitated moments of personal awareness for young people and adults through their interaction with adventure activities. The perceived risks they encountered created moments of fear and uncertainty, allowing them to address constraining limits of self-perception. As a consequence of their achievements on the rock faces, on the rivers, on the sea, in the mountains, on the high ropes courses and so on, they came to understand the limits they set for themselves were merely perceptions and they were capable of much more. As Kurt Hahn said;

"There is more to us than we know. If we can be made to see it, perhaps for the rest of our lives we will be unwilling to settle for less."

There was no doubt despite the severity of my situation, I was gaining a huge amount of self-awareness from the experience. I was living my private Outward Bound course.

It happened without warning. I was caught in a clapotic upsurge and found myself precariously perched on the tip of a peaking standing wave. It all occurred in a millisecond but felt like slow motion. The kayak and I toppled sideways towards the deep, gaping trough below. I had no way of supporting myself, my right-hand blade slicing thin air. A capsize was sure to follow and I readied myself for the eventuality, calmly leaning forward to set myself in a position to execute a roll. Miraculously *Sahwira* held her own, merely smoothly sliding sideways into the hole without fuss, then riding easily up the slope of the following wave, my paddle now offering me on its steep face, the support I required. A pulse of adrenalin surged through me, and I shook my head with relief. Remaining upright was a rewarding surprise. That I held my own and not allowed myself to panic bolstered my confidence and even though I was slightly shaken by this close call with capsizing, I looked ahead with renewed enthusiasm. It was later when in my tent I fully processed the experiences of the day and concluded I really did have the ability to kayak solo in demanding conditions. A belief I had yet to fully embrace, despite kayaking the hundreds of miles I had done to that point.

I was now kayaking below the cliffs of Yesnaby where sadly many of the Stromness Lifeboat's call outs are directed to. The high cliffs dropping sheer to the raging sea are a popular location for people choosing to take their lives. Attending suicides is a tragic role which many lifeboat crews around the country must face.

I was nearing the Bay of Skaill and the sea conditions were easing. Ahead lay another seven miles of demanding conditions without respite before I would reach Brough of Birsay where I had planned to stop for the night. I was worn out after my nerve shaking paddle from Stromness, so I decided to call it a day in the Bay of Skaill. Besides, this would provide the opportunity to visit Skara Brae, the much-vaunted Neolithic Settlement administered by Historic Scotland which was to be found there. There was a sting in the tail to the day when I entered the bay and found myself caught in a perfectly formed surf wave as I crossed a shallow reef. It took my heart the few minutes of paddling to the beach for it to settle. What a relief it was to arrive safely after probably the most demanding day of paddling I had faced so far.

I waited for the crowds to disappear for their hotels and holiday homes before I ventured down the beach to the Skara Brae site. I had the whole archaeological site to myself and I spent a delightful couple of hours carefully and respectfully exploring every inch of it. It was difficult to imagine the lives people lived here because of the manicured nature of the site. The grass was cropped to tennis lawn grade and neatly trimmed along the edges of the designated pathways. However, it was when I crawled into the narrow spaces of the semi-subterranean buildings, I appreciated some of what existence here may have been like, five and a half thousand years previously. What was striking was the ingenious use of the natural flat-bed sandstone to create 'furniture' such as cupboards and tables. I sat by the hearth of a fire in one of the central rooms and attempted to imagine the families who once occupied this home. It's rather like wondering about the universe because try as I might, the enormity of the concept was too much to equate. The buildings of Skara Brae had been lived in for over six hundred years before being abandoned two thousand five hundred years ago. The unusualness of the architecture also made it difficult to make a connection with past lives, and so it was with some disappointment I climbed out of the ancient drystone walled hollow and wandered back to my waterproof coated nylon tent.

A little later, as the sun was setting, I wandered up to the top of the cliffs and sat by an impressive cairn of rocks, gazing down on the ruffled sea far below. The crashes and the booms from the thumping waves seemed muted in comparison to those I experienced earlier in the day. The clear air afforded a stunning view along the line of cliffs and the far-off looming hills of the Island of Hoy, with the distinctive Old Man of Hoy sea stack standing alone, as if it were gazing westwards to the glorious sunset. From this elevation the surface of the sea appeared benign, belying the turmoil I had experienced earlier. The day was drawing to a peaceful close, the sun lowering itself as if with a heartfelt end of a working day sigh, below a sky artfully scattered with fragmented clouds.

I sat with my back resting on the cairn, finding a position of comfort within a discordant pile of stones, and pondered my day. It would be easy to pass it off as just another day at sea and only concentrate on what lay ahead, but I recognised it was important to review the decisions I had made and how I had responded to the challenges I encountered. I considered my wisdom in putting to sea in the first place. Before I had launched, a fisherman had warned me of the likelihood of heavy seas on the west coast as a result of the westerly winds. He had in fact described with some accuracy the nature of the seas and the size of the waves. I had chosen not to heed his information. No-one said I shouldn't go, but they warned me of the likely conditions I would encounter. What was it I wondered, which impelled me to ignore such sage advice? Did I consider I knew best? Was I showing off, bragging about my kayaking ability? Was I subconsciously aware of my ability and so unperturbed by the warnings? I found no answers to these questions.

I went on to consider the risks I had taken and whether I had placed myself in harms way. There was no doubt the answer to this was an affirmative. I looked out towards the horizon, somewhat chagrined by my severe internal review. I had quite literally 'pushed the boat out' and had exceeded the safety parameters I had established for myself. Yet I had come through without incident. This was largely due to my kayaking skill. I may have felt at the time I was at the limit of my ability and fearful of capsizing, but the reality was I held my own with considerable ease. A smile touched my face at this point because I'm not quick to praise myself about my ability.

Should I have been out there today? I looked skywards, giving myself time to consider this rhetoric question. Probably not, especially because I was on my own. I looked horizon-wards again noticing the yellow globe of the sun now seemingly melting into the sea, flattening at its base, molten globules of gold and yellow spilling about. The clouds in the sky were transforming too, chameleon like, into streaks of opalescent golden shades. Suddenly annoyed with my self-interrogation, I heaved myself to my feet and angrily stomped further along the cliff, stopping at the crumbling edge and looked out to sea again. I told myself belligerently, I would make the same decision again and the next time I have the knowledge I'm up to the demands of the conditions. I berated myself further, how else would I test my limits? How else would I learn my ability? How else would I grow? Out there on the chaotic tempestuous sea, I had learned valuable lessons which would have been beyond my reach if I had not stepped across the limit of my comfort zone and trusted myself.

The following day dawned beautifully, and I had yet to decide my route ahead. Was it to be northwards towards North Ronaldsay and the hope the weather would be fair for a crossing to Fair Isle, or continue around mainland Orkney to Kirkwall? My experience the previous day had dampened my ardour for high adventure and so without much vacillation, I chose to continue to Kirkwall. Accepting I would be travelling to Shetland by ferry, I reckoned I would make peace with myself regarding the ethics of my journey. I began this process by acknowledging a primary motivation of remaining safe.

It was a splendid dawn, the surface of the sea in the Bay of Skaill perfectly calm, mirroring the broken clouds high above. Around terns flapped jerkily and screeched their interminable cries. They, along with oystercatchers, are the sound of summertime sea kayaking. I was packed and away in under two hours, effortlessly slicing the sea towards the Point of Howana Geo. Around this headland and I was out in the open sea again, with a residual heavy Atlantic swell, though it was nothing like the day before. I could clearly see the distinctive whale back shape of the Brough of Birsay ahead and this is where I made for.

Keeping a kilometre off the cliffs because of the confused seas, I made good progress. With new confidence I coped with the lumpy and unsettled waters with ease. The sky was clearing, and the day was gaining in warmth. It promised to be wonderful throughout. Atop Marwick Head stood the distinctive crenelated Lord Kitchener memorial. In June 1916, the armoured cruiser HMS Hampshire purportedly struck a mine and sank in the seas off Marwick Head. She was on a top-secret mission, carrying the Secretary of State for War and the famous face and pointing hand on the *'Your Country Needs You'* poster, Field Marshall Kitchener to Archangel. His task was to persuade Tsar Nicholas II, to keep Russia fighting in the Great war. Of the seven hundred and forty-nine crew aboard, only twelve survived. Kitchener's body was never recovered. He was a Victorian hero who had been instrumental in successful African military campaigns, including the Second Boer War during which under his direction, concentration camps were conceived and where over twenty thousand Boer women and children died through disease and starvation. He was a military leader of his time and gave no quarter.

The loss of the ship and Kitchener became a cause celebre of the time, akin to the conspiracy theories of President J.F. Kennedy's assassination in 1963. Rumours abounded; had Kitchener actually been aboard? Had he been assassinated by the IRA for directing the brutal suppression of the Easter Uprising in Ireland that year? Or was the ship lost to a German U-boat directed to the kill by Fritz Joubert Duquesne, a Boer (and a German) spy, disguised as a Russian diplomat and who managed to escape to the submarine before the sinking? Why were troops sent to the coast to prevent local folks from attempting to rescue survivors? Where was the gold bullion said to have been aboard to 'bribe' the Russian emperor? These questions have been lost in the mists of time, but the memorial remains and is a notable, if tragic, navigational aid for Orcadian mariners.

I stopped briefly to explore the impressive, ruined remains of a Viking village on the Brough of Birsay before pressing on for Costa Head and the entrance to Eynhallow Sound five miles away. Relatively sheltered from the westerly swell, this stretch of coastline was delightful with at one point a hundred metre tunnel through Whitaloo Point.

Sea caves hold a strong attraction. Exploring them when conditions allow, is like entering an ephemeral world, concealed from everyday folk high on the land above. A sea cave is a realm of semi-darkness, booming echoes, gurgles, sudden splashes, gleaming walls, and sometimes the melancholy spectral singing of resting seals from deep inside. Often there is an iridescent otherworldly light emanating from within the sea at the entrance to a cave. The shades of aquamarine blues and emerald greens are captivating and when I stare into the depths, I become mesmerised by the intricate motes of light within which infinitesimal plankton dance and swim. Once I'm inside a cave I like to turn my kayak and sit still, holding my craft steady with lightly controlled paddle strokes. The outside world where I existed a moment earlier, appears to belong to a parallel reality and it was easy to understand how subterranean places held mystical awe for the ancients, suggesting a threshold between a world of normal reality to one where time and reasoning cease to exist. To enter a sea cave on my own in a kayak requires care and commitment. Every one of my senses is brought to bear, to ensure full awareness to my surroundings and safeguard a trouble-free passage back to the daylight world. The risk of being caught by a surging swell is high, so my judgement is key. This frisson of exhilaration enhances my overall experience, intensifying a sense of presence in the moment, resulting in this becoming enduringly imprinted on my conscious.

Through sheer enjoyment, I paddled under the headland through the tunnel a couple of times before pressing onwards. The tide was due to alter direction and I needed to be through Eynhallow Sound before this occurred. The flow runs at seven knots here and it wouldn't do to find myself against it. I rounded Costa Head into the Sound with the last hour of the tide in my favour. The flow should have been weakening because of this, but I was still swept through at a decent six miles an hour. Places along the shore with unusual names passed by, causing me to wonder about their origin and their meaning. Reading them in succession from the map was an entertaining process, almost if they were the list of characters in a fantasy novel; Loop of Crooie, Ramly Geo, Oyce, Skea, Ramna Geo, Haafs Hellia, Fisk Hellia, Buckquoy, Grit Ness, Reeky Knowes, Scara Taing, and Harpy Taing. Orkney is alive with heritage. The past is visible in just about every corner of the archipelago, dynamically connecting the living with the ancestral Orcadians. The richness of archaeology can be overwhelming to the point it is almost discounted because of its normality. I reluctantly paddled past many historic sites which I would dearly have enjoyed exploring; the monastery on Eynhallow island, Gurness Broch, Rendall dovecot, countless ancient chapels, churches, tumuli, chambered cairns and I counted seven brochs shown on the map along the coastline I was traversing. I did pull ashore to view one of these brochs and enjoyed finding a section of dry-stone wall, four layers high, atop the crumbling edge of a low cliff. I reverentially reached out to the stones thinking of the people who would have placed them there two thousand years previously. I looked from the vantage point on the tussocky knowle, down onto *Sahwira* pulled up on the shale beach below, imagining the craft of the Iron Age peoples in very much the same position. I experienced a deepening sense of connection, especially considering the method I was travelling along the historically redolent Orcadian coastline.

Before long, I was crossing the cold expanse of Wide Firth with accompanying tuneful singing from a harem of seals lounging on nearby Quanterness Skerry. Kirkwall was in sight and I readied myself for my re-immersion into a busy town. The seal chorus dwindled behind to be replaced by the noises of industrious humans who were unaware of a lonely sea kayaker making his way into the bustling harbour.

Making sure I avoided the frequent ferries which serve as the life blood throughout the islands, I arrived at Kirkwall Lifeboat station, landing on the cobbled slipway with a huge sense of relief. I had enjoyed a long day of kayaking, roughly thirty miles, and it was both surreal and believable I was finally here. I was warmly welcomed by the station mechanic, Dupre Strutt, who handed me a cold can of beer before a mug of tea! I enjoyed my two-day stopover in Kirkwall, exploring the narrow streets and wandering around the magnificent cathedral. I was interviewed by BBC Radio Orkney too. However, my mind was distracted by Shetland and what lay ahead.

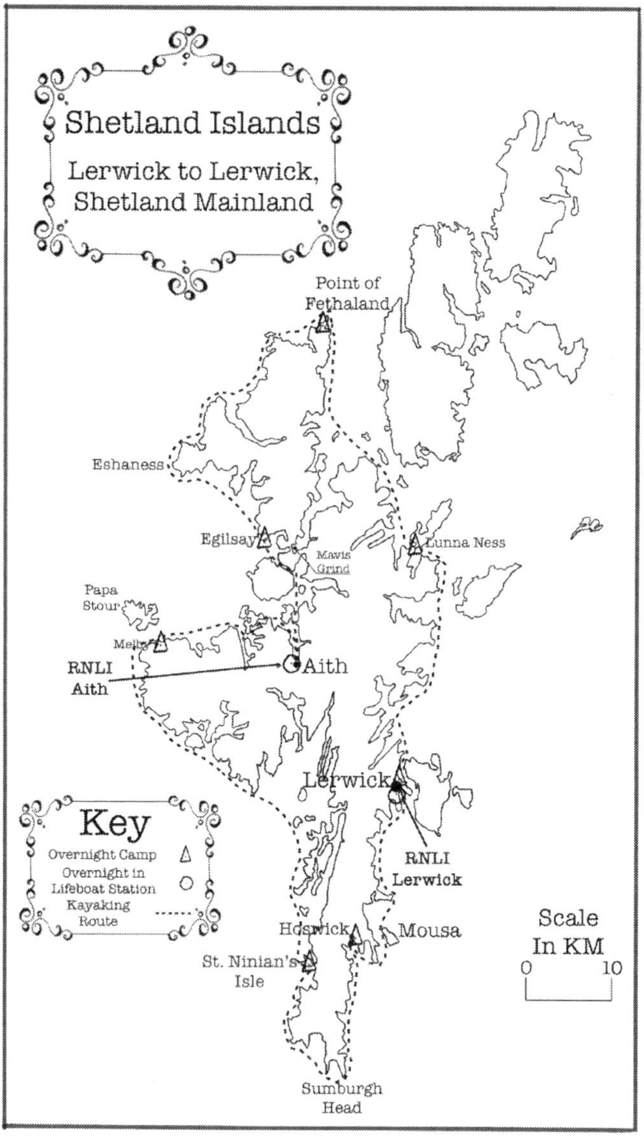
Shetland Islands
Lerwick to Lerwick,
Shetland Mainland
Point of
Fethaland
Eshaness
Egilsay
Mavis
Grind
Lunna Ness
Papa
Stour
Melby
RNLI
Aith
Aith
Lerwick
RNLI
Lerwick
Key
Overnight Camp
Overnight in
Lifeboat Station
Kayaking
Route
Hoswick
Mousa
St. Ninian's
Isle
Scale
In KM
0
10
Sumburgh
Head

Shetland Islands
Lerwick to Lerwick, Shetland Mainland

Chapter 29

The North Link ferry from Aberdeen to Lerwick, stopped en route in Kirkwall at 11pm. Not wanting to bother anyone, I didn't ask for a lift with my kayak and belongings to the ferry terminal a good distance from the lifeboat station. On the evening of my departure, I packed my kayak and paddled the mile and a half to the ferry pier. Here I had to unload my kayak and carry it, and my kit, precariously clambering over huge boulders up to the road and then out onto the pier. It took three hours before I was ensconced in the waiting room. Thankfully on embarkation, all I had to carry onto the ship was my kayak because my four IKEA bags were transported aboard in luggage trolleys. This was a rare moment when I would have liked a kayak-trolley with me.

The sailing to Lerwick was uneventful, arriving in Shetland just before 8am. It took another couple of hours to carry my kayak and bags of kit along the streets of Lerwick, to a patch of rough ground by a small harbour where I made camp. I used the rest of the day to prepare myself before my departure around mainland Shetland the following morning.

My expedition ethics did not allow me to introduce myself to the lifeboat station in Lerwick without first having arrived by kayak. Neither would it be permissible to simply launch into the sea nearby and paddle a few hundred metres to the station as a means of negating this self-imposed requirement. So, early in the morning the day after my arrival on the ferry, I set off from Lerwick southwards, thus embarking on my clockwise circumnavigation of mainland Shetland. I was filled with anticipation and my customary nervousness. Shetland held an awe-inspiring reputation because of its far northern latitude and wild rugged coastline. It was an unknown seascape, despite having hungrily devoured descriptions of sea kayaking in the islands in guidebooks and on the internet. Ahead were significant headlands with accompanying fearsome tides, empty stretches of coastline with immense cliffs, scores of islands with equally as many channels to choose from, with powerful tide streams to match, hundreds of caves, sea-arches and incredible sea stacks.

I had long wanted to visit the Shetland Isles and now I was here, it was the happy realisation of a dream. The Shetland archipelago consists of over one hundred islands, fifteen of which are inhabited by an overall population of twenty-two thousand people. Situated where it is in the warming seas of the Gulf Stream, the lands enjoy a relatively mild and damp climate. There was a feeling of the exotic when I first arrived, as if I had travelled to a foreign land with distinctive architecture and language. I had never been to Scandinavia, but it was clear the links between Shetland and its Scandinavian roots continued to thrive with considerable strength. For example, I learned while I was there many new houses built in Shetland are supplied from Norway. Genetically sixty percent of the male population stem from Norwegian lineage, which is not surprising since Norway is only two hundred miles away to the east. The Norse administered the islands as their own from 800AD to 1471 when it was annexed, or rather mortgaged, to Scotland by Denmark as part of the dowry for Margaret, a Danish princess on her marriage to James III of Scotland. The

Norse heritage is interesting, but I was particularly looking forward to encountering Shetland's pre-history, that of the Pictish peoples and those before them, the Neolithic. Here, like Orkney, there are brochs galore and many other ancient archaeological sites to get excited about.

More recently North Sea oil has been a mainstay of the Shetland economy. This was evident as I departed Lerwick, kayaking silently under the berthed cruise liners utilised as barracks for the small army of eight hundred construction workers, for a massive oil and gas construction project next to the Sullom Voe oil terminal. I imagined the boost to the Lerwick night-time economy and wryly created an image of a wild west gold rush town. As if to prove Shetland was not only about oil and construction, an otter surfaced a few metres away on my starboard side and swam for the shore, whereupon it appeared to guide me along the Lerwick foreshore by lolloping alongside as I paddled southwards.

The day was blustery and chilly, and the sea was correspondently choppy. I had the tide in my favour, and I made steady progress down Bressay Sound, the body of water between mainland Shetland and the sizeable island of Bressay less than a mile offshore. Soon I left the gradually awakening town behind, and I settled into an enjoyable paddling rhythm, keeping a safe distance from the cliffs and making the most of the southward tidal flow. I could see from my map I was passing some interesting historical features but because of the height of the cliffs, it was impossible to see these. Like Orkney, the names of places were intriguing, and I wondered about their origins and meaning. For example, places such as Torvald's Geo. Who was Torvald and when did he live? Was he an ancient Norse farmer or a warrior? Again, a headland named 'the Nizz'.

What on earth does Nizz mean? Surely not a person's name? And there were many more; The Grood, Stack of Pulli, Trumba, Skerry of Okraquoy, Taing of Bloggars-hellia, and Buggie to name a few. I wasn't amused by the names; I was intrigued and would like to have understood their meaning. I find our Ordnance Survey maps an incredible source of information for gaining insights to places through reading their names, and associating their possible meaning to history, people and landscape.

Mousa is a small island just over nine miles south of Lerwick and under a mile offshore from the mainland. I cut into the Sound of Mousa after a decidedly uncomfortable two-mile open water crossing and landed on the island in a sheltered rocky gully, where the waves were less forceful. I was excited, for here on the island was the only fully intact iron-age broch in existence. I considered the Broch of Mousa akin to the important archaeological sites in the world, the Pyramids of Giza or the Acropolis in Athens. I had read about it; I had seen countless pictures of it, and I had long held a strong desire to visit and see it for myself. As I clambered out of the gully after ensuring *Sahwira* was safely out of the tide's reach, I could see the broch, like an ancient cooling tower, proudly standing where it had done since 100BC. My mouth was dry with anticipation as I almost scampered the five hundred metres towards it.

Found mainly in the northern realms and islands of Scotland, the Iron Age brochs are substantially constructed dry stone dwellings. There are well over five hundred recorded remains of these enigmatic structures around Scotland and each vary in size. They share similar characteristics of being hollow walled circular designs rising to a considerable height. Mousa's walls for example, stand at

13 metres. They have a single entrance leading to an open lower-level space, from which a staircase climbs within the wall void, to an upper level where there will have been a wooden floor and probably where the family lived. It is assumed the ground floor space was for livestock. The stairway in the void continued upwards to the ramparts of the dwelling, offering unequalled views across the landscape where the brochs were situated. Little is known about the purpose of these structures. There has been much academic speculation which includes defence and displaying high status. There is no doubt viewing these buildings from afar, would have indicated a family of some importance lived there. It's because they are enigmatic which intrigues me so much about them. The Iron Age is an era of British history which holds much appeal. We are fortunate in Scotland to have thousands of sites from this period to seek out and explore. Many have yet to be excavated and interpreted by archaeologists and will merely remain as names and features on Ordnance Survey maps until they are. With the advent of the internet, as a lay person, it's possible to easily research these sites, to discover what is known of them.

My fascination for prehistory began when I was a boy. Growing up as I did in the wild African bush of Zimbabwe, I would take myself off to the granite rocky hills known as kopjes (pronounced: koppies) and clamber over them, around them and through them, searching for anything of antiquity. These natural rocky bastions were favoured by early humans for the vantage points and the safe havens they provided, in the forested savannah. As such, these humans left their mark in the form of beautiful rock paintings. In my youth we knew these as 'bushman paintings' because they were created by the San, the indigenous hunter-gatherer people of Southern Africa. It was a joy to discover even the smallest of galleries with lively scenes of ochre coloured stick people hunting elephant, kudu, eland and even giraffe. The paintings could be found anywhere; in a cave, under an overhang, even on exposed natural granite walls. They were painted up to eight thousand years ago and some of them appear to be as vivid as the day they were created. I was transfixed by them, and even though I was not of indigenous African heritage, I felt a deep connection to the long-vanished peoples of the African bush. Once, I was scratching in the talcum powder like dust of Inanke Cave deep in the wild Matobo Hills of Matabeleland in Zimbabwe, when I happened upon a stone arrowhead. It was a thing of beauty, intricately chipped to form a distinctive rounded arrow with a point so sharp, it pricked a drop of blood from my twelve-year-old finger. Even at that age, I sensed within my hand I held an object which had last been touched by another human, many thousands of years before. It was both beyond comprehension and easily understood too. A connection to the distant past through sensation and wonderment.

Mousa Broch reawakened this feeling of wonderment within me. I walked around the base of the broch, my left hand lightly caressing the dry stone, enjoying the tickling feeling of the wisps of grey green lichen, which adorned the outer wall. Each stone had its place, no mortar held it in position and yet the wall was as solid as any constructed in the modern age. From the base I had to arch my neck backwards to view the upper reaches of the wall. It was perfectly constructed with a wasp waist, bowing inwards halfway up before leaning outwards towards the top, similar in look to modern coal fired electricity cooling towers. I stood for a minute by the low entrance, gathering my thoughts before pulling open the wrought iron gate and ducking low to avoid banging my skull on the substantial stone lintel. Inside I was immediately struck by a sense of serenity. I was the only person on the island and had the building to myself. As opposed to the manicured presentation of Skara Brae on Orkney, Mousa had the appearance of only recently being abandoned by the Pictish family who had lived there. Rocks were tumbled on the floor and there was no attempt to make the building seem anything more than it was, an inscrutable ruin from our prehistory. There was no imported gravel to line the ground under the feet of visitors, or interpretation boards plastered about the walls. It was empty of all that, leaving room for individual imagination and contemplation. I stood for a length of time, gazing around and allowing my mind to soak up all I could see, while imagining voices, laughter, shouts, busyness, lowing cattle, the smell of wood smoke, cooking and always the presence of the sea.

It was amazing this structure was open for all to visit. There were no limitations in the form of cordons or fences. I was free to wander as I wished and so stooping, as the inhabitants would have done a couple of thousand years before, I ducked into the dark void between the two walls and climbed the smoothed stone stairway upwards. The floor for the upper dwelling was no longer in place and it required some creativity to imagine a thriving living space where the family went about their lives. The stairway carried on upwards and I was soon out on the rampart into the open air. There was an immediate sense of exposure, a feeling of being higher than the thirteen metres of the edifice. My breath was taken away. Here I was, at the top of a prehistoric structure, no other person within sight, gazing out on a view which two thousand years before, others will have done the same. I wandered along the rampart walkway, imagining swinging a cloak of rough cloth over my shoulder, gazing across to mainland Shetland over a ruffled sea. It was clear to see why this must have been a desirable place for a broch.

The strong breeze tugging at my imaginary cloak reminded me not to linger too long. The forecast was for strengthening winds and I wanted to progress further southwards. With great reluctance I pulled myself away from the expansive, timeless vista, making my way down the foot worn stairs and out of the broch. Walking back to my kayak, once again the nature of my transience impacted me. I was forever on the move, never stopping for longer than necessary, always looking to the far horizon. I would have liked to have made camp on Mousa, on the close-cropped grass next to the broch, enjoying creating a deeper connection with the island which had been a home for humans for thousands of years.

Out at sea again, the conditions had deteriorated with a destabilising chop. I was losing heart for fighting the weather and almost decided to return to the Mousa shore. Instead, I made for the mainland after taking a few last photos of the broch standing proud against the horizon. My chosen destination for the day was Grutness, close to Sumburgh Head, but given the conditions, this was going to be an unlikely achievement. Instead, I arrived in Hoswick after a buttock clenching paddle in rough seas around the crashing headlands of No Ness and Cumlewick Ness. I had the feeling of needing to adjust myself and my expectations to the Shetland seascape. It was unfamiliar and consequently I felt nervous in the lively seas.

I went for a wander around Hoswick in search of a shop and a café where I could charge my electricals. I walked past a young man wandering down the road towards me. He suddenly turned and asked, "Are you Nick the sea kayaker?"

Taken aback I replied, "Yes, how did you know?"

"My friend and I listened to your interview on Scotland Outdoors and we hoped we would meet you when you came to Shetland!"

I was flabbergasted. Here I was, arbitrarily in a small village in Shetland and I bump into a man who listened to me speak about my trip on the radio on a programme which airs before eight on Saturday mornings! I suddenly felt a little famous. It transpired Mark and his friend are sea kayakers too, so we chatted about my journey and what the highlights had been so far. When it came time to part, Mark said, "Just wait till I tell Simon I met you. He'll be really jealous!"

I ambled off up the road feeling even more celebrated. If I had a walking stick, I would have been idly swinging it with a self-satisfied cocky air. In seriousness though, this recognition was good for me. I'm not an academic or show prowess in any other field where I am acknowledged for the contributions I make. This journey was where I gained recognition for something worthwhile and for which I was good at. This was not about celebrity fame but knowing I held significance within the society I was a member of. It was heart-warming to learn how my journey was an inspiration to others.

The following day I was to round Sumburgh Head, one of the significant headlands on my journey. One which I was in awe of, and which I held considerable fear for. There is a notorious tide race off this southernmost tip of mainland Shetland called the Sumburgh Roost. Indeed, the name

Sumburgh is a derivation from Old Norse *"the head onto the loud tide-race"*. The night before in my tent, I assiduously studied my planning notes and while making my breakfast in the morning, I did so again. I doubled checked my workings for the tidal streams and times, not wanting to make a mistake with either of these. I was satisfied I had prepared myself fully for what lay ahead. The sea was unsettled but the wind had eased which was a good sign. The forecast for the day was hopeful and I looked forward to enjoying at least some sunshine. I arrived at Grutness well ahead of my schedule. This allowed a couple of relaxing hours ashore beside the Fair Isle ship pier, to wait until the tide turned in my favour to take me around Sumburgh Head. My plan was to arrive at the headland in the early stages of the flow when it was at its weakest.

I was anxious to get going but resisted the temptation to set off ahead of schedule. I'd learned from my earlier mistakes, not to discount tide times. The hour arrived and with a tight knot of anxiety I paddled away from Grutness and down the coast towards the headland. The sea was lively, ensuring I pay close attention to my paddling as I made my way southwards. The cliffs to my right slowly gained in stature until once again I was a mere human speck on the sea, dwarfed by natural grandeur. The tide was flowing much faster than I expected, so I eased back on my paddling. There was a short cut I could take through a channel which separated a rocky bastion called Little Tind, from Sumburgh Head itself. I had read the entrance to this channel could be easily missed, so I was careful to stay as close to the shore as I dared. This seemed a rather precarious choice, given the confused conditions of the sea and the breakers smashing onto the rocks.

The tide pushed me along faster than I wanted and despite easing back on my paddling, I realised with a shock, I had travelled further along the coast than I thought. I consequently nearly missed the entrance to the gut, which was indeed difficult to identify as a viable route through to the other side of the headland. Entering the channel was akin to stepping off a busy city thoroughfare into a secluded cathedral cloister. Calm descended in a palpably welcome manner. Even the numerous wheeling sea birds who criss-crossed the skies above, appeared to ease up on their cacophony. I was relieved but not relaxed, because I was unsure what lay ahead. Would I leave the gut and kayak out into the mighty Roost? I paddled forward slowly through the channel, the water beneath swirling with silent eddies and upwelling burp-like surges from deep below. Craning my neck, I could just make out the protruding lighthouse foghorn, high on the cliffs above pointing out to a sea it no longer mournfully boomed out to. Fog horns have ceased to be used around our coast since the advent of GPS navigation.

Abruptly, I found myself in the open sea again, this time it was calm with no confusion or roaring tide race. In fact, I couldn't spot any of this at all. I was confused and slightly disappointed, because I had expected to engage with at least the fringes of the Roost. Nevertheless, I was pleased to have arrived at this point unscathed and with the weight of worry lifted off my mind, I looked ahead to the rest of my circumnavigation of Shetland with renewed excitement.

It all seemed so innocuous now. The seas washed onto the rugged shoreline of Garths Ness with some vigour but not in a manner which would elicit surprise or fear. It was a different story though, early in the morning on January 5th,

1993. MT *"Braer"*, an oil tanker laden with over eighty-four thousand tonnes of light crude oil, on passage from Norway to Canada, lost engine power and ended up adrift a few miles off southern Shetland. There were gale force winds and mountainous seas which drove the stricken ship onto the rocks of Garths Ness, where she immediately began breaking up with dreadful consequences. Thankfully there was no loss of life to the thirty-four people aboard, who were rescued by helicopter. As the storm raged and the mighty two hundred and forty-metre-long ship disintegrated, the television images of the broken vessel lying forlorn in a tempestuous sea, awash with various shades of dirty black crude oil, had the British nation transfixed. This was the largest disastrous oil spill in British seas since the *'Torre Canyon'* disaster in the Scilly Isles in 1966. Because of the storms and the immediate destruction of the tanker, there was no hope of preventing further crude oil washing into the ocean and all eighty-four thousand tonnes disappeared into the ecosystem. The gale force winds drove some of the oil as sticky black spume far inland, causing forty-five square kilometres of rough Shetland pasture to become excluded from grazing.

Surprisingly, the environmental impact on land was not as disastrous as expected, with only 1% of the oil washed up along the shoreline. Tragically though, over seven thousand birds were killed and it's not certain how the marine life was affected. The spilled crude oil was light and lacked the viscosity of other crudes, which meant it was easily broken up and dispersed by the action of the chaotic seas. It was difficult to comprehend the disastrous scene, as I slowly paddled past under the cliffs, through the same seas which would have been littered with debris and slick with pollution. I put my left hand in the cold clear water beside my kayak and swirled it around, trying to imagine the sensation of lifting it out, coated in a filthy, slick, avarice-coated slime. I felt shame to be a human, who, as does most of the earth's population, relies on the extraction and the movement of crude oil around the earth to conduct my life. Through this complicity, my disregard for our planet is shameful. Whenever I fill the tank of my car, I never think of the cliffs I was sitting under, silent of sea bird cries because their occupants will have perished, coated with stinking black sludge, suffering a gruelling death. It was now twenty-two years after the disaster, and as I lifted my paddle from the sea beside me and set off along the long line of high cliffs, I was happy to have five Black Guillemots fly low overhead, to land with clumsy splashes not far ahead. Life had returned.

Rounding the eponymous Fitful Head was a highlight of my day. The raw wildness of the sheer four hundred and fifty-foot-high cliffs caught me by surprise. I hadn't expected to feel so isolated and as tiny, as I paddled through a bumpily fragmented sea, far beneath them. Looking westwards I could clearly make out the lonely island of Foula, twenty-eight miles away with a population of thirty-eight hardy souls. Along with Fair Isle to the south in the channel between Shetland and Orkney, Foula is one of Britain's two remotest permanently inhabited islands. Gazing across to it as I paddled in my tiny craft, dwarfed by the immense cliffs above, I acknowledged how incredibly wonderful Scotland is with these remote outlying communities, which many people have little awareness of.

My destination for the day was the delightful St Ninian's Isle. It isn't an island really, connected to the mainland by a magnificent white sand tombola beach. Landing here was a huge relief and after I had made camp, high on the close-cropped bowling green slopes overlooking the beautiful sands, I sat back with a welcome cuppa and reviewed my day. Quite simply, it had been one of the highlights of my journey so far. After I had heartily wolfed a large dinner of pasta, I wandered off to search for the remains of the medieval St Ninian's chapel. There were only the footings of the chapel and an outline of associated structures. On returning to my tent, I noticed a stranger had generously left three bottles of locally brewed craft beer and a small tub of fruit trifle. As luck would have it, I saw a figure striding away across the beach, so I shouted after him. Simon was Mark's friend, the young man I had met in Hoswick in what seemed an age back but was in fact only the previous day! We stood by my tent and chatted for a good length of time about sea kayaking and his life in Shetland. I was touched by his generosity and assured him I would enjoy the beers, one each night for the next three days.

Chapter 30

My destination goal on the west side of Shetland was Aith, where the most northerly R.N.L.I. lifeboat station in Britain is situated. From St Ninian's Isle it would have been a two-day paddle to reach there, but I was held up due to strong winds, taking shelter for an extra day, in the hamlet of Melby, overlooking the island of Papa Stour. Sadly, the rough conditions prevented me from making a foray to the island and enjoying its incredible subterranean passages and caves, accessible only by kayak. In my planning for my journey, I allowed myself a few days here to explore the caves, but there was no chance of this now. I was well behind time and the forecast was looking grim, meaning I would be forever attempting to make ground against the clock. This was a huge disappointment and emphasised the vagaries of expedition kayaking. Remaining flexible and not adhering to a dogmatic plan was essential for the success of any adventurous pursuit.

There was no fanfare when I arrived in Aith on a blustery day, after a long hard slog up the fjord like voe, to the small harbour at the head of it. It was dominated by an impressive lifeboat station and of course the sedate and proud Severn Class lifeboat, berthed alongside the harbour wall. I was made warmly welcome by Hylton Henry, the larger-than-life coxswain for the boat. I was ushered into the crew room with the most magnificent vista from a lifeboat station, I saw anywhere on my travels. It far outstripped even the view from the Tighnabruaich crew room, all the way back in the Clyde Estuary, which I'd held as the benchmark until now. A huge picture window looked right up the length of the empty and starkly beautiful Aith Voe. It took some sinking in to realise I had made it to the most northern lifeboat station under my own steam. Admittedly, I had used the ferry from Orkney to Shetland, but to all intents and purposes I had kayaked from the Solway Firth this far north. I think it was by now the nature of what I was experiencing, the scale of my achievement did not register with me. Arriving in Aith was simply another destination.

I stayed an extra day in Aith, where I immersed myself in the moment, chatted to the people I met, laughed, shared stories and set about planning my future progress. One task I had to achieve was my laundry. There was a washing machine at the lifeboat station, and I made full use of this facility, hanging my freshly washed clothes to hang in the blustery sunshine, on a rudimentary clothesline I had created from my kayaking towline. I laughed to myself as I hung my clothes over the rope in a haphazard manner, thinking of my wife who never allows me to hang out the washing at home. According to her I never do it properly! There's not much to do in the hamlet of Aith, so I happily spent my day off kicking back in the crew room and gazing out of the picture window at the magnificent view up the Voe. I worked out I had four days of paddling ahead to complete the circumnavigation of mainland Shetland to reach Lerwick. The forecast was mixed with strong winds promised for much of the time. There were a couple of exposed sections of coastline to contend with, particularly Esha Ness with a reputation for rough seas and few places to hide. For the briefest of moments, I pondered portaging from the west side of mainland Shetland to the eastern side into Sullom Voe over the curiously named Mavis Grind, a neck of land which separated the west seas from the east. Mavis Grind it turned out when I asked Hylton, wasn't a 1950s dance but a derivation from Old Norse meaning *gate of the narrow isthmus.* The isthmus, under thirty-five metres wide at its narrowest section, is the land link between the Northmavine Peninsula and mainland Shetland. Even though portaging here would considerably reduce my journey to Lerwick, I wanted to enjoy the achievement of kayaking around the whole of the island.

In hindsight, as Hylton suggested, I ought to have stayed at Aith another two days, because shortly after setting off I found myself struggling into the teeth of a minor gale. The winds were from the northwest from the direction I was heading. I paddled slowly out of Aith Voe, one laboured paddle stroke after another, realising I was exiting an excruciatingly long natural wind tunnel. I cursed my stubbornness in insisting I would press on, no matter what. As I struggled to gain forward momentum, my conscience niggled with criticisms of my impetuousness. I mouthed silent thanks I had left Aith too early in the morning for folks to spot me struggling away up the voe.

Eventually I passed Papa Little Island and crossed to the island of Muckle Roe. Along the shore here I was out of the worst of the wind, and I caught up with myself a little, this easing my bad temper. Despite the fierce wind, the day was gloriously sunny, the sea glittering with thousands of dancing diamonds. I looked up at the Scandinavian influenced farmsteads and dwellings and felt again the exoticness of being somewhere wonderfully foreign. I turned from Busta Voe, a name which made me smile because it sounded like a 1980s Ska singer, under the bridge linking Muckle Roe to the mainland, and into Roe Sound. Ahead through the narrow stretch of water was the expansive St Magnus Bay across which, nine miles away, was the headland of Eshaness. The wind was blasting down Roe Sound and once again I found myself digging my paddle blades deeply hard with a sweat inducing effort to make headway.

I was less than a mile from Turvalds Head, (who was Turvald I wondered?) This was the point where I faced a choice to turn eastwards for Mavis Grind and the short portage into what assuredly would be the easier seas of Sullom Voe or press onwards towards the Eshaness headland. Choosing the Mavis Grind route would ensure the wind would be gratifyingly behind me whilst I paddled the remainder of the route to Lerwick. As I reached forward over another choppy wave and pulled hard, this choice was an attractive consideration. I was sorely tempted by the prospect of easier paddling. I was half an hour away from having to make my decision.

The forecast assured the strong north westerly winds would persist for at least two days, possibly three. I would struggle against them if I continued up the west coast of Shetland. The seas off Eshaness would be nasty and recalling my fearful experience along the west coast of Orkney, I didn't want to face those conditions again. It seemed wisdom should prevail and with a heavy heart I was close to acceding to the inevitable. The glitter went from the day despite the diamonds continuing to dance about. Notwithstanding the prospect of encountering easier conditions in Sullom Voe, my disappointment was palpable. My heart was set on completing a circumnavigation of Shetland mainland. It seemed my journey was in danger of unravelling. I was losing purpose. My original somewhat ambitious plans for my adventure, had included paddling right up to Muckle Flugga, the most northerly piece of land in the British Isles. In the cosy comfort of the small saloon aboard our yacht, and with the alluring aid of Google Earth, I had glibly drawn a route to this most northern point without much thought for the reality of the weather conditions I now faced in a rather bleak Roe Sound. As ever with a decision such as this, there were variables to consider, each validly presented. My task now was to sort through these in a logical fashion to arrive at an eventual choice.

The natural realm, the great outdoors as we often like to call it, tests me in many ways. From the dawn of time, humans have pitted themselves against the elements. I would imagine for hunter gatherer peoples, the natural environment was the milieu where they lived, thrived, and coexisted with wild beasts, in a mutually shared space. I could not imagine they sought to climb a mountain simply because it was there, or paddling a log boat along the coast, because they saw this purely as a personal challenge. I imagined for them, life held primary purposes, gathering food, finding shelter, and protecting their children. As humans moved away from a transient lifestyle to one of settlement and permanent shelter, our aspirations through the millennia shifted and altered, to the point where here I was a modern human, sitting in my kayak, on a wind whipped Shetland sea, enjoying the luxury of fulfilling a personal aspiration to kayak around Scotland. If there was no life sustaining purpose being here, then what did this moment serve? What did it matter if I chose to cross Mavis Grind and curtail my circumnavigation of Shetland, instead of pushing further westwards to realise my aspiration for a Shetland circumnavigation?

I discovered the answer was this; the personal purpose of my adventure was indeed life sustaining. It was offering an important opportunity for growth and development. Physis is a Greek word which describes an innate natural force within every living entity which drives us to grow. In humans, physis refers to the energy invested in health and the expansion of our personal horizons. This is the urge to do something different, the aspiration to be who we want to be, and to choose our destiny. Good mental health is not only the outcome of sound relationships but also the fulfilment of essential universal drives within us, including belonging, self-fulfilment and survival.

Physis involves change. No living thing can avoid change, we are constantly in the process of evolution. However, because we crave equilibrium, continuity, and safety in our lives, change is often difficult to accept. We hold onto what we know because this provides us with certainty. This desire for stability is called homeostasis, the opposite to physis. Humans are therefore pulled by these two opposing forces, homeostasis and physis. It is this unresolved struggle which underpins many of the unhappy responses we have to our life choices.

My struggle with clinical depression is most likely an outcome of this internal tussle, which is why, suddenly, the decision to complete the circumnavigation of mainland Shetland or cut it short, had become a vitally important one to resolve. It wasn't simply a matter of portaging into Sullom Voe to avoid the winds. It was about the importance I placed on facing, or not facing, the challenge the strong winds presented. Homeostasis determined I would seek the less demanding route, to ensure I maintained my schedule and avoided the probability of serious and demanding sea conditions. Physis on the other hand, invited me to push on, even though success was uncertain and there was a high probability of becoming storm bound with inevitable delays. As so often when faced with this process, it is conducted beyond my consciousness. What I am aware of though, is rationalising the presenting facts of the issue, and ascertaining the consequences if these facts are ignored or considered. The underpinning factor is personal safety, so an indication the task being considered was completely reckless, would determine an immediate avoidance. If though, the risks were such harm may occur but with care, could be avoided, then the task was worthy of consideration.

It would be simpler to avoid the complexities within the decision-making process, for me to not heed the desire for self-understanding, but this would diminish my opportunity for self-awareness. I consider this to be integral to an adventure experience. Without understanding, there is no wisdom to be gained. It was clear from the outset, my journey around Scotland was so much more than simply visiting the lifeboat stations. It was an opportunity to gain deeper insights into my 'self'. This would help me grow into the older man I hoped to become. I didn't want to slide into my old age. I wanted to arrive with as much energy and enthusiasm for life as I had when I was in my twenties.

I decided to continue a full circumnavigation of mainland Shetland. With renewed determination in my paddling, Turvals Head slowly slipped behind. I made my way out into the steep and uncomfortable waves of St Magnus Bay. Jitterbugging the Mavis Grind would be enjoyed another time.

Despite my resolve to face my adventure head on, shortly after setting out into the bay, uncomfortable sea conditions seriously challenged me. I had previously coped with trickier seas but somehow, I wasn't in a sound frame of mind to deal with this continuous onslaught of broken waves, and the powerfully gusting head wind. Searching as far ahead as I was able to, I saw conditions around Lang Head, my next headland, were dreadful. Even from my low sea level elevation I could see an angry race kicked up by wind over tide. I was faced with another crucial decision. I was able to turn back to Mavis Grind or I could find somewhere to stop nearby in the hope conditions eased during the day. Pressing on around the headland with those heavily breaking seas was not an option.

I resolutely held onto my desire to round Shetland. I pressed on another mile as best I could, through extremely lively seas to a small island called Egilsay, where with a relieved scrunch, I landed on a shiny pebble beach. A small cohort of common seals welcomed me in, snorting and splashing in the waters behind. I pulled the kayak up the stones and wandered over to the far side of the island where I would gain a better view of Lang Head. From the raised elevation on land, it was immediately clear I had made a wise decision not to attempt to get around. It would be a nasty piece of water to be kayaking alone in these wild conditions. I wandered back to the boat and dug out my flask of lemon and ginger tea, always a soothing drink when my mind is troubled, and I needed to think things through. I had managed only ten miles out of the thirty I had hoped for in the day. If I stopped here, the wind would only increase in strength and I would be stuck for a couple of days at least, the seas around Lang Head worsening in the near gale north-easterly. I looked morosely back to where I had come from minutes before. The entrance to the short voe leading to Mavis Grind was clearly visible, only a mile away. With the wind behind, I would reach there in no time at all, and within the hour I would be unpacking my kayak and portaging my kit, my boat and myself across into Sullom Voe and assured easier seas beyond. I sighed deeply, noticing the seals looking back at me, almost it seemed with sympathetic gazes.

"Fuck!" I shouted and was immediately answered with a few splashes in the small bay as my profanity caused some alarm. "Fuck! Fuck! Fuck!"

I was fed up with the winds and I was fed up with what seemed to be a continual process of evaluation and re-evaluation. Why couldn't I simply enjoy a carefree passage along this stunning Shetland coastline? Was fate trying to tell me something?

I refused to entertain the idea of giving up on my circumnavigation of Shetland, and this belligerence mobilised my inert body. I heaved myself to my feet and set about unpacking the kayak, making an elegant camp on wonderfully comfortable cropped turf, a few metres away from the beach. My mind was unyielding. I would sit out the gales for as long as they blew, after which I would endeavour to complete my desired goal.

The small island of Egilsay became my home for two days and three nights. This enforced castaway existence became one of the magical experiences of my journey. There was no phone signal and therefore no internet connection either. For some reason I could not pick up Coastguard broadcasts on my VHF radio too. I was unable to communicate beyond the shores of the island. I was not concerned about unnerving others of my safety because I knew the YB-Tracker would indicate my location, even accurately pinpointing where I had placed my tent. Nevertheless, I did wonder if the Aith Lifeboat would pay a visit because they might wonder what had occurred. Without communication there were no on-line distractions, which pleasingly offered the opportunity to appreciate uninterrupted solitude. When I was a boy, the tale of Robinson Crusoe enthralled and I've ever since wanted to experience island solitude, the unique alone-ness which a body of land surrounded by water affords. The coastline of the island was a natural boundary beyond which I was unable to venture without paddling in my kayak. Devoid of other humans, my company was the small group of seals, screeching terns, skittering oystercatchers, rather dreamy fulmars, and a cantankerous black-backed gull. To the east, over a mile into Mangaster Voe there was an ubiquitous fish farm. Thankfully with the wind from the direction it was, I wasn't disturbed by any noise this produced. I chose to ignore it most of the time. One vital thing the island did not contain, was a fresh water supply. Not for the first time or last, I acknowledged with gratitude my obsession, insisting I carry at least ten litres of fresh water every day.

The joy of enforced time ashore creates a delicious sensation of relaxation. There is permission to lie in bed late into the morning, brew coffee and tea whenever I felt like it, read, write, read again, or simply wander and explore. The time is also valuable for making and mending, attending to bits of kit which require caring for, and re-evaluating plans for future route options.

I embraced my island solitude with enthusiasm. The angst about losing time was easily forgotten and replaced with a tranquil enjoyment of my island surroundings. I explored every inch of Egilsay, clambering along the rocky shoreline, striding over the sheep cropped slopes and ambling along the small beach, eyes cast down in the hope of finding interesting flotsam. I looked for signs of ancient human heritage, a Viking grave perhaps, or evidence of an iron age home. I carried my binoculars everywhere and would sit motionless on the rocks gazing out to sea, wondering if I would spot a killer whale. I desperately wanted to see a killer whale. I sang to myself, loudly and out of tune, idiotic made-up songs which were bawdy and full of nonsense. I read, and I slept. I caught up with my journal. Then I wandered around the island again, and again, and again. At six hundred metres long and two hundred and fifty metres wide, it didn't take long to stride around the glorified skerry.

At one point I pondered solitude as an experience in its own right. When I worked for Outward Bound, one of the most significant experiences we offered on the classic three-week courses was what we termed, 'solo'. This important course element would occur midway through the programme (a personal development course for adolescents and young adults). This was the point when self-awareness was becoming apparent for the participants. Ideally, the solo experience lasted for forty-eight hours; two nights and two days of solitude. Each student was provided with rudimentary materials to construct a basic shelter, a change of spare clothes, their sleeping bag, enough water and minimum rations. They were encouraged to keep a written journal but not allowed the distractions of watches, cameras, phones, music players, or books. The purpose of the solo was mindful self-reflection. Out in a forest or a wild area, each person was placed so they were out of sight of the other group members. They were given clear boundaries for their solo site and asked not to wander, both for their safety and not breaking another person's solo. Their safety and welfare were monitored throughout the forty-eight hours by the course instructor, such as me. The solo was a pivotal moment for many students during the course, when significant personal insights were achieved. This opportunity for true solitude is rarely attained in our modern lives.

I was enjoying my personal enforced solo, though I did have a watch and other distractions which broke the rules. I quickly became aware the effect my presence on the island was having on the lawful inhabitants. Unwittingly, I had pitched my tent a few metres from a tern's nest. Thankfully this did not disturb the guardian birds who took flight when I emerged from my tent quickly returning when I had wandered away. In the hidden seclusion of my tent, I enjoyed listening to the parent's soft chuckles as they went about their egg warming duty. The seals were extremely nervous, and I wondered if this was due to the proximity of the fish farm. However, by the time I came to leave, one or two of them appeared less eager to slip into the sea from the beach any time they glimpsed me wandering around the island. The highest point of the island belonged to a large male black-backed gull who protected his domain with a vengeance. Anytime I dared come close to his spot, he launched into the sky with screeching cries, wheeling above, gaining height before turning like a fighter plane, accurately diving for my head, causing me to involuntarily duck. I usually scuttled away. The flock of terns were just noisy! If I wandered too near where they were perched, as one entity they would rise into the air, yelling and screeching in their high-pitched tones, all the while flapping like wooden bird marionettes. I attempted to minimise my disturbance on the island but recognised too there was little I could do about my presence. I was not there to cause harm to any creature.

Chapter 31

Despite enjoying my island idyll, I was relieved to find on the third morning the wind had sufficiently dropped to proceed with my journey. I said my farewells to my feathered neighbours and enjoyed the company of a few seals for a fair distance after I had paddled away. I think they were seeing me off their property. Lang Head presented no problems, and it wasn't long before I was crossing St Magnus Bay towards the eponymously named Drongs, a magnificent cluster of bare and jagged stacks standing a mile offshore. These were the first natural highlight of what developed into one of the finest days on the sea during my journey. The sea state was lumpy but not unmanageably so. Crucially the wind had diminished and shifted to become a now helpful south westerly.

St Magnus Bay is thought to be the remnant crater of a massive meteor strike on the earth. Looking closely at the map I could see this to be possibly true, its circular perimeter bordered by Papa Stour to the south, Muckle Roe and the mainland to the east and Eshaness to the north. I also learned the depth of the bay was an astounding one hundred and sixty-five metres deep. I kept to the edge of the bay and pulled ashore a few miles later to visit the small folk museum in the settlement of Tangwick, only to find it closed and locked up. I had hoped there would be an internet connection I could use to acquire a weather forecast. I wasn't perturbed by not achieving this, happily continuing my way. The day was fair and there were no warning signs in the skies above, which indicated an approaching front. If the wind happened to rise, the direction it was blowing from would benefit me.

The day became a litany of superlatives. Not far from Tangwick I paddled the few hundred metres out to the mighty Dore Holm, a substantial sea stack owning an impressive natural arch, which appeared to protrude from the island and drop into the sea, not unlike an elephant drinking with its trunk. I took great delight in kayaking backwards and forwards through the arch and exploring a huge echoing cave, which hollowed the base of the island. The restless sea sloshed around the rocks, reminding me to take care and not allow my playfulness to cloud my judgement. I was now close to the Eshaness headland and a nervousness set in. This stretch of incredibly rugged coastline, set about with gnashing skerries bore the brunt of unimpeded North Atlantic seas. To add another level to the possible excitement, the tidal streams were powerful here too. Once again, the wonderful place names lured me onwards, almost as if I were kayaking through a fantasy novel. Ahead Utstabi marked my entrance to this fascinating stretch of Shetland coastline. My earlier knot of nerves had now been replaced with excited anticipation. I was particularly looking forward to exploring a couple of large sea caves the area was renowned for.

I paddled forward cautiously, confirming the conditions were safe enough to proceed. The sea was lively with a sharp-edged chop, but this did not cause any discomfort. I made good use of the ink black skerries which kindly provided moments of shelter from the oceanic swell. I hustled between them and enjoyed hunkering down behind them one by one. This was a moment when I would have enjoyed sharing this experience with another kayaker. Not because I felt the need for a safety buddy, but because it would have been lovely to share the excitement and playfulness of exploration. I was in sensory overload and I had only just begun my traverse of this magnificent section of coast. The cliffs weren't particularly high by the standards I had experienced elsewhere, but I understood why people said this was serious coastline. I certainly wouldn't have enjoyed being here a couple of days earlier when I paused on my castaway island. This would have been a serious undertaking!

I made my way through an attractive gap between a set of skerries delightfully called The Bruddans, and I created a TV show of the same name, where a fly on the cliff series follows the Bruddan seal family through their everyday lives.

It's an odd phenomenon, but when I paddle in the calm lee of a skerry on the opposite side to where a lively sea is piling up, I have a sensation of kayaking at a much lower level. It's a crafty natural optical illusion. It's incredibly atmospheric when waves thunder onto the far side of the skerry, launching spume into the air or ice cream thick white-water cascading over the rocks with a vibrating rumble. It's awesome to be sheltered and secure with a kayak level grandstand view of the whole spectacle. This was exhilarating, and I felt wonderfully alive. Sneaking past another thunderous skerry, this time aptly named, The Cannon, I found myself completing the bulge of the Eshaness headland and I was soon under the cliffs atop which stood the Eshaness Lighthouse. I was on tenterhooks because around this area I knew there was a huge sea cave with multiple entrances. I had been told it was probably the largest sea cave in Britain and I certainly wasn't about to paddle past without exploring. One of the entrances when I eventually saw it might have had 'Enter Here' painted over the lintel, it was so inviting!

As I do when entering all caves, I approached with extreme caution, my senses alert for any changes in the patterns of the waves, the way the sea moved in and out of the cave, and the amount of room I had to manoeuvre. I rarely if at all reverse into a cave as some kayakers like to do because this gives them a view of the outside sea and importantly, the opportunity to paddle away from any oncoming threat. I accept I may find it difficult to hurriedly reverse out of a tight spot if required, but I would far rather see where I'm going and enjoy the completeness of exploring a cave in a natural fashion. I need not have had any concerns about the Eshaness cave. It was truly magnificent! I was immediately struck by the tranquillity within, almost as if I had entered a sanctified space, a cathedral even. The sea irritably choppy outside, was pervasively calm inside with the lightest of movement to indicate the sloshiness of a maritime swell. The roar of the surf crashing on the skerries outside was muted. The clamour superseded by tinkling dripping and musical splashes around. The space within was cavernous, enabling me to paddle freely from corner to corner, end to end. A boyish exploratory inquisitiveness playfully surfaced within, and I spent a happy half hour paddling in and out of the three entrances, around the chamber and sliding the nose of the kayak into as many hollows and intriguing slots I could find. Because I was prepared for exploring the caves, I had kept my head torch handy and put this to good use for the darker corners. I would have loved to share this moment with my kayaking friend Phil. It was just the thing we would have enjoyed doing together.

Eventually, I tore myself away from the peace of the cavern and exited through Calders Geo into the tetchy sea. Not far ahead was another subterranean feature I wanted to explore, and I kept my eyes peeled for the entrance. I ended up backtracking to reach it because I missed the camouflaged entrance, but The Holes of Scraada were everything I hoped for. Once again, my inner child was delighted with the narrow tunnel, the promise of daylight shining from around a corner deep within, and the sound of an echoey sea washing in and around the hidden nooks of the tempting void. Emboldened I paddled in, confident in my ability to cope. I dislike the term 'playground' as an attribution to the outdoor realm. This infers a disrespect for the landscape and Nature per se, but here, I felt playful, and this tunnel was inviting me to play. I found myself once again missing the company Phil who I would have enjoyed sharing this moment with. We would have been like a couple of excitable boys.

I edged my way through a short tunnel which contained a gentle dog leg, unexpectedly finding myself in an amphitheatre of rock, sea and sand. This was a tremendous experience. I half expected to look up to see lines of Roman spectators on the edge of the hole cheering my probable demise when wild beasts were inevitably released to devour me. I hadn't been aware of a swell in the tunnel, but here in the open hole, there was a definite wash up and off the sandy beach at the far end. I landed on the sand hauling myself out of my kayak as fast as I could, before being swept back off the steep beach. My lack of agility nearly saw me tumble backwards. I avoided a dunking by gripping a deck line to hold myself steady. Ashore with my customary lemon and ginger tea to celebrate the moment, I wandered around the beach, up to the back of the vertiginous rocky hole, and gazed with amazement at a seemingly discarded weighty tree trunk. It looked as if it had been carefully sandpapered and shaped into an object of great beauty. What amazed though was the question of how it found its way into the hole? It was a huge tree with a bulbous foot, stripped of its root system. I shuddered to think of the storm which must have driven the behemoth through the tight entrance and dog legged tunnel to leave it ignominiously redundant here. Discarded around the trunk was the miserable detritus of human thoughtlessness, myriad pieces of plastic and nylon rope, infant in their process of breaking down, their eventual decomposition a millennium away.

The Hole of Scraada was once a massive sea cave, its roof now collapsed, leaving a gaping skylight to the world above. I wondered about this cataclysmic event, assuming it happened in one massive crash, and attempted to philosophise, if a cave collapses and no one is around, does it make a sound? Whatever the case, it must have been an impressive occurrence. My mind wandered on, "What are the chances of being in a cave and the roof collapsing?" I laughed out loud at my fanciful thinking before sitting on my kayak to enjoy the uniqueness of being in this incredible setting. It was another one of those realisations, I had arrived here, all the way from Kippford on the Solway Firth!

Out on the sea once more, I pressed onwards. Eshaness was a rich area to explore but sadly I lacked the time to do so, and anyway, I was feeling a mantel of loneliness descending upon me. The delights I encountered had lacked the joy of sharing them with another. There are moments in life when I crave the company of friends, to enjoy peak experiences in the outdoors such as these. Rather than allow despondency to settle, I paid attention to the landscape ahead. Beyond the tight entrance to Hamna Voe, a lovely looking bay, were a fine line of cliffs stretching towards an incredible looking natural arch aptly named The Faither. I kept a good distance away from the shoreline because of the uncomfortable sea conditions. I had little desire to do battle with a clapotic sea, simply to view the cliffs from a closer perspective. Paddling through The Faither appeared to be a daunting prospect, the swell now pushing me towards it in a manner which demanded my full attention. I couldn't allow the kayak to run away with a wave and thus lose control if we surfed toward a rocky ledge at the base of the cliffs. There was an increasing sense of confinement as I tentatively paddled towards the gaping arch. I was being drawn forward, almost as if this were a star-gate, a portal to another dimension, which I was compelled to travel through. On my left, a long rocky ledge was frequently awash with the rising and falling Atlantic swell, the rumbling of the wash echoing off the stark walls of the arch. A colony of cormorants warily observed my stealthy approach, one with its wing's half open in an absent-minded fashion. The kayak rode the chop with ease, my lower body independent of thought, fluidly matching the movements, my upper body tense, ready for a swift paddling response if this was required. I gazed around in awe and absorbed yet another intensely pleasurable moment of the day.

The Faither was indeed a portal to another world. Amazingly the landscape altered and the jagged ruggedness of the Eshaness coastline was left behind. It became another memory, another experience to be fondly recalled in my years to come. Ahead lay softer contours and softer features. Even the sea calmed, no longer agitated by the resolute cliffs and skerries of the headland behind. Seals swam around me, ahead and behind me, splashing in mock surprise whenever I turned to look at them. They kept me company most of the way to Uyea, a knob of land, almost an island, with a tropical white tombola beach linking it to the mainland. Instead of choosing to kayak around this small headland, I decided to land on the beach and drag my kayak over, according to the map a matter of only seventy metres. I was persuaded to take this course of action because a nasty tide raced around the protruding lump. The sea looked uncomfortably messy, and anyway, I was keen for a comfort break and a leg stretch. It's a good thing this natural feature is a popular attraction in Shetland, because when I landed and stood on the sand, I sank up to my ankles! I knew from bitter experience attempting to drag my loaded kayak across soft, cloying sand is a near impossible task. I managed to pull it only a few metres over the sugary sand before I flopped down onto my behind, puffed and defeated. A young man scampered over the rocks from where he was sitting with his family. He offered to help. He was a godsend! It transpired his father filmed the whole thing, including me launching the other side and being caught in a breaking wave which pulled one of my spare paddles off my deck, and posted this on the internet.

Four miles after leaving Uyea, I arrived at the Point of Fethaland on a tide building in strength. This looked as if it would sweep me onwards towards Ramna Stacks, an impressive set of skerries a mile distant. It was a moment which was considerably important. This was the furthest north I would journey on my trip, this being the northernmost point of mainland Shetland. I pragmatically conceded the far north skerries of Muckle Flugga would wait for another day. My focus was now centred on turning the northern point, and setting a southward heading, homeward bound. There was no relaxing just yet because the tide had me in its grip and I needed to be wary of being caught in unexpected disturbance. As luck would have it, like Sumburgh Head in the south, there was a cut between an outlying stack and the mainland which allowed me to round the point clear of the tidal race. So, it was with calm ease I found myself safely through the gap and looked down at my compass to watch my bearing swing to a southerly direction. Despite some hefty weather, I had successfully kayaked from Lerwick and up the west coast of mainland Shetland. Above gulls mewed their congratulations. I gazed around, taking in the surrounding scenery. After the ruggedness I had encountered along the west coast, the caves, the huge arches, the finger like stacks, mighty cliffs and the rumbustious seas, this landscape seemed genteel in comparison. It was an odd feeling. A part of me wished I were still exploring the rugged west coast and had the many wonderous sights still to look forward to, but another part was simply relieved. Relieved I had made it to this point without mishap. I was now anxious to reach Lerwick in good time.

My camp on the Fethaland peninsula was one of the most delightful of the journey. I pitched my tent overlooking the sea to the east and realised instead of watching the setting sun dip below the horizon, it would be tomorrow's dawn I'd be enjoying instead. Around were a cluster of abandoned cottages in various states of ruination. This was once a busy herring fishing community from where men would row sixty to eighty miles into the Atlantic Ocean, in small craft known as sixareens. Out there in the rolling ocean, they would remain for days on end, until they had caught enough fish and row back again. In a relative fashion, having experienced the might of the Atlantic, solo in my kayak, I found it difficult to imagine the exposure these courageous men faced. They existed out there in small craft with no shelter, eking a living in a most hazardous manner. In the evening I wandered along to the tip of the peninsular and sat for a long while gazing out to the seas beyond. I was enjoying a healthy sense of wellbeing, a pride in achieving my arrival here. I was particularly pleased not to have yielded when faced with the decision to portage Mavis Grind or not. I reflected on this further.

It would have been the easiest thing to have avoided the northwest section of Shetland. I would be in Lerwick by now, or even heading south on the ferry to Orkney. There would have been no shame in a decision to cut short the circumnavigation. A decision to do this on the grounds of safety would always be accepted as a valid response to the prevailing conditions. So, this was not a choice I would need to justify to others. It was a choice I had to justify to myself and live with forever. Regret is a powerful emotion which we expend needless amounts of energy assuaging. I know I would have regretted a decision not to press on up the west coast if I had chosen the Mavis Grind option. It took courage to stick with my conviction to complete the whole of the island. I had put myself under pressure to make up for diminishing time and was mindful of remaining within my margins of safety. These were self-imposed limitations which sometimes proved difficult to overcome. A fulmar glided past, head height and turned to look me in my eyes. It slipped along the edge of the cliff, before sweeping downwards and out low across the ruffled surface of the sea. I recognised it then, the answer to the question I pondered. If the limitations are those which I set myself, then so are the choices for change, the path I choose to follow. I was not bound by my self-imposed rules any more than I would bind anyone to theirs. The trail I was forging on this journey was of my own creation.

From Fethaland, it was a wonderful journey along the indented east coast of Shetland. What the coast lacked in high cliffs and remote ruggedness, it offered in small islands, many stacks and skerries, history, wildlife and birdlife. With the winds from the west, I enjoyed sheltered waters and the pleasure of not being continually wary in wild seas. I stopped for the night on the narrow neck of Lunna Ness where during the Second World War, the seventeenth century house was used as a base for the 'Shetland Bus' operations. This was the use of wooden Shetland fishing boats to clandestinely transport men and equipment to and from Nazi occupied Norway. The links between Shetland and Norway were tragically clear, when I came across graves to unknown Norwegians found drowned at sea. It was sobering to encounter our country's connection with the Norwegians. It was a relationship I had been aware of but had never come face to face with.

It was a straightforward paddle from Lunna to Lerwick, again along delightful coastline, through watery alleyways between intricate stacks, hopping between seal inhabited skerries and generally cruising in easy conditions. I relaxed without worry. There was no obligation to be attentive, constantly evaluating my options as each headland was attained. Navigation was straight forward, and the way was clear. In the early afternoon I rounded Kebister Ness to find myself close to the northern and narrow entrance to Bressay Sound. The return to the busyness of Lerwick was a dramatic transition from a wild and lonely existence. I suddenly found myself surrounded by shipping, industrial waterfrontage and the ever-present noise of vehicles and machinery. The tide too seemed to have a sting in its tail by running strongly against me, so much so, I had to paddle hard to make headway past a couple of berthed oil rig service ships. I was worried I would be forced into their looming steel hulls. Eventually though I made it past the docks to the small harbour where the lifeboat was berthed. I slipped through the entrance and stopped paddling. I was weary and a wave of emotion welled up from deep within. I had managed to circumnavigate mainland Shetland. This was quite something, possibly even greater than much of what I had managed to complete before. I think this was because of the remoteness of Shetland, the sense of being somewhere foreign, and being alone. The aloneness was a powerful factor in my self-awareness during this leg of my journey. There wasn't the option of making a phone call and having Karen come and meet me. Neither was there anyone to welcome me into Lerwick, to stand on the quay and whoop congratulations with hearty waves. I arrived unnoticed and unrecognised. My achievement was a private affair.

Landing on a wooden dock, I wandered up into the impressive Lerwick lifeboat station. In its day, the edifice must have been an authoritative harbour building. With a sense of trepidation, I made my way up the impressive stairway and into a huge crew room with an adjacent office. John Best, the full-time mechanic for the lifeboat, greeted me with genuine warmth, making a pot of tea and passing me a plate piled high with biscuits. There was no question of where I was to stay because as he said with a wink and a wry smile, the couches in the crew room make excellent beds. I didn't enquire why he would know this, but gratefully accepted the invitation. After the tea and biscuits, the scalding hot shower was restorative heaven. *Sahwira* was unpacked and laid up alongside the harbour wall. This was going to be home for two nights and I was looking forward to spending time exploring Lerwick. That evening I was invited to join the crew for a training exercise on the lifeboat. It was exhilarating to sweep down Bressay Sound along the rocky shoreline I had crept past early in the morning eleven days earlier. I felt heroic as I stood there on the thrumming deck, dressed in the bulky 'yellows' of an R.N.L.I. crewperson. The July evening light just above sixty degrees north lasted long enough for us to return to Lerwick close to eleven, under a fiery red sky, the sun setting far beyond the western side of the island. It was close to midnight when I finally slipped into my sleeping bag on one of the comfortable crew room sofas with a couple of welcome beers inside me.

I had a busy time in Lerwick. I was invited onto the Lerwick / Bressay ferry by Mike who is the captain of this vessel. He is a crew member of the lifeboat. It's a short run across the sound between the islands but an impressive operation, nonetheless. I was given the full tour and even joined the crew for their break of tea and biscuits in their tight crew room, where I desperately attempted to keep up with the conversation without having to say "pardon" or "excuse me" too often. I was not tuned into the lyrical Shetlander dialect. I did know 'peerie' was small, but that wasn't a word which was used very much on the Bressay ferry. Another invitation was from Peter, also on the lifeboat crew, who is a meteorologist with the Met Office in Lerwick, to visit their weather station when they launched the daily weather balloon. This was a fascinating interlude in my journey though I didn't understand a huge amount of the science.

I visited Clickimin Broch situated on the edge of town, beside the lochan which gives it its name and juxtaposed with twentieth century urban development. It was incongruous to wander around the site overlooked by modern housing. Like many historical sites with a high tourist interest, the remains were prettily maintained, with well-tended lawn like grass and loose stone chip paths. Despite this though, I couldn't help but be impressed by the sheer size of this prehistoric homestead, with the thick-walled central broch structure surrounded by attendant buildings, all within a defensive wall with a single gateway. Wandering around I was struck by the richness of our historical heritage in Scotland and how readily accessible it is. I wondered how it was structures of this nature survived through the millennia. It's always been easy to assume it's our generation who are the enlightened ones with a sense of history and place. It never occurred to me humans of the past will have venerated their heritage as much as I do now. Why wouldn't a man in his fifties in the 16thC wandering around these ruined iron age buildings hold them in as much awe and reverence? I mulled this over as I wandered along the asphalt pavement back into the bustling town.

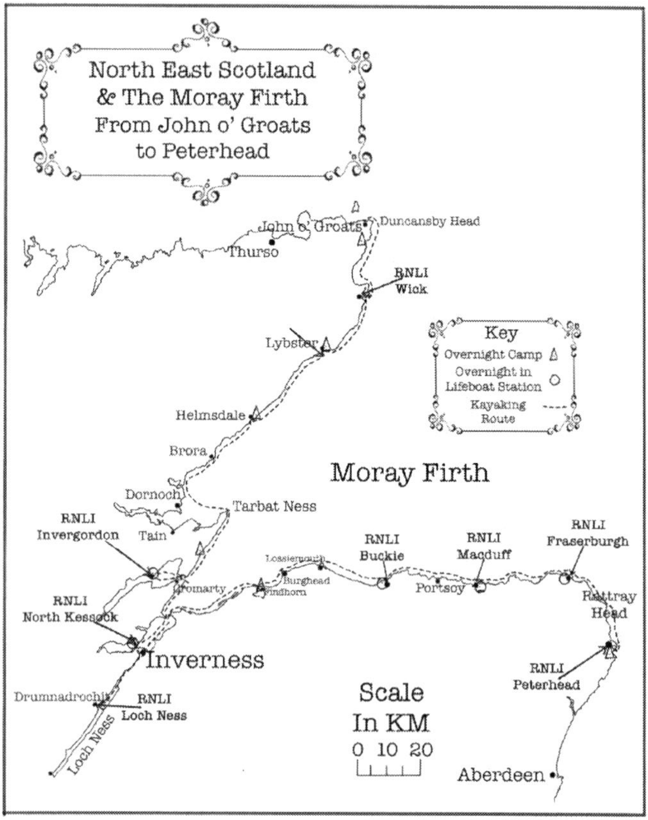
North East Scotland
& The Moray Firth
From John o' Groats
to Peterhead
Key
Overnight Camp
Overnight in Lifeboat Station
Kayaking Route
John o' Groats
Duncansby Head
Thurso
RNLI
Wick
Lybster
Helmsdale
Brora
Moray Firth
Dornoch
Tarbat Ness
RNLI
Invergordon
Tain
Cromarty
Lossiemouth
Burghead
Findhorn
RNLI
Buckie
Portsoy
RNLI
Macduff
RNLI
Fraserburgh
Rattray Head
RNLI
North Kessock
Inverness
RNLI
Peterhead
Drumnadrochit
RNLI
Loch Ness
Loch Ness
Scale
In KM
0 10 20
Aberdeen

Northeast Scotland and The Moray Firth John o' Groats to Peterhead

Chapter 32

The time arrived to embark on the Northlink ferry back to the Orkney Islands from where I'd continue my journey southwards. I was gifted a complimentary passage by the ferry firm which was incredibly generous. The late afternoon passage was smooth and on arriving in Kirkwall late in the night, I realised I once more faced serious decisions regarding the ethics of my adventure, because of another unfavourable forecast. If I chose to paddle onwards from Kirkwall, making my way to the Pentland Firth, I was in danger again of battling strong winds when I least wanted them, namely along the northeastern coastline of mainland Scotland. I was now fast running out of time to complete my whole journey in a gainly fashion. So, finding myself delayed on the Orkney Isles would have a serious impact on my ability to gain momentum.

It was a tough choice, but in the morning, I put a call out on a Facebook group for any Orkney kayakers to kindly give me a lift to South Ronaldsay, where I could take the ferry across the Pentland Firth, back to the mainland. In a matter of minutes, I received a response, and I was kindly given a lift by a kayaker called Iain from Shetland, who had been attending the sea kayaking symposium being held in Orkney. Everything seemed to happen with haste and before I knew it, I was once more loading my kayak and bulging IKEA bags onto the small passenger ferry to John o' Groats. Once back on the mainland, I set to, preparing myself to go to sea, even though by now it was close to the early evening. I wanted to press my advantage and round Duncansby Head while the weather was benign, and I was assured a fair passage through what were notoriously turbulent waters.

I was patient enough to wait for the tide to turn, because the tide race around Duncansby Head wasn't one I wanted to become entangled in. Despite the late hour, I was confident I would make it to Freswick Bay in time to establish camp and enjoy a restful evening. Ahead was another significant moment of my journey and which marked what I had long viewed as the penultimate stretch of coastline, leading to my finish down at Eyemouth. Somehow though, I didn't appreciate the enormity of the moment, instead glancing anxiously at the swirling waters of the Pentland Firth beyond the John o' Groats harbour. I could make out the looming corner of the headland which marked the far north-eastern corner of mainland Britain but not the seas at its foot. I searched for tell tale signs of white capped waves and a rushing tide race, but there were none.

Eventually the moment arrived to load my kayak and put to sea. I was nervous but now I had come so far and faced so much, what lay ahead was well within my stride. It seemed the East Coast was a mere formality, and, in a few weeks, I would be crossing my finish line. It was a lovely late afternoon with light winds, which helped ease the low-grade anxiety I was feeling. The tide had turned, and I found my passage eased towards the ominous cliffs of Duncansby Head. I scanned the surface of the slight sea ahead, searching for any signs of a tide race to be avoided. I was so intent on this; I almost missed the moment I turned the corner and set a new course southward. So as it happened, another significant chapter of my odyssey began without fanfare. Looking down at my compass, I was delighted to note my bearing was now one hundred and eighty degrees. What lay ahead was largely unknown and as I had done until now, I faced the uncertainty with equanimity. I would take each day as it arrived. Now though, I allowed myself the self-congratulatory pleasure of rounding the last great headland of my journey – or so I thought at the time. I was out of the unpredictable seas of the north coast and now venturing down what I assumed to be the easier waters of the east. Certainly, if the conditions I were enjoying at that moment were an indication of what lay ahead, then it would be plain paddling.

A couple of figures atop the cliff high above on Duncansby Head, provided the perspective I needed to help feel the enormity of my location. The cliffs were as all others I had traversed until now, and I noticed how blasé I had become. Even the tide picking up its pace and sweeping me faster through the channel between the huge stack known as the Knee and the mainland, on a building and exciting wave train, didn't stir my spirits. To spice things up I cockily paddled closer inshore, feeling the significant swell lift me towards the flat sheets of sandstone which adorned the fringes of the cliff bases. I was enjoying toying with the sea and an element of recklessness had taken grip.

The mighty and thick set Stacks of Duncansby, were a delight to paddle past. Seals abounded in the clear waters around their bases, and I enjoyed the company of a couple of them, as they swam close alongside checking me out. They seemed less fearful than the seals over on the west coast. I surmised this might possibly be due to no fish farms along the east coast, and consequently they weren't shot at for disturbing the fish. I ambled along beneath the inspiring scenery, drifting a little and then paddling slowly. The stacks form one of Scotland's iconic coastal landscapes and photographs taken of them from the high cliffs can be found in calendars, coffee table books and many Scottish websites. It was again quite an experience to be there, alone in my kayak, threading my way through the rocks around their bases.

The cliffs, layered as they were with sheets of guano spattered sandstone, were from time to time punctured by mighty chasms or geos. I was never sure how to pronounce geo. Was it *jee-oh* or *ghee-oh*? I chose the former. Wife Geo was a chasm too tempting to paddle past without entering and exploring, on the map it carried the alluring word – caves! Prudence dictated because I was alone, I ought not go too far into the geo for fear of having an accident in the sizeable swell, which boomed in and out of the abyss. This would be a messy place to extricate myself on my own. Nevertheless, I made the decision to head into the cleft and have a nosy. I told myself I could always retreat if I wanted to.

I edged in, noticing for the first time the swell was substantially larger than I had assumed. I stopped forward progress when a large set of waves washed through, creating soulful echoey booms from deep within the hollow cliff. As I waited for the sea to settle while the waves swept out seaward again, I doubted my wisdom. My inquisitiveness was piqued however, and I wanted to explore further. Accompanied by other kayakers, this would have been an easy undertaking but now, with the booms from deep within and the rolling swell lifting and dropping with gut swooping regularity, I was beginning to feel unsure. The only person egging me on was myself, so I had no one to blame for my decision to edge in further. The cleft I was in was wide enough to turn my kayak which is what I did. Looking seaward, I was rewarded by the spectacular sight of an eggshell blue sky, framed by the cave like entrance of the geo. Outside, a flight of guillemots skimmed by, low over the sea and perfectly silhouetted as they passed the geo entrance. I used this opportunity to assess the swell, waiting a good length of time to count the sets and to ascertain their steepness. What seemed to be a scary rush of water when I first entered, now felt manageable. I decided to proceed further inwards.

I turned a corner and found myself in what felt to be a wonderful natural theatre. A boulder strewn beach at the back of the large void was the stage, while the high greasy walls with white streaked bird inhabited ledges, were the stalls. I was in the watery auditorium. I imagined the gulls and the kittiwakes looking down with disdain from their lofty roosts. It would have been easy to turn and make my way out through the geo I had entered. However, there was an intriguing passage leading to another blind corner. Emboldened I chose to explore this and pressed onwards, just as a larger than normal set of waves swept into the natural theatre. As if a crowd were rising to their feet to cheer and applaud, the waves crashed and thundered onto the stage of boulders, refracting back to create a moment of mayhem of confused and chaotic sea. This was exhilarating and if it had been possible, I would have lifted myself off the seat of my kayak and cheered and applauded too. As it was, I allowed myself an uncustomary whoop and a holler which echoed around the walls with the deafening crash of the waves. The spectating birds continued to look down with disdain.

Warily, because of the suddenness of the previous set of waves sweeping into the geo, I paddled into another open chasm and saw ahead a widening exit to the open sea. Suddenly I spotted to the left, the entrance to a narrow slot, through which a substantial amount of water was flowing. I was intrigued. Peering into it, I couldn't work out if it was navigable or not, but by the amount of sea water being washed through, I guessed whatever passageway lay beyond was a substantial one. I edged closer, deftly working my paddles to hold my position in the swirling waters while I attempted to gain a better perspective of what lay beyond the opening. I was feeling playful and adventurous, and I wanted to enter the slot and explore further. Discretion ought to be the better part of valour, especially when one is kayaking solo in a laden expedition sea kayak, within the tight confines of a Caithness geo in a sizeable easterly swell.

In an instant though, I made up my mind and I was nudging *Sahwira's* prow into the entrance of the slot. I was in! I noticed with some unease, now I was in the confines of the chasm how tight it was. I didn't have room to paddle normally and instead had to dip each blade tight against each side of the kayak, the opposite blade vertically above my head. Once in the slot I realised too, to make any further progress I had to commit myself to making my way through a dogleg, despite not being able to see what lay beyond this. Given what I observed of the geology of the geo, I assumed the slot would continue beyond the dogleg without narrowing any further. However, what I couldn't be certain of was whether it might be choked by fallen boulders. I knew once through the dog leg; it would be near impossible to reverse the route and I would be committed to moving forward. As it was, it was going to be tricky to exit the situation I had placed myself. The sounds of the sea echoing through the passageways of the geo and the cries of the lofty sea birds added a level of excitable ambiance to the impasse. I didn't linger and made the decision to move forwards.

The sound of my paddle blades scraping on the rough grit of the sandstone rock, was more unbearable than the fear of what might be on the other side of the dogleg. With my heart in my mouth and now committed, preparing myself for the worst, I worked my kayak through the tight turns as best I could, without scraping her fragile gunwales on the rough sandstone sides of the chasm. I found myself in a tight slot and with a rush of relief, I saw daylight about a hundred metres away at the far end. There was no impassable obstruction either. I worked my way forwards towards the light. The passage was too narrow to paddle properly, and it was easier to use my hands on either damp wall to pull myself through. Suddenly it seemed as if the tunnel was darkening, as if the light was diminishing. I looked ahead and was alarmed to see a high wall of water coursing down the passageway towards me! A wave was working its way down the channel and there was no escaping it. I was in the tightest section of the cleft and realised when my kayak and I were lifted, and then dropped by the swell, there was a chance we would be wedged between the walls below the water level in the following slump, when the wave receded. I frantically pulled myself forward a metre just as the silent body of North Sea water reached me, and effortlessly and gracefully lifted *Sahwira*, leaving the impression of being raised skywards. As fast as the crest had reached me, so did the following trough and the descent into this was considerably less pleasant. The drop must have been three metres and there was a distinct gut swooping sensation, as *Sahwira* seemed to slide down between the walls of the cleft into what appeared to be a bottomless dark pit. I tensed my buttocks fearing an almighty crunch as the kayak's hull was dropped onto rocks, waiting below the surface. Thankfully none occurred, and the second wave swept through with the consequential following trough, and then the final and larger wave of the sets. Feeling rather shaken I pulled myself forward to the point a few metres ahead, where I could once again make use of my paddles and made best haste for the chasm's exit. Emerging into the open air was akin leaving a cinema after watching a matinee action film. My pulse was drumming.

On the open sea again, I experienced a curious sensation of euphoria. The fear I felt had been real. This had been exacerbated by the knowledge finding myself stuck within the chasm, would result in a dire situation. I berated my foolishness and decided I had been unnecessarily risky. Yet, despite this recrimination, the elation of facing up to the challenge of exploring the geo on my own, was an affirmation of my strong sense of adventure. It felt good to have come through this and to have succeeded, with a task which to all intents and purposes, looked unlikely.

I only had a few miles left to paddle before the wide expanse of Freswick Bay and these were covered in good time. Camp was made on a comfortable patch of sheep hewn grass and I enjoyed my first night on the east coast of mainland Scotland, knowing in the morning it would be the rising sun I would see. From now on, the sun would set behind me, over on the west.

Chapter 33

The far north easterly once busy fishing port of Wick was my next destination, where there was the first of the remaining twenty lifeboat stations to visit down Scotland's east coast. From Freswick Bay I had a wonderful paddle beneath the rugged sandstone cliffs and intriguing ruined castles, particularly the impressive façade of Keiss Castle. From the perspective of the sea, it looked as if it was a substantial castle ruin, when sadly, it was just one remaining wall perched precariously on the cliff edge. Wick was clearly a port and town which had once seen and enjoyed much prosperity. Sadly, it seemed a shadow of these previous times but the welcome I received from the lifeboat crew, was nonetheless effusive in generosity and warmth. Because I'd arrived in the late morning and I was keen to paddle onwards, I did not accede to the kind invitation to stop the night and make use of their facilities. When I declined, I was instead generously given money by Ian the coxswain to buy myself a slap-up lunch, before I carried on my way. It was another wonderfully warm gesture of selfless humanity. Before we said our goodbyes, we agreed I would attempt to meet them and their lifeboat much further along the coast at Helmsdale, where there was an annual late summer gala they always attended.

I enjoyed a lovely afternoon of easy paddling along the base of high sandstone cliffs with wonderful names such as Twinkie, Tod's Gote, Gote a' Sly, Muckle Red Craig and Creag-a-backyard to name a few. My stop for the night was at the curiously shaped harbour of Lybster. Here I encountered the fiercest midges of my whole journey. They were unrelenting in their intensity, causing me to hide in my tent despite the lovely summer evening. I was saved from this predicament by a friend and his wife who took me out for dinner, driving me all the way back to Wick where I'd been earlier in the day.

I set off at dawn the following day and in fair seas, I ploughed a lonely but determined twenty-mile route to Helmsdale further down the coast. I was determined to arrive in good time for the gala and spend time with my new Wick lifeboat friends. Sadly, as it had been on previous days in my adventure when I'd set myself a determined target, I paddled hard and fast without giving time to appreciate the wonderful scenery I was passing. I was paddling past coastline steeped in history with several landmarks I would've liked to explore more thoroughly. It is with some regret I chose not to meander and appreciate the spectacular nature of the far northeastern coastline. However, I was fixated on reaching Helmsdale and I did so in five hours of hard paddling. I was grinning from ear to ear when I sidled up to the shingle of the inner harbour shoreline and I heard my name announced over the tannoy, as the kayaker who was kayaking around Scotland for the R.N.L.I.. That afternoon I enjoyed receiving warm congratulations from strangers and feeling included as one of the lifeboat crew, who were giving guided tours of their lifeboat. The Helmsdale gala was everything one would imagine of a small fishing village celebration, of their local culture and heritage. People had made a huge effort to provide substantial quantities of home baked goods and food. There was music, singing and dancing, and an air of happiness and gaiety lifted my spirits. I was pleased I'd made the effort to join the lifeboat crew as part of these celebrations. I even got to meet the town's local celebrity who was there to support the event. Edwyn Collins (of Orange Juice fame) was generous in the interest he showed in my venture.

Once the festivities had ceased at the end of the afternoon, I wandered up to a local hotel with Ian and the rest of the lifeboat crew for a huge meal, and more beers than I should really have consumed. By the time I climbed into my sleeping bag, my head was swimming, somewhat literally but mostly metaphorically. It'd been a long and rewardingly full day and I slept soundly.

After another early rise and a hasty visit to pay my respects to the 2007 emigration monument overlooking the town, I quietly slipped away from Helmsdale. Invergordon a few days away in the Cromarty Firth, was my next lifeboat station destination. As I paddled southwards in the early morning sunshine and on a pleasantly rolling sea, I reflected on my visit to 'The Emigrants'. This is the statue which commemorates the huge numbers of economically poor highlanders, who were forced from their ancestral lands to find new homes, some if they could in Scotland, but most compelled to sail abroad, to populate growing British colonies. The 'Clearances' as this period of ethnological Scottish history is termed, remains the cause of debate today. Some view the eviction of impoverished tenants a necessary economic choice for embattled landowners. Others view the practice a form of cultural genocide leading to the collapse of a way of life and a system of society, which had served Scotland's north and west for hundreds of years. Knowing for myself what it's like to be uprooted from the country of my birth and to establish a new life in a foreign nation, I couldn't help feeling a sense of distress at what the thousands of highland people faced. The closing line on the dedication to the statue remained with me; "*Their voices will echo forever thro the empty straths and glens of their homeland."* It reflected the poignancy I experience when I come across the tumbled ruins of these peoples' long-gone homes and communities. I will forever wonder about them and the lives they lived before they were banished.

I was now kayaking waters I was familiar with, having spent many happy years living in the quaint town of Cromarty on the Black Isle, situated on the edge of the firth it gave its name to. Knowing where I was, and knowing I needn't worry about what lay ahead, infused a delightful sense of calm and ease to my paddling. The weather was settled and for once the winds were light, providing easy days of kayaking. I spent the night with new friends at Littleferry before crossing the Dornoch Firth to Tarbet Ness with its distinctive red and white lighthouse, and then making my way down the coast to the entrance of the Cromarty Firth. I had to stop for the night at the small village of Balintore, because I'd only paddled half the day, due to a late departure governed by the tides. It was here I encountered what would become a somewhat delicate issue all my way down the east coast. On the west and north coast of Scotland I found myself used to the wildness of the landscape around where I camped for the night. There was always little human habitation nearby. Here on the east coast, there were not the isles and skerries to camp on and neither were there many wild and empty stretches of coastline. Because of the geography, wherever it was suitable to camp, it was also suitable for habitation and so I often found myself camping in full view of people's homes and businesses. This caused some unease when it came to my ablutions. The ability to live wonderfully feral in this regard, as I had been doing till now, simply wasn't possible. In the short term, I managed with long muscle strained walks to the fringes of bays and beaches for the privacy and the ability to use the sea as a natural flush. As time went on and the coastline became busier the further south I journeyed, the opportunity to plan and use public facilities made this aspect of adventuring easier.

Entering the Cromarty Firth through the Sutors, the high headlands on either side of the narrow entrance, felt like returning home. These were now waters I knew intimately, having paddled here innumerable times during our five happy years in Cromarty. I kept myself well offshore from the town's sea front and made my way through increasingly lively seas towards Invergordon, seven miles further into the firth. My way to the industrial port of Invergordon was lined with anchored oil drilling rigs, looming above like the immobile machines from the War of the Worlds. Suddenly, the Invergordon lifeboat appeared through the rough seas, crashing her way with ease towards me, ploughing the waves aside and creating a satisfying wake of white foam. I was warmly greeted with much waving and loud shouts of encouragement. It was particularly special they had come out to greet me, because I'd worked closely with them in training exercises and on actual missing persons searches, when I was a voluntary Coastguard Rescue Officer at Cromarty.

It was lovely to reconnect with many of the crew who I remembered from just four years previously. We crowded into their crew room, and I was plied with food and copious mugs of coffee. We laughed at remembered incidents and they listened intently to my tales of my journey. I felt once more comfortably surrounded by friends. In an act of wonderful generosity, I was given bed and breakfast at a hotel in the town. It felt odd to leave my rather rancid pile of belongings at the lifeboat station and wander into the hotel with a single dry bag of clean clothes. Despite the comfort of the hotel, I felt out of place, almost as if I were a person who'd never experienced anything like this before. I think I cut quite a wild figure when I arrived and hopefully when I left the next morning, I had been somewhat restored to civility.

The next day I had a short hop back down the firth to Cromarty where I planned to stop for a couple of nights to catch up with the many friends I was lucky enough to have there. On arriving I set myself up on the Links, the stretch of mowed grass behind the golden sanded foreshore, enjoying the notion of camping in familiar surroundings. I spent the next day and a half wandering the town, dropping into the homes of people I knew and enjoying catching up on the gossip. I also used the opportunity to take the bus into Inverness where I bought memory cards for my camera and generally spoilt myself with a wander around the large supermarket, purchasing luxuries such as fresh doughnuts! The night of my arrival in Cromarty I took myself to the Cromarty Arms, the pub we frequented when we lived in the town. Here I splashed out on one of Helen's steak dinners, always my choice when we ate there. The pub filled up with friends and by the end of the night there was a happy throng of us in one of the corners, recounting tales with much laughter and hilarity. It was a memorable and happy night.

Refreshed and invigorated by reconnecting with so many friends and with their generous words of encouragement ringing in my ears, I set off early a morning later, heading for North Kessock near Inverness and then on to the city itself. I was joined on the water by Mike Armitage, my section manager from my Coastguard days. Being an avid sea kayaker himself, he was keen to paddle with me which was lovely. As we headed out through the Sutor narrows at the mouth of the Cromarty Firth, we were joined by a sizeable pod of bottlenose dolphins. The magnificent mammals are the furthest north of their species, and it was always a joy to share the seas with them. They were intent on their feeding but later in the morning we watched them leaping and cavorting from afar, when they were further out in the Moray Firth. Mike and I paddled happily together, reminiscing about our coastguard experiences and me learning of his youth lived over on the west coast of Scotland. We stopped at Chanonary Point to meet with the inspirational Charlie Phillips who is a feature of this natural gravel point, where it's possible to sit and watch in delight as the dolphins leap, play and feed in the powerful incoming tide. His incredible photography of these creatures has earned him just praise as one of the finest wildlife photographers in the country. Aside from his photographic skill, I found myself truly impressed with his knowledge about the dolphins he watched every day. He knew each one by the name it had been given by the wildlife researchers, its age and who it was related to. I could have sat with him for the rest of the day listening to him speak with passion and love for these beasts.

However, I had to press on to North Kessock where I was due to meet some of the crew of the North Kessock inshore lifeboat. I was now paddling through the upper reaches of the Moray Firth, still in waters I knew very well. Drawing closer to the high Kessock Bridge which gracefully reaches across the firth from Inverness to the Black Isle, I could see the distinct flashing blue lights of a cluster of emergency service vehicles a third of the way across the bridge. I then saw on the water beneath the bridge the bright orange flanks of the North Kessock lifeboat, as it slowly patrolled the waters about. I realised immediately with sadness there was an incident involving a person who was on the parapet of the bridge, agonising whether to leap to complete their suicide or not. I held back, not wanting to find my way into the midst of the drama and with relief, soon saw the lifeboat turn towards me and roar over to my position on the flooding tide. The blue lights on the bridge above disappeared and it was clear the situation had been safely resolved.

The crew of the Atlantic 85, a semi-rigid lifeboat with two powerful outboard engines, shouted their greeting and their welcomes while they roared around in a large arc. With that they sped back to the lifeboat station a few hundred metres away. After I'd arrived and pulled my kayak up the shore, I was invited for a burl on the lifeboat which I eagerly accepted. For the next twenty minutes, dressed in my kayaking clothing but wearing one of their chunky and substantial helmets, I held on to my hand grip for dear life, attempting to lean with the violent turns while at the same time trying to ride the saddle seat with some semblance of grace in the lumpy seas. It was an adrenaline-charged finish to my paddling day. It was enjoyable too to help them retrieve the boat and then wash it down and ready it for the moment, at any time day or night, when its services might be required. Being accepted so naturally in this manner was always reaffirming. It was here at North Kessock a couple of my followers on Twitter introduced themselves. Richard and his wife were incredibly generous in having gone out of their way to travel to North Kessock to say hello.

Chapter 34

After North Kessock I headed inland. The next day I once more met with Mike, who was going to paddle with me to the only Scottish inland R.N.L.I. lifeboat station at Drumnadrochict, on the northern shore of the mighty Loch Ness. The first few miles of the day's journey were along the sheltered and calm waters of the Caledonian Canal. It had only been a few years earlier when Karen and I had motored our small yacht, then our new home, along this route on our way to begin a new life on the west coast. For a while during the paddle that day I pondered the path I'd followed which had led to where I found myself in that moment. Three years ago, I'd never suspected I'd be kayaking these waters, especially as a part of a major solo expedition around the Scottish coastline. The weather was grey, and a strong wind blew right through the Great Glen from the west. There was no warning when we rounded the last bend in the canal and entered the dark peaty waters of Loch Ness, of the waves we found ourselves encountering. The full twenty-two-mile uninterrupted fetch of the loch meant there was a sizeable two metre swell running by the time it reached Dores, at the eastern end close to where we were. To reach Drumnadrochit and the lifeboat station there we had seven miles of incredibly bouncy conditions to paddle through. Despite the strength of the head wind, I was thoroughly enjoying myself. It felt novel to be kayaking in fresh water and not have the taste of salt in my mouth every time a wave crashed over my deck, and it was fun paddling alongside Mike, watching him seemingly disappear behind what seemed to be huge wave, so that only the top of his head was visible. Any thoughts of meeting the Loch Ness monster were swept away in the waves and the gale.

We eventually arrived at the lifeboat station which was in its infancy at the time. There had been a rescue service on the Loch which had been operated by the Coastguard, hence Mike's interest in my visit here because of his involvement in those days. The R.N.L.I. took over responsibility for the provision of a rescue service and R.N.L.I. Drumnadrochit was established. One wouldn't normally consider there to be a need for a lifeboat on an inshore body of water in Britain, but Loch Ness is not an ordinary body of water. It is incredibly long and deep, containing more water than all the lakes in England and Wales combined. Because of its location in the Great Glen, the natural geological fault running southwest to northeast across the Scottish Highlands, the surface conditions of the loch are governed by the winds which strongly blow up or down the glen. The loch is an important link in the ship bearing Caledonian Canal which cuts through the Great Glen and so mariners of all sorts must use the loch during a passage from east to west or vice versa. The Caledonian Canal is popular for pleasure boaters and holiday craft and it's these who often find themselves caught out by the sudden and surprisingly fierce conditions on the loch. As a result, the lifeboat on the loch is one of the busiest in Scotland.

We were warmly received at the lifeboat station when we arrived, with Mike clearly proud of his involvement with the establishment of this service. I was shown several impressive helmet camera films of previous rescues where the crew went to the aid of boaters and canoeists alike. At the time of my visit the station was fundraising for the construction of a dedicated lifeboat building where the crew could train, and equipment stored. After a couple hours of enjoying the hospitality of some of the crew it was time to head back to Inverness. Mike and I enjoyed a speedy wind assisted surf back down the loch and into the calm waters once more of the canal. Where the River Ness divided from the canal I said my goodbyes to Mike, because it was my intention to paddle down the river to where it emerged into the sea at Inverness. I knew the river conditions were low and I'd probably spend much of my time gingerly lifting my kayak over the rocky shallows, but it seemed a fitting conclusion to my foray inland, I should paddle on the river rather than the canal. It'd been an aspiration of mine to paddle the Ness, and this was the finest opportunity I had.

The ten kilometres of the river Ness from the loch down to the sea were hugely entertaining and not as difficult as I anticipated. There was enough water to scrape, albeit painfully sounding, through the shallows and down the various weirs. Sometimes the river gained in speed and strength to create short rapids which I loved taking my sea kayak through. Within an hour I arrived in Inverness and before I set a course seaward I dropped into an old place of work on the banks of the river where it met the sea. Once more sustained with tea and biscuits, I was back on my saltwater path and my onward journey.

It was late in the afternoon when I eventually arrived at the mouth of the Findhorn River where thankfully the tide was sweeping into Findhorn Bay and not out of it. Alarmingly I arrived at the same time as a violent electrical storm which shook my nerves to their core. With every retina searing flash of lightening, there immediately followed a gut reverberating roll of thunder, indicating the storm was right overhead. Floating on the surface of the sea as I was, I felt completely vulnerable and clenched my buttocks in fearful anticipation of being the lightening's next target. Thankfully the storm moved away up the coast to be replaced with the most incredible downpour I'd experienced in my kayak. The tropical sized rain drops exploded with crackling force on the kayak deck and beat a frenzied drumming tattoo on the surface of the sea around. It was amazing to watch the globules of freshwater skittering over the sea's surface in every direction. It'd been a long day and it was with considerable relief I pulled up onto the shore of the bay to find somewhere to camp.

Despite the desultory conditions that evening, I enjoyed numerous visitors to my hidden spot behind the dunes ranging from family friends, kayaking acquaintances, a former Outward Bound colleague and being taken under the wing of a group of young and vibrant female marine biologists, who were living in a nearby caravan. I enjoyed a hot shower and more tea and cake through their kindness, followed by a slap-up meal with my OB friend, Alan, in a local Findhorn pub.

I slipped out of Findhorn Bay before the sun had risen the next day to make my way to Buckie along the Moray coastline. I was once more in unfamiliar waters, and I enjoyed viewing the coastal landscape from my sea level vantage. I was particularly interested in spotting the remnants of dry-stone walling which would have constituted the Iron Age Pict settlement of Burghead. A period of Scotland's history which fascinates me. Beyond Burghead lay the wide expanse of Spey Bay fringed by empty stretches of golden sandy beaches. I stayed out to sea, well offshore to avoid the breaking swell and sent myself into one of my absent-minded reveries to keep me entertained, as I paddled away the long unbroken distance.

I arrived in Buckie early in the afternoon and made myself known to the lifeboat personnel at the station which was set prominently overlooking the sadly empty harbour. Buckie had once been a haven for the great fishing fleets which plied the Moray Firth waters and further out into the North Sea. There was a somewhat sad feeling of neglect to the surroundings which dampened my mood a little. Nevertheless, I was made welcome and invited to use the station as a place to stay for the night. Never one to turn down the opportunity for a hot shower and the comfort of indoor living, I readily accepted. Later that evening a few of the crew came to the station to meet me, and I spent a thoroughly convivial evening with them, whilst at the time being trounced by their skills on their crew room pool table.

Onwards from Buckie the next morning, my destination for the day was the old fishing port of Macduff. I was now paddling the outer fringes of the Moray Firth towards the distinctive eastern geographical bulge one can see on maps of Scotland. The coastline was excitingly new, and I relished the opportunity to paddle as close to the shoreline as I could. There were landmarks I'd heard of which I was looking forward to seeing. The first of these was Bow Fiddle Rock, just outside the small harbour town of Portnockie which itself is situated adjacent to the wonderfully named harbour town of Findochty. It was with boyish pleasure and joy, I paddled backwards and forwards a few times beneath the uniquely shaped natural arch of rock, looking very much like a violin bow, thus bestowing its name. This landmark is regularly featured on Scottish tourist literature and glossy photographic calendars. I loved the fact I'd arrived here under my own power and was able to enjoy seeing it in my inimitable way.

Next on my tourist list for the day were the ruins of Findlater Castle high on the edge of the cliffs. I wasn't disappointed when I passed under the crumbling walls. Portsoy was a harbour I'd long wanted to visit because of its continued connection to traditional boat building and celebration of wooden craft. Again, I wasn't disappointed, as I crept slowly through the harbour labyrinth into the inner basin. All about I saw the paraphernalia of a busy fishing port from a bygone age. I was impressed at how dedicated the local populace were at sustaining the feel of a traditional fishing town. There were wooden fish boxes neatly piled on the quays, wicker work fenders, numerous yawls of various sizes and even a couple of handcarts with wooden wheels. I was delighted to have arrived at somewhere so quaint and I snapped away with my camera. It was still early in the morning so there was no one around, I had the harbour to myself. Then I began to doubt what I was seeing. It all seemed too manicured to be a working harbour. In fact, there were no modern boats at all, and I would've expected to have seen a few, even in a dedicated traditional setting such as this. And then I saw them, standing neatly upright in the corner of the harbour between two stone buildings. They were a gantry of spotlights used for film production. I looked around again and realised with mirth I'd been taken in by the elaborate film set that was for the time being, Portsoy Harbour. I took a few more photos before deciding to slip away and continue onwards. It occurred as I did this, it was fortunate I'd arrived early in the morning before filming was under way and I might've interrupted a crucial scene. I later learned the remake of the film *Whisky Galore* was being filmed there. I wonder what Eddie Izzard, one of the lead actors, would've made of a scruffy sea kayaker stealing into shot?

I arrived in Macduff in the early afternoon to be greeted by lifeboat crew and R.N.L.I. volunteers cheering me in from high up on the harbour walls. Macduff was very much a working harbour, so it was useful to be guided by them safely through to the place where I could land and unpack. The lifeboat station wasn't far from the harbour, but it was unique in Scotland, because the inshore lifeboat here is 'berthed' on the back of a truck with a crane. Whenever the call comes to activate the lifeboat's service, the crew assemble and change at the lifeboat station, then drive to a best launch spot according to the needs of the situation, and lower into the sea from the truck. This negated the need for a fixed launching location for a stretch of coastline, which is peppered with small harbours, all of which provide perfect launching spots from the vehicle. Like all the lifeboat crews I'd met so far, they were incredibly proud of their vessel and the life saving service they provided. The truck was driven out of the garage where it was kept, so I could appreciate their set up more fully and I was impressed. They proudly stated their launch times were comparable to those of regular lifeboat stations and I didn't doubt their veracity. After taking a few photographs of *Sahwira* lying alongside the truck and lifeboat, we collected in the crew room where a wonderfully restorative cold beer was pressed into my hand.

With considerable apology, I was told I couldn't sleep overnight in the station because they had a community event which prevented this. Instead, they'd arranged for me to stay in a local Bed and Breakfast. I insisted it didn't matter if I found a patch of ground for my tent, and I impressed it wasn't necessary for them to be responsible for my lodgings. They wouldn't hear any of my protestations, so as I did in Invergordon, I collected what I needed and wended my way through the quiet Macduff streets to find my hosts for the night. I found the house where I was to stay was one of many similar fishermen's homes, unremarkable from the exterior though adding to the quaint attractiveness of the town architecture. My host invited me in and I was once more offered a warm welcome with a pot of tea and slabs of buttery shortbread. After, I was shown to my room and on entering I fear I may have gasped out loud, for centrepiece to the small space was a heavily ornate four poster bed, draped in wisps of chiffon. It was the last thing I was expecting, especially on a kayaking expedition such as mine. I was taken aback, and my host must have wondered if it wasn't to my liking, because she suddenly went silent. I couldn't have been more delighted by the exoticness of it all and I said as much. Sadly, though I don't think my host was mollified by my assurances and simply said, "I'll be leaving you now, here's a key to the front door." I felt like I'd broken the magic, and I wanted to begin the moment again from the time I arrived at the front door.

I fed myself on a fish supper that night, sitting above Macduff harbour gazing out over the coastline I'd paddled along earlier in the day. A moroseness was beginning to settle within, and I felt tired. I decided an early night was in order and I took myself off to my four-poster boudoir. Going to bed that night with the chiffon hanging about me, I was reminded of my childhood in Africa where I slept every night during the rainy season under a mosquito net. Like I used to then, I found myself making sure none of the chiffon would find itself on my face during the night. I slept soundly.

Chapter 35

The following morning quite a large group of lifeboat personnel had gathered at the station to meet me and wave me off. Rather than carry my kayak the few hundred metres to the slipway in the harbour where I was to pack and launch from, everything was put on the back of a small truck and with everyone standing in the back, each firmly holding *Sahwira* so she wouldn't fall, we drove slowly to the dockside. We looked like a funeral cortège where the coffin was on the back of the truck with the pall bearers crowding about it as it was slowly and respectfully driven through the streets. The one difference to my conjured scenario was the loud jocularity surrounding me and once more I was reminded of the strong bond the lifeboat crews held. Once unloaded from the truck I set about packing the kayak. I expected farewells to be made and I'd be left to my devices, but it was quickly apparent, everyone was eager to watch me perform what was for me a standard daily task. I sensed they thought it improbable I'd fit everything into slim and slender *Sahwira.* There were murmurs of amazement as I steadily worked my way through the contents of each bag, placing the items into their preset places in one of the three kayak compartments. I felt like a magician performing unfathomable street magic in front of their incredulous gaze. It was with a distinct flourish I firmly tapped the last hatch closed and stood from my position by the kayak with a broad grin. I should've shouted "Ta-daa" and affected a flamboyant wave of my hands as I did so. I paddled away from Macduff with a line of new friends waving from the harbour wall, some shouting words of encouragement over a widening gap of sea.

My goal for the day was Fraserburgh and ahead I knew I'd some fine cliff scenery to savour. The wind had risen but the weather was settled, and the sea wasn't rough. It was going to be a lovely nineteen-mile day. I ambled along the coastline taking delight in my proximity to the shore and paddling between the outlying skerries. Troup Head is the largest gannet colony on mainland Scotland with over two thousand nesting pairs. Accompanied on the high cliffs by thousands of guillemots, kittiwakes, razorbills and puffins, they created one of the greatest natural spectacles of wild Scotland. As soon as I paddled around the headland past the tiny hamlet of Crovie, next to Gardenstown, I could see the sky was dark with wheeling birds above the Troup Head cliffs a mile or so away. It was an incredible sight, which only gained in impressiveness the closer I paddled. Before long I could hear the raucousness of the colonies, the screeches and strident cries of thousands of individual birds creating a discordant, yet beautiful chorus around. The air was full of their noise, almost as if it was swamped by their calling. My senses were overloaded. Around me birds flashed by as they swooped and dived, soared and flapped. Gannets thumped with force into the sea around like large bullets fired from a canon on the cliffs. I sat and watched them with awe, noticing the precision with how they entered the water, folding their sleek wings alongside their white bodies at the last minute and disappearing beneath the surface, a stream of small bubbles leaving the only clue of their sudden immersion. A few short minutes later, the gannet would appear suddenly on the surface like a popping cork, a few feet away. After a quick glance around, they then unfolded their long wings and effortlessly lifted themselves from the sea's clinging surface, hauling themselves into the sky to once more begin patrolling before maybe again, turning inverted and diving for the sea like a dart. With so many birds doing this around, I found my head was swivelling in every direction, attempting to take them all in. There was a pervading odour of bird guano which provided a pungent, almost acrid, olfactory backdrop to the overwhelming setting.

It gladdened my heart to find myself amidst such natural vibrancy. For many years I'd been aware of the dire tales and warnings of our declining sea bird populations, all caused by the excesses of human consumption and neglectful stewardship of the oceans. In fact, there were many times during this journey when I found myself feeling noticeably depressed when I learned from local folks, sea bird colonies near them, had declined over recent times. Here though, it felt wild nature was in command and through the brilliance in their improbable aerial displays, the magnificence of their sheer numbers and the uninhibited joyfulness of their squawking, I was humbled into accepting myself as one very small part in the grandness of life.

I could've lingered in the feather and guano strewn sea beneath the gannetry for ages, absorbing the breathtaking atmosphere. Sadly though I had to press onwards. I'd arranged to meet the volunteer press officer for the Fraserburgh lifeboat in the hamlet of Pennan at lunchtime and I didn't want to keep him waiting. It was with considerable sadness I left the teeming sound-filled skies behind.

Arriving in Pennan was the realisation of a secret ambition. One of my favourite films of all time is the quintessentially Scottish film, *'Local Hero'*. A film of the early 1980s, it tells the story of an American oil executive with a

Scottish surname, sent to a remote coastal village in Scotland to make a deal, on behalf of the oil giant he works for, with the locals to buy a huge swathe of their land for an oil refinery. It is a lighthearted comedy with a happy outcome. Through the film there are delightful scenes where the locals take 'Mac' under their wing, and he experiences the quirkiness of Scottish rural life. The film was filmed in two main locations, on the lovely white sanded beaches of the Keppoch coastline on the west coast, close to Mallaig and here in Pennan.

Like many of the small fishing communities on the east coast of Scotland, Pennan consists of a single row of houses and buildings set on a narrow strip of foreshore at the base of steep cliffs behind. It has its own harbour which would have served their small fishing fleet in days gone by. It is both an unremarkable village and a picturesque one too. As I drew closer to the shoreside hamlet I saw I was being vigorously photographed which made me smile. I enjoyed a fleeting moment of feeling famous. I pulled into the harbour to be warmly greeted by the Fraserburgh R.N.L.I. press officer. I took the opportunity to wander up and down the single main road of the village, easily recalling the scenes from *Local Hero* which were filmed here. The hotel was real, but the famous old fashioned red phone box was a prop. It was through the payphone in this box, the protagonist would telephone his boss in America, always a moment of comedy in the story. When you see the film, as I urge you to do, you'll smile with me when I mention the tearaway youth on the small motorbike roaring up and down this single street. Just one of the many subtle delights adding to the quality of the story.

I continued on my way, agreeing to keep an eye out for the press officer who wanted to photograph me at various points along the coast to Fraserburgh. The stretch of coast beyond Pennan Head was some of the finest I encountered on the journey. It felt wild and remote with jagged reefs and skerries cutting through the surface of the sea. There was a small cave like opening through one sizeable reef which invited me to paddle through it. As I did so, I enjoyed the distinct feeling of passing through a portal of some sort, from one world to another. I slowed my pace to enjoy picking my way through the rocks, while seals seemed to take delight in playing hide and seek with me by inquisitively following, and then dramatically splashing under water when I turned around in my seat to look at them.

I met the photographer one more time where there was a lovely sea arch guarding a small sandy beach. I didn't mind paddling backwards and forwards through this a few times to provide him with the shot he was looking for. The last few miles were through a gathering sea to Kinnaird Head and the opening to Fraserburgh Harbour. The lifeboat came out to greet me when I arrived at the head, just when the tide had changed, creating extremely uncomfortable short sharp metre and a half waves. After such a wonderfully relaxing day of enjoyable paddling, it was a shock to find myself having to concentrate hard on not getting caught out and tipped over. After greetings were cheerfully made between me bouncing around on the waves in my kayak, and the yellow garbed crew gazing down from their comfortable lofty perches on the orange lifeboat, I set about paddling for the harbour. As I approached the entrance, the intensity of the confused sea suddenly increased. For the final couple of hundred metres of the day's journey I was focussed intently on remaining upright, my buttocks as tightly clenched as the concentrated expression on my face. It simply wouldn't do to capsize in front of the Fraserburgh lifeboat.

Thankfully all ended well, and it wasn't long before *Sahwira* was unpacked and along with my four IKEA bags of worldly belongings, I was ensconced with the lifeboat crew in the large and welcoming station crew room. I then discovered another challenge, understanding Doric, the unique dialect of the Aberdeenshire east coast. It was like a language I'd never heard before and the bemused consternation must've shown in my face, because with much hilarity Vic, the coxswain, mercilessly laughed at my confusion. No one attempted to tone down their fast-running dialect, but neither did they seem bothered I kept asking "Pardon?" after just about every sentence, they uttered. It wasn't long before I managed to grasp the rudiments of their conversations and contribute more than nodding along dumbly.

An hour after my arrival, a call came from Aberdeen Coastguard requesting the Fraserburgh lifeboat launch to the aid of a large yacht, stricken with a mechanical fault and unable to make headway to safety. Immediately, in split seconds the jocularity dropped away to be replaced by a palpable intenseness of purpose. Within minutes, further crew members were running into the lifeboat station while those already there were making their way to the lifeboat, dressed in their foul weather clothing. In under ten minutes, the lifeboat with her compliment of eight crew was building up an impressive speed as she exited the harbour entrance. This was the first actual lifeboat launch I'd witnessed on my journey, and I was mightily impressed. It was a thrill to have a front row view of the whole event and I found myself feeling emotionally moved by the experience. I forced away a lump in my throat because there was no need for it, but it was there, nonetheless. I was reminded again, of the selfless nature of lifeboat service, how women and men who volunteer to crew these craft, are prepared to lay aside whatever they're doing to go to the aid of a stranger. It is one of the most humanist acts of selflessness I can think of. It wasn't lost on me as the Fraserburgh lifeboat crew ran for the station in response to their pagers, they did so past the poignant statue of a lifeboatman, the 2010 memorial for the thirteen lives of the Fraserburgh crews lost when the lifeboat capsized in 1919, 1953 and 1970. I admire them hugely.

A couple of hours later, the news arrived the lifeboat was returning into the harbour with the yacht in tow. I watched again with quiet admiration how deftly and gently the crew eased the powerless yacht into a waiting berth, and without rancour or any sense of patronising grandiosity, made their farewells to the crew of the yacht, who were effusive in their gratitude. When we were all gathered in the lifeboat station crew room once more, Vic with his customary good humour shouted out, "Where were we then?"

Such was the warm hospitality of all the Fraserburgh crew, I chose to take a rest day here and simply hang out in the station with them. It seemed in any coastal town which had an all-weather R.N.L.I. lifeboat station, this building became a community hub. I saw this in Portpatrick, Portree, Longhope, Stromness, Aith and Wick. It was lovely watching how the locals enjoyed the welcoming open-door policy of the stations, dropping by for a blether and the craic. It all served a serious purpose too. The lifeboats crews were kept aware of what was occurring in the local boating and fishing communities and like wise, they were able to speak about safety and any current maritime concerns they needed to impart. Fraserburgh was no different and I enjoyed being introduced to all visitors as the "crazy kayaker", meant with obvious respect and affection.

Sadly, after a day of rest and my sides continually split with laughter, the like I hadn't enjoyed in years, it was time to move on again.

Chapter 36

I've no idea how it happened, but I'd discharged the battery on my Garmin GPS. I discovered this only when I was well out of Fraserburgh Harbour. The sea conditions were unsettled, and I wasn't keen to turn around, head back in, dig out spare batteries from the forward compartment and continue my way. I wasn't worried so much about not having a GPS affecting my navigation for the day, more annoyed because I would not have a recorded log to refer to. It was eighteen miles to Peterhead and although the sea was restless, the wind forecast was for calm. I didn't anticipate any problems, so I pressed on. If only I had decided to stop on Cairnbulg beach before rounding the point, I wouldn't have had the day I did.

This was not a stretch of coast to be taken lightly. I was rounding Rattray Head, a notable landmark on Scotland's northeast coast. Like Ardnamurchan on the west coast, it features as the changeover point between inshore weather forecast sectors. It also has a formidable reputation as a danger to shipping and several wrecks can be seen littering the sands of the surrounding beaches. In planning for the day, I hadn't been too concerned about what lay ahead. I had faced more difficult seas when planning for other notable headlands such as the Mull of Kintyre, Cape Wrath and Duncansby Head. Rattray Head was not bounded by cliffs and there were no long stretches of difficult coastline to be worried about.

The weather was calm but an ominous quality to the day was beginning to emerge. Heavy grey cloud was building, the sky darkening, without definition. The horizon disappeared. In winter where the falling snow creates a horizon-less landscape, it's referred to as a white-out. This was similar. It wasn't foggy, but without the horizon or any features on the sea, I had little idea of judging distance. Without the ability to do this, I found it challenging to gain a sense of my progress. I had chosen to paddle at least a mile out to sea to avoid becoming caught in any tide races running close around the Headland. Vic had warned me to be wary of the surf which can pile onto the beaches on either side of Rattray Head, by ensuring I was well off the headland where the lighthouse stood. *Sahwira* rose and fell on an unseen and substantial swell, sweeping stealthily shoreward, like ranks from a silent army intent on a surprise invasion.

I could make the lighthouse out but not with the clarity I would have liked. It was difficult to see what the sea state was at its base. An opaque surf driven mist hung low along the shoreline creating an optically confusing impression of land blending with sea. With no visual evidence of the surf tumbling onto the beach, I had little idea of how large it was. I could hear it though, without interruption, rumbling and crashing, a threatening soundscape for the morning. I had a sense of being moved along by a strong tidal flow but without my GPS I had no idea of the speed I was travelling. It was an odd sensation, feeling the tug of the tide southwards while a large swell washed in from the east. I began to lose perspective and unease rose like bile within. I was becoming disoriented, visually and audibly. My head began to swim. When I was sixteen, as an R.A.F. Air Cadet at school, I went on a weeklong summer camp to learn to fly gliders. There were ten of us who were taught the rudimentary skills for launching, flying a circuit of the airfield, and landing. I was not a natural pilot, and I was one of the last to be allowed to fly solo. When my turn arrived, I was launched by cable into a sky heavy with cloud. At about eight hundred and fifty feet, climbing almost vertically on the winch cable, I flew into cloud, thick, clammy and opaque. I could hardly see the wing tips of the glider. A cable launches a glider to a height normally of a thousand feet, however because I was alone and slight of frame, the glider continued to climb further into the cloud until at eleven hundred feet I felt the nose of the plane begin to dip and the speed drop away. I pulled the cable release, and I was alone in the sky. The problem was I couldn't see a horizon ahead or the ground below. The only instruments I had to refer to in this open cockpit plane made from wood and cloth, were the altimeter, telling me my height, and the airspeed indicator. A piece of red string flying from the nose of the glider was my guide to whether the plane was slipping sideways. I had seconds to act, because the normal length of time for a glider to reach the ground from a thousand feet was three minutes. I pushed the control column forward and dived, I had to get clear of the cloud. I was completely disoriented, and I had no idea if I was flying level or otherwise. This was what I was experiencing now in my kayak. I felt slightly giddy with disorientation and became increasingly alarmed.

I believed I could hear a tumble of a tide race ahead, even though I knew this not to be a possibility. The tidal flow certainly appeared strong enough for a tide race to form and I began to doubt my preparations and the information I had gleaned about the hazards of this stretch of water. The seeds of doubt now sowed, sprouted within my mind and took root, dislodging rationality. The sound I was certain I could hear, was this the surf on the beach or was it over-falls close ahead? I became aware I was tensing my body, tightly gripping the shaft of my paddles so my knuckles turned white. I was perplexed, after all I had faced to this point, why would I be so fearful now? I had to get a grip of myself, slow the rate of my rising panic. A well-practiced process of grounding works well in these types of situations, where irrationality threatens to overwhelm. It's quite simply opening my awareness and noticing the small things around me, what my sensations are, the smells, the sounds and the sights. It's a process of slowing my heartbeat down, encouraging me to breathe slower. I noticed how tense I was, the feeling of tightness of my buttocks on the kayak seat, the claw like posture of my hand gripping the paddle shaft, my swift turns of my head as I gazed around attempting to determine my position in relation to the coast. I went on to become aware of the sound of my paddle blades cutting the dark grey surface of the sea, the familiar splash of entry followed by the scoop of exit slightly behind my hip, with tell tale drips of water falling from the exposed blade.

Calming myself, I settled into a steady rhythm, soon leaving the fret shrouded Rattray Head lighthouse astern. (By the way, I landed the glider safely after performing a near perfect final leg turn, with my wingtip almost touching the ground. I went on to volunteer at the gliding school for a couple of years, clocking up many happy hours flying solo.)

Peterhead lay ten miles ahead, three hours away. The time passed by without anything remarkable occurring, apart from unexpected over-falls running over the reefs next to Peterhead. I entered Peterhead Bay through the breakwater entrance and dithered over whether to enter the harbour or not. The large size of the oil rig support vessels and their rather intimidating angular lines put me off. More to the point though, I doubted if there would be a suitable place to land and secure my kayak. I opted instead to land at the back of the bay where I pulled *Sahwira* high onto the council-maintained grass, disrobed and wandered off to the harbour to find the lifeboat station. It was somewhat surreal to be wandering through the streets of a town I had little knowledge of, apart from the fact it has a notorious prison. I didn't have a plan for where I was going to stay or any other plan for that matter. I had arrived and that's what was important.

I was expected and warmly welcomed by Ali Wilson, the mechanic for the station. I couldn't spend the night in their crew room and instead camped on a comfortable patch of grass beside the broad reach of Peterhead Bay. Here I was something of a novelty for the many dog walkers who kept me entertained with stories about their city. It was late when I climbed into my sleeping bag, extremely tired after what had been a demanding day. Just as I was drifting off, I heard my name being called.

"Nick! Nick! Are you awake?" It was Ali from the lifeboat station.

Rather groggily I replied I was awake, and he asked what time I was departing in the morning. The next day I wanted to be away early to make use of the tide, "About six I think", I replied.

"Great" said Ali and then, "Sleep well." With that I listened to his footsteps disappear into the darkness. I was so tired I didn't give the exchange much thought, before I dropped into a deep sleep.

It was a stunning dawn the following morning, one which took my breath away. It was so lovely I was slow in my packing, taking my time to stand and absorb the slowly changing orangey red hues over the rugged Peterhead city skyline. I launched and headed out into the bay making my way for the open sea beyond. I was feeling nervous about the day's paddling because this was when I would reach the waters around Aberdeen, by far the busiest seaport on the northeastern Scottish coastline. As I was picking up speed with my customary long reaching paddle strokes, I heard the briefest of 'toots' on my left and glancing over, my heart leapt to see the Peterhead lifeboat making its way across the bay towards me. Everything suddenly fell into place as I recalled the brief conversation, I'd had with Ali late in the night before. He had organised the crew to give up a relaxed early Sunday morning to come out and wave me off. Not for the first time did I feel a gulp of emotion rise within.

I eased up on my paddling and allowed *Sahwira* to slowly drift to a stop, watching with interest as the lifeboat circled and I was photographed by yellow clad crew. The boat eventually pulled alongside and with many hands reaching down to hold my kayak steady, I clambered out of my cockpit and up onto their deck. I was immediately embraced in warm hugs and had my hand firmly shaken by other maritime calloused hands. This was wonderful and I was beaming from ear to ear. Someone had a thermos of coffee, and I gladly accepted a mug, standing with it in my hands as I'd hold a pint while chatting in the pub. Once again, I enjoyed feeling intimately integrated with the R.N.L.I. and chatted amiably with the crew about my trip so far and enquiring from them, the service they provided to the seas around Peterhead. Somehow, I managed to find my book of the R.N.L.I. in Scotland and passed it around for each of the crew to sign, as I had done for all the other lifeboat stations where I'd met crew so far.

The sun was climbing steadily into the sky, and I was loathe to break the magical spell of new friendship, but I knew I had to be on my way. After another round of handshakes and hugs, I lowered myself back into my kayak, snapped my spray deck around the rim, pushed away from their gleaming dark blue hull and set my course once more for the open sea. Breaking out through the walled entrance of Peterhead Bay, I again met the swell I'd been nervous about the day before. It seemed more pronounced, but each set passed easily beneath, or rather I passed easily over each set. The lifeboat stayed with me as far as the hamlet of Boddam, turning back towards Peterhead with a mighty roar and an impressive wake in its trail. Some of the crew stood on the stern waving farewell as I made for the sea spangled rocky shore of Buchan Ness. I had now rounded the most easterly point of mainland Scotland and a quick gaze at my compass, confirmed my southerly heading. It suddenly felt as if I were on the homeward leg.

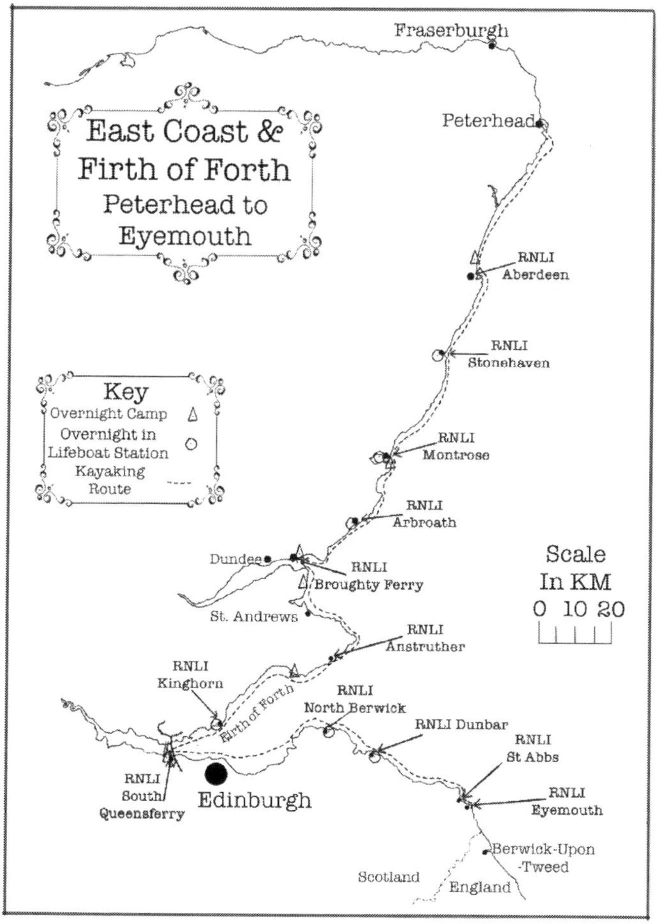
Fraserburgh
Peterhead
East Coast &
Firth of Forth
Peterhead to
Eyemouth
RNLI
Aberdeen
RNLI
Stonehaven
Key
Overnight Camp
Overnight in
Lifeboat Station
Kayaking
Route
RNLI
Montrose
RNLI
Arbroath
Scale
In KM
0 10 20
Dundee
RNLI
Broughty Ferry
St. Andrews
RNLI
Anstruther
RNLI
Kinghorn
Firth of Forth
RNLI
North Berwick
RNLI Dunbar
RNLI
St Abbs
RNLI
South
Queensferry
Edinburgh
RNLI
Eyemouth
Berwick-Upon
-Tweed
Scotland
England

East Coast and Firth of Forth Peterhead to Eyemouth

Chapter 37

The coastline south of Buchan Ness was delightful and I wished I could've given time to exploring the intricate geos, natural arches and many inviting caves. Instead, I pulled hard on my paddles and maintained a steady speed. For a few hours a thick fog rolled in from the sea, obscuring what had been a bright and warm sun. I found shelter in the quaint harbour of Collieston while I tussled with a desire to stop and camp early. I managed to overcome my feeling of slothfulness and paddled onwards through the now fracturing fog and into sunshine once more. Out to sea, a few miles away I saw long lines of anchored and unemployed oil tankers. I knew it'd be impossible to paddle into Aberdeen Harbour because as a kayaker, I was not allowed to. I therefore needed to decide how I would visit the Lifeboat station there. The swell sweeping from the North Sea had grown and I was reluctant to make a landing through the surf onto the Aberdeen beach. I was also feeling tired. I decided to visit the station the following day and I altered my course for the mouth of the river Don. I don't like camping on beaches at the best of times and neither did I want to camp where the city came down to the sea front. The wildish land surrounding the river Don estuary, offered the privacy I enjoyed. Because of the sizeable North Sea swell I was keen to avoid a landing through the surf if possible. Surf landings are often when I'm most vulnerable in my kayak, because of the reduced control I have of my laden craft. Entering the Don estuary enabled me to avoid this surf and pull onto the estuary shoreline with far more grace than I would on the Aberdeen Beach. There was a sand bar guarding the mouth of the river opening where waves steepened and broke, but then washed through and onwards up into the estuary. I navigated this bar successfully, albeit with my heart in my mouth and was soon paddling with relief, towards a calm patch of shingle on the south side of the river.

As I'd anticipated, the area was perfect for a secluded camp and with practised ease, I had my tent up in minutes, was changed out of my paddling garb, and soon cooking my dinner. It'd been a long and rewarding day and I was hungry. As I was wolfing down my simple fare of rice and vegetable chilli, I spotted a group of youths wandering along the shore of the river towards me. One of the teenagers was pushing an incongruous small child's vibrant pink scooter. I inwardly groaned and steeled myself for a possible problematic encounter with the local gang of unruly kids. It annoys me how my sense of middle-class entitlement often kicks in, and I become irritated at the prospect of being disturbed by youngsters. They were animatedly chatting and laughing as they wandered straight towards me. My hope they would pass by without us interacting dwindled, to be replaced with resignation.

What followed was one of the joyful encounters of my journey around Scotland. The youngsters, about twelve of them ranging through the teens, were an absolute delight and had me telling them about my journey, the notable experiences and showing them *Sahwira* and my kit. They were genuinely interested in everything, even if their expostulations of amazement would've filled a sizeable swear jar in a matter of minutes. I made a pan of coffee, and two mugs were solemnly passed between them while we continued to chat away. In turn, they spoke of their lives locally and how this place, hidden away amongst the dunes and reeds, was their haven. Here they'd light fires, spend summer nights out and get up to whatever they wanted. In my outdoor instructional years, I worked a lot with young people who were termed hard to reach and at risk of criminal behaviour. These youths, from the way they dressed and spoke, clearly fitted this demographic and I wondered how our interaction would've been, somewhere different without the wide-open Aberdeenshire sky above, the lazily flowing river beside us and the nearby sound of the surf. Here, in this small place of wildness on the fringes of the old grey city of Aberdeen, we shared a common bond. We didn't need to pretend to be any different to who we were. I didn't have to behave in a manner to ingratiate their respect, and they certainly didn't alter their behaviour to account for my obviously middle-class English accent. For a few hours we were sharing the intimacy one human does with another, in the natural realm without rancour or judgement. The sun had long set, and a heavy dew was forming when we agreed it was time to call it a night. Without affectation, we said our goodbyes and shared good wishes, and then they were gone. I slid into my sleeping bag with a happy smile on my face.

The next day landing on the Aberdeen beach, close to the harbour walls was far easier than I anticipated. I heaved and dragged my kayak up the beach to ensure she was out of reach of the rising tide, and I set off through the maze of streets of the harbour city, to find the Lifeboat station. This I did without difficulty, only to discover the boat was out on a 'shout' and there was no one from the crew I could meet. I found out from the one person who was in the building, a trainer from the R.N.L.I. office in Scotland, the lifeboat had sadly been called to search for a crew member of a fishing vessel who'd been lost overboard. I hung around for a while but concerned about the rising tide and my kayak alone on the busy beach, there seemed little point in lingering. I was soon back by my boat, dragged her to the sea and launched once more on a course southward.

My goal for the day was Stonehaven, where there was an inshore lifeboat station to visit. Again, I found myself paddling hard along coastline which would normally have held great appeal for exploration in my kayak. As ever, I resolved one day I'd return and give the east coast the attention it deserved. The sizeable swell prevented me venturing close in to the cliffs but I could make out wonderfully intriguing caves and gulleys.

It was mid afternoon when I kayaked into Stonehaven harbour and pulled up onto the sandy foreshore. Being an inshore lifeboat station, there wasn't a permanent presence, and all was locked up. Thankfully I'd been expected, and it wasn't long before the operations manager arrived, unlocked the door and invited me in. Little did I suspect I'd end up here for four days. It was fortunate then I was made warmly welcome and once again found myself immersed in the tight camaraderie of the R.N.L.I. volunteers. I was forced to remain in Stonehaven because a large storm swept through on the first two days and the sea conditions on the subsequent days proved far too rough to safely traverse the coastline down to Montrose, my next destination. I was entertained with generous fish suppers, taking part in their weekly training exercise and kindly given a comprehensive guided tour of the area, as well as visiting local landmarks. I found myself deeply attracted to the town because of its distinct personality and culture. While holed up here, it entered my awareness, the end of August was in sight and September was around the corner, with the sense summer was ending, and Autumn about to begin. Although I enjoyed the generous hospitality I received from the folks in Stonehaven, I itched to continue my way.

While at Stonehaven, I enjoyed the pleasurable opportunity to meet Jono Dunnet. He was windsurfing solo around the British mainland and arrived in Stonehaven after sailing from Port Errol, north of Aberdeen. Unlike me with my sea kayak and my watertight compartments, Jono carried his belongings in a small rucksack on his back and in a sizeable plastic screw lid tub, which was strapped firmly to the deck of his wind surfer. Somehow, the people helping him while he was passing through the area, had got to hear of my venture and I was invited to join Jono for a Scottish Television interview, which I thought was incredibly generous. Jono and I met for the first time on the Stonehaven beach, and I felt an immediate connection with his genuine, unassuming demeanour. Together we performed for the camera, me in my kayak and Jono on his windsurfer, before each going ashore for an interview with the television presenter. I was in awe of Jono. While out on the water I'd enquired of him what he used for a tent and his reply was disarmingly understated, "I don't have a tent, I sleep under my windsurf sail." Given the weather we'd experienced through the summer, in my opinion, this one fact placed him as a hard-core adventurer.

However, we viewed the other, it was clear we identified as men who were not in this for fame or glory. The quality of the experience was key for each of us, not the substance or whether it made a good Instagram moment or a snappy Facebook story. Sitting in the pub with Jono, enthralled by his descriptions of his experiences so far, I understood what mine meant for me. I determined afterwards, it did not matter if he slept under a sail and me a tent. What mattered was our individual intent and purpose. We each faced our adventure with equanimity, hoping to gain as much from every experience we possibly could.

Where the wind was my nemesis, it was Jono's friend, and it was with a tinge of sadness I watched him sail out of the harbour early the next morning. He headed off seawards over the heaving swell, with considerable grace and ease. Although our meeting had been brief, I realised I would miss him and the loneliness I'd been holding at bay behind the guise of glorious solitude, managed to take hold for a good few hours that day.

I tried on my third day in Stonehaven to make headway, but I only managed a mile out of the security of the harbour before deciding to turn back and run for shelter again. It was the first and only time during the journey I had forced myself back, and on this occasion, it wasn't a difficult choice to make. The sea still carried the large swell which swept in from the expansive and shallow North Sea. With this too, there was an uneasiness to the movement of the sea. Maybe I was feeling out of sorts, but I was unnerved by the depths of the troughs and the sloppy nature of the wave peaks. I didn't feel in control. Gazing searchingly along the miles of unbroken cliffs into the far distance, I could see the result of the heaving swell, as plumes of heavy white water burst skywards. I remembered my experience kayaking along the Yesnaby cliffs in Orkney and the feeling I'd been fortunate to have come away from that day unscathed. Like that stretch on Orkney, there was no safe break in these cliffs from Stonehaven for over twelve miles. Inverbervie seemed the only option but even this would have meant a heavy surf landing on what was marked on the map as a stony beach. Thus, well and truly spooked, I turned unsteadily and headed back into Stonehaven to be greeted by the harbour master who simply said, "I thought you were silly to go out in that. It'll be OK tomorrow."

Chapter 38

Paddling down to Montrose the following day was unremarkable, except for the fact I kept well out to sea, away from the refracted energy of the waves meeting the cliffs. With the wind in my favour, I made good time and arrived off Scurdie Ness in the early afternoon. The sea was still running high and all about waves were peaking and collapsing with thunderous rumbles. There seemed no way I'd reach the haven of Montrose without running the gauntlet of the breakers. I forced myself to stop, take a breather, have a bite to eat and consider my options more thoroughly. Despite the danger of being caught in a breaking wave, and unceremoniously dumped in the obviously shallow waters, I was tempted to cut the shortest line possible from my position out to sea, to the harbour mouth I could see a mile or so away. Wisdom determined this was not the best option, so I pulled my map out of my deck bag to have a closer look. With relief I saw a clear channel which ran the length of the Scurdie Ness shoreline right into the harbour. All I had to do was paddle as close as I could get to the conspicuous and handsome lighthouse on the promontory, then follow the channel in. Half an hour later I found myself in the narrow sea way leading into the harbour, where reassuringly there were no breaking waves.

I'd placed myself under considerable pressure to arrive in Montrose a few days earlier, when they took delivery of their new Shannon class lifeboat. This craft was the first of its class to be deployed in Scotland and was a big occasion. The Shannon, unlike predecessor lifeboats, was propelled by a water jet system and consequently, was highly manoeuvrable. Because I now felt privy to the inner workings of the

R.N.L.I. in Scotland, I was aware of the great excitement amongst the other lifeboat station crews about this. Few had actually seen a Shannon lifeboat, and I was party to many enthusiastic discussions about the merits of the new design. Indeed, by the time I arrived in Montrose, I was keen to see for myself what the excitement was about. What I eventually saw as I paddled slowly past, was a sleek craft with a modern design, relatively small and undoubtedly specified for operating in demanding conditions. However, the Luddite I am, I couldn't help thinking the much older and rugged looking Tyne class lifeboat sitting alongside it, held more appeal. The Tyne class lifeboat was the Montrose station's current boat which remained on service while the crew trained on the new Shannon.

I pulled ashore on a shingle beach on the harbour foreshore and wandered up to the lifeboat station door, where I was met with a hearty greeting by the coxswain. Without demurring I was invited to bring all my belongings into the building and make myself at home which I gratefully did. As was usual on these occasions, I enjoyed sitting in the crew room chatting amiably about my journey so far and finding out about the service they provided from Montrose. It interested me to know what their likely rescue scenarios were, and what were the more common 'shouts' they attended. Montrose wasn't a big industrial harbour, but it was an important one for servicing the offshore support vessels for the North Sea oil and gas fields. Not long after five in the evening when everyone departed for home, I was left to my devices with the invitation as always to help myself to whatever I found in the cupboards or the fridge. Each lifeboat station had its unique character, and this was demonstrated through the volunteers, the décor of the crew rooms and interestingly, the contents of their cupboards in the kitchen. For example, if I opened the fridge and saw piles of barbecue food, I'd assume the crew were a sociable bunch. The friendly way I'd been greeted, and the walls lined with photographs from through the years and a plethora of framed certificates of merit, told me this was a station who were extremely proud of their heritage.

The weather deteriorated through the night, and it was clear from the strength of the wind and the heavy rain, the conditions next day were not ideal for paddling. However, because the volunteers were intent on their intense training on their new lifeboat, I was reluctant to ask if I could stay for a couple of days until it was safe to head out. Instead, I kept my counsel and headed out in the foul weather. I didn't even make it as far as Scurdie Ness, because as I paddled down the narrow channel out of the harbour, I was assailed by a steep swell sweeping in from the sea. One look at the crashing seas beyond the lighthouse on the point, told all I needed to know. I pulled ashore while I could and made camp overlooking the channel. I wandered up to the point where the lighthouse stood and realised with a sense of relief, I'd made a wise decision. The sea was a maelstrom, and it would have been my undoing of if I'd ventured further than I had. For two days I disconsolately waited for the conditions to ease. For a while they in fact deteriorated with the visibility reducing to a few metres. The only entertainment I had was watching the large ships steaming in and out of the harbour through the narrow channel. It occurred to me this required considerable seamanship given their proximity to the rocky shore on one side and the shallow breaker laden sand banks on the other. It was fun too to watch the Montrose lifeboat heading out and back from their training out at sea, cutting with bronco-like ease through the heavy swells.

Thankfully the conditions eased, and the time arrived to move on, and I launched into a much calmer sea. My destination for the day was Arbroath, only twelve miles away. This was to be my last day of sustained cliff scenery and for this reason I chose to paddle as close as I dared to the shoreline. I'm pleased I did, because towards the end of the day, I found a magnificent cave and arch which proved to be the last subterranean kayaking experience of my journey. I think I knew this was the case, because I lingered for a good while, enjoying sitting within the cave, listening to the slaps and gurgles of the hidden sea in its deep dark recesses. The sea was different now to what I'd been used to. The clear steel blue grey of further north was now opaque, almost brown, and there were swathes of foam covering the surface. There seemed to be a strange metallic tang to the air which I couldn't quite fathom.

I received another warm welcome when I arrived at the Arbroath lifeboat station in the early afternoon. The lifeboat here is the last slipway launched boat in Scotland, the traditional method of launching one associates with the R.N.L.I.. The red roofed building eschewed an air of history and walking into the gloom of the shed to look at the gleaming lifeboat, I had the feeling of stepping back in time. It was easy to imagine through the decades, the countless moments of intensity the lifeboat would have been released from its restraining shackles, to rush headlong down the ramp with a mighty splash into the waiting sea below. Ron Churchill, the full-time mechanic at the station proudly gave a thorough tour of Arbroath's Mersey class lifeboat, explaining in detail almost every working part. For someone mechanically challenged as I was, it was both interesting and overwhelming at the same time. His detailed tour served to highlight the professional dedication required to maintain the lifeboats to a high operational standard. There were no shortcuts in their maintenance because lives relied on the boat being always serviceable.

The winds rose overnight and were forecast to continue blowing hard for the next three days, too powerfully to safely paddle the short distance along to Broughty Ferry, the next lifeboat station to visit. The sun shone brightly over the three days which made the enforced time ashore even more frustrating. However, my stay in Arbroath was sweetened by a few friends choosing to visit and take me out for meals. I was also interviewed for the 'Scots Magazine' who kindly wrote a piece about my journey. The hours I hung out in the crew room at the station, I was kept company by Blair, a young man who was deeply passionate about the R.N.L.I., especially his home lifeboat of Arbroath. I was fortunate too to be invited out on a training exercise with the crew aboard the lifeboat. It was a thrill to sit on the foredeck of the boat when it ploughed into the sea after a short and exhilarating slide down the ramp. The shouts and the blaring of a horn at the point of launching added to the atmosphere of daring excitement. The exercise for the evening was navigational training and a familiarisation passage to Montrose harbour and back. Despite the keen wind it was a glorious night to be at sea, and the passage back to Arbroath was in the deep orange hued glow of a magnificent sunset.

The weather relented and time came to move on, and as it happened, it was my fifty second birthday. In lumpy seas and blustery conditions, I paddled the short distance to Broughty Ferry past the famous Carnoustie Links. I'd timed my paddling as always to coincide with the favourable direction of the tide and yet, I was taken aback at the speed with which I was swept around Buddon Ness and up into the Firth of Tay. I hardly had to paddle at all as the watery travelator swept me past the impressive Broughty Castle which loomed authoritatively above. Landing by the lifeboat station I was disappointed to find it was closed for the rest of the day, so I set up camp on a scrappy piece of grass on the foreshore by the building and set off into the town to buy myself a celebratory birthday drink and a meal.

My start the next day was an early one, to ensure I caught the ebbing tide. I intended to set off at the end of the flood so I would arrive at a point in the estuary where I could portage across a few metres of sand into a cut called Pool Channel. From the map, it looked as if this would provide easy access to the expansive St Andrews Bay. If I managed to succeed, I would avoid the five-mile slog along the Abertay Sands, leaving me far out in the bay beyond. The day promised to be a challenging one, simply because it involved traversing long empty stretches of beach coastline. Psychologically this is not my favourite kind of sea kayaking. I was therefore counting on finding the crossing in the channel through the sands and thus easing a long day of featureless paddling.

On setting off I realised I'd misjudged the tide times and the flow was already strongly on the ebb. I missed finding the point where I would disembark on the sands of Abertay and portage into Pool Channel. As I careened along the steep edges of the muddy sandbank, I realised I needed to be spot on with my navigational decisions to pick the exact point to stop, unpack my kayak, and lug all my belongings the hundred metres over to the channel. If I got it wrong the consequences were multiplied in their hundreds. Even with my GPS I wasn't confident in stopping, climbing out of my boat and trudging through the deep sand and mud to ascertain if I was in the right place or not. The scutter of the whole rigmarole overwhelmed my determination, and I easily acceded to the inevitability of paddling out into the sea along the five miles of Abertay Sands. With a sigh, I realised I was in for a long day.

The only consolation for the time being was the ease with which the tide was pushing me seawards. Halfway along the sands I happened on a huge grey seal colony, with what appeared to be hundreds upon hundreds of large, well-fed seals hauled out onto the dark brown sands. It was an incredible sight to behold. For a moment I wondered if I would drift silently past without disturbing them. I eased my paddle into the water by my left stern to guide me away from their side of the channel, but this subtle movement was enough to spark a stampede the likes of which is difficult to describe. I remember when I was working in Zimbabwe with Outward Bound, I was running a course in the Lowveld wilderness. There were twelve students, me, my friend Mick as a co-instructor and an armed wildlife guide. When walking through a wide grassy vlei, we were stampeded by a huge herd of buffalo. If fifteen humans could stand on a single coin, then we would have managed this! Instinctively we huddled together, fearfully waiting for an inevitable bovine crush. The noise of their thudding hooves was incredible, as was a distinct thunder-like shimmering in the air. I remember clearly the unmistakable sound of Gibson, the wildlife guide, cocking his automatic weapon, and not feeling reassured by his determined act. Seemingly, on some unspoken cue, the lead buffalo wheeled a few metres away from us and slowed down to a walk, encircling us from behind. In a matter of seconds, the charge had ended, and we were now surrounded by huffing and snorting boss headed beasts, who merely gazed at us with their languid eyes. The fifteen of us simply began uncontrolled giggling in response.

It felt the same now. I was drifting down the channel and to my right, wave upon wave of weighty and ungainly seals, lumbered with impressive and graceless speed over the sand and into the sea, so forcefully there were tsunami type waves sweeping towards me. For a few seconds I was concerned for my safety. I'd never heard of seals attacking sea kayakers, but this wasn't to mean a concerted onrush like this didn't have the potential to overwhelm me. My needless fear was quickly replaced with guilt, because it was my presence alone which had caused them to abandon their rest and slumbers, and rush headlong into the sea. It took minutes for all the seals to thunder into the mud churned water, and then all was silent. Afterwards, I was followed for a long way by inquisitive seals who now they were in the water, appeared to have the confidence to swim up close to my kayak.

I was met in St Andrews Bay by a strong head wind and an uncomfortably confused and lumpy sea. Up until this point I'd been sheltered by the long uninterrupted bank of the Abertay Sands. From expending little effort as the tide swept me along, to now battling for every paddle stroke, my spirits began to diminish at a rapid rate of knots. I could make out the faint outline of the town of St Andrews over seven miles away and it suddenly seemed like an impossible quest. In my planning for the day, I'd hoped to paddle with ease along this shoreline and make good time. Suddenly my paddle strokes seemed sluggish and ineffectual. My mood was dipping alarmingly and with it my concentration. A deep recovery stroke when a crackling wave tumbled me into the jaws of a waiting trough, shook me out of my despondent reverie. I had to pull myself together, but I lacked the will to do so. I knew from my experiences on my journey so far, I'd the fortitude and the ability to make it across the bay, but somehow this awareness did not equate to action. I simply gave in, and I hated myself for doing so.

I chose to make a run for Tentsmuir Beach four miles away, where I eventually landed pretty much at low water. It seemed the punishment for my tardiness was now a gruelling portage of my four laden IKEA bags, and my kayak, across half a kilometre of soft cloying sand. It felt the rest of the day was spent shuttling backwards and forwards across the unending beach, heaving the bags with straps which cut into my aching shoulders, and carrying my kayak which was constantly caught in the strong wind and blown out of my hands. In the end, as much as I hated doing so, I dragged poor *Sahwira* by her forward toggle across the sand as if she were a petulant child. Eventually camp was made in the heath like landscape between the dunes and the forest, and it became one of the finest camps of my whole expedition. I was the only human present in this unspoilt landscape with a wonderfully wild feel. I was sheltered from the wind which beyond the protective dunes, whipped up sweeping flurries of stinging sand across the beaches. All was still and peaceful and the anguish I'd faced earlier in the day was forgotten. I was happy to be here and for the remaining few hours in the day, I allowed myself to totally unwind and rest my body.

Chapter 39

After a restorative night in the Tentsmuir heathland, I enjoyed an easy paddle past the ancient university town of St Andrews (where my wife Karen, had studied) and along the coastline to the distinctive point of Fife Ness where I finally turned into the Firth of Forth. It was a notable moment because I was now within sight of the final stretches of my expedition. Suddenly, the effort, the hundreds of hours, over a thousand and five hundred miles, and innumerable incredible experiences, were condensed into this final body of water. My journey was nowhere close to ending yet, but the end was in sight.

The East Neuk of Fife coastline seemed so much softer. Suddenly it seemed as if all the coastal challenges Scotland had to offer were behind me. I was now being graced with a gentle end to my long sea kayak journey. Indeed, the picturesque harbour town of Crail seemed to emphasise this fact. The sea conditions had eased too with easy paddling throughout the day. I stopped in Anstruther to visit the lifeboat station there. It was a Sunday, so the full-time coxswain was on his day off. Nonetheless he kindly came down to say hello when the lady in the R.N.L.I. gift shop, much against my wishes, gave him a call. It was the briefest of meetings but lovely, nonetheless.

After Anstruther I enjoyed a truly lovely paddle along the historically interesting Fife coastline, studded with ruined castles, chapels and intriguing caves. At one point shortly after passing St Monans, I was joined by a small pod of bottlenose dolphins who swam alongside, from time to time gracefully leaping from the surface to delight me. They were close enough to hear them breathe, with a powerful exhalation and a whistling inhalation. I camped for the night at Shell Bay where my good friend Charlie met me with a delicious fish supper and a generous portion of chips. We sat by my tent talking of adventures and all I'd encountered on my journey. I had last seen Charlie in Troon nearly four months earlier. Then, I was only weeks into my journey with little idea of what lay ahead. Now, I felt a seasoned traveller with a quiet self-confidence I hadn't possessed back then.

The next day paddling to the village of Kinghorn and the next lifeboat station, *Sahwira* sliced through a mirror calm glassy sea. It was a hot and sunny late summer day, glorious for being out at sea in a kayak. My paddle strokes were long and powerful, but such was my level of fitness now, I wasn't exercised by the effort. I was scenting the end of my long journey and there was a keenness growing within to bring it to a close. It was strange to look across to my left, southwards to the Edinburgh coastline across the firth, and know reaching there would signify the penultimate days of my adventure. It was important I didn't wish away the remaining couple of days and one day regret not fully immersing myself in my paddling experience right to the very end. Now I was in sight of the finish, I found myself being drawn more and more into thinking about my future, living settled in one location, once more being at home with Karen and Ziggy. For the previous four months I'd easily slipped into an existence of immediacy, living in the moment, absorbing the many experiences I encountered each day. Of course, there was planning required for the days ahead, but I rarely found myself worrying unnecessarily about what the future held. Instead, I responded to the weather and tides each day presented, accepting them without rancour or wishful thinking. This isn't to say I didn't have anxieties and fears, I did, many times, but I always knew with certainty I had the faculty and skill to see my way through the challenges I faced.

Kinghorn was a delightful seaside village to arrive at. There remained a festive holiday air to the surroundings, with children on the beach and cafes selling teas and ice creams. I was assured of a warm welcome here having been in touch with Sylvia, one of the volunteers, before arriving. Indeed, despite this being an inshore lifeboat station there was someone waiting to greet me. I was shown into the building and up to their crew room which afforded a wonderful view across the firth. This would be my home for the night. That evening quite a few of the lifeboat crew came down to the station, each of them bringing something to contribute for dinner. That night I enjoyed one of the most happy and convivial lifeboat gatherings on my trip. I felt so at ease in their company and equally warmly accepted. Everyone sitting around the table, giving up an evening to spend with me, were doing so because they were R.N.L.I. volunteers. They were passionate about the life saving service of the charity and the importance of the lifeboat within their community. There was no hint of a braggadocios motive for their service, simply the natural humanistic generosity of compassion, which has the potential to exist within all of us. After everyone had left fairly late at night, I stood by the open window of the crew room gazing out into a darkening world, with the lights of shipping and navigation buoys flickering out on the sea. Tomorrow I would be out there again.

The first thing I remember ever learning about Scotland when I was a child was the legend of the painting of the Forth Rail Bridge, once it has been finished, the process begins again. When I was in kindergarten, we had reading cards which we worked through as our reading levels improved. Each card was a story or a snippet of information and the one card I remember above all, was one about the Forth Rail Bridge. This is a fifty-year-old memory from when I was in my class in Triangle, the Lowveld town in Zimbabwe (Rhodesia then) where sugar cane was grown. Since then, I have become acquainted with the bridge as a train passenger on the many journeys I made from Inverness to Edinburgh and vice versa. Rumbling slowly across the red ochre bridge and peering out of the window at the Forth far below, was always an anticipated moment on these journeys. When I gazed at the dirty grey waters swirling beneath, I wondered what it would be like to one day kayak down there and be looking upwards.

It may seem odd as an inveterate wilderness lover and a person who is essentially anti-industrial development, I'd be excited about kayaking under a huge steel rail bridge. I enjoyed a delicious air of anticipation from the moment I departed Kinghorn, eventually spotting with excitement the bridge superstructure from afar. My anticipation was such, I paid scant attention to the fine ruins of St Colm's Abbey on the island of Incholm. In normal circumstances I would have landed on the isle and explored the intriguing ruins, but I was focussed on reaching the bridge only three and a half miles away. With the tide in my favour, it took less than an hour to finally find myself beneath the immense construction and gaze skywards as I'd long dreamt of doing. There was nothing to disappoint about this experience because it was all I'd expected. The muddy waters of the firth swirled noisily around the massive stone stanchions, causing me to remain attentive and wary. I sat for a good forty-five minutes beneath the bridge gazing at its shape, its colour and listening to its sounds. From time to time a train would trundle through the arches high above, the rumbling sound echoing downwards and evoking within a boyish excitement. I used to have a train set when I was a lad, and I always loved the sound the model train made when it crossed the set's toy bridge. Deep within there's something liminal about bridges, because they're the point where I cross from one side to another. So often this is an experience out of my awareness, but I think there are certain structures which invoke this feeling within, and the Forth Rail Bridge is one such structure. To be sitting beneath it now in my kayak, having reached it after well over a thousand miles of paddling, felt a powerfully symbolic moment. Passing beneath it for the first time in my kayak, I think was the exact moment when I decided I was ready to bring my adventure to a close.

There were still five lifeboat stations to visit before I could end my journey, and one of them, the South Queensferry station was right at the foot of the rail bridge on the south shore of the Forth. I landed on the weed slimed slipway which would have once served the ferries which plied the crossing of the firth before the opening of the first road bridge in 1964. I wandered up to the modern lifeboat station which again contained an inshore lifeboat and met with one of the volunteer crew who was waiting to greet me. It'd been just a morning's paddle to South Queensferry, but space had been arranged for me to camp at the water sports centre at Port Edgar a little way upstream. Additionally, I'd arranged two meetings for the evening, so despite the gnawing need within to press on, I set up camp and relaxed for the rest of the afternoon.

My close friend Mick and his family who live in Edinburgh, drove down to spend time with me and it was a wonderful experience. Mick has known me through thick and thin, which is why it was a special feeling to sit with him, Bridget and their daughters Holly and Poppy, and recount my tales. After they left for home, I then met up with Nick Hancock, who in 2014 had spent forty-five days alone, on the singular rock bastion of Rockall, over two hundred and thirty miles west of the Outer Hebrides, in the mighty Atlantic Ocean. He had hoped to be out there for sixty days, but his adventurous tenure of the isolated rock was cut short by a violent storm. Nick and I had been in regular contact, each interested in the other's quest for adventure. It was a rewarding evening spent with him talking about our experiences and sharing what these meant at a deeper level for us. Listening to him interpret his views on his experiences, helped me fathom some of the questions I was asking of myself, namely, what was it all for? Essentially as in Nick's case, there was no rhyme or reason to choose to sit alone on a speck of rock deep in the Atlantic. Yet as I understood it from him, there was every reason for him to undertake the challenge. It validated his desire for a life less ordinary, one which fulfilled within him a sense of personal accomplishment and the opportunity for deeper self awareness. My thoughts about my own reasons for my long solo journey, powerfully echoed and resonated with his words.

I slipped away from Port Edgar into the dark waters of the Firth. It had been a restless night where I tossed and turned attempting to inveigle sleep to drift me away. Instead, my mind was filled with thoughts of the few days ahead. Heading out of the Firth of Forth was one of those significant moments in my journey, the moment which marked the ending of my adventure. Once I left the Firth, I faced only two remaining days of the voyage. In the stark reality of the daylight, this was difficult to comprehend. The Firth stretched ahead, offering no real challenge or any potential coastal enjoyment. It was early in the day and thankfully I had the tide to sweep me oceanward.

It was an unremarkable day, something of an anti-climax from the day before. Even paddling beneath the rust-coloured rail bridge again didn't offer the sense of awe I experienced the day before. I considered kayaking as close to the shore as possible with the hope I would take in the architectural delights of Leith and Edinburgh. However, Sahwira made her mind up and our course was a beeline from the Point of Leith to Gullane Point. The crossing of the bay passed without incident, my mind far away, restless like the sea at times, always avoiding thinking of the final hours of the trip. I did not want to think of these until the last day of the journey. I was purposeful in my paddling, preferring not to linger. The seaside town of North Berwick was my next point of call where the R.N.L.I. station used a D-class Lifeboat.

It was with considerable shock I found myself in an unexpected and feisty tide race around Gullane Point. So unprepared was I, I found myself slapping the steep breaking waves with flailing paddle strokes, almost as a novice kayaker would do. My heart was in my throat, adrenalin coursed through me and the lower portion of my body was tense with every jolting confused wave. I was terrified I would capsize. The race was against me, so it was hard work against the current to make it around the point. I made it through unscathed and sat in still water above the race allowing my pulse rate to return to normality. I told myself in the sternest fashion I could, to stay aware and disallow complacency. It occurred to me, now I was nearing the end of my long trip, I was beginning to ease up, paying less attention to the hazards still ahead.

With greater caution I made my way towards the skerry of Eyebroughy, which in my opinion marked the moment I exited the Firth of Forth. Excitement rose within and a few gulps of strong emotion wracked my upper body. From this point on, it was southwards to Eyemouth, thirty-four miles away, in effect just two days paddling.

I was soon joined out on the sea by the North Berwick lifeboat. It seemed so small in comparison to the previous lifeboats I'd encountered on my journey, and it appeared to be crewed by young lads! With skill and panache, they drew up alongside and greeted me with warmth and enthusiasm. I was pleased they'd come out to meet me, because they could point out the safest passage through the teeth like skerries which lined the shore and protected the entrance to the small North Berwick harbour. The North Sea had kicked up a large swell again and it was running hard ashore. This would have been great for surfers but in my kayak, it proved a daunting prospect, especially with the rocky skerries to contend with too. The lads were reassuringly relaxed when pointing the line, I needed to take before they roared away, their small craft scudding with resounding and plucky thumps on the rumpled sea. As I paddled into the harbour, I inadvertently picked up one of the steep waves running into the entrance, and for a few gut clenching seconds I wondered if I would hopelessly breach myself and end up bringing my day to a tumbling close. Thankfully all was well and with a deep breath I ran *Sahwira's* prow up the sand. The small lifeboat followed me in soon after and I was once again amazed at the deft skilfulness of the helm as he brought the craft in through the rushing sea. I helped them retrieve the D-class and joined them in the crew room which would be my home for the next three days.

The winds blew hard from the east for three solid days, kicking up a huge swell. It was incredibly frustrating to be so close to my finishing point and yet unable to safely put to sea. I had to fight the temptation to throw caution to the wind and make a run for it anyway. However, I knew it would be a fool's errand and would probably end ignominiously if I did. There were few places of refuge between North Berwick and Eyemouth and all of them were affected by the heavy easterly swell. I couldn't have been held up in a more delightful town than North Berwick. It was the end of summer, now early September and yet there was a wonderful gaiety to the place. People seemed happy. There wasn't much to do except sit and wait. I enjoyed friends visiting me, meeting new Twitter friends who'd been following me, and my dear Mum and Dad drove from where they were ensconced in their caravan, close to Berwick Upon Tweed to see me. They'd loyally driven up from their home in Herefordshire to welcome me into Eyemouth when I eventually arrived. Thankfully they were happy to enjoy an extended caravan holiday while they waited.

Chapter 40

On the third morning I judged the conditions safe enough to paddle onwards and I packed quickly and headed out into the swell laden sea. The weather was fine and for now the wind had eased. To my left the impressive guano painted bulk of Bass Rock dominated the horizon. However even this was regularly obscured from sight from my sea level perspective, because of the undulating swell. I paddled cautiously maintaining a safe distance from the shore. I was wary of outlying skerries and the possibility of being caught in the surf zone. This was to be the penultimate day of my journey, and it was clear now it was unlikely I'd be held up from finishing the next day. Around gannets swirled in the skies and dived with their inimitable courage into the water, chasing the fish I could never see. If I'd wanted to, I could've pressed for reaching Eyemouth in one day from North Berwick. It was twenty-eight miles away and certainly achievable given my level of fitness. However, I didn't want to rush my last remaining stretch of the journey. There were still two lifeboat stations to visit before I reached the final one in my list at Eyemouth. I wanted to give them the attention I'd given all the others before. Dunbar was my destination for the day and the entrance to the harbour was soon within sight. It was a nervy entry into the small port because of the skerries on either side of a difficult to distinguish channel, onto which the relentless swell crashed with fury. It was clear I needed to maintain a high level of alertness right up until the last few paddle strokes of the day. Dunbar's all-weather lifeboat isn't always berthed in the harbour, sometimes taken to another berth a few miles down the coast which enables them to put to sea at all states of the tide. However, the coxswain was there to greet me as was Rebecca, a member of the crew who I'd met a few days earlier at the South Queensferry lifeboat station. Suddenly I became aware of the enormity of the moment. Things which had been commonplace and second nature over the preceding four months were now, 'the last time'. The last time I'd unpack *Sahwira* as part of my journey. The last time I would sleep on a R.N.L.I. crew room floor. The last time I would look at my homemade almanac and work out my passage plan for the next day. The last time I'd climb into my sleeping bag alone in my solitude. This did not feel real and yet it seemed the most natural of experiences. I'd not really pondered what the ending of my journey would look like and consider how I'd be feeling. I guess, like how I'd approached most of my experiences throughout the adventure, I assumed I'd deal with this as it occurred. Rebecca had invited me to dinner with her and her husband that evening, so I was focussed on that. In fact, it was a lovely evening spent with them because I was able to recount all the important events, I'd enjoyed over the previous four months. Being able to tell my story like this, especially to an audience who understood my motivations for undertaking the challenge, was important. I was recounting my tale as much for myself, as it was for them.

The story began of course in the Solway Firth, the body of sea which set me straight with my complacency and taught a valuable lesson about over confidence. Then came the Firth of Clyde and my surprise at how wild and challenging it proved to be. The west coast and the Hebrides followed, with the challenges of long distances and crossings, as well as tides and the wind. Every day through seas and along coastline which took my breath away. Cape Wrath on its own was a highlight of my journey, an accomplishment I'd long wanted to undertake. The North Coast again surprised me with its rugged beauty and left me wanting to return to explore it more thoroughly. The Orkney Islands came next with their powerful tides, the solemnity of the Longhope Lifeboat Memorial, and of course the nerve-wracking passage along the Yesnaby cliffs. I waxed lyrical about Shetland and the paddling I enjoyed there. It was good to recall how pleased I was to arrive at Aith, the most northerly lifeboat station in Scotland. Finally, my long and enjoyable passage down the Scottish east coast with my foray inland on Loch Ness. Throughout this stretch I was tested by the winds and the swells but by this stage, I was confidently taking difficult conditions in my stride.

It wasn't just about the physical attainments of the journey, but the wonder and the extraordinariness of the natural realm I journeyed through too. Here the story became almost overwhelming in its telling, such was the richness of the daily natural experiences I'd been privileged to enjoy. Rebecca and her husband listened quietly in deep appreciation, as I described just a few of the hundreds of bird laden cliffs I'd kayaked beneath, where the air was rent with their incessant calling and their dynamic constant wheeling in the skies above. The sheer numbers of these birds with their activity, their noises and pungent scent created a pulsating susurration which assailed my senses.

I was wary of over telling my tale, bringing the evening to a close by stating I was tired and needed a good sleep for my big day tomorrow. It had been a lovely evening and a perfect way to celebrate the final night of my journey. Back in the crew room at the lifeboat station, I blew up my inflatable sleeping mat and threw my now well used sleeping bag across it. I stood still for a few long minutes looking down at it, again processing the enormity of the moment. This was the last time on this journey I would sleep alone.

Whether it was the delicious richness of the evening meal or my fevered state of mind, my night was restless and uncomfortable. I began my day groggily but ensured I ate breakfast and had a coffee before I packed *Sahwira* for the final time. I paddled away from Dunbar, alone and unseen, in the early morning light. It was going to be a lovely clear day to finish on. The sea state though told a different story. It was heavy with a lazy swell, yet jumpy and confused as well. My ultimate destination for the day was Eyemouth and the lifeboat station there, twenty miles away. Before reaching there, I had one more lifeboat station to visit, St Abbs. It was a close-run thing, but I was thankful to be visiting the lifeboat station there because the following day it was being closed by the R.N.L.I. as being superfluous to the charity's provision in the area. There'd been considerable debate about this at the lifeboat stations I visited from early into my journey when it was announced this would be happening.

The crew and the supporters of the St Abbs lifeboat vociferously appealed the move and established a widely shared public campaign, to persuade the R.N.L.I. to reverse their decision. Towards the end when it was clear there was to be no reprieve, the campaign sadly became rancorous and latterly, the conversations during my visits to lifeboat stations were dominated by the issue. As far as I could ascertain, the general feeling was one of deep sympathy but a sad acceptance this was the right course of action. I think for some stations I visited, there was a feeling of 'there but for the grace of God' because there were fears a review of their service might lead to a similar conclusion. It's a fact with the advent of modern rescue vessels and technology, the operating range of lifeboats has been greatly extended and where there once required a coastline lined with lifeboat stations, this was not necessary anymore. As it was, St Abbs was just a mile and a half from the larger lifeboat at Eyemouth.

I steered a careful course of not embroiling myself in the politics of the situation when the conversations followed those routes. Instead, I often found myself wondering about the human impact this was having. Being told your services are redundant, for whatever reason, can be a painful experience. Especially so if you've dedicated a large part of your life on a voluntary basis to provide this service. I felt for all the crew and volunteers at St Abbs on this count. I imagined how I would've felt if one of the mountain rescue teams where I was an active volunteer, were suddenly closed and our 'area' was handed to another team. I surmised I'd be angry and hurt, much like the St Abbs folks were by the time I came to meet them. However, their story wasn't unusual because I'd seen many abandoned lifeboat stations around the Scottish coastline where their service had been halted because of innovation and no longer a need for their boat on that stretch of coast. I recalled thinking at the time when I passed these old buildings, some of which were now homes but many in a sad ruinous state, how their crews, volunteers and communities responded to their cessation.

I was mindful it wasn't just the crews and volunteers who were affected, the communities too lost a valuable focus of their town or village identity. For many of the communities I'd seen on my journey around the coast, the lifeboat station was an important focal point within their existence. Sometimes, like Aith in Shetland for example, it was just about the only service of note in the community. With outsourcing and globalisation, a fact of modern life, I felt as keenly as any in these communities what the loss of their lifeboat service would signify. We live in a period of rapid change where sometimes coping with this change can be challenging and difficult to manage. For the small village of St Abbs, their lifeboat had been an important facet of their community since the early 20th century.

Chapter 41

The tide was with me and despite the rough sea conditions, I was making good time. It was mid-morning when I arrived at St Abbs head, thc last notable headland of my journey. It was a gloriously wild section of steep cliff scenery with azure waves crashing with mighty booms onto the rocks at their base. I suddenly found myself in a patch of uncomfortably odd water and I began to flounder. My breath rate increased, and I began talking to myself, urging me to be careful and pay attention. I think I was in a stretch of violently refracted sea with a running tide and because it was my last day, I was possibly out of sorts. I became concerned for a few minutes I'd be the very last rescue the St Abbs lifeboat would perform. As if on cue and seemingly out of the blue, such was my concentration at the time, their lifeboat appeared on my left shoulder. They had come out to meet me and I was incredibly moved by this. Deep within an uncontrolled sob rose which was thankfully unseen by the waving crew. In this one small moment, a myriad of realisations swamped my consciousness. It was almost an out of body experience when the clarity of what I'd undertaken crystallised with magnificent brilliance.

My journey had been about transformation, my growth and maturing change. In this moment of ending as epitomised by the close presence of the soon to be defunct orange hulled lifeboat, I realised all I had achieved through the four months would mean nothing if I didn't embrace the change within, which was sure to follow. My journey had been about service. Highlighting the selfless service of countless R.N.L.I. volunteers around Scotland and how this collaborative act of compassion, offered a powerful insight into how best we could choose to live our lives. In essence I had been in service of myself too. I'd given myself dedicated, uninterrupted time to explore who I was, understand my strengths and realise my potential. I'd been responsible for my safety and my wellbeing. I'd placed myself in front of challenges I'd never experienced. I'd motivated myself to continue, to keep going, to reach the end. I'd processed thousands of crucially important decisions and I'd called upon deep inner resources to make these work. Many times, I'd faced my inner darkness and had come away unscathed, if not invigorated by what I learned there. I found out life was worthy of my existence, and I was as crucial a part of it as the thousands of birds I'd seen and heard crying out joyfully, proclaiming their places in the biosphere. I experienced my frailties and drew strength from the awareness this was merely what they were, and not the character flaws I so often imagined them to be. I'd felt unbridled joy, the like of which I'd forgotten how to notice when it occurred. It was a powerful realisation when I accepted, I was allowed to feel happy. Also, I learned happiness is not something to be searched for. It occurs through simplicity. Living simply and adopting the pace of Nature allowed me to rediscover the pleasure gained from simply living. If I attended to my vital needs, I gained valuable time to be attentive to all which was happening around, especially the minutiae of life. It was through noticing the smallest of things, I gained insights into larger matters. I learned about being human and what this entails. Vitally, I saw within Nature life isn't perfect and there's vulnerability within existence. However, I saw how life meshed to sustain all beings, if it was lived collaboratively and in tune with the natural order. I experienced deep sadness, often when I became aware of how as humans, we disregard this natural order for our insatiable consumptive gain. I also discovered within the capacity for hope, especially when moments of depressive thinking became too much to bear. Through the fecundity of natural life around me, I realised the adage of "where there's life, there's hope", is powerfully true. As I'd covered each long mile in my kayak, I'd been paddling towards hope all the time.

Every day, the ocean's vastness had been a mirror, reflecting the limitlessness of my life. The daily distant offing invited me to gaze beyond my horizons, and not accept the apparent restriction set by the faraway point where the sea and sky converged. Immersion in this magnificent landscape where every day for four months, I woke to wild solitude, surrounded by the profusion of Nature, taught me more and more about what it means to be human. In recent years, as my consciousness focussed more on my place in the world, I struggled with the notion of being human in a natural world, viewing myself separated from it, forever seeking how I could alter this self-limiting perception. I sought intimacy with Nature where I considered my existence to be equal to her, not superior.

This solo four-month journey was one of celibacy. In many respects it was akin to a monkish retreat. A choice to renounce the pleasures of the flesh. Healthy sexual fulfilment is a recognised psychological drive within humans. This goes beyond the basic need for copulation, importantly comprising our emotional responses of arousal, romance, passion and love. Yet, because of the physically celibate nature of my four-month adventure, I was reminded of the importance of intimacy in my life. I am an intimate being and discovering intimacy in my relationship with the natural world was like rekindling a long-lost love. It was exciting. I found myself aroused by the fecundity of life around, on the skerries, on the high cliff ledges and across the wide sandy strands. In truth, I fell in love.

The love I experienced for the wild world I was living in; was as real as any love I have ever felt for another. It was passionate and uncomplicated. It was intense and committing. What I gave, I received back, and more. There was not a moment, even in the toughest times, I didn't relish the intimate companionship of the Natural world around. In fact, when the chips were down and I faced a grim passage through wild seas, it was the uncomplicated proximity of wildness which settled my nervous disposition. I was often calmed knowing I shared the space with Fulmars, Kittiwakes, Gannets and every other sea bird. Their presence, and those too of seals and otters, encouraged me to become at ease with my celibate oceanic existence.

Looking around as I paddled along the rocky St Abbs coastline, I smiled to myself. I doubted if the seals were wracked with guilt after copulating, or the terns laughed at puerile innuendo, or indeed any wild creature spend so much time pondering with angst about their sexual behaviour. I was reminded again the simplicity of life is fully encompassing. Being human does not set ourselves apart from other living beings. It is us who choose to muddle our existence.

Now my journey was close to an end, and soon it would be time to return to the human world I inhabited. What would sustain my transition from my itinerancy to a more settled existence, would be the embodiment of the spirit for life I'd encountered in Nature, in the lifeboat crews, the R.N.L.I. volunteers, Scotland's coastal communities and finally, myself. Holding onto the hope life will be fulfilling and living simply in a manner to ensure this, was a singularly powerful realisation for me.

The sloppy sea didn't allow me to disappear into an introspective reverie for long. I could now see the tight opening to St Abbs harbour and with the lifeboat keeping close to my port side, I eventually safely made it into the calm waters beyond. There, on the slipway opposite the lifeboat shed, were Karen and Ziggy waiting. Our greeting was both incredibly intimate and loving, and it was open to the public gaze too. I was vaguely aware of the applause and the shouts of congratulations from the many R.N.L.I. volunteers and crew who'd turned out to greet me. Ziggy was beside himself with excitement and Karen joked maybe she should emulate his excited yaps and boundless energy. My parents were there to greet me too and it was with great meaning they were. Even as a fifty-two-year-old, it meant a lot to have Mum and Dad proudly see me complete my achievement.

Karen and I wandered up to the lifeboat shed where we were taken into the crew room for tea and biscuits. It felt incredibly poignant to be there, the day before a R.N.L.I. truck was due to arrive to take their lifeboat away. The crew were gracious in their plaudits of my journey and the fundraising motivation behind it and I could tell at the same time too, they were in anger and in pain at losing their lifeboat. I wanted to give them my time, to talk to them about what the closure of their lifeboat station meant for them, but it wasn't appropriate to open conversations I had no hope of focussing on. I was suddenly in demand for photo opportunities and to meet folks who'd been following my progress. The hour or so I spent at the St Abbs station felt blurry. Again, an out of body feeling where I wasn't fully in control.

It was now early afternoon and eventually I made my farewells which seemed sadder than the ones I'd made over the past four months. I wished the folks at St Abbs well, expressing the hope they eventually find peace with the occurrence of their loss. The crew on the lifeboat insisted on journeying with me almost to Eyemouth, ostensibly to point me in the right direction. Eyemouth was an hour's paddle away and I really wanted to have this last hour on the sea on my own. However, it would have been unforgivable to turn their support away because at an unspoken level, we all knew this voyage with me along the coast was likely the last they would make with their lifeboat.

I paddled slowly away from St Abbs into a now manageable lumpy sea and set my course for Eyemouth. The St Abbs lifeboat shadowed me for about ten minutes before blasting off across the sea to Eyemouth, returning shortly later to tell me the Eyemouth lifeboat was on its way out and they were in effect handing over to them. We shouted our goodbyes and I watched with sadness as they roared off out to sea for one more burl in their boat before returning to St Abbs.

I was just a mile away from Eyemouth when I saw their lifeboat slowly emerging through their harbour entrance. Flying from the bow of their craft was a huge R.N.L.I. flag. Yet again I found myself gulping back a sob of emotion. They saw me and roared towards me, parting the sea with their customary foamy white wake. As they drew up, the shouts of congratulations reached me across the water. Their cheers brought a wide grin to my face, and I felt a deep glow of satisfaction. It was an incredibly rewarding experience.

Andrew, the coxswain of the lifeboat leaned over the edge of his bridge to both congratulate me and point out the channel I'd to follow into the harbour. They motored ahead and I followed behind.

On entering the harbour, I looked up to see a small crowd of family, friends, and well wishers cheering and hollering me in. This was a far more raucous ending to my journey than my beginning had been, just over four months earlier all the way on the other side of Scotland. The lifeboat joining in with the congratulatory shouts, sounded its horn loudly and so, soaking in the moment as best I could, I paddled up to the floating pontoon where willing lifeboatmen hands helped me out of *Sahwira* and lifted her with gentle ease out of the water to lie beside us. Amongst the melee was Karen, and we once more greeted each other with deep fondness. Then there was a loud pop and champagne was handed to me in a plastic cup. That was the moment my journey ended, sharing this important moment with my wife and the Eyemouth crew who epitomised the warmth and generosity of spirit I'd experienced from the R.N.L.I. volunteers around Scotland.

Shortly after the champagne had been quaffed, we made our way up to the lifeboat station where more drinks were shared out in the crew room. This provided the opportunity to chat with friends who'd travelled to Eyemouth to greet me and the well wishers who'd given up their Sunday too. For the last time I passed my Scotland R.N.L.I. Lifeboat Station book around for the crew to sign and found I'd happily gained the signatures and wishes from the many folks who were present.

The inevitable moment arrived. With what seemed ungainly haste, I unpacked *Sahwira,* loaded up the car, strapped her onto the roof, made my farewells to everyone, and drove away from Eyemouth docks, my mind swimming with all which had just occurred. I'm not certain in that moment if I fully appreciated what I'd achieved.

However, I did smile to myself because while being helped to load *Sahwira* onto the car, one of the Eyemouth crew remarked, "She's a beautiful canoe."

"She certainly is," I responded, before unnecessarily adding, "She's been an incredible kayak."

"Sorry, kayak," was his reply. "What's the difference between a canoe and kayak then?"

Nick Ray

Bibliography

Adam Nicolson, Sea Room, An Island Life in the Hebrides, Harper Perennial, Revised edition, 2007

Brian Wilson, Blazing Paddles, Birlinn, 2019

Doug Cooper, North & East Coasts of Scotland, Sea Kayaking, Pesda Press, 2014

Nicholas Leach, The Lifeboat Service in Scotland, Amberley Publishing, 2013

Local Hero, 1983, Enigma Productions, Goldcrest Films International, Celandine Films. Directed: Bill Forsyth. Written: Bill Forsyth

Out of Doors, current, BBC Radio Scotland

The Author

Nick Ray lives in the colourful harbour town of Tobermory on the beautiful Isle of Mull, in Scotland. Here he makes jewellery from items he combs from the island's coastline. He continues to enjoy extended sea kayaking adventures, exploring Scotland's incredible coastline. This is his first book.

For further information about Nick, please visit his website:

LifeAfloat.co.uk

Printed in Great Britain
by Amazon

85092622R00253